DESIGNING WRITING TASKS
FOR THE
ASSESSMENT OF WRITING

Writing Research

Multidisciplinary Inquiries into the Nature of Writing

edited by Marcia Farr, University of Illinois at Chicago

Arthur N. Applebee, *Contexts for Learning to Write: Studies of Secondary School Instruction*

Barbara Couture, *Functional Approaches to Writing*

Carole Edelsky, *Writing in a Bilingual Program: Había Una Vez*

Lester Faigley, Roger Cherry, David Jolliffe, and Anna Skinner, *Assessing Writers' Knowledge and Processes of Composing*

Marcia Farr (ed.), *Advances in Writing Research, Volume One: Children's Early Writing Development*

Sarah W. Freedman (ed.), *The Acquisition of Written Language: Response and Revision*

Judith Langer, *Children Reading and Writing: Structures and Strategies*

Leo Ruth and Sandra Murphy, *Designing Writing Tasks for the Assessment of Writing*

William Teale and Elizabeth Sulzby (eds.), *Emergent Literacy: Writing and Reading*

IN PREPARATION

Christine P. Barabas, *Technical Writing in a Corporate Setting: A Study of the Nature of Information*

Robert Gundlach, *Children and Writing in American Education*

David A. Jolliffe (ed.), *Advances in Writing Research, Volume Two*

Martha L. King and Victor Rentel, *The Development of Meaning in Writing: Children 5–10*

Anthony Petrosky (ed.), *Reading and Writing: Theory and Research*

Bennett A. Rafoth and Donald L. Rubin (eds.), *The Social Construction of Written Communication*

David Smith, *Explorations in the Culture of Literacy*

Jana Staton, Roger Shuy, Joy Kreeft, and Leslie Reed, *Dialogue Journal Communication: Classroom, Linguistic, Social and Cognitive Views*

Elizabeth Sulzby, *Emergent Writing and Reading in 5–6 Year Olds: A Longitudinal Study*

Stephen Witte, Keith Walters, Mary Trachsel, Roger Cherry, and Paul Meyer, *Literacy and Writing Assessment: Issues, Traditions, Directions*

DESIGNING WRITING TASKS FOR THE ASSESSMENT OF WRITING

Leo Ruth
University of California, Berkeley

Sandra Murphy
San Francisco State University

Ablex Publishing Corporation
Norwood, New Jersey 07648

Copyright © 1988 by Ablex Publishing Corporation

Printed in the United States of America

Library of Congress Cataloging-in-Publication Data

Ruth, Leo.
    Designing writing tasks for the assessment of writing / Leo Ruth, Sandra Murphy.
        p.   cm.—(Writing research)
    Bibliography: p.
    Includes indexes.
    ISBN 0-89391-339-1. ISBN (invalid) 0-89391-430-1 (pbk.)
    1. English language—Rhetoric—Ability testing.   2. English language—Compo-
sition and exercises—Ability testing.   3. English language—Rhetoric—Study and
teaching.   4. English language—Composition and exercises—Study and teaching.   I. Murphy, Sandra.   II. Title.   III. Series: Writing research (Norwood, N.J.)
PE1404.R88   1987
808'.042'076—dc19   87-19688
                                                                                    CIP

Ablex Publishing Corporation
355 Chestnut Street
Norwood, New Jersey 07648

Contents

List of Tables — xi
List of Figures — xiii
Preface to the Series — xiv
Authors' Preface — xv

1 INTRODUCTION — 1

The Need to Study Writing Tasks — 1
The Plan of the Book — 5
A Note on Terms — 6
Dimensions of Writing Tasks — 8
Basic Issues in Designing Writing Tasks — 12
Sources of Knowledge for Studying Writing Tasks — 16

2 RECOMMENDATIONS FROM PRACTICE — 17

Professional Wisdom as Knowledge — 17
    The Limits of an Experimental Research Model — 17
    The Need for Contextual Research — 18
    The Role of Practical Knowledge in Research — 18
    Toward a Theory of Practice — 19
    The Nature of Practical Knowledge — 19
    Establishing an "Ensemble of Practices" — 20
Professionals in Action — 21
    Philosophy of the Assignment: Fred N. Scott (1903) — 21
    Subject Plus Predication Equals Topic: Josephine
        Miles ([1962], 1979) — 22
    Providing the Occasion for Writing:
        The Commission on English (1965) — 24
    Two Basic Assignment Patterns: Arthur J. Carr
        (1965) — 25
    Criteria for Composition Questions:
        The Commission on Writing (1968) — 25
    Audience, Purpose, and Voice: Edmund J. Farrell
        (1969) — 26
    Creating Meaningful Topics: William F. Irmscher
        (1979) — 27
    Avoiding Excessive Instructions: Marjorie Kirrie
        (1979) — 28

39776

Finding the Best Essay Topics: Gertrude Conlan
(1980, 1982)   29
Primary Trait Scoring: National Assessment
of Educational Progress (1974)   32
Summary   36

3   KNOWLEDGE FROM RESEARCH ON TESTING   39

Psychometric Research: Contributions and Limits   39
Early Attitudes Toward Essay Tests   39
Statistical Methods for Analysis of Topics   40
The Limits of Psychometric Measures   41
Topic Effects: "Hidden" Variables in Writing Research   42
The Kincaid Study (1953)   43
The Godshalk, Swineford, and Coffman Study
(1966)   43
The Starch and Elliott Study (1912)   44
The Choppin Study (1969)   45
Topic Effects in Faigley and Skinner's Review
of Research (1982)   46
When are Topic Effects Real? The Significance
of "No Significant Difference"   47
Summary   49

4   KNOWLEDGE FROM RESEARCH ON WRITING: TOPICS   51

Research on Selecting Subjects   51
Knowledge Requirements of Subjects   51
When Students Select Subjects   55
Summary   59
Research on the Language of the Topic   59
A Psychometric Perspective on Wording   59
Psychometric View of Bias   60
Studies of Effects of Wording Changes   62
The Inconclusive Nature of Experimental Studies   68

5   KNOWLEDGE FROM SCHOLARSHIP AND RESEARCH
ON WRITING: TASK INSTRUCTIONS   69

Specifying Rhetorical Context   69
"Circle of Readers"   69
"Task Environment"   69
Effects of Full Rhetorical Specification   70
Concepts of Audience   73
A Definition of Audience in School Writing   76

The Effects of Audience Specification in School
    Writing   77
Specifying Mode   78
    The Problem of Discource Classification   78
    Effects of Mode or Type   79
    Difficulty Level of Modes   80
    Research on Influences from Testing Contexts   83

6   KNOWLEDGE FROM THEORIES AND MODELS   88

Discourse Theory   88
Categorical Systems   88
    Bain's Classical System   88
    Rockas's Concrete and Abstract Modes   89
    D'Angelo's Conceptual Rhetoric   90
    Kinneavy's Aims of Discourse   91
Relational Systems   92
    Moffett's Realm of Discourse   92
    Britton's Functions, Roles, Audience   94
Psychological Models   95
    Emig's Composing Process   95
    Flower and Haye's Rhetorical Problem   95
    Bereiter and Scardamalia's Cognitive Processes
      in Writing   98
    Bruce's Cognitive Science Model   98
The Domain of Writing and the Specification
    of Competence   99
    Polin on the Assessment of the Writing Process   100
    Mellon's Taxonomy of Compositional Competencies   100
    Odell on Defining and Assessing Competence
      in Writing   102
    Purves's and Vähäpassi's Specification
      of the Domain of School Writing   105
Theory and Research-Based Assessment Models: Special
    Cases   108
    Skills Models and Discrete Point Measures   108
    The Primary Trait Model   110
    A Research-Based Model of Writing Task
      Development from E.T.S.   110
Models of Large-Scale Assessment   113
    An English Model: Assessment of Performance Unit   113
    A Canadian Model: Ontario Writing Assessment
      Projects   114

7   THE WRITING ASSESSMENT EPISODE: A MODEL
     FOR INVESTIGATION   117

     Foundations of the Model   117
        Introduction   117
        Problems of Meaning in Topics   118
        Current Theories of Comprehension Applied
           to Topic Interpretation   119
        Social Interaction in Testing Contexts   123
        Methodological Concerns   124
        The Nature of Models   126
     A Model of the Writing Assessment Episode   127
     General Description of the Studies   130
        The Main Research Questions   130
        Sources of Knowledge Studies   131
        Subject and Wording Effects Studies   131
        A Study of How Students Read Topics   132
        Variations Among Communities of Readers   134
        Student Rhetorical Task Construction Across
           Grade Levels   134

8   HOW TOPIC WORDING AND TESTING CONTEXT AFFECT
     RESPONSE   136

     Introduction   136
     Effects of Rhetorical Specification on Performance   137
        The Nature of the Topic and the Degree
           of Specification   140
        The Interaction of Variables   140
        Problems in Comparing Versions of a Topic   141
     Effects of Topic Wording Not Measured by Score   141
        The Influence of Wording on Choice of Form   142
        The Effects of Wording Variation on Composing
           Strategies   145
        Variations in the Planning Process   148
        Effects of the Testing Context   149
        The Influence of Testing Context on the Student's
           Conception of Task   149
        The Effects of Time Limits on Performance   151

9   HOW STUDENTS READ TOPICS   155

     Central High Study of the Construction of Meanings
        of a Topic   155
     Sources of Information in the Study   156

The Topic and Alternative Interpretations   156
The Interviews and Patterns of Interpretation   159
The Interview and the Essay Compared   164
Methods of Developing an Argument   171
  Narrative and Evaluative Elements   171
  Attribution   172
  Generalized Attribution   173
  Generalization   174
  Comparators   174
Sources of Variation in Interpretation   176
  The Nature of the Topic   176
  The Context of the Writing Performance   176
  Learned/Taught Writing Strategies   176
  Selective Reading Versus Misinterpretation   178
  The Text of the Topic   178
Summary   179

10 HOW DIFFERENT COMMUNITIES OF READERS INTERPRET
    TOPICS   181

Divergence in Interpretation of Topics by Students
  and Teachers: Data from the Central High Study 182
  The Interview Data from the Teachers   183
  The Questionnarie Data from the Students
    and Teachers   185
  The Questionnaire Responses and Holistic Scores 188
The Evaluation of Papers by Students and Teachers: Data
  from the Rhetorical Specification Study   191
  The Raters As Subjects   192
Agreement Within and Among Three Groups of Raters   193
  Interrater Reliability Estimates   193
  Agreement Among Groups   194
  Score Distributions for Three Groups of Raters 194
The Data from the Training Sessions   196
Summary   202

11 HOW WE ASSESS DEVELOPMENT IN WRITING   203

Introduction   203
Definitions of Progress in Writing   204
  Linguistic Definitions   205
  Cognitive Definitions   206
Students' Definitions of Writing Tasks   220
  Problems of Classifying Responses to Open Topics 221

A Taxonomy of Student Text-Types   223
Measuring Development of Writing Ability Over Time   225
    The Nature of the Sample   225
    The Limitations of the Sample   226
    Coding the Papers in the Sample   226
    Analyses of the Data   227
    Patterns of Task Interpretation   232
Problems and Limitations in Developmental Studies   233

12   GUIDELINES FOR DESIGNING TOPICS FOR WRITING
     ASSESSMENTS   236

Introduction   236
Overview of the Process of Topic Design   237
The Planning Phase   238
The Developmental Phase   247
The Evaluation Phase   283
Conclusion   290

References   291
Author Index   309
Subject Index   313

List of Tables

1.1   Writing Assignments in Teaching and Testing Contexts   9

6.1   Bain's Forms of Discourse (Derived from D'Angelo, 1976)   89

6.2   The Writing Situation (Adapted from D'Angelo, 1980)   90

6.3   Aims and Purposes of Writing (Adapted from D'Angelo,
      1980)   90

6.4   Topics of Invention or Methods of Development (Adapted
      from D'Angelo, 1980)   91

6.5   Schema of Discourse: Progression of Speaker-Audience
      Relationship (From Moffett, 1981)   93

6.6   Progression of Speaker-Subject Relationship (From Moffett,
      1981)   93

6.7   Nature of the Writing Stimulus (Derived from Emig, 1971)   96

6.8   Taxonomy of Compositional Competencies (Adapted from
      Mellon, 1977)   101

6.9   Dimensions of a Writing Assignment (Adapted from Purves,
      et al., 1984)   108

8.1   Means and Standard Deviations of Proficient Students' and
      Less Proficient Students' Total Holistic Scores by
      Class, Section and Grade Level   143

8.2   Frequencies for the Different Forms of Writing Produced
      by Topic Version A and Topic Version B   143

8.3   Mean Total Holistic Scores by Proficiency and Form
      Selection   144

8.4   Results of Questionnaire Data by Topic Version   145

8.5   Total Holistic Score Means, Standard Deviations
      and Numbers of Students by Topic Version
      and Planning Time   147

8.6   Total Holistic Score Means and Standard Deviations
      by Topic Version, Planning Time, and Re-Reading   147

10.1   Responses by Students and Topic Authors/Raters
        to Selected Questionnaire Items   185

10.2   Kendall's Correlation Coefficients: Responses to Selected
        Questionnaire Items with Total Holistic Score   189

10.3   Reliability Data for Three Groups of Raters   193

10.4   Agreement Between Groups of Raters   194

10.5   Scoring Distributions for Three Groups of Raters   195

10.6   Scores Awarded to Sample D During Training   197

10.7   Scores Awarded to Sample E During Training   198

10.8   Scores Awarded to Sample I During Training   201

11.1   Cognitive Scale: Index of Levels of Abstracting (Based
        on Freedman & Pringle, 1980b)   209

11.2   Preferred Task Constructions by Topic/Year   227

12.1   Composite Framework of Writing Tasks for Ages 11
        and 15   251

List of Figures

6.1   The Communication Triangle (Based on Kinneavy, 1971)   92

6.2   Functions of Writing (From Britton, 1975)   94

6.3   The Rhetorical Problem (From Flower & Hayes, 1980)   97

6.4   Tasks in Relation to the Domain of School Writing
        (From Purves, et al., 1984)   106

6.5   Model of Discourse (From Lloyd-Jones, 1977)   111

6.6   NAEP Model of Discourse (From Lloyd-Jones & Klaus,
        1977)   111

7.1   A Model of the Writing Assessment Episode: Participants
        Processes, and Texts (From Ruth & Murphy, 1985)   128

8.1   A Diagram of the Differences in Planning and Writing Time
        for Versions A and B   146

10.1   Distributions of Scores Awarded by 3 Groups of Raters   195

11.1   New Score Means for Overall Sample and Individual
        Groups   229

11.2   New Score Means for each Grade Level Compared
        to Overall Sample Means for each Topic/Year   230

12.1   The Processes of Designing a Writing Task   239

Writing Research

Multidisciplinary Inquiries into the Nature of Writing

Marcia Farr, series editor
University of Illinois at Chicago

Preface

This series of volumes presents the results of recent scholarly inquiry into the nature of writing. The research presented comes from a mix of disciplines, those which have emerged as significant within the last decade or so in the burgeoning field of writing research. These primarily include English education, linguistics, psychology, anthropology, and rhetoric. A note here on the distinction between field and discipline might be useful: a field can be a multidisciplinary entity focused on a set of significant questions about a central concern (e.g., American Studies), while a discipline usually shares theoretical and methodological approaches which may have a substantial tradition behind them. Writing research, then, is a field, if not yet a discipline.

The history of this particular field is unique. Much of the recent work in this field, and much that is being reported in this series, has been conceptualized and funded by the National Institute of Education. Following a planning conference in June 1977, a program of basic research on the teaching and learning of writing was developed and funded annually. The initial research funded under this program is now coming to fruition, providing both implications for educational improvement and directions for future research. This series is intended as one important outlet for these results.

Authors' Preface

This book for teachers, evaluators, and researchers focuses on a "neglected variable" in writing assessment and research—the nature of the writing task and its interpretation. In this report we analyze the results of a series of investigations into psychometric assumptions about the nature of tasks used for the assessment of writing and about the uniformity of writing task interpretations by all the participants in a writing assessment—the task authors, the student examinees, and the teacher raters (readers). Our analysis of these investigations led us to formulate a number of recommendations about selecting subjects and wording writing tasks, about specifying audience and mode, and about framing instructions. This set of practical guidelines for designing tasks for assessments is based on the work of the Writing Assessment Project (1980–1982) conducted under the auspices of the Bay Area Writing Project (BAWP), Graduate School of Education, University of California, Berkeley, with funding provided by a grant from the National Institute of Education (NIE-G-80-0034).

Our work has benefited from the help of many colleagues associated with the Writing Assessment Project. In particular, we are grateful to James Gray and Miles Myers, then Director and Associate Director respectively, of BAWP, who provided needed professional and personal support in initiating and fostering the Project. But without the contributions of many other people, the research presented here could not have been accomplished. Therefore, we are deeply appreciative of the collaboration we enjoyed with BAWP Teacher-Consultants from local schools as well as other faculty at several San Francisco Bay Area public schools who contributed to the research.

The success of the project was also dependent upon the dedicated scholarship of those graduate students in the School of Education at Berkeley who collected and analyzed data and co-authored chapters of the 1982 research report to NIE. In particular, the project was fortunate to have the teaching and writing research expertise that Catherine Keech (Lucas) brought to her role in developing several studies for the Project. Each of our research associates—Karen Carroll, Charles Kinzer, and Donald Leu—made unique contributions essential to the success of the Project. Faculty at Berkeley—especially Paul Ammon, Sarah Freedman, and Judith Langer as a Visiting Scholar—provided valuable advice. Special recognition is due also to Mary Ellen McNelly, Ann Robyns, and Elissa Warantz who co-authored portions of the original report and to Deborah Dashow Ruth whose extensive editorial assistance on both the 1982 report and on the present analysis was invaluable. Our thanks must go also to Michael Brady, who helped us survive several emergencies in preparing the original report.

For his initial suggestions about the content, style, and form of this volume, we thank John Mellon. To Marcia Farr our debt of gratitude is broad and longstanding, beginning with her supportive recommendations as our NIE project officer and continuing through her wise counsel as editor of this series. And finally, we are indebted to all the other fine scholars, researchers, and teachers whose professional knowledge and wisdom about writing and its assessment are represented in this report. They comprise the real foundation of this volume.

Lastly, we give our deepest thanks to Deborah Ruth and Dennis Murphy—and Kris, John and Bill Murphy—who endured postponements and gave us the time, the understanding, and the support we needed to complete our own writing task.

The current report represents a thorough update, expansion, re-analysis, and re-writing of the 1982 report to NIE. Hence, any misconceptions or omissions are entirely our own. Although much of the content of this report is based upon work supported by grant number NIE-G-80-0034 from the National Institute of Education, Department of Education, the opinions expressed in this publication do not necessarily reflect the position or policy of the National Institute of Education, and no official endorsement should be inferred.

Leo Ruth and Sandra Murphy,
Berkeley, California,
July 1987

ONE

Introduction

RESOLVED: That before essay tests are used, the complexities of such tests shall be carefully considered. More importantly, topics shall be designed with great care . . . . [From the CCCC Resolution on Testing (1979)]. Adopted April 1, 1978

The Need to Study Writing Tasks

Topics assigned in "essay tests" need to be "designed with great care" because they initiate and direct the act of writing that produces the sample for evaluation. But what is a "good" topic? Surprisingly little research has been done on this question. While there is an extensive research literature describing procedures for creating valid and reliable objective measures of certain kinds of academic attainment, the literature on the assessment of writing through the collection of writing samples offers few scientifically established principles to guide the development of the topics, questions, or exercises given to students in the examining rooms. We do have a growing literature on how to *score* writing samples, and to some extent advocates of several competing methods do address themselves to the problem of developing good topics. In fact, extensive work on the relation of test topic to scoring plan has been done by developers of a method called *primary trait scoring* (Mullis, 1976; Lloyd-Jones, 1977). But the title of this approach identifies its focus as mainly a *scoring* system, as with several other assessment procedures, for example, the holistic or analytic scoring methods (Spandel & Stiggins, 1980).

Professional test developers attempting to design good direct measures of writing ability are willing to admit for the most part that the act of creating good topics remains more an art than a science. Up to now, deciding when a topic is good has typically been more intuitive than objective. This observation is corroborated by two well-respected authorities in the field of educational measurement in their comments on the state of the art in designing essay test questions or topics. Thorndike and Hagen (1969) preface their recommendations for writing essay questions with the following disclaimer:

> Writing good questions is an art. It is a little like writing a good sonnet and a little like baking a good cake. The operation is not quite as free and fanciful as writing the sonnet, but not quite so standardized as baking the cake. It lies somewhere in between . . . The point we wish to make is that there is no exact science of test construction. Most of the guides and maxims that we shall offer have not been tested out by controlled scientific experimentation. Instead, they represent a distillation of practical experience and professional judgement. (pp. 76–77)

A.G. Wesman (1971) of the Psychological Corporation shares Robert Thorndike's view that the creation of test "items" or questions is an "art form:"

> Item writing is essentially creative—it is an art . . . . Principles can be established and suggestions offered but it is the item writer's judgment in the application—and occasional disregard—of these principles and suggestions that determines whether good items or mediocre ones are produced. Each item, as it is being written, presents new problems and new opportunities.

> Extensive use of statistical methods for the analysis of responses to test items has seemed to imply that test production can be made a statistical science in which the skill of the item writer is of secondary importance. This notion is based on a misconception of the role of item analysis. Item analysis is evaluative—not creative. Its role is essentially a negative one. It serves to identify clearly bad items: those which are too difficult, too easy, or otherwise nondiscriminating. It does not assure the goodness of an item; it in no way lessens the skill and care requisite in the original item writing. (p. 81)

Until the mid-1970's, a few large national agencies, notably the Educational Testing Service (ETS) and the National Assessment of Educational Progress (NAEP) devised most of the nationally administered essay examinations. During this period, the design of exercises, questions, or topics for the assessment of writing remained in the hands of skilled topic writers who were subject to the guidelines for quality control required by the agencies they served. But the rapid growth of local assessments in schools and colleges across the nation soon made evident the lack of public guidelines for use by novice test makers. It can be argued that current practice does not represent a disciplined approach but rather an ad hoc response to the exigency of getting writing assessments done. For example, it is rather common practice to borrow topics from other assessments, as if any topic could serve an all-purpose function in the measurement of writing. But assessment purposes vary. Can we simply assume that minimum competence, program effectiveness, instructional needs, appropriate placement, and different kinds of writing can all be determined by the same topic?

Those local school assessors who do provide an all-purpose essay topic and then generalize broadly on the basis of student response are assuming that "good writing" is a unitary concept and that a single topic can measure all aspects of what constitutes "good writing." Similarly, some schools offer topics intended to stimulate exposition or argument but which instead function more as a measure of the writer's general knowledge than the writer's capacity to mount an argument or sustain a piece of exposition. For example, the following topic, intended to stimulate writing in the argument mode, presupposes a knowledge of the history of women in the United States (Myers, 1980, p. 13):

> Explain your agreement or disagreement with the following statement: The history of women in our country is the history of oppression.

The topic was eliminated from the assessment after two female teachers admitted that they did not know enough about the history of women to write a sound essay on the subject themselves. Of course, if the students had just completed a class in the history of women, the topic would have been appropriate. And in that case, the topic would test mastery of course content in addition to writing competence.

Another problem arises when test makers think that students should know the specific "audience" that they are ostensibly writing for, without recognizing the impact this will have on writing performance. In a California writing assessment, the audience was specified as follows: "Write a letter to your pen pal." But a study by Marion Crowhurst (1978) indicates that students produce more sophisticated and complex syntax when writing for a teacher or general reader than when writing for a peer. If an assessment purpose is to evaluate maturity of syntax, then a topic specifying an unsophisticated audience should be avoided.

Still another problem is that researchers as well as local school authorities are not sufficiently aware of the effect of the topic or task itself on the performance of writers. The researchers Bereiter, Scardamalia, and Bracewell, as cited by Polin (1980, p. 8) have noted that:

> Developmental research in writing has generally proceeded by assuming that the task was construed the same by all subjects and therfrom (sic) inferring differences in competence. But this is quite an inadequate way of going after any deep understanding of cognitive development in writing. (1978, p. 5)

The writing topic is a stimulus, a springboard, propelling writers into the creation of essays. But each writer uses that springboard differently and performs uniquely. This metaphor suggests that researchers and assessors need to recognize the interactive characteristics of the transaction that occurs between the writer and the topic—the linguistic, cognitive, and social reverberations that such a transaction may set off in the writer. As far as we can determine, there seem to be a number of potential interactions between a topic and a writer that have yet to be investigated. We need to understand more about the nature of the interaction evoked by the subject as well as by any accompanying instructions, written or verbal. If choice of topic does not affect the performance of the writer, how do we know whether the topic is actually enabling the student to perform typically in the areas we would like to assess?

There is potential for invalid writing assessments arising from interpretations on the part of both student readers and teacher raters. But we are just beginning to understand the kinds of issues that topic designers must consider. Some of the critical questions that we must seek to answer include:

1. How do local assessors and national test developers create essay test topics? What practical knowledge guides them? What theory and research guide them?
2. How are "good" writing topics generated and tested systematically?
3. How does topic wording affect response? Which of the test maker's cues does the writer recognize, understand, and use?
4. How do students read topics? How do students construct an understanding of a writing task?
5. What is the nature of the transaction between the writer, the topic, and the composed text?
6. What changes occur in maturing students' responses to topics in successive annual assessments, and what do these changes reveal about how we should be assessing developing abilities in writing?
7. How do different communities of raters interpret the same topic? Do teachers and students have the same interpretation of a particular topic?

The literature is silent on most of these questions, for it is only recently that specialists in writing assessment have begun to recognize the importance and complexity of exploring some of the many crucial questions about the properties of topics and their effects on writers. The purpose of the present volume is to describe the results of studies of topic effects conducted by a team of researchers working under the auspices of the Bay Area Writing Project (BAWP) with funding from the National Institute of Education (Gray & Ruth, 1982).Together, these studies provide (1) a comprehensive review of current sources of knowledge about designing topics for writing assessment, (2) a theoretical model of the writing assessment episode, (3) data gathered in five interrelated BAWP research projects, and (4) a set of practical guidelines for researchers and evaluators using topics to gather data about accomplishments in writing. In devising our model of the writing assessment episode and our topic design guidelines for practitioners, we have been intentionally eclectic. There is a need to identify the existing bits and pieces of knowledge existing in scattered documents and to synthesize this information into a coherent structure. Although we may not be able to propose answers to all of the questions that we raise in regard to issues of topic design, our work may serve as a starting point for developing a literature on topic design, helping designers of tests to better understand the complex and dynamic nature of the relationship between reading the topic and responding to it. The topic initiates a sequence of processes, culminating in an evaluator's judgment of writing competence that presumes to say something meaningful about the written response of the student in relation to the task instructions received. Thus, the conception of a writing task not only requires a model of discourse forms and functions but also a theory of the nature of the writing process and a theory of reading comprehension.

The Plan of the Book

Chapter 1 provides an introduction to the project. Chapters 2 through 6 review current sources of knowledge about designing writing tasks. Chapter 2 examines the role of practical knowledge in research and gathers examples of recommendations from the practice of experienced teachers and test makers. Chapter 3 then reviews knowledge from psychometric research and considers how topics act as "hidden" variables in testing and in research on writing. Chapter 4 presents knowledge from the research on writing that takes account of topic effects, while Chapter 5 continues the exploration of what writing research says about topics, but with a focus on writing task instructions such as the specification of audience and mode. Chapter 6 looks at knowledge from discourse theory, reviewing several rhetorical systems and psychological models. Chapter 7 is the focal point of the volume, presenting a model of the writing assessment episode, a construct that guided the several research studies in our Writing Assessment Project. This chapter also presents an overview of the Bay Area Writing Project topic effects studies which are described in detail in chapters 8 through 11. More specifically, Chapter 8 outlines our preliminary investigations of how topic wording affects response. Chapter 9 then presents the key research study of the whole Project, which sought to answer the question: How do the participants in a writing episode read and respond to topics? Hence, this chapter examines the variation in interpretation given to a single topic by various participants in a writing assessment episode—test makers, student writers, and teacher raters. Chapter 10 compares how different communities of readers—students, teachers in training, and expert teacher raters—interpret and evaluate topics. Chapter 11 describes several approaches toward studying how skill in writing progresses in relation to the students' psychological and social development, and it provides a preliminary classification of student responses to "open" writing tasks with regard to form and function. Chapter 12 consolidates information from various sources of current knowledge about assessing writing into a practical guide for designing writing tasks for use in assessments. The volume ends with a reference list and indexes.

A Note on Terms

Research in writing constitutes a relatively new field, and there is not yet consensus on the use of a number of terms. It is therefore necessary to designate how particular terms will be used in this volume.

Assessment and Evaluation

The two terms, assessment and evaluation, tend to be used interchangeably in the literature, although considered strictly there are key distinctions in the two processes. An *assessment* may occur formally or informally whenever one person seeks and interprets information about another person. An "assessment of writing" occurs when a teacher, evaluator, or researcher obtains information about a student's abilities in writing. This information may be gathered in classrooms through observations, class assignments, or formal tests. Assessment information may be gathered without tests or without any kind of measurement that implies fixed standards. Assessment procedures do not require the comparison and ranking of students, or the attaching of a letter or number score to the performance. Assessments can be descriptive without being evaluative. In everyday usage, however, the two terms—assessment and evaluation—tend to be synonymous.

An *evaluation* attempts to identify and judge the results of teaching either from the perspective of student performance or from the perspective of course or program content and structure. Evaluation is an essential step in the instructional process and in determining the accomplishments of school programs.

Writing Test or Essay Test

Multiple choice tests of usage and editing skills are often called *writing tests* or even *composition tests* although no writing or composing is required. In this volume, however, the term *writing test* will refer only to those tests which call for one or more samples of actual student writing. We will also follow common practice in using the term *essay test* as synonymous with writing test, even though many writing tests do not call for essay forms.

Writing Sample

The term *writing sample* refers to the writing produced for writing tests, whether by a single student or by an entire student population. When we use the term *writers,* we mean *student writers.* Hence, the designing and administering of the *writing test* is followed by the collecting and scoring of the *writing sample.* Generally, those who score the *writing samples* are simply called *readers,* but in order to avoid confusion with other common usages of this term, we sometimes use the term *raters* or the more cumbersome forms *teacher readers* or *teacher raters.*

Writing Assessment and Scoring

Writing assessments differ mainly in their scoring procedures. An assessment using *holistic scoring* tests writing by calling for a group of students to produce samples of writing, which later are read and rated according to systematic procedures variously derived. One type of holistic scoring involves rapid *general impression* ranking of the papers in the tested population on a scale such as a 4 or 6 point continuum. Since the procedure provides no information about the nature of the writing itself, it is limited to ranking papers within a class, a school, or a district, or in some other particular population such as freshmen entering college.

An assessment using *analytic scoring* determines the quality of the writing in response to the topic by ranking the papers on a scale against clearly specified criteria. For example, Diederich's (1965) Analytic Scale requires raters to consider such features as *ideas, organization, flavor, wording, sentence structure, punctuation, spelling, handwriting,* and *neatness.*

An assessment using *primary trait scoring* operates somewhat differently. Based on a theory of discourse, the method assumes that different writing tasks engage different writing strategies. Thus, when the task is created, certain rhetorical strategies are identified and then cued in the task itself. An extensive scoring guide designates the characteristics of writing that seem appropriate to the particular task, enabling raters to judge how closely papers approximate the expected "traits" or characteristics of the particular type of discourse being assessed. In this case writers are not ranked against one another but against an absolute criterion.

"Given Task," Topic, Stimulus, Prompt, Exercise, Question

The writing task *given* to students for a writing test will be referred to variously as *the topic, the task, the prompt, the test question, the writing stimulus, the writing instructions, the assignment,* and some of these terms will be used interchangeably—especially *the writing topic, the task, the prompt, the test question*—to refer to the *whole* writing assignment. The assignment generally consists of two main parts: (a) the subject, or stimulus—the tester's identification of *what* the writer will write about; and (b) the instructions—the particular suggestions about or limitations on the content of the writing and the tester's specifications about *how* the writer is to address the subject.

"Constructed Task"

This is the task that the writer sets for himself on the basis of the *given* task. It reflects the writer's interpretation and understanding of the given task. There may be a high degree of congruence between the given task and the *constructed* task, or there may be virtually none.

Class Writing Assignments and Writing Tests

It is necessary to distinguish carefully between the nature of the writing tasks in two different school contexts that require writing. In current practice, the topic that appears in a *testing context* usually functions autonomously: No help from the proctors in interpreting the task is permitted; no preparatory context is provided; no motivating impulse is stimulated. Usually only the command, "Write, as directed" initiates work upon the task provided. The conditions for the participants are carefully controlled so as to be depersonalized, formalized, and standardized. The underlying psychometric assumption upon which the stability of such measurement relies is the belief in the uniformity of the stimulus properties for each student responding to the topic. Each head bent over the page is presumed to be getting the same message to direct the writing performance.

By contrast, the topics or writing assignments that appear in a *classroom instructional context* function in a setting that encourages negotiation or interpretation. The teacher may offer a good deal of guidance, making clear the expectations as well as the possibilities of the assignment. The teacher may orient the class to the area of experience to be drawn upon and, through discussion, may enlarge the ground of shared knowledge. The teacher may give examples of appropriate and inappropriate strategies for discovering and structuring the essential material of the composition. And if the writing occurs in class, the teacher can assist in repairing any of the breakdowns that may occur, if initial attempts to progress through the writing assignment fail. The process is personal, informal, non-standardized, and keyed to the proposition that differential interpretations of the topic are inevitable but also reconcilable through negotiation. A display of the major contrasts between teaching and testing contexts as occasions for writing follows in Table 1.1.

The *writing test topic* and the *class writing topic* constitute two types of assignments that must meet different criteria to perform their unique functions. Thus, assignments for teaching and testing are not easily interchangeable without substantive modification.

Dimensions of Writing Tasks

In designing a writing task, the test maker must provide students with something to write about, a *subject or another form of stimulus*. The test maker usually also formulates a set of instructions to accompany the statement of the subject. Commonly these two elements, *subject and instructions*, comprise the structure of a writing task. These two elements are intended to work together to elicit the particular kind of writing performance the evaluator is interested in judging. At this time, we will not attempt to de-

Table 1.1.
Writing Assignments in Teaching and Testing Contexts

Participants, Texts, Processes	In a Teaching Context	In a Testing Context
1. Population	Class members	Assembled students
2. Leader	Teacher	Unknown proctor
3. Evaluator	Teacher, peer	External examiner
4. Text	Negotiable assignment	Autonomous topic
5. Teacher Expectations	Known or negotiable	Specified and/or implicit
6. Student Expectations	Student constructed	Student constructed
7. Interaction	Allowable with peers, teacher	Prohibited
8. Writing Process	Informal, interpersonal, reciprocal, sequenced	Standardized, depersonalized, one-way, truncated
9. Conditions	Restricted but negotiable and variable	Uniform and nonnegotiable location, time limit, length, etc.
10. Evaluation	Flexible, contingent, graded	Fixed standard, ranked, scored

scribe or classify the *content* of either topic subjects or instructions. We will, however, discuss some general properties of both subjects and instructions from a functional perspective.

A subject for writing is selected with the expectation that the student's composition will address the given subject, and the student's response to the subject will be matched against the interpretation of the subject expected by the evaluator. In designing a topic to assess competence in writing, the evaluator usually is not interested in appraising student knowledge of a particular subject nor does he aim to identify clever students who can decipher complicated instructions. Rather, the test maker hopes to select a subject and accompany it with clear instructions which fit the purpose of the test. Personal subjects are often popular with designers of tests because they do not require special knowledge on the part of the student, and they are easily accessible to a broad range of participants in assessments. Thus, they are useful for general competency testing purposes. Other kinds of writing tasks may serve other purposes such as assessing ability to analyze a literary passage. Clear instructions are necessary in any writing task if the test is to fulfill its function. But even when the instructions appear to be clearly written, the evaluator cannot always be sure that students will interpret the subject as intended and respond to the instructions appropriately. Sometimes a single word may mislead the students as in a case described by Tanner (1981):

> Some years back (about 1971 or 72, I think), the first question on the AP [Advanced Placement] English test used a passage from an Orwell essay as a

springboard. The instructions went something like this: "Demonstrate how the author of this passage establishes his attitude toward the coming of spring." I was question leader on that question, and early on in the reading I was puzzled to have large numbers of papers brought to me blank. Many obviously fine candidates, who did fine essays on the other two questions, simply skipped the first question entirely. And then I had a notion: I suspect that a great many students took the word "Demonstrate" to mean that they should pick a subject of their own and imitate Orwell's manner of expression. I was led to this belief by one paper in which a good candidate had actually *done* that as he "demonstrated" his own attitude toward the beach. (B.R. Tanner, letter, February 8, 1981)

Not all writing prompts provide a fully formed subject for the writer to develop into an essay. Sometimes the subject is just a title, a word or a phrase, requiring the student to generate a *predication* to form it into a statement for development. Josephine Miles (1979) has noted that giving a subject in abbreviated form—for example, "My Home Town"—does not provide the writer with a thesis or a generalization which might generate a coherent essay. The writer must discover his own thesis by shaping a *predication* for his subject that is susceptible to demonstration and development; for example, "My home town provided a rich environment for the development of a bad character."

The conception of *subject* which requires students to generate their own predications is exemplified in *A Thousand Topics for Composition* Rev. 4th ed, *(Illinois English Bulletin)*, 1980, or in *What Can I Write About? Seven Thousand Topics for High School Students* (Powell, 1981). These two volumes do indeed list thousands of subjects in the form of short phrases without instructions that might serve as titles of student essays: "my home town," "a childhood memory," "my favorite object," "sex education," "capital punishment," "making tacos," "the case for/against dieting." (See Chapter 2 for an expanded discussion of the limits of this approach.)

So far we have considered only one form of stimulus for writing, the subject expressed in the form of a mini text, which might be as brief as a word or phrase or extend into a half-page long scenario. The stimulus may, of course, take other forms: a famous quotation, a complete poem, a controversial statement, a fragment of an essay or story, a photograph or drawing, a piece of music, a taped conversation, a film clip, a news bulletin, or an advertisement. In these cases, the accompanying instructions may, with varying degrees of specificity, direct the writer with regard to what kind of writing to do, what line of development to take, and so forth. The student writer might be directed to respond to a photograph, for instance, by creating an imaginative piece which relates a personal experience, recounts a stream of consciousness, or tells a story. But when the student is asked to describe, comment on, criticize, evaluate, agree or disagree with, explain, or in some way to write *about* the given stimulus, then a line of development has been indicated and the stimulus plus the instructions become the full prompt for writing.

The following topics (Keech, 1982a) illustrate some of the distinctions we are making between the subject and the instructions:

Topic 1a

Think about the word *trees*. Write about what the word suggests to you. (Keech, 1982a, p. 137)

Note that the subject in Topic 1a is designated in one word: "trees." In this case, the instructions, "Think about the word" and "Write about what the word suggests," are quite simple and provide almost no constraints.

The same topic as revised in 1b or 1c could be accompanied by an alternative, more elaborate set of instructions which would encourage students to move away from writing only for self-expression toward writing for literary or even for academic or social purposes.

Topic 1b

Think about the word *trees*. Write a story in which trees play an important part. This may be a real experience or an imaginary story. You may even write as if you *were* a tree. Be sure that trees play some part in your story. (Keech, 1982a, p. 137)

Topic 1c

Think about the word *trees*. Write an essay in which you explain one of several possible ideas this word may suggest to you. You may write about a special kind of tree, a special use of trees, people's attitudes toward trees, or something else that interests you about trees. Focus on one idea—do not attempt to list all the things trees can mean. (Keech, 1982a, p. 137)

In these two examples, it is not the subject but the writing instructions that structure the cognitive demands of the task, determining whether the test is one of general fluency calling for self-expression and free exploration of internal feelings or whether it calls for demonstration of control of specific composing strategies leading to particular forms of discourse—for example, narrative as in topic 1b, or essay as in topic 1c. The instructions may call for the writer to take into account a number of features of discourse: genre, audience, role, purpose, style, or tone. The instructions may also announce certain requirements: length, time limit, use of pen and lined paper, and so forth. The instructions may identify criteria indicating that success depends on using correct grammar, spelling, punctuation. The instructions may also offer guidance about organization—"give examples"—and about process—"make a rough draft first."

In summary, then, the typical writing task has two main parts: (a) it announces the subject for writing (the *what*); (b) it offers instructions, including recommendations for approaching the subject, limitations of the assignment, and sometimes criteria for evaluation (the *how*). The topic writer's challenge is to reduce the student writer's uncertainty about the nature of the desired response by providing adequate guidance without introducing stifling constraints. Just how a creator of writing tests undertakes this challenge is the subject of the rest of this volume.

Basic Issues in Designing Writing Tasks

This volume raises a question basic to writing assessment: How should students be asked to write and what should they be asked to write about, if we wish to measure their real writing abilities? The assigned writing task plays a critical role in determining how students perform and whether testers are measuring what they think they are measuring.

Creating a good prompt is not easy. Students write best when they find something they want to say to someone. No matter how highly motivated they may be to perform well on a writing test, no matter how concerned they are to achieve a good score, they will not be able to do their best if they find the topic dull, confusing, or intimidating. They need to seize on the germ of an idea and begin writing with confidence if they are to generate a complete piece of writing in the time allowed.

There is increasing awareness that wording and other properties of writing tasks will have a marked effect upon the writing process and the product. But the research still provides little to consult when one is designing prompts for writing assessments. It is curious that so little work has been done on the properties and effects of assigned topics on writing processes and products,[1] despite the fact that Braddock, Lloyd-Jones, and Schoer (1963), in their landmark report on the state of knowledge in composition, had identified "the assignment variable" as one of four key variables to consider in the conduct of research in writing (1963, pp. 7–10). Yet when we began our study of the properties of writing tasks in 1980, our literature searches revealed that no systematic investigations had focused on the study of topics. Since 1980, besides our own studies, there have been several others that have examined particular dimensions of topics: Brossell (1983), Hoetker (1982), Greenberg (1981a), Purves, Söter, Takala, and

---

[1] A work is now in press (Freedle & Duran) which may offer insights about the cognitive processing of writing tasks. *Cognitive and Linguistic Analyses of Test Performance,* though devoted to items intended to assess verbal and reasoning skills, promises to shed light on the issue of how the act of test taking and the language of the test items interact with the assessment of the targeted skills.

Vähäpassi (1984).[2] As might be suspected, given such a small literature, there remain a substantial number of unanswered questions. Among those writing scholars commenting on the gap in our knowledge about the development of topics for writing assessment have been Odell, Cooper, and Courts, (1978); Odell, (1979); Greenberg, (1981b); Hoetker, (1982). The kinds of questions that these scholars are asking suggest the areas where information is needed and the directions that future research investigations might take.

Scholars' Questions About Writing Tasks

Questions Raised by Odell, Cooper, and Courts (1978, p. 11)

How should researchers frame a writing task so as to obtain the best possible work from students?

Must researchers, as Sanders and Littlefield (1975) claim, provide a full rhetorical context, that is, information about speaker, subject, audience, and purpose?

Is there any aspect of the rhetorical context that we need not include in a writing task? Would an assignment that, for example, specified speaker, subject, and audience but not purpose, elicit writing that differed significantly from writing prompted by an assignment that specified a full rhetorical context?

Questions Raised by Odell (1979, p. 41)

Is it in fact true that different kinds of writing tasks elicit different kinds of writing performance from students?

Are there some kinds of tasks in which purpose seems a more important consideration than it does in other kinds of tasks?

Does one writing task elicit a greater number of abstract (or connotative or formal) word choices than do other tasks?

Do different writing tasks lead students to use, on average, longer T-units (or more final free modifiers or more adjective modifiers. . .) than do other tasks?

Do different tasks lead students to use different types of transitional relationships or to use paragraphs that fill different types of functions?

Questions Raised by Greenberg (1981b, p. 8)

How do students read writing tasks? Which aspects of the directions do they understand? Or use? Or ignore?

[2]Just as we went to press, we became aware of Hamp-Lyons's (1987) very important study of task-related influences on writers who are responding to academic writing essay tests. Hamp-Lyons has developed a model for analysis of the rhetorical structure of an essay test question which offers a means of appraising the effectiveness of a test item and the responses of raters to papers it elicits.

How do students interpret writing tasks? What kinds of details do they think that the task is asking for?

How do students react to writing tasks? What factors in a task cause a student to perceive it as "easy" or "difficult?"

How are students' responses to writing tasks influenced by situational factors (test vs. nontest context, in-class vs. out-of-class assignment, timed vs. untimed composition, student-initiated vs. teacher-initiated tasks, and so forth) ?

Meanwhile, as these scholars were asking their questions, we had begun to formulate a set of our own which proved to correspond closely with their interests. Expanding on the main question that comes from practice, "What is a good topic and how do you word it?", we devised these questions:

Research Questions about Writing Tasks

1. Questions about the Content and Form of Tasks
   Selection of the Subject
      What considerations need to be taken into account in selecting the subject?
      How does choice of subject affect writer performance?
   Subject Matter Information Base
      What should be given and what should be assumed?
      How does the quantity and the character of the information supplied affect writer performance?
   Procedural Information
      How does the extent of rhetorical specification affect the writer's performance as measured by score? as measured by how tasks are defined?
         Zero specification
            +   mode
            +   role or voice
            +   audience
            +   purpose
         Full specification (all of above)
      How do special cues affect the writer's performance?
         Hints about planning, organization
         Questions to cue content
         Admonitions (to be clear, etc.)
   Contextual Information
      How does knowledge of the purpose of the assessment affect performance?
      How does specification of evaluation criteria affect performance (be careful about grammar, spelling, punctuation, etc.)?
      How do constraints such as time limits and word limits affect performance?

Wording

    How does the wording of writing tasks affect their comprehensibility?

    What semantic or syntactic choices make tasks harder to grasp?

    What language best enables writers to access both content and procedural knowledge?

2. Questions about Reading and Interpreting Tasks

    The Process of Interpretation

       How do students read writing tasks?

       Which of the task-writer's cues and constraints does the writer notice, understand, and use?

          What aids readers to attend to critical portions?

          What makes important content salient?

          What leads to confusion, uncertainty?

       How do different topics and task specifications activate different cognitive processes?

       How does consciousness of the testing context affect interpretation and performance?

       What makes student writers judge tasks too hard or too easy?

       How does interest in a task affect performance?

       In what sense can writing tasks be said to be of equivalent difficulty?

3. Questions about the Raters' Interpretations of Tasks

       How does the rater determine the intention of the test maker?

       How does the rater determine the intention of the student writer and take this into account?

       How do the raters' biases—preferred discourse model, notion of the relevance or irrelevance of scribal skills, preference for displays of creativity, originality, reasoning, or the lack of these—enter into the assigning of quality ratings?

       In short, how does the rater's interpretation of the task influence the rating?

4. Questions about the Process of Designing the Task

       How do implicit or explicit rhetorical theories affect the design of tasks?

       How does the assessment purpose govern task design?

       What criteria can be used to sort and classify tasks?

       How should the test-maker proceed in selecting or generating tasks?

       How do we test topics to assure user understanding? to assure reliability?

       What research processes are available for evaluating and determining the effects of topics?

       How do test makers take into account the development of writers?

Starting with these questions, we wondered what sources of knowledge might be available to begin answering some of them. So we first reviewed the literature to determine the ground already covered before attempting to discover new ground.

Sources of Knowledge for Studying Writing Tasks

As Marcia Farr has indicated in the Preface to this volume, "Writing research
. . . is a field, if not yet a discipline." Writing research has only recently
emerged as a distinct field of inquiry. As an interdisciplinary field it draws
from branches of linguistics, psychology, anthropology, education, cognitive science, social science, and literary study. Although our own cross disciplinary review of current studies is more lengthy than usual, even it cannot
be considered exhaustive. Of necessity, we have been selective in the disciplines we have chosen to review, and within those disciplines we have also
been selective. Our rationale for including particular theory and research
documents in the following review is based on a criterion of relevance. That
is, we looked for sources of knowledge that held promise for answering the
types of questions that people in the field are asking about the properties of
writing tasks. At the start of our research in the fall of 1980, we found in the
standard data bases (ERIC, *Dissertation Abstracts, Psychology Abstracts, Social Sciences Index,* etc.) very few items dealing directly and exclusively with
properties of writing tasks. We found most of our leads and bits and pieces
of information embedded in studies serving larger research interests in writing and in other fields. We found, as Thorndike and Wesman have suggested would be the case, little empirical support for practices in the design
of writing tasks and a good deal of reliance on professional judgment. The
main sources of knowledge that provided background for our studies proved
to be professional wisdom and recommendations from practice, multidisciplinary writing research, psychometrics, and discourse theory from the
perspective of written and spoken language. The findings from these
sources are presented in some detail in subsequent chapters.

TWO

Recommendations from Practice

Professional Wisdom As Knowledge

The Limits of an Experimental Research Model

Educational researchers have traditionally adopted the methods employed by researchers in the natural sciences. The model of the experiment and the statistics it generates has been the primary means of formulating conclusions in the numerical terms that the general community of educational researchers considers binding. For a long time even the most rigorous rational analyses of human activity did not count as research. Appeals to common sense and practical knowledge generally have been even more suspect, dismissed as "mere anecdote" or "journalism." Eventually, by the mid-1960s, certain sociologists, cognitive scientists, and other social theorists began to question the more narrow models of research in education and social science. Sociologist William Bruce Cameron (1963), for example, noted the limits of knowledge based on numbers as applied to the complexity of human affairs: "not everything that can be counted counts, and not everything that counts can be counted" (p. 13).

Some years later, at the 1981 Cognitive Sciences Conference held at the University of California, Berkeley, cognitive scientist, Robert Abelson (1981) of Yale's Artificial Intelligence Project characterized the competing research traditions in the study of human cognition as being between the "neats" and the "scruffies"—in other words, between those "whose canons of hard science dictate a strategy of the isolation of idealized subsystems which can be modeled with elegant productive formalisms" and those other scientists who seek to deal with "the rough and tumble of life as it comes" (p. 1).

Connors (1983) has questioned the appropriateness of the scientific model for research in writing. Connors characterizes the field as "tending strongly in the direction of scientific forms of inquiry" (p. 1). He approves of conducting empirical research in writing where it is appropriate, but too often in composition research, Connors finds a mindless aping of the experimental method of the physical sciences that succeeds only in producing a "barren enactment of imitation science" (p. 19). Connors considers this scientific model to be inadequate when it is applied to human processes, primarily because it so often fails to accommodate "the complexity and interdependence of mental processes, which make . . . disembedding [and isolation] of discrete phenomena difficult" (p. 12). Connors concludes:

> Empirical research has much to teach us, but it cannot teach us who or what we are. If we surrender to the role-playing of scientism . . . our work can only result in a false objectivity.

17

The Need for Contextual Research

Connors has not been the only one to call for adopting a broader range of research strategies in studying composition. Marcia Farr (1981) too, has described the need to adopt new methodologies in writing research:

> We are devising our own tools, choosing from among a variety of social-science disciplines and approaches as we go along. We must create structure out of what we find—out of the data. Writing is a human activity; as such, what we really need to do in order to get valid information is pick our way along and eclectically use methodology from here and there, selecting techniques to help us learn what we want to know. Being eclectic, of course, does *not* preclude being rigorous in our thinking. (p. 13)

Marcia Farr (1981) called for research to start with practice, to deal with the real life in writing classrooms:

> Often researchers get too far from the social contexts in which their work could be useful, and their work becomes so esoteric that it requires much further work to "translate" the findings into practice. It is also important for those who teach writing every day to participate in formulating the research questions. . . . (p. 13)

It does seem to make good sense then to turn first to those who actually teach writing every day to see what their practical knowledge has to offer as starting points for investigation.

The Role of Practical Knowledge in Research

Given the revered status of "scientific knowledge," it is not surprising that "practical knowledge" tends to be undervalued and to carry very little authority in an educational research community that seeks to emulate natural-science ideals. It is, therefore, still necessary to argue the case for recognizing professional wisdom as a respectable source of knowledge and to explain why we have taken practical knowledge as the starting point for our own analysis. The case for elevating the status of practical knowledge has been strengthened by the recent work of social theorists such as Anthony Giddens (1979) who has acknowledged "the rediscovery of natural language and common sense" (p. 250) in determining what counts as knowledge. According to Giddens, social theory must recognize that social actors are knowledgeable about the social systems they produce. Giddens explains the implications of his theory for creating descriptions of any kind of social conduct:

> The social world, unlike the world of nature, has to be grasped as a skilled accomplishment of active human subjects; the constitution of this world as "meaningful," "accountable" or "intelligible" depends upon language, regarded however not simply as a system of signs or symbols but as a medium of practical activity; the social scientist of necessity draws upon the same sorts of

skills as those whose conduct he seeks to analyze in order to describe it; generating descriptions of social conduct depends upon the hermeneutic task of penetrating the frames of meaning which lay actors themselves draw upon in constituting and reconstituting the social world. (1976, p. 155)

Applied to research in writing assessment, Giddens's "method" would require investigators to take as their starting point "common sense knowledge," the "mutual knowledge" generated by "lay actors" (writing teachers) in a particular "meaning frame" (assessing writing). First, observers would identify the "lay concepts" guiding the skilled performances of the writing teachers as "lay actors" on the stages of their own classrooms. To discover the "recognizable" characterizations of a particular activity, such as assessing writing, the investigators would immerse themselves in many "forms of the life" of that activity. To generate descriptions which would become social-scientific discourse, the investigators would participate in an "ensemble of practices." Critical inquiry, according to Giddens (1976), begins then in the context of practice as it is organized through "practical, common sense" knowledge (pp. 159–162).

Toward a Theory of Practice

Because he recognizes "retrospective generalization" or "personal history" as a key source of knowledge, Stenhouse (1981) has provided a philosophical rationale for collecting and using the wisdom of individual professionals. In a very important essay, he asked the question, "What counts as research?" He discusses how the "history-as-research" method of retrospective generalization helps to define the conditions for future action by summarizing experience and by suggesting considerations that people need to take into account as they make judgements about how to act. Thus, in any given case, people's judgments can be founded on "stock-taking," state-of-the-art reports, which function as special types of "contemporary histories." Such "histories" document practical knowledge, the experience of action, in such a way as "to strengthen judgment . . . in the planning of acts." Furthermore, the documents of history take most of their terms from the actors and the events they record. Thus, one great strength of a personal history is that its vocabulary is accessible to other practitioners who are interested in the same pursuits, according to Stenhouse (1981).

The Nature of Practical Knowledge

Practical knowledge is often less orderly than the carefully processed knowledge of science. Yet practical knowledge has virtues recognized by other practitioners but often overlooked by scientific researchers: Practical wisdom is rich in recognizable content; it is tied to specific, familiar contexts; it has been tested under fire. It is particularly valuable when it has withstood tests of situational verification and retrospective generalization. Often, however, much practical knowledge remains private. It does not circulate, and therefore it does not profit by criticism from members of the community it might serve. This step of critical refinement is crucial. For when personal knowledge comes under the scrutiny of fellow professionals, a heretofore particularized body of ideas, experiences, hypotheses, theories, and practices comes into contention with the experiences of others in the same community of practitioners. It is in these encounters during the informal exchanges directed toward mutual learning that the limits to the validity of the ideas offered are discovered and that responsible experience-based generalizations are formed. The process enriches knowledge because the collective image of the reality derived from several "frames of meaning" enables the group of participants to take on a variety of perspectives more comprehensive than that of any individual contribution. Yet the process still preserves the acceptability of individual disagreement.

Practical knowledge develops through a continuing involvement in the unique and particular experiences of the profession, but it remains essentially an individual theory of practice so long as it stays private. However, some privately held theories of practice eventually "go public" through textbooks, curriculum guides, and other media. Once public, these works too are subjected to critical processes which may lead to their verification, validation, and refinement or even rejection. Thus, in time, there develops a form of theory that William Reid (1978) has called "a theory of idealized practice." Dr. Reid, a specialist in curriculum studies in England, believes that a "highly idealized and misleading account of what scientific inquiry is and how it functions" (p. 18) has narrowed our conception of what counts as theory. As he explains:

> When the question of theory as inquiry in the field of curriculum is raised, we tend to visualize a type of theory heavily laden with "scientific" characteristics—offering causal explanation, using precise measurement, lending itself to the repetition of experiments, to hypothesis testing, and so on—a whole range of features which contrast sharply with the nature of practice as we experience it. But this is only one approach to inquiry. It is part (and a somewhat debatable part) of a wide range of concepts and techniques which make up the broad spectrum of theory as inquiry.
>
> A reassessment of the nature and status of scientific theorizing leaves the way clear for an attempt to see whether other types of rational thought or action may not, after all share in some, at least, of the characteristics of theory making. (Reid, 1978, pp. 19–20)

Establishing an "Ensemble of Practices"

Because that reassessment of the nature and status of scientific theorizing and research with respect to composition studies (cf. Connors, 1983) is still in flux, we have provided a lengthy rationale for initiating our study with a source of knowledge too often disdained and neglected in educational research. We believe the practical knowledge of professionals can provide a common sense foundation for designing writing tasks. We are aware of a rich store of practical wisdom in the experience of teachers and other professionals creating topics for writing assessments. It needs to be collected, sorted, appraised, and selectively used to formulate an "ensemble of practices" to guide the design of topics for testing writing.

A full scale search would require a substantial project to collect and synthesize systematically a true sample of the available accounts of practice in designing writing tasks. In this chapter, however, we can offer selected examples from different periods in the history of teaching writing in the United States. This "sample" (in no sense a scientific sample) will suffice to indicate the nature and quality of the professional wisdom that is available to provide a basis for developing a theory of practice. For this sampling of professional wisdom, we have selected ten examples of professionals in action whom we consider to be "exemplars" of wise practice. Each exemplar is a renowned scholar, teacher, testing expert, or a professional body, who in our judgment, is a model of reflective practice. We do not consider this small sample to be a definitive "stock-taking" of practice but rather a starting point for collecting and collating a sorely needed state-of-the-art body of literature grounded in professional action.

In the main, we have selected professionals who have shared their procedural knowledge about one or both of the two dimensions of topics identified in Chapter 1: (a) the subject and (b) the instructions. We have not limited our exemplars only to those persons dealing with the design of topics for assessment. Several of the people presented here address the creation of writing assignments in the context of classroom instruction; however, we consider their procedural recommendations adaptable to an assessment context.

Professionals in Action

Philosophy of the Assignment: Fred N. Scott (1903)[1]

At the turn of the century, Fred N. Scott (1903), a professor of English, contributed his "Philosophy of the Assignment" to an early book on methods of teaching English. Scott divided the making of a classroom writing assignment into five steps:

1. the announcement of the subject,
2. stimulation of interest in the subject,
3. arousal of a desire to write upon it,

---

[1]We are indebted to Alfred H. Grommon, Professor Emeritus, Stanford University, for calling our attention to this source.

4. suggestion of a method or procedure in writing,
5. precautions against wasted effort.

Much of Scott's discussion is devoted to consideration of the principles for selecting an interesting subject. Although he recognizes some value in allowing students to select their own subjects, he argues that freedom of choice does not work in practice because too much of the effort expended is "mis-directed and desultory" (p. 321). Interestingly, Scott's early account of his practical experience with allowing the self-selection of subjects anticipates the findings from current psychometric research which indicate that when students are given a choice of topics in an examination, they are often unable to select the one upon which they will make the highest score (Coffman, 1971a, p. 291).

Scott offers two main principles for choosing subjects for writing: (a) the subject chosen must be one that is interesting to the teacher and (b) the subject chosen must be one that is interesting, or that can be made interesting, to the students, as Scott explains:

> It must be borne in mind that after the essays are written they must be read, and it is the teacher who will read them. He ought to read with intense interest and a kindling enthusiasm. But if the subjects are distasteful to him, his reading, despite the most conscientious efforts, will be half-hearted and ineffectual. (p. 322)

In discussing the desire to write, Scott claims that "such a desire, when it is natural, springs from two healthy impulses: the impulse to give expression to one's thoughts and feelings, and the impulse to communicate one's thoughts" (p. 324). Again, Scott's early-day professional wisdom anticipated the positions of the latter-day discourse theorists, James Moffett, James Britton, and others, who also have advocated making assignments that elicit personal, expressive writing for real audiences.

Scott makes a particularly forceful statement about the importance of the audience to writers. His words deserve careful consideration by designers of writing tasks:

> In assigning the work, the teacher should be at some pains to provide an audience or a reader. Sometimes the audience will be real, sometimes it will be imaginary, but it should never be lacking. (p. 325)

Designation of an audience is important because, as Scott states, "the consciousness of waiting auditors" is "the most powerful of all stimuli to expression" (p. 325).

Subject Plus Predication Equals Topic: Josephine Miles ([1962] 1979)

Josephine Miles (1979), Regent's Professor of English at the University of California, Berkeley, always believed that the solution to the problem of controlling the magnitude of subjects lies with training the writer to formulate a "responsible predication" for any given topic. She considers no subject to be too large or too small or too complicated so long as the writer controls what he has to say about it. In her monograph on composing, she argues that control comes in selecting a *supportable predication* about the subject from the writer's own experience or knowledge. Miles has suggested that one can take even an abstract subject such as "death" and formulate a predication that is "responsible" and "supportable" in terms of what a writer knows: for example, "When death appeared in my life, it didn't frighten me" (p. 3). Miles explains that the verbs in the predicates of these two clauses cue the structure of further development. The verbs in the "death" predication initiate a retrospective account of an event as it happened. The temporal locative *when* in association with the sequence of verbs, *appeared* and *didn't frighten,* together require a commitment to develop the natural temporal sequence they suggest. This event, the appearance of a "death that didn't frighten" is what the writer outlines, not the subject by itself, for the subject alone is inert.

Miles (1979) always believed that it is necessary for students to learn how to recognize the implicit structure in their own predications and in the questions they receive in assignments. She explained why assignment by topic poses difficulties for students:

> Assignment by topic is artificial, not only because it is unmotivated, but because it is too far removed from the central unit of thought, the statement. It is the question to be answered, rather than the topic to be predicated, which gives the student the central clue to the order and structure. Only after he can handle questions easily can he move easily to those mere half-questions which are topics. (p. 20)

Miles formulated her theory on the basis of years of experience in teaching freshman English and through informal "experiments" conducted between 1950-1952 in collaboration with Berkeley's Committee on Prose, an early effort to improve the writing of prose across the disciplines (the summary report is reprinted in Miles, 1979, pp. 10–13). The committee concluded that the "problem of student writing is fundamental to student learning" and "therefore suggested a further and deeper integration of writing with learning throughout the University" (p. 11). The Committee also sought to improve writing across the disciplines by teaching the cues to the structure of predications in statements and questions.

When we select subjects for writing, Josephine Miles recommends that we provide opportunities for students to develop ideas in essays where they can make "statements based on interest and speculation and [support] them by adequate evidence pro and con" (p. 23). The power of students to compose their thoughts comes from working through ideas, taking care to see that they are responsibly developed. Thus, Miles criticizes the common practice of offering assignments on personal subjects which virtually exclude rational processes.

Providing the Occasion for Writing:
The Commission on English (1965)

In 1965, the Commission on English, an agency of the College Entrance Examination Board, published its report on the teaching of English, *Freedom and Discipline in English*. The Commission's report contains a section on composition assignments which declares, "No part of an English teacher's job is more important . . . than the making of sound, well-framed assignments, what is called 'providing the occasion' " (p. 92). The authors propose the following criteria for a good assignment:

Criteria for a Good Writing Assignment
(Adapted from Commission on English Recommendations, 1965)

A good writing assignment

1. evokes the best from the writer and gives the teacher the best chance to be helpful;
2. aids learning and requires a response that is the product of discovery;
3. furnishes data to start from;
4. may take the form of, or be construable into, a proposition;
5. limits either form or content or both;
6. will stipulate the audience to be addressed, wherever feasible. (pp. 93–96)

The members of the Commission recommended starting an assignment with data such as contradictory criticism of a literary text, opposing arguments, incongruous bits of common sense (e.g., contradictory maxims), or even a picture or a cartoon, but they thought that *usually it should be on the literature studied*. Because the Commission advocated giving students material to work with and clear direction, it recommended converting a topic into a proposition in the following manner:

> "The view from my window" has the virtue of inviting invention but the serious fault of giving the writer nothing to control his attention. Translated to propositional form—"That the view from my window makes me dread (or welcome) getting up in the morning"—the same topic suggests a focus and even a tone for the writer to exploit . . . The provision of a predicate immediately puts the writer into a posture of defense or attack and calls for the summoning and ordering of evidence or arguments. Instead of a circle circumscribing undefined matter, the proposition supplies an arrow pointing out a clear direction of movement. (p. 94)

With respect to audience, the Commission observed that "Too many English themes seem addressed . . . to the teacher . . . or, in a vague romantic way, to the world or posterity or some Saroyanesque 'You Out There' " (p. 95). The Commission would remedy this lack of attention to audience by having teachers vary their stipulations, beginning with fairly simple exercises: "Write a letter to the governor arguing that . . . ," "Write a petition to the student council or the principal requesting that . . . ," "Write an essay on the proposition that . . . " etc. (p. 95). The Commission expected the student eventually to define his or her own audience and "to define it, not in so many words, but by tone and content alone" (p. 96).

Moreover, the Commission acknowledged that "for the novice" especially, it might be inhibiting rather than helpful to require that he think of a specific audience for a poem or for any of the range of forms that are more 'literary' than expository or argumentative" (p. 95). The Commission's writing assignment models actually go beyond naming an audience to specifying mode or genre as well as propositional content. Thus, these Commission assignments rather explicitly circumscribe and define the essay that is to be written.

Two Basic Assignment Patterns: Arthur J. Carr (1965)

Arthur J. Carr (1965), a professor of English at the University of Michigan, made a kinescope called *Student Writing Assignment Based on 'Fire Walking in Ceylon'* for the Commission on English in the early 1960s. Carr shares the convictions of the members of the Commission that the design of the assignment significantly affects the quality of writing that students may produce in response to it. His kinescope production relates his experience with the writing assignment on "Fire Walking," which had produced a terrible set of papers. But instead of berating his students for their obtuseness, he takes himself to task, asking, "What went wrong with my assignment?" After analyzing what had gone wrong in making the assignment—failure to prepare the students, lack of clarity in the statement of the assignment, lack of a defined purpose in making the assignment—Carr described two basic assignment patterns. One type of assignment would emphasize structure and form; the other would emphasize ideas. If the instructor specifies the form, then he should liberate ideas, leaving the subject open to choice. If the instructor names the subject, then he should liberate form, leaving the kind of discourse open to choice. Carr believes in carefully selecting and controlling the number of constraints a student must cope with in a single assignment. He views the making of assignments as an art to which true professionals should give considerable thought. Well-designed assignments take more time and imagination than most people give to them. Haphazard assignments flung out in assessments without adequate development and trial reap a harvest of false and superficial response, of spurious, invalid results.

Criteria for Composition Questions:
The Commission on Writing (1968)

In 1968, the Commission on Writing of the Education Council proposed one maxim and four criteria for preparing composition questions (R. Clark, et al., 1968):

Criteria for Preparing Composition Questions
(From the Commission on Writing, the Education Council,
Clark, et al., 1968)

Maxim: Be sure that any question you ask insures the possibility of a rhetorically effective composition.

1. A good question should be stimulating: it should present a subject matter with which a student can readily become engaged and it should present the subject in such a way that he can make an assertion about it. Not "My Summer Vacation" but "What do you think was the point of failure in your summer vacation?"
2. A good question should be fashioned to the interest and abilities of the students. Like any writer, the poser of a question must be aware of his audience.
3. A good question should seek to elicit a specific response. Although one may at times wish a student to generate his own topic, generally one should seek to show the student the specific area in which he is to organize his essay and the audience for whom the essay is intended. A teacher should beware of his own power and not force the student to "write to the teacher."
4. A good question should be clear and precise in its instructions. In all respects, the demands on the questioner are identical with those on the writer. (1968, p. v).

Audience, Purpose, and Voice:
Edmund J. Farrell (1969)

Drawing upon his experience as a supervisor of student teachers in secondary English at the University of California, Berkeley Campus, Farrell (1969) culled a number of writing assignments that he felt exemplified various sorts of lapses. He observed that:

> Common to these assignments is the absence of a stipulated audience and/or purpose which would help the student to define himself in context, which would lead him to adopt an appropriate persona or 'speaking voice' in his composition. (p. 430)

Farrell joins a long line of professionals who advocate specification of audience, role, and purpose in the writing assignment. But Farrell goes further than some other professionals in suggesting patterns for creating assignments with built-in "selves" which function as cues to suggest the particular roles (and "voices") that the writer may adopt in relation to the given audience and purpose. Farrell (1969) offers four possibilities:

The Writer's Role and Audience
(From Farrell, 1969)

1. The "self" of an assignment may be internal to the selection, the purpose unspecified, and the audience private. (Example: Assume that you

are Lady Macbeth and that you keep a diary. Write the five entries which precede your suicide.)

2. The "self" and the audience may be internal to the selection and the purpose specified. (Example: You are Tom and have been away from home now for three months. Write to Laura trying to explain to her why you left.)

3. The "self," audience, and purpose may be external to the selection. (Example: A friend of yours comes to you with a copy of Macbeth and says, "I understand you've read this play in class. What should I look for so I can most fully understand it?" What advice would you offer?)

4. The "self" may be internal to the selection and the audience and the purpose external. (Example: You are one of the inhabitants of Spoon River who has died. You have an opportunity to speak out from the grave, summarizing your life in a paragraph or two. What comments have you to make?) (pp. 430–431)

Farrell concludes that if students are given good assignments that enable them to adopt appropriate voices, "their writing should be more pleasurable to read and much easier to evaluate" (p. 431).

Creating Meaningful Topics: William F. Irmscher (1979)

A past president of the National Council of Teachers of English, a former chairman of the Conference on College Composition and Communication, and a former editor of its journal *College Composition and Communication*, William F. Irmscher (1979) brings a wealth of experience to his pedagogical guide, *Teaching Expository Writing*. He opens his chapter on topics with the sentence: "Assigning topics for writing is one of the most important things a composition teacher does" (p. 69). Irmscher's discussion of topics echoes in many respects the principles espoused by the other professionals so far presented here. Like Scott and Miles, Irmscher would not give certain personal experience topics to freshman students because he would not want to read the cliche-filled essays that they would produce. Such topics, says Irmscher, "are not springboards for writing; they are traps. They don't give students a chance to reveal that they can think inventively" (p. 69). Instead, Irmscher discusses each of five criteria that a good topic ought to meet (pp. 68–72):

Criteria for a Good Topic
(Based on Irmscher, 1979)

1. A good topic ought to have a purpose.
2. A good topic ought to be meaningful within the student's experience.
3. A good topic ought to prefer specific and immediate situations to abstract and theoretical ones.

4. A good topic posing a hypothetical situation should be within a student's grasp.
5. A good topic ought to encourage a student to write.

In elaborating on his criteria, Irmscher explains that a "meaningful" topic is not necessarily a "personal" topic, though it should be involving. He observes that students do distinguish what they are willing to talk about in the dormitory from what they are willing to talk about in the classroom. That is , students do consider some topics "too personal" (p. 70). In view of the widespread use of personal topics in writing examinations, we need to learn more about how to identify topics that may be considered "too personal."

Irmscher discusses his notion of specificity in a topic by contrasting the abstract topic, "Discuss freedom" with another one that is more concrete. "List the freedoms you enjoy where you live and the freedoms you are denied. What is the reason for the denials? Do you accept the reasons? Write an essay on the subject" (p. 70). Finally, Irmscher evaluates the effects of topics which require writers to project themselves into hypothetical situations. He reads the following topic as an overly-imaginative stimulus which implicitly invites satire: "If you were the first chimpanzee to be landed on Mars, what message would you deliver to Earthlings?" (p. 71). Yet certain hypothetical topics do provide an indirect vehicle for expressing thoughts that otherwise would be difficult to share: "Write an extended obituary notice for the newspaper upon the occasion of your own death" (p. 71). This kind of hypothetical topic actually concerns the values a student currently holds even though it seems to project these values into the future. Thus, Irmscher says it functions very differently from one that addresses a seventeen-year-old by saying, "If you were an old man or woman . . . ." This type of hypothetical projection is very ill-advised, according to Irmscher because "If the purpose is to find out what it is like to be old or how the old think, it would be far preferable to have young people talk to old people and report their impressions" (p. 71). Irmscher endorses allowing choices among topics, but he concludes that "limitless choice ('Write on anything you want to') usually proves self-defeating. Students flounder when they can choose anything in the world" (p. 72).

Avoiding Excessive Instructions: Marjorie Kirrie, (1979)

As both a professor of English and a chief reader for the College Entrance Examination Board, Marjorie Kirrie (1979) explains in a brief article for the *National Writing Project Network Newsletter,* how topic writers, in a well-intentioned effort to be specific, are likely to unwittingly introduce factors that produce unwanted side effects. These side effects are the result of what Kirrie calls "overwriting" the prompt. She cautions against "shoring up topics with all kinds of directions: 'You are writing to . . . ,' 'You have met a . . . ,' 'Tell about . . . ,' 'Tell how . . . ' " (p. 7). Such instructions dictate structure and lead to "a stringing together of attempts to cope with each 'Tell' in the exact order given in the prompt" (p. 7).

Kirrie further cautions against asking students to address a specific unreal audience, to imagine themselves in situations alien to their world, or to imagine themselves as other entities. The topic that begins "If you were . . . " can only be written in the subjunctive or conditional modes and sets "traps for all except the highly skilled" (p. 7). In contrast to the views of other professionals already presented, Kirrie insists that specifying an audience makes the writing task needlessly difficult and calls for greater skill than many students possess. "Besides, " says Kirrie, "students never forget the real audience for assessment writing [the teacher and other evaluators]" (p. 7). Also Kirrie noted a further complication in specifying an audience: "Some audiences call for less sophisticated diction and syntax than we would like to see students produce in a test situation" (p. 7).

So what should topic authors do in order to design a topic that works? Kirrie advises keeping the topic as "nondirective as possible" and using "any word, phrase, or brief statement which invites a variety of interpretations and responses" (p. 7).

> A statement should give students as many options as did the quotation from Pogo used in last year's College Entrance Examination Board Test essay in 1978, "We have met the enemy and he is us," which elicited everything from historical exposition to commentaries on language usage. As for additional directions, variants of "Write an essay on what . . . means (suggests) to you," together with the advice that examples may be helpful and that good writing will be appreciated, are all that are needed. (p. 7)

We should bear in mind that Marjorie Kirrie's recommendations are intended to support methods of developing topics which will be used in assessments where holistic or general impression scoring procedures will be used.

Finding the Best Essay Topics:
Gertrude Conlan (1980, 1982)

Gertrude Conlan (1982), a senior examiner at Educational Testing Service, has worked for more than 20 years on the development and scoring of a variety of essay tests. Citing a number of vivid examples from her experience, she describes how difficult it is to create good essay topics:

> At ETS, even after years of experience, even after the combined efforts of the qualified teachers who create and approve the topics, only one topic in ten, on the average, passes the trials of pretesting. (p. 11)

Conlan cites, as an example of a problem topic, one that had been approved for pretesting by the Committee of Examiners (experienced English teachers) responsible for the College Board's English Composition Achievement Test:

> Waste is a necessary part of the American way of life.

Conlan reports that the members of the committee had been thinking about the roles that planned obsolescence and attractive packaging have played in our economy, and no one was prepared for the interpretation that showed up regularly in the 300 papers written during the pretesting:

> "Waste," these papers said, "is produced by all animals. Americans have bodily wastes to dispose of, too. Of course, waste is necessary to American life." The wording of the topic was changed and eventually students taking the English Composition Test were asked to write on a topic that began with the words, "Wastefulness is part of the American way of life." (p. 11)

A number of unpredictable factors may influence the student's interpretation of the topic; therefore, it is always desirable to try out topics on a population matching the one that ultimately will be tested.

In this same article, Conlan (1982) evaluates a number of other trial topics, one of which is:

> Nothing in America stands still for very long, including the people.

Her trenchant description of the results of the trial of this topic reveals that:

> The candidates isolated "standing still" for definition—out of context. They documented the statement instead of agreeing or disagreeing with it; they did not focus on the question posed. They did not deal with the idea of progress. The topic invites Fourth of July oratory. As it stands, the topic does not contain the germ of argument. A possible revision might ask the candidates to draw a line between what is simply hectic movement, busyness, haste. (p. 11)

During a panel presentation, at the 1983 National Testing Network in Writing Conference on Assessment, Conlan (1983), drawing further on her years of experience at ETS, made a number of observations about problems in developing essay topics. The recorder's report follows:

> Every essay measures "an almost infinite universe of knowledge and skills;" topics and questions do not equal each other.

> There is no formula to produce effective test questions.

> Any change in the topic—including what was on TV the night before the test—may change the task, often in unpredictable ways.

> A question must be able to be scored. It cannot be too emotion-charged, or too boring for the readers. (p. 10)

Gertrude Conlan (personal correspondence, August 22, 1980) provided

Catharine Keech, one of the research coordinators for the Writing Assessment Project, with a set of broad guidelines for designing essay questions:

Suggestions for Writing Essay Questions[2]

1. The question should be clear.

    Students should not have to puzzle over the instructions. The topic is intended to test the ability to write and not the ability to guess what the test maker intends. Besides, students have only a limited amount of time, time that should be spent writing and not analyzing unnecessarily.

2. The question should be as brief as clarity allows.

    Restatement may sometimes be necessary to avoid misunderstanding. But, then, perhaps one should consider whether the restatement should be used without the original because the restatement does not need additional clarification.

3. The instructions should be definite.

    Students should know what is required. For example, *Discuss, citing specific examples from one novel.* Or, *Pay attention to the correct form of the business letter.* Or, *Be sure to use complete sentences.*

4. Avoid questions requiring only a yes or no answer.

    Example: *Do you agree?* Where does the student go from there?

5. Average students should be able to write average answers to the questions, and yet bright students should be able to show their brightness.

    A good topic permits the ranking of all students according to their ability.

6. The vocabulary used and the concepts expressed in the topic should not be too difficult for the ordinary student to understand immediately.

    A difficult topic distinguishes only between the very bright and the rest of the population. Besides, difficult reading changes the test to a reading test.

7. The question should not call for cliches as answers.

    A topic worn out by overuse produces worn-out responses. On the other hand, some good questions merely twist cliches. For example, *What's right with television? In what ways are teenagers more conservative than the over-thirties?*

8. The question itself should provide an organizing principle for the essay.

    Example: Compare and contrast . . .
    Briefly describe . . . and then analyze . . .

[2]From: *Suggestions for Writing Essay Questions.* G. Conlan, 1980. Reprinted by permission of Educational Testing Service, the copyright owner.

Discuss your answer to this question, giving the reasons for your answer and citing specific examples to support those reasons.

9. The question should not elicit responses which affect either the writer's or the reader's judgment.

Politics, racial issues, and other inflammatory topics are to be avoided. Also to be avoided are topics that are dishearteningly dull. For example, even a seemingly innocuous topic such as *Who has had the greatest influence on your life?* cannot be scored easily. If the candidate writes on the wrong political figure (from the reader's point of view), the score is either too high—because the reader is making up for his or her own bias—or too low because the reader has succumbed to that bias. On the other hand, the fifth essay on the greatness of the basketball coach is not scored at the same standard as the first. Readers are human; they do become bored.

10. The question writer should write out the answer expected and determine whether the question really calls for that answer. The question writer should also try to answer the question in the allotted time, just to see whether it is humanly possible to do so. The question should be revised in the light of any discoveries made.

In heeding her advice, it is well to remember that Gertrude Conlan's suggestions for designing topics, like Marjorie Kirrie's, pertain to the development of prompts that will be used to elicit writing samples for evaluation under a holistic or general impression marking scheme.

Primary Trait Scoring: National Assessment of Educational Progress (1974)

While Gertrude Conlan has illustrated the difficulty in predicting what response an essay question will elicit and Marjorie Kirrie has explained why a writing prompt should have "the widest possible evocative range," there are other professional test-makers who have adopted the point of view that a writing task should be defined more exactly. The *primary trait* approach— developed by Richard Lloyd-Jones, Karl H. Klaus, and their other associates for the National Assessment of Educational Progress (Lloyd-Jones, 1977, p. 37)—calls for a writing "exercise" with precisely defined rhetorical specification of subject, audience, and role (See the "Children on the Boat" exercise later in this chapter). Another principal developer of the primary trait system has been Ina V.S. Mullis, senior research analyst for the NAEP at the Education Commission of the States until 1983 and since then associate director for NAEP at the Educational Testing Service. She has described the characteristics of the writing "exercises" devised for NAEP assessments according to the primary trait model put to use beginning with the 1974 assessment. Afterwards, some NAEP items were released to the general public with the hope that "this information [would] be useful both to those interested in using NAEP items and to those interested in adapting this scoring procedure to their own writing tasks" (Mullis, 1976, p. 1). As Mullis portrays this model:

> The essence of the primary trait system is to narrowly delineate the situation of the writer, by defining the variables. With this approach responses should all address the same task and can be judged using the same criteria . . . This means that for each exercise three things must be specified: (1) the identity of the writer (whether the respondent is himself or is given a role to play), (2) the audience (who the writer is writing to) and (3) the subject matter (what the writer should communicate to the audience). The more structured the task, the less difficult the scoring, since the essays or letters will be more uniform in focus. For example, if persuasive writing is chosen as an important skill to measure, it could be decided that students should be able to use writing to influence decision-makers. The task could be "Write a letter to someone important about a problem in this country." A better task would be, "Write a letter to your principal suggesting a way to solve a problem in your school." If the nature of the problem is further defined, e.g., the lunchroom, the task would be even better. With a national sample, it is difficult to identify universally applicable situations. (pp. 8-9)

Rexford Brown (1978), Editor of Publications and Test Developer for NAEP, also has argued for developing exacting specification of the writing task in an assessment:

> If you want to evaluate an essay for certain characteristics, then you must be sure that you have requested them in the assignment. This is not a trivial matter; it is extremely difficult to write assignments that define precisely the rhetorical imperatives that will either be met or missed by the students. If you want to know whether they can elaborate upon a role expressively while maintaining control of a point of view and tense then you have to set the task up in such a way that they must do so, and define acceptable levels of achievement that are concrete and realistic. (p. 5)

The primary trait assessment procedure begins then with the design of a task containing rhetorical specifications that are intended to direct the writing process. An evaluation procedure of this sort presupposes a theory of rhetoric, but we shall reserve discussion of that until Chapter 6, which is devoted to an exploration of the sources of knowledge from discourse theory. However, to clarify the distinctions between this system of topic design and others, we provide here abridged versions of the two examples given by Richard Lloyd-Jones (1977) in his comprehensive account of primary trait scoring:

Example No. 1

Writing Task: Children on the Boat

> Respondents were given a printed photograph of five children playing on an overturned rowboat. The picture is copied in NAEP report 05–W–02, "Express-

ive Writing" . . . The task was presented to a sample of ages 9, 13, and 17 in 1974. The actual task and the original draft of the scoring guide are reproduced here. The final scoring guide given to raters follows that. These guides do not appear in the report . . .

Directions: Look carefully at the picture. These kids are having fun jumping on the overturned boat. Imagine you are one of the children in the picture. Or if you wish, imagine that you are someone standing nearby watching the children. Tell what is going on as he or she would tell it. Write as if you were telling this to a good friend, in a way that expresses strong feelings. Help your friend FEEL the experience too. Space is provided on the next three pages. (pp. 47–48, 60)

Following the task is the NAEP Scoring Guide. This is a detailed guide running several pages, much too lengthy to quote here. It begins with a background section which identifies the *primary trait* as follows: "Imaginative Expression of Feeling through Inventive Elaboration of a *Point of View*." The second part of this section is a rationale which states exactly what the task seeks to test and then proceeds to show how particular words and features of instructions will cue the desired response. For example, this passage sets forth these expectations:

The test is whether a writer can project him/herself into a situation, find a role and an appropriate audience, and then reveal an attitude toward the material in relation to the role—a complex writing task . . . the writer must *choose* appropriate facets of the situation consistently to serve a *purpose* . . .

Note the important features of the instructions. "Look carefully at the picture." The writer is expected to study the facts, to perceive detail . . .

The writer is given one of two roles—that of a child in the picture or that of a person nearby. The latter may be a child or adult . . .

Finally are the three verbs of crucial instruction, "Tell, " "Write, " and "Help." "Tell" suggest an oral manner, although it probably does not require it, but "as he or she would tell it" provides additional pressure to be natural. In fact, it encourages role playing, a strong "I" voice, and that can cause some difficulty in reading papers by mature writers who are trying to imitate children [and so forth]. (p. 48)

Then comes a section of the scoring guide called the Rubric, which describes how to judge and mark the papers received. It provides a scale which specifies degrees of control of the subject from

1   *(no real entry into the imaginary world of the picture* [to]
5   *(temporal and spatial point of view maintained; shapes the facts of the situation into a highly structured, intelligent statement).*

Included in the guide are sample responses at each scoring level for each of the three populations under assessment (Lloyd-Jones, 1977, pp. 47–60).

Example No. 2

Writing Task: Woman's Place Essay

> Some people believe that a woman's place is in the home. Others do not. Take ONE side of this issue. Write an essay in which you state your position and defend it.

The task is accompanied by a scoring guide that sets up a scale of value based upon whether or not the writer takes a position and defines it clearly and then defends that position with reasons. The scale specifies degrees of clarity in the position and ranks response according to the quantity of elaborated or unelaborated reasons. Types of appeals to reason are also taken into account (Lloyd-Jones, 1977, pp. 60–66).

The primary trait system was developed in response to a considerable amount of professional criticism leveled at the ETS-type essay topics and holistic scoring procedures used in the first NAEP writing assessment. An influential report, *National Assessment and the Teaching of English* by John Mellon (1975) on behalf of the National Council of Teachers of English, offers an extended evaluation of the form and content of the first round of NAEP composition exercises and kinds of information they provided before the primary trait system was adopted at NAEP.

Seven essay topics were developed for use at ages 9, 13, and 17. Mellon lists all of these topics in the form they were given, but for the purpose of this discussion we shall quote only two of them here:

Essay Topic for Age 9: Going to School

> Think about what happens when you go to school. Write a little story that tells what you do from the time you leave where you live until you get to school. Be sure to include everything that you think is important.

Essay Topic for Age 9: Forest Fire

> Here is a picture of something sad that is going on in the forest. Look at the picture for a while. Do you see the forest fire? Write a story about what is happening in the picture. This is an important story because you want people to know about this sad event. [The picture depicts a forest fire with animals swimming across a river rapids to obtain safety.] (Mellon, 1975, p. 21)

Mellon (1975) expressed deep concern over the quality of writing produced in response to each of the NAEP topics, finding it "diffuse and unfocused as to discourse structure and devoid of a single sense of audience and unified voice and tone (p. 35). As an example of the problem he observed, he described the wildly unpredictable range of responses elicited by the "Going to School" topic:

Some writers developed fantasy occurrences while others stuck to the mundane facts of daily life. Some wrote about a real happening they had once seen, such as a traffic accident; others gave maplike directions for getting from home to school; still others merely described scenes along the way. The words "sad" and "important" in the "Forest Fire" essay led some writers to downplay what was happening in an attempt to express and describe their feelings. Others tried to explain why forest fires constitute important events, and a few ventured into the Smokey Bear idiom and wrote essays on fire prevention. (p. 35)

Mellon attributed these results to "imprecisely formulated topics [which] prevented the National Assessment from measuring students' ability to handle specific rhetorical tasks defined in terms of mode, purpose, voice, and audience" (Mellon, 1975, p. 36). Thus, he applauded the development of the second-round set of NAEP topics formulated with rhetorical specificity and primary trait scoring in mind. In summarizing the results of the first writing assessment Mellon speaks of the need to "refine our instruments of measurement" (p. 37) and to recognize that " 'writing ability' spans a wider range of rhetorical occasions, and [that] we should attempt to formulate topics with enough precision to enable student writers to experience as many of these as possible" (p. 38).

Summary

We do not intend to slight the significance of educational research, for that is the subject of the next chapter. But Stenhouse (1981) suggests that readers of educational research can hardly fail to notice that it often deals in data so highly abstracted, so remote in form of expression that the people who were the original creators of the data often can barely recognize their connection to the reported results. Only rarely do these results portray particular human beings interacting in particular human contexts. This is to be expected, of course, since so much educational research deals in the study of *population samples* rather than in the study of *particular human cases*, a key distinction explained by Stenhouse:

> The portrayal of cases offers to inform the judgment of actors—the administrators, teachers, pupils, or parents—rather after the manner of history, by opening the research accounts to recognition and comparison and hence to criticism in the light of experience. Such a refinement of experienced practical judgment eludes the psychostatistical model which strips data of recognizable characteristics and content, and presents "findings" or "results," which are accessible to criticism only by replication or by technical attack on the design or conduct of the research. (p. 107)

We have considered it important to begin our study by reviewing informally the work of particular professionals—teachers and test makers who are skilled practitioners in creating classroom essay topics and tasks for writing assessments because we wanted to tap this well of individual professional experience at the start of our account before we turn to the formal reports of the "mean results" found in the research literature. Because in our own experience as teachers and researchers we had noted that "practical knowledge" is undeservedly overshadowed by an ostensibly more valuable "scientific knowledge," we have decided to broaden our own conception of what counts as valid forms of knowledge in an educational investigation. In certain respects, our philosophy of science and our work seem to be compatible with the ideas now being advanced by Schön (1983) who has called for development of an "epistemology of practice." Schön urges us to take a new view of professional action as a primary source of knowledge. He believes that reflective knowledge from practice deserves to be as honored and valued in academia as knowledge based in research.

The data that we have gathered here by noting the contributions of individual professionals "reflecting-in-action" reveals several themes. A certain consensus emerges in this collation of their views of the process of creating writing assignments. There are differences of opinion about the proper degree of rhetorical specification, but there are some agreements on other matters. What follows is our effort to piece together some principles that seem to have stood the "tests of time" in practice. As we began with Scott's 1903 "philosophy of the assignment," so we end with our own contemporary "Principles for Designing Assignments for the Assessment of Writing" based upon our own experience and the wisdom of the professionals presented in this chapter.

Some Principles for Designing Writing Assignments for the Assessment of Writing: An Evolving Consensus

Leo Ruth and Sandra Murphy

Maxim: *A well-framed topic for a writing assessment provides an occasion for writing in which the student's powers of expression and communication are stimulated to their maximum.*

Principles:

1. The subject chosen should be potentially interesting to the student writers.
2. The subject chosen should be potentially interesting to the evaluator of the essays written.
3. The assignment should furnish data to start from.
4. The assignment should be meaningful within the student's experience, neither too difficult nor too easy, permitting assessment of all students according to their ability.
5. The assignment should seek to elicit a specific response and should place limits on content or form or both.

6. The assignment may suggest a carefully chosen audience beyond the teacher or evaluator when the subject and the presupposed world knowledge of the test-taker make such specification feasible.
7. Assignment by subject or essay title alone without a predication is artificial and yields a lack of focus in the development.

    Coda: A well-framed assignment, clear and precise in its instructions, shows awareness of the audience of "waiting examinees."

These principles are put forth tentatively. They await further refinement as fellow professionals test them both in practice and through carefully designed research. Now we shall turn to what the available research does say about designing writing tasks for assessments. The next three chapters deal with issues in conducting research on topics and present examples of research in psychometrics and in writing which have a direct bearing on the design of topics for writing assessment.

THREE

Knowledge from Research on Testing

Psychometric Research: Contributions and Limits

Given our nation's long reliance on the written examination, we might expect to find a substantial research literature covering such matters as problems of meaning, unintended wording effects, and other issues in designing essay questions. But such is not the case. Psychometrics, the science of testing, virtually ignores this whole area.

Early Attitudes Toward Essay Tests

For over one hundred years, written examinations have played a large part in the lives of youth in American schools. Emerging in the middle of the nineteenth century, written examinations became the dominant means of assessing learning. In the mid 1930s the very term *examination* was synonymous with *written examination.* Thus, a 1936 report on written examinations to the Carnegie Foundation for the Advancement of Teaching was called *Examinations and Their Substitutes in the United States* (Kandel, 1936). The *substitutes* for the "real" examinations were what were then known as the *new type test* composed of *objective* questions.

As claims for the superiority of the new type of objective test grew stronger, people attempted to formulate essay questions that could be marked more objectively and yield more reliable results. But as Kandel (1936) pointed out, objectivity exacts its cost in altering the form and function of the essay test: "the more accurately and carefully this is done, the closer will be the approximation to the new type test and the less in the long run will be the real educational value of the essay" as a means for training in expression (p. 85).

We cannot, of course, truly label any test as objective. Elements of subjectivity enter into the creation of all test questions (or items) and their scoring systems at various steps in their making. Consequently, some testing experts have sought more accurate terms of classification. Thorndike and Hagen (1969, p. 50), classifying tests by item format, call the two main kinds *free answer-type* and *structured answer-type.* Anastasi (1976) calls the test where an examinee is given a task bearing little resemblance to the real-life criterion behavior under evaluation an *indirect* test (p. 588).[1]

In time, there developed a scientific testing movement called psychometrics—actually a kind of applied statistics—dealing with a restricted range of issues in determining the "quality" (defined

---

[1](e.g., a multiple-choice writing test which requires no writing. See the Note on Terms in Chapter 1 for further clarification of terms.)

psychometrically as reliability) of tasks to be used in assessing writing or any other subject. As Gilbert Sax (1974) defines the field: "Educational measurement . . . requires the quantification of attributes according to specified rules" (p. 3). These rules deal with the quantifiable properties of tests to resolve issues of reliability, validity, objectivity, and standardization in the development, administration, scoring, and interpretation of tests, including writing tests. Textbooks on educational measurement commonly deal with test construction, but they tend to concentrate more on developing objective *items* than on creating the essay questions that comprise writing tests.

Statistical Methods for Analysis of Topics

Since the measurement people have concentrated mostly on issues of reliability in essay testing, (Coffman, 1971a) without particular regard for the form and wording of the content of essay questions, the literature on psychometrics does not offer guidance beyond the most general sorts of principles for actually designing and wording the writing tasks. But psychometrics does offer statistical procedures for appraising the "behavior" of questions or topics for writing during both field trials and actual test administrations. Psychometric *field test* procedures tend to be costly and time-consuming. To design an essay test that will distinguish between good writers and poor ones, the examiners create several essay questions, administer them to a sample of the population to be tested, observe whether they predict performance along the lines expected, and eliminate or change questions that do not work. We need to recall that Wesman (1971) has called this essentially a negative process: It identifies "clearly bad items," but "it does not assure the goodness of an item" (p. 81).

There are special rules for sorting out desirable and undesirable topics using procedures of *item analysis.* Often misinterpreted, as we noted in Chapter 1, item analysis is a statistical method of deriving an *index of difficulty* and an *index of discrimination.* The *difficulty level* of an item is calculated on the basis of the proportion of students who pass at different levels on the scale in use. The *index of discrimination* shows how "good" and "weak" students scored on particular topics during the *field trial.* These indices enable test-makers to predict how populations comparable to the ones participating in the tryout are likely to do on particular questions. This procedure succeeds in weeding out grossly inadequate topics—ones that fail to sort out ("discriminate") the weak students from the strong ones. But even though the numbers obtained through these procedures are useful, they do not reveal the sources of problems of interpretation. Gilbert Sax (1974), a leading measurement expert, has acknowledged that item analysis, as it is conducted psychometrically, "cannot reveal if ambiguity results from the students' lack of knowledge or from poorly written items" (p. 233).

Through the "field trial," psychometrics provides an evaluative procedure for eliminating faulty essay questions or other test items, but psychometrics does not have empirically derived analytic methods for determining what has gone wrong in framing the essay question in the first place (Payne & McMorris, 1967). The essay questions that survive the field trial are presumed to be "meaningful" to the larger population to be tested. Although psychometrics strives to be scientific, the procedures used to construct and validate essay questions are essentially subjective and scientifically crude in the sense that there is no theory of information processing or of cognition underlying the design of writing tasks. (See Thorndike and Hagen (1969) and also Wesman (1971) as quoted in Chapter 1.)

The Limits of Psychometric Measures

Standardized objective testing procedures assume that the examiner and the examinee share a common language and congruent interpretations of tasks. Yet Mellon (1975) has shown us how wide the variation in interpretation of a topic can be. In Chapter 2, we offered Mellon's comments on the difficulties encountered by the NAEP assessors in formulating writing topics (even with the help of experienced personnel from the Educational Testing Service). Mellon wondered why a seemingly straightforward topic such as "Going to School" produced, on the part of some writers, mundane accounts of scenes along the way, while it elicited descriptions of fantasy occurrences in others. There is also the "Waste" example offered by Conlan which shows how topics do not guarantee the activation of uniform interpretations, particular levels of thought, or even expected forms of discourse. The function of a writing task as a stimulus event cannot be understood until the examiner determines how constraints of language use and interpretation are operating in the writing assessment situation.

Despite the fact that researchers in educational measurement have acknowledged question-wording effects (French, 1966; Coffman, 1971a), the larger theoretical issues of essay task wording and typology have seldom been addressed. Wording effects have tended to be treated anecdotally or incidentally in the context of other objectives of a writing measurement study. (For example, see anecdotal treatments of wording effects in Godshalk, Swineford, and Coffman (1966); Winters (1980); Smith (1980); Lloyd-Jones (1977); Michigan Survey Research Center (1969) *Interviewer's Manual,* etc.) Current procedures for "item analysis" do not include "analysis" of the linguistic properties of the texts of essay questions which might affect their interpretation by persons responding to them.

Statistically oriented designers of tests do not seem to be aware that the psychometric approach to measuring achievement necessarily presupposes an information-processing model of communication—that is, a human actor receives, in some social context, the linguistically coded message of the test item and processes it mentally to extract the intended meaning. Therefore, these test designers have not attempted to study the influence of psycholinguistic and sociolinguistic variables on the process of interpreting

either objective items or essay topics. Rather, the emphasis in psychometrics has been on manipulating and treating products in measurement
schemes rather than on developing an understanding of the cognitive processes that might be involved. From the beginning, psychometrics has dealt
with concrete matters in the measurement of a product. As defined by
Edward L. Thorndike in 1918, educational measurement has been based on
the following theory:

> Whatever exists at all exists in some amount. To know it thoroughly involves
> knowing its quantity as well as its quality. Education is concerned with
> changes in human beings; a change is a difference between two conditions;
> each of these conditions is known to us only by the products produced by it—
> things made, words spoken, acts performed and the like. To measure any one
> of these products means to define its amount in some way so that competent
> persons will know how large it is, better than they would without measure-
> ment. (cited in Kandel, 1936, p. 80)

Given the empiricist bias reflected in Thorndike's statement, it is not surprising that he and other like-minded early educators devoted themselves to
devising "new type" tests—"real" measures which yielded numerical results
that were supposedly objective and more reliable and accurate. This reduc-
tion of complex natural phenomena to sets of discrete measurable properties made relevant the application of statistical techniques to the study of
writing. Early on in the scientific testing movement there developed an ob-
session with checking the reliability of essay tests. I.L. Kandel (1936), reporting to the Carnegie Foundation on the state of knowledge in conducting examinations, observed that investigations had been "limited in the main to a
study of the reliability of the making of examinations" (p. 3). Thirty-five years
later, William E. Coffman, a researcher for the Educational Testing Service
and the College Entrance Examination Board, could still confirm Kandel's
earlier observation about the dominance of issues of reliability in the study
of essay testing. Coffman (1971a), in the standard reference, *Educational
Measurement,* says that most reasearch on essay testing "has dealt in one
way or another with the question of reliability" (p. 298). Hoetker's (1982)
recent review of research on effects of topics on student writing corrobo-
rates the earlier findings. After conducting his comprehensive review, James
Hoetker (1982) also concluded that "research attention has been devoted
almost entirely to issues of rater reliability, ignoring for the most part the
issue of validity as well as the other two sources of error in an essay
examination—the topics and the writer" (p. 380).

Topic Effects: "Hidden" Variables in Writing Research

Braddock, Lloyd-Jones, and Schoer (1963) were, perhaps, the first writers
about research in composition to call attention to what tends to be a "hidden," ignored variable in much of that research, "one which can be con-

trolled but often is not—the assignment variable, with its four aspects: *the topic, the mode of discourse, the time afforded for writing, and the examination situation"* (p. 7). Even 20 years later, the topic still tends to be ignored in much research on writing. Hoetker (1982) observes that "Until the past few years, reports of research studies and testing programs usually did not bother to include the texts of essay topics" (p. 380). There is little uniformity in the practice of providing the texts of writing tasks and other relevant details. But the importance of including full information about the writing task variable cannot be overstated. There is a twofold loss when insufficient information is provided: It becomes impossible to independently judge the claims the researcher is making about the writing task characteristics, and it also becomes difficult to build a cumulative knowledge base about the properties of writing tasks. Hence developers of writing tests lose opportunities to learn more about the nature and effects of writing tasks.

The Kincaid Study (1953)

An example of the potential for the reinterpretation of past studies when adequate topic information is provided can be found in the Braddock et al. (1963, p. 8) report already cited. Ten years earlier Gerald Kincaid had concluded in his study that the performance of poor writers varied significantly according to the topic assigned. But when Braddock and his associates reinterpreted Kincaid's three topics, they noted that the content of each one was actually very similar, though the topics did require different modes of discourse. Thus, Braddock et al. (1963) concluded that the Kincaid study suggested that the "variation of the assignment from expository to argumentative mode of discourse did not seem to affect the average quality of the writing of a group of freshmen who were better writers as much as it did a group who were worse writers" (p. 8). On this basis, Braddock et al. argued that until more could be known about the effect of mode on writing performance, it seemed necessary to control for this element in planning assignments to be used for research on writing.

The Godshalk, Swineford, and Coffman Study (1966)[2]

Unfortunately, too many reports of research results tend to gloss over or ignore topic effects. When topic effects are not the focus of experimental interest in a study, the information reported about the topic—its actual text and the presentation of any effects noted—tends to be cursory and oblique. For example, the widely heralded Godshalk, Swineford, and Coffman (1966) investigation of the validity of the multiple-choice response mode in the mea-

[2]See the Breland, et al. (1987) report of the effort to replicate the Godshalk study. This new investigation of the relative merits of multiple-choice and essay assessments of writing skills does take into account many factors that were not considered in the earlier study. It offers a detailed account of the procedures of task development and full text of these tasks.

surement of writing does not quote the actual texts of the five criterion exercises used. Godshalk et al. follow the rather common practice of *describing* rather than *presenting* the exact wording of the topic(s) used in their investigations of writing. This reporting practice effectively prevents a reader of the study from making an independent appraisal of the experimenter's conception of the task and its rhetorical, cognitive, and subject knowledge demands. It is a practice that can lead to confusion about the meaning of results.

The Starch and Elliott Study (1912)

Failure to understand the researchers' conception of the task can lead to misleading generalizations which may continue to circulate for decades. Consider, for example, the "classic" study of the reliability of the grading of essay tests in English which was conducted by Starch and Elliott (1912, 1913, 1914). This and studies in other fields provided the "research" base for their famous assertion about the unreliability of essay test ratings: "It is almost shocking to a mind with more than ordinary exactness to find that the range of marks given by different teachers to the same paper may be as large as 35 or 40 points" (Starch & Elliot, 1912, cited in Sax, 1974, p. 118).

Given the way this claim is worded, one might get the impression that this "same paper" so notoriously elusive to evaluate was an essay on a single topic. Acutally the two "papers" used in the English part of this study were not even essays. They had been written to answer a set of six discrete questions, among which were the following:

> 2) Give five requirements to be observed in the structure of a paragraph; 3) Write a business letter; 4) Define narration, coherence, unity; classify sentences rhetorically and grammatically. Illustrate or define. 5) Name all the masterpieces studied this year and name the author of each. (Starch & Elliot, 1912, reprinted in Payne & McMorris, 1967, p.55)

What is truly shocking is that such poor data and misleading findings are still being cited 60 years later to bolster claims about the "disadvantages and limitations of essay tests" (cf. Sax, 1974, p.117). Starch and Elliot's so-called essay test is obviously a test of knowledge of discrete items and not an "essay" test at all in the sense we use that term today. If one thinks of an essay test as a composition requiring a sustained piece of writing on a subject, this research clearly is not applicable. Fortunately, Starch and Elliott included the text of their "essay test" in the original report making it possible to reexamine their data and correct the misleading generalizations still circulating. The point is that one cannot even be sure what the term "essay test" is intended to mean, unless one has an adequate description of the actual instrument or can actually examine the topic. One must wonder about the nature of the other early studies of reliability which contributed to an increasing lack of confidence in essay examinations during the 1930s and 1940s and that ultimately led to their virtual abandonment for the next three decades in favor of the "objective" test, which was supposedly superior because it could be more reliably scored.

The Choppin Study (1969)

The Choppin study is an example of an investigation where the researcher seems unaware of the impact of the question variable on the results attained. (Choppin & Purves 1969). Choppin set out to study the differences in the effects of two response modes used to measure literary understanding. Two short stories, "The Man by the Fountain" by Georges Hebbelinck and "My Childhood" by Maxim Gorki, provided the basis for both multiple-choice and open-ended tests. Choppin concluded from the results that the study offered "no evidence that the multiple-choice questions *per se* measure anything different from open-ended questions *per se*" (p. 22). In other words, multiple-choice questions could be as valid a measure of literary understanding as the open forms. This finding is not so surprising when one examines the structure and content of the "open" and "multiple-choice" questions. The so-called "open" question was really as restricted in scope as the multiple-choice question in that it called for a factual as opposed to an interpretive response. Short answer "open" questions inviting factual answers in a phrase or a sentence are not far removed from multiple-choice questions. The following examples, based on Maxim Gorki's "My Childhood," illustrate this point:

Open-ended: Why did Maxim yearn to make the brothers aware of his presence?

Multiple-choice: Which of the following best explains why Maxim yearned to make the brothers aware of his presence?

     (A)   They were old acquaintances and he was sick.
     (B)   He wanted them to become his friends.
     (C)   He had been rejected by other children.
     (D)   His grandfather wanted him to meet them. (Choppin & Purves, 1969, p. 17)

In a separate set of "Comments" at the end of Choppin's report, Purves made several observations. While Choppin is content to attribute "at least half of the nonerror variance to characteristics specific to the text under consideration," Purves states:

I would suspect that the items play as great a part as the texts. The stories are different, although both deal with children, and the questions they demand are different as well. The Gorki passage elicits questions about character relationships and symbol; the Hebbelinck questions about single characters, plot, and mood. These are related kinds of questions but we have not ascertained whether students perform differently or in the same fashion given different types of questions. Too often the difference is simply glossed over as being a difference between works. (Choppin & Purves, 1969, pp. 23–24)

We would have to concur with Purves that the basic question of validity in this study has not been answered. Purves himself explains the confounding of variables which weakens any conclusions that might be drawn from it:

> In both forms of the test the student's attention has been directed to certain parts of the literary work. What is being compared is a greater or lesser degree of direction in the questioning. What remains unknown is the relationship between performance under some set of conditions of direction and performance in an undirected situation. From this study, therefore, we may conclude that the two measures are measuring the same thing or similar things, but we have not fully defined the nature of the thing they have measured. (Choppin & Purves, 1969, p. 24)

Topic Effects in Faigley and Skinner's Review of Research (1982)

It is virtually impossible to know how great is the magnitude of topic effects in current writing research. We tended to stumble across undeveloped references to topic effects fairly often as we were reading the literature in preparing this review. We have no precise empirical data about the frequency of topic effects or about their nature. But is is interesting to note how often incidental references are made to topic effects as various pieces of research are described in Faigley and Skinner's (1982) comprehensive review of the research on "Writers' Processes and Writers' Knowledge." Six of the nine cases are quoted (page references are to Faigley and Skinner, 1982):

> [Mischel, 1974] The student spent less than one minute engaged in pre-writing planning on autobiographical assignments but twenty minutes on a memoir writing task. (p. 3)

> [Caccamise, 1981] conducted two experiments that examined what hinders writers from retrieving ideas from long-term memory . . . Under the more constrained conditions—the audience of children and the unfamiliar topic—students generated a smaller range of ideas, and these ideas were less cohesive . . . in the more constrained conditions students were more likely to repeat ideas. (p. 8)

> One implication for composing is that organization in some text types, such as simple stories, is easily achieved (Applebee, 1978), but the ability to organize other types, such as classificatory essays, develops much later (Stein & Trabasso, 1982). (p. 9)

> [Britton, 1975] Writers did not seem impeded when they were writing a narrative, but more complex tasks, such as persuasive tasks, proved to be very difficult. (p. 10)

Beach (1979) noted a significant effect among writing topics on the degree to which writers revised. He theorized that "differences in topic, even within one discourse mode, affect revising" (1979, p. 119). (p. 33)

Beach also found that differences in topics—which varied along a familiarity-to-writer dimension—affected to some extent the revision strategies of the subjects. (p. 35)

We have observed a number of cases where the researchers themselves knew when a topic effect had occurred and noted it in passing, but neglected to examine and explain it. The impression we have of this fairly common practice of ignoring topic effects is apparently similar to that of Alan Purves, who noted in a recent account (Purves, Söter, Takala, & Vähäpassi, 1984):

Much research in the area of written composition has foundered on the assignment issue, and much evaluation of written composition has been challenged on the basis of the assignments used to assess writing. In general both evaluators and researchers tend to pay little attention to the nature of assignments for student writing and how that nature might affect the writing itself. (pp. 385–386)

We conclude this section by wondering how researchers can have confidence in their results if they do not take steps to control for topic effects. And we consider it a matter of utmost importance for researchers and evaluators to report the full text of the topic used to elicit the samples of writing collected.

When Are Topic Effects Real? The Significance of "No Significant Difference"

We have so far presented considerable evidence to demonstrate that topic effects are real. Yet often when researchers attempt to design experiments to test hypotheses relating to the wording of topics, the selection of subjects, or rhetorical specifications, the results show "no significant difference" between variations in topic texts. We need to ask, then, what is the meaning of this common finding in so many studies?

We do not intend to engage in any technical discussion here about procedures in statistics for testing for "significance" or for determining "confidence intervals." Any textbook on educational measurement will treat this subject, but only a few clarify the distinctions between the usage of significance as a statistical term and as a term we know in everyday language (Atkins & Jarrett, 1979, pp. 86–109; Rowntree, 1981, pp. 116–121; Katzer, Cook, & Crouch, 1978, 128–131; Morrison & Henkel, 1969, pp. 131–140). In everyday language, on hearing of a "*significant* new discovery," we would know that something important had happened. Likewise, if we heard that there is *no significant difference* between two kinds of catsup, we would interpret this to mean that any small difference that might exist could be considered unimportant. In other words, *significance* in ordinary language connotes matters of importance. It is easy for naive readers of statistical reports to confuse the ordinary language meaning with the much more restricted statistical meaning. The *significance* level that is reported statistically designates the degree of certainty with which one can accept so-called "significant" findings as being not caused by chance. (We shall take up so-called "nonsignificant" findings in a moment.) Thus, when any researcher reports that his results were "well beyond the .01 level of significance," he is saying that there is only one chance in one hundred that his results could have been caused by chance, and that there is a very strong probability that a genuine relationship exists between two variables under comparison.

However, in statistical thinking, a "significant" result does not necessarily mean that the result is of theoretical or practical importance. Katzer, et al. (1978) describe the limits of the application of this concept:

> Statistical significance states only that the findings are probably real, that they will affect the real world. Statistical significance does not state *how much* the findings will affect the real world. This is an important difference. Frequently, we have noticed among our students a tendency to equate statistical significance with meaningfulness or what is sometimes called *social significance*, (pp. 129–130)

Katzer, et al. also provide an interpretation of the so-called "nonsignificant" finding:

> . . . statistical decision making is one-directional. If a finding turns out to be significant the author may argue that the finding is real. If, however, the finding is not significant, the author should not argue the opposite. Researchers cannot use their findings as proof of non-realness. In statistical inference, it is rather difficult for researchers to obtain significant findings. But it is easy, especially for untrained researchers, to get nonsignificant findings. Every mistake made by the researcher pushes the result toward nonsignificance . . . [and] findings of nonsignificance cannot generally be used to conclude anything. (p. 129)

Hopkins and Stanley (1981) warn against another common error of interpretation, that of assuming that something called a statistically *significant* relationship is therefore a large relationship: "A relationship may be *statistically* significant and yet be very small if it is based on a very large sample" (p. 95). The test of significance does not allow statements about *strength* of associations, only about probable associations. Because significance tests are based on probability theory, accurate interpretation of the results of significance tests rests on understanding precisely their conceptual and logical limits. Henkel (1976) reminds us of some of these limitations:

The correctness of probability estimates obtained through the use of a test of significance is a function of the extent to which the assumptions which underlie the techniques are met by the data on which the test is performed. . . . In particular, the correctness of probability estimates is contingent on the appropriateness of the sampling procedure used. . . . If the sampling procedure is nonrandom (due to non-response, a nonprobability design, or whatever) the probability calculation has no meaning in the sense of classical statistical inference. (p. 76)

Furthermore, according to Henkel, "statistical inferences are limited to the population from which the simple random sample was drawn" (p. 84).

Our purpose here is not to present a full discussion of statistical significance; that is better done by an authority such as Henkel (1976). Rather, we wish merely to alert readers who may be less familiar with the field of statistics that the use of tests of significance in social science research has become increasingly controversial (Henkel, 1976, p. 7). Even under optimum conditions for using the tests, the designations "significant" or "nonsignificant" have narrowly restrictive statistical meanings requiring the most cautious application and interpretation. And always we must remember that we cannot tell from statistical levels the meaningfulness of any findings. Attaching a value to such findings must be done on nonstatistical grounds.

Summary

Full discussion of the mathematical and statistical procedures for determining the psychometric properties of topics, such as reliability, validity, powers of discrimination, and other quantitative means of appraising topics is beyond the scope of this volume. However, information on these subjects can be found in any standard book on educational measurement, but mostly with regard to "objective" items. Our purpose here has been to outline some of the problems and issues arising from a rather narrowly constrained psychometric view of essay examinations as instruments of measurement. We have looked at how some of current practice has evolved, and by focusing on traditional psychometric interests still largely dominant today, we have brought to light the neglected areas of study in direct assessment of writing, especially with respect to the point where writing assessment begins: the writing task. In 1971 Coffman remarked:

It should be recognized that in the area of essay testing, as in most areas of human endeavor, few of the important questions have been answered in any final way. (p. 296)

As we turn to consider what current research in writing conducted across several disciplines tells us about the development of topics, we shall see that Coffman's observation is still true today. We have been able to find little research directly focused on the study of the properties of topics; that is why we embarked on several studies of our own which will be described in Chapters 7 through 11 of this volume. But as general background to our own studies, we will now review selected pieces of composition research. Even though many of these studies were directed toward answering other questions, they nevertheless provide some knowledge useful in the study of topics.

FOUR

Knowledge from Research on Writing: Topics

Research on Selecting Subjects

Teachers, evaluators, and researchers all seem to agree on the importance of wisely choosing the subject that starts the student off in a writing assessment episode. The subject assigned is of great consequence because ideally it is structured to attract attention and interest, to invoke powers of observation and imagination, to initiate thought and reflection, and to be within the range of all students' mental reach. William Harpin (1976) recognizes how critical the subject is in the assignment of writing. From his perspective as a classroom researcher in England, he explains that:

> A theory of function and audience, no matter how elegant, is incomplete without reference to the experience that is to be worked on and aimed at a reader. Many teachers and certainly the majority of those who collaborated with us in producing the writing, see choice of subject or starting point as the most formidable challenge, dominating all other concerns. (p. 93)

Knowledge Requirements of Subjects

Designers of tests usually recommend selecting subjects that are "neutral" and that are not "content-specific." Hence, they often turn to personal topics which they consider to be accessible to the broadest range of participants. It seems reasonable to take this position because writing assessments are intended to be measures of competence in writing, not measures of content knowledge. Tanner, however, challenges the claim that subjects can be content-free. In reviewing an early Writing Assessment Project document which made this claim, Tanner (in Ruth, 1982) raised a number of questions about the role of knowledge in affecting the writer's stance, purpose, and vocabulary. Tanner insists that writing itself is "subject specific," that a person must have something in mind to write about, some *knowledge of a subject.* And how that subject is developed affects the way the reader judges its merit. Tanner elaborates on these points:

> One can write about history only when he has learned some history and learned a bit about how history can be written. The subject makes demands on vocabulary. It makes demands on the writer's stance. It makes demands on what facts should be selected and how they should be put in order . . . Some people may want to use writing prompts to find out if a student can write about chemistry, or metal working. . . .
>
> When we holistic readers respond . . . we are responding to *subject matter sense* rather than to mere writing skills. The irony is that one can write error-

51

free prose about nonsense. When we read AP [Advanced Placement] papers for ETS [Educational Testing Service] we are reading holistically for BOTH content and quality of expression. We are facing the SUBJECT SPECIFIC demands on any worthwhile writing. . . .

What I am saying is this: No "transactional" prompt can be truly broadly successful *without depending on reading skills* or *without being intentionally the culminating act to some body of study or learning experience.* Hence in the nature of things one must evaluate such writing on a basis of subject matter as well as writing skills. (B.R. Tanner, letter, February 8, 1981.)

Another source of information about the knowledge demands of subjects is the National Study of Writing in the Secondary School. The first report on this study presented survey data on the state of classroom writing instruction across several school disciplines (Applebee, 1981). Of special interest to us are Applebee's accounts of approaches to setting writing tasks. Applebee found that a preponderance of writing assignments simply required a mechanistic "slotting in" of missing information. Even when students were not occupied with these fill-in-the-blank exercises, the writing tasks that students were given merely required repeating information already presented by the teacher or the textbook rather than extending or integrating new learning.

Applebee found that this emphasis on writing to evaluate prior learning turned writing into a routine, mechanical performance. There was little attention to writing process activities such as prewriting or providing help during the writing. The given subject functioned mainly to cue information that was to be repeated from memory. In his later report on the National Study Applebee (1984) noted that they had found many examples of subjects that are "in a real sense impossible to write on":

Western Europe on the eve of Reformation was a civilization going through great changes. In a well-written essay describe the political, economic, social and cultural changes Europe was going through at the time of the Reformation. (23 points)

——9th grade social studies (p. 4)

This subject is "impossible," unless it is viewed as a school writing task intended to cue only the relevant learning in memory from prior study.

Applebee's evaluation of school writing tasks continues in his monograph on the second phase of the National Study of Writing in the Secondary School reported in another volume of the Ablex Writing Research Series (Applebee, 1984). Whereas the first report focused on the nature of writing instruction within the national sample of 68 teachers and classrooms in general, the second report centers around case studies of the development of the writing skills of 15 students during 16 months of study. Here again, Applebee (1984) looks at the types and functions of school writing assignments. Informational writing dominated 89% of the school writing tasks collected in the sample; about 88% of the school writing reflected either generalized summary or analytic writing. Most of this writing was based on information from either the teacher or the text.

In another study reported in this same volume, Langer (1984) looked at how the focus of an assignment interacts with subject knowledge to affect writing and noted that "the specific effects of subject knowledge on written expression have been ignored" (p. 136). Four tenth-grade American history classes were assigned two writing tasks at two points during the semester. Various prior knowledge measures were taken before the study began. Each sample was scored on five separate dimensions: overall quality, coherence, syntactic complexity, audience, and function.

The results of the analysis showed that the knowledge measures had the strongest relationship to the holistic score (r = .30, $p<$ .001, p. 139). Langer (1984) also found a relationship between the choice of audience and function and the knowledge that the students brought to the tasks: "Mean scores for the combined measure of subject knowledge . . . were somewhat higher for the papers addressed to the teacher-as-examiner ($p<$ .12); so were the holistic scores of the writing that resulted ($p<$ .13)" (p. 145). Langer commented: "Not surprisingly, the data clearly suggest a strong and consistent relationship between topic-specific background knowledge and the quality of student writing" (p. 146).

Of particular relevance to our general study of topics, however, is the other evidence of topic effects that Langer found. Her analysis of the content of the four teacher-developed assignments indicates that the assignments carried implicit demands for two different response patterns: a *compare/ contrast* organizational pattern and a more general *thesis/support* structure (Langer, 1984, p. 141). For example, the following two assignments, each by a different teacher, were judged to require the thesis/support structure:

1. Write a one or two page essay on your version of a Utopian society, the kind you would like to live in.
2. It has been stated that in the 18th and 19th centuries the South was a deferential society. In one or two paragraphs, explain why this was true. In your answer, be sure to discuss the concepts of prejudice and acquiescence and how each related to this conclusion. (Langer, 1984, p. 137)

Obviously, one task seems to be more fully structured than the other one, yet both assignments "prompted similar types of writing from students" (Langer, 1984, p. 141). Langer (1984) observes that "in our analysis, the type of argument required to respond appropriately to a prompt proved to be a more influential factor in task complexity than the amount of structure that seemed to be provided by the prompt itself" (p. 144). Langer (1984) concludes her analysis of topic differences with these observations:

For the two topics that required compare/contrast essays, the measure of organization of background knowledge was strongly related to essay quality. For the two topics requiring details to elaborate upon a thesis statement, the amount of information available (reflected in the fluency score) was important and the organization of that information was not.

These findings imply that different assignments, given for different purposes, tap different aspects of a writer's knowledge of a topic. A low score on a particular paper might not mean that a student does not know the information, but that knowledge that was available was not organized in a useful way for that particular assignment. (p. 144)

Langer's analysis of the nature of the interactions between topic knowledge and writing performance, too detailed to be reported in full here, is one of the first substantive studies devoted to this issue, and it deserves careful consideration by anyone interested in the problem of prior knowledge in writing assessment.

A striking demonstration of the effects of a subject upon the display of writing competence occurred when a team of British researchers, Rushton and Young (1974), set out to define the concepts "elaborated" and "restricted code" with respect to distinctions in the writing performance of middle-class and working-class people.[1] The authors conducted an experiment in which they compared essays written by sixth-form public school[2] boys with essays written by adolescent factory workers of the same age who, while working in a car factory, were attending a general course in industrial training at a college of further education.[3] Over a period of some months both groups were given nine essay titles on which to write under very broad time limits. Three types of topics categorized by the style and treatment of subject matter which they were intended to evoke were included in the study. Examples of the three style categories and the titles include:

1. Imaginative descriptive: "The city at daybreak"
2. Opinionative discursive: "The world in fifty years time"
3. Technical explanatory: "A workshop lathe: What it looks like and how it works"

On the typical school subjects (numbers 1 and 2) the essays of the two groups of boys showed the expected language differences between "elaborated" and "restricted" codes. But on the technical subjects (number 3) the linguistic disadvantage of the working-class boys disappeared. That is, the

[1]These terms were introduced by the British sociologist Basil Bernstein (1971) to distinguish between speech that is "restricted" because it can be understood only by people with relevant shared experience and the more "elaborate" forms of speech that are not so dependent on context.

[2]The English "public" school would be called a "private" school in the U.S.

[3]A college of "further education" is similar in function to a college "extension division" in U.S. higher education.

working-class boys, "without formal educational qualifications and with an almost uniformly depressed verbal intelligence score, were able to produce in their technical writing, a higher frequency of complex nominal modification than were a sample drawn from the science sixth form of a major public school" (Rushton & Young, 1984, p. 186). The authors concluded:

> Choice of [subject] or essay title does appear . . . to be the powerful influence upon syntactic selection which previous research had suggested it might be. Moreover it appears to have the power to influence the level of linguistic performance of even linguistically "deprived" groups. (Rushton & Young, 1974, p. 186)

When Students Select Subjects

The interaction between students and essay test questions has been recognized and demonstrated by psychometric research (Coffman, 1971a, p. 289). For example, among the sources of error in scores based on tests requiring actual writing, one investigator (French, 1966, p. 588, as cited in Foley, 1971, p. 801) defines the variation in student response to a single essay question as "test error": "The composition test is almost like a one-item test. Some students may happen to enjoy the topic, while others may find it difficult and unstimulating; this results in error." Coffman (1971a) goes so far as to say that "some students do better on some questions while other students do better on others. To some extent the grade a student obtains depends on which questions appear on examinations" (p. 289; see also Rosen, 1969).

Despite the fact that researchers in educational measurement have acknowledged topic effects, the larger theoretical issues of essay task construction and typology have seldom been addressed. There has been little concern about determining the frequency, magnitude, or underlying nature of essay task effects. Topic effects have tended to be treated anecdotally or incidentally in the context of other research objectives. For example, the research that is most often cited to confirm the validity of the use of multiple-choice questions as predictors of students' writing ability is a study done by Godshalk, et al. (1966).[4] All five writing exercises that constituted the criterion were administered to one class of eleventh-grade and one of twelfth-grade students of English in each of 24 secondary schools. A geographically representative sample of classes of average ability and achievement in both public and independent schools was selected. The subjects of the topics used are *described* by Godshalk et al. (1966), but unfortunately, the original wording of the exercises is not given:

1. the description of an interesting element in the student's home town, as told to a foreign student in a pen pal letter;

---

[4]Martin Steinman (1967) has challenged the conceptual validity of this famous study.

2. write in narrative form an imaginative story about an experience (as participant or observer) or about a commonplace inanimate object;
3. an exposition, with reasons, supporting or attacking the idea that teenage students are much more conventional than their elders;
4. an opinion essay requiring the student to decide upon and defend a course of action toward an errant student (The student, secretary-treasurer of the student body, has neglected his duties.);
5. a character analysis based upon the brief talk of a college freshman given to the student body of his high school alma mater (Because the talk had to do with the freshman's ideas about college, the resulting essays might, and usually did, elicit arguments, or statements about the writers' opinions, in addition to the exposition that was based upon the required analysis of the speaker's character.). (p. 8)

This study revealed significant variation in ratings assigned to the essays produced in response to the five topics used in the study, as reflected in the mean score for topics. The investigators point out that these differences in ratings would have consequences under certain examination conditions:

> If the five topics had been assigned as alternate topics from which one or two could be chosen by students, a student's rating might depend more on which topic he chose than on how well he wrote. Or if one topic had been assigned to one form of a test and another topic to a second form, then some method of equating the scores would be required; otherwise the magnitude of an individual's score would depend partly on which form of the test he wrote. (Godshalk et al., 1966, p. 13)

Although the topic effect was recognized as important in the Godshalk study, it was considered only in connection with the estimation of the score reliability; topic effect was identified as a source of variability in the reliability of the test score, but it was not discussed as an interesting phenomenon on its own, worthy of further investigation.

Unfortunately, the current statistical procedures used to check topic effects often fail to reveal the presence of effects. For example, when Brossell (1983) conducted his study of rhetorical specification, he did not find significant differences in the mean scores awarded to essays written on six different subjects. Although the statistical analysis did not reveal topic effects, Brossell and his associate, Barbara Ash, noted "strikingly superior" writing on one of the topics, whereas all the others elicited essays that they found to be "a desultory lot." On one version of a topic about "violence in the schools," the writers addressed the task more quickly, had more to say, and wrote papers that were superior as a group and received the highest mean score.

Hoetker, Brossell, and Ash (1981) also field-tested 33 topics with a population of undergraduates in education to create a pool of validated topics for future administrations of the Florida Teacher Certificate Examination. Unfortunately, these topics cannot be revealed because of the need to keep the pool secure for future administrations of the examination. But the researchers found that although some topics were clearly more "popular" (chosen more often) than others, "except in two extreme cases, popularity was quite unrelated to mean scores of essays written on the topics" (Hoetker et al., 1981, p. 10).

The students in this study had completed a questionnaire which asked them to explain whey they had rejected the topic on which they did not write. Hoetker et al. (1981) note:

> The student comments made us realize that we had ignored another equally important dimension of the matter: the source of the essay's content. We had not taken into account that, even if all students are to write personal essays, it makes a difference whether the topic allows students to give their opinions on a public issue or demands that they introspect and report their inner lives. (p. 10)

The researchers found that they could classify the topics into "public" and "private" categories. When so classified, mean scores were almost identical, but because student preferences were expressed strongly and often, they recommended "that student preferences be taken into account by choosing one public and one private topic as options for each form of the examination" (Hoetker et al., 1981, p. 11).

Karen Greenberg (1981b) also has reported information about student preferences relating to nine questions field-tested at the City University of New York for the CUNY Writing Skills Assessment Test. Greenberg provides a "popularity" index for the topics which indicates the percentages of native English-speaking and ESL students who liked each question. At the time Greenberg reported her index, it had not been established whether the preferred topics elicited better writing. Both populations gave the following topic the highest ranking (83% native speakers, 81% ESL):

> It is the responsibility of parents, not teachers, to give children information about sex. Sex education is a private matter. It should not be taught in private or public schools.

Both populations gave the following topic the lowest rating (38% native speakers, 24% ESL):

> The government is considering drafting young men into the army. Young women have been asking for equal rights and equal responsibilities. In all fairness, young women should be drafted into the army if young men are drafted.

Both groups gave the same rank orders to all the other topics except one on which there was a substantial difference of opinion. Seventy-nine percent of the native speakers but only 52% of the ESL students liked the following question:

Some people work too hard and too much. In their efforts to succeed at school and at work, they often do not have time to build good relationships with their families and friends. This effort to succeed is not worth it.

Peter Evans (1979) reported on "topic bias" (topic effects) observed during an evaluation project in which students in grades 12 and 13 were directed to write a 250 to 300-word essay on one of eight topics. A fellow investigator from the Ontario Institute for Studies in Education (OISE) had used scores on a reading comprehension test and a language test as a predictor.

> The topics chosen by the more able students gave these students positive additional advantage in the holistic scoring while the choice of topic by less able students tends to disadvantage them further. This bias was especially acute for Topic #1 chosen by many less able students and for Topics #3 and #4 chosen generally by more able students. This finding reinforces our recommendation of strict mode and topic control in formal appraisal of student writing. (Evans, 1979, pp. 16–17)

These are the topics alluded to:

1. Should scenes of violence in books, in films, or on television be censored?
3. "The progress of science guarantees the progress of civilization."
4. Secondary schools should not demand that students take particular courses or pre-requisites; students should be free to choose courses of interest to them. (Evans, 1979, p. 15)

There were several sources of data that indicated that even though these students had a choice of topic, they "lacked motivation." "Many students did not take the assignment seriously . . . the most serious problem with most of the writing was not error frequency, but sheer dullness: a lack of personal commitment and interest" (Evans, 1979, p. 17).

Some evaluators have assumed that attitudes toward particular subjects can affect the way students perform; therefore, they have felt it desirable to allow students a choice of topics. Yet there is some evidence that given a choice, students are unable to choose the one that will give the best indication of their performance (Godshalk et al., 1966, p. 13; Coffman, 1971a, p. 291; Evans, 1979, p. 17). In a study of the effects of student attitudes toward topic on performance, Freedman (1983) found that although individual topics did affect student scores, the students' sense of the ease or the interest level of a topic was not the source of that effect. She hypothesized that students might have perceived them one way when they encountered the topics in the questionnaires that were administered, but when they wrote their essay, they might have perceived the topics another way: "topics that appear easy on first glance turn out, in fact, to be difficult. Likewise, topics that appear dull become interesting as writers explore their depths" (Freedman, 1983, p. 323).

Summary

The discovery of appropriate topics for use in writing assessments—ones that are neither too large, too insignificant, nor too abstract—continues to be an art rather than a science, because there is insufficient research to enable us to explain differential performance in relation to topics used to elicit writing samples. We have mainly anecdotal information to tell us which subjects "work" and which do not. And even the anecdotal information remains scattered and unanalyzed.

It is easy to propose a number of maxims about the selection of subjects for use in assessments, but it is somewhat more difficult to be "scientifically" exacting in selecting the subject matter that we ask our students to give their heads and hearts to during an examination. We know that we must somehow find relevant and accessible subjects that students will greet with enthusiasm. But just now, research provides only a few glimmers of how this goal might be accomplished.

The findings of the several studies reviewed here suggest that when students are given a choice in the selection of topics, the choice they make is not random. Students respond differently to different topics and not always wisely. The findings indicate that evaluators may also respond differently to different topics. Hence, to assure greater reliability in holistic scorings, evaluators should consider only writing that is elicited by a single task. As Peter Evans (1979) put it, "Topic restriction is *more* rather than *less* fair" (p. 17).

Research on the Language of the Topic

A Psychometric Perspective on Wording

Psychometric literature recognizes the possibility of wording effects on the perceived difficulty of writing tasks, but it views the issue broadly and nonanalytically. Standard textbooks in educational measurement offer only a few general principles to guide the wording of essay test questions. For example, under the rubric, "Constructing Good Essay Tests," Hopkins and Stanley (1981) give these suggestions specifically related to wording:

2. Make sure that questions are carefully focused.
3. The content and length of questions need to be structured. (p. 221)

Mehrens and Lehman (1973) are somewhat more helpful. Under the rubric, "Writing Good Essay Questions and Preparing Good Essay Tests: Some General Considerations," the authors offer 10 suggestions, including four related to question wording:

2. The question should be written so that it will elicit the type of behavior you want to measure.

3. A well-constructed essay question should establish a framework within which the student operates.
   a. Limit the area covered by the question.
   b. Use descriptive words.
      Words such as "define, select, illustrate, classify, summarize." "Discuss" is ambiguous without specific instructions. "Explain," "compare," and "contrast" should also be defined.
   c. Aim the student to the desired response.
7. Don't start essay questions with such words as "list," "who," "what," "whether."
8. Adapt the length of the response and the complexity of the question and answer to the maturity level of the student. (pp. 216–223)

Even though this textbook offers a much fuller treatment in its single chapter on essay tests, it still does not begin to cover the most important issues. We need to take into account that these texts deal with essay tests in content fields, not writing tests per se.

Coffman (1971a) advises the testmaker to be sure that essay questions are "so worded that all candidates will interpret in the same way the task to be done" (p. 287). But Coffman offers no suggestions for accomplishing this goal other than to present the essay questions to colleagues for review or to try them out, following the standard psychometric model for field testing.

Psychometric Views of Bias

Most users of national standardized tests, thinking that they have been protected from test bias, would probably be surprised to learn that the study and control of bias constitute a rather late development among psychometricians. Donald Ross Green (1982) acknowledges that when the California Test Bureau became part of McGraw-Hill in 1966, it had "no explicit policy concerning test bias and no stated procedures for dealing with the matter" (p. 231). Carleton and Marco (1982) discuss "past practices" at Educational Testing Service, and explain "that the current process [for detecting and eliminating bias], although incorporating many procedures that were already in place for some testing programs, is relatively new, having been developed in 1979 and 1980 and implemented only recently" (p. 279). Joanne M. Lenke (1982) describes procedures used at the Psychological Corporation and remarks that

> it has only been since the mid-1970's that attention has been focused on ways of determining whether or not a particular item is statistically biased. It is for this reason that tests published prior to 1976, though examined for surface bias, were not routinely subjected to item bias procedures during their development. (p. 256)

The preceding reports are from Berk's 1982 *Handbook,* billed on publication as a "state-of-the-art" review of the methods of detecting test bias. In his

Introduction, Berk (1982) defines a biased item as one that will "favor or disfavor one particular population compared to another population" (p. 3); he notes that present conceptions of bias tend to be related to the current "trinary conceptualization of validity (Jensen, 1980, Reynolds, 1982): content, criterion-related, and construct" (p. 2). Hence, we hear about content bias, predictive bias, and construct bias, and sometimes situational bias. However, Berk sees problems with this conceptualization because the categories overlap. He considers the recent trend toward a unified conceptualization of validity (Cronbach, 1980) as providing a more useful framework. These newer concepts enable designers of tests to focus on methods of detecting bias at the test-item level, which Berk (1982) views as "the most fundamental level of content analysis and the foundation for [score] inferences . . . item bias studies are necessary for all tests (p. 3)." Though "item discrepancy methods" were developed for use with items for objective examinations, we may find them helpful in evaluating essay topics.

Berk (1982) recommends that any investigation of bias should include the following three steps:

1.   *judgmental review* to detect stereotypic, culture-specific, and offensive language and to asure fair representation in the work roles and life styles of sex, racial, and ethnic groups;
2.   *statistical analysis* based on an appropriate experimental or quasi-experimental design to detect performance discrepancies in relation to item, construct, and/or predictive bias;
3.   *a posteriori analysis* of the statistical results to discern whether true item or test bias is present and, if it is, to deduce explanations for why it occurred and consider procedures for eliminating it.
     In essence a study should begin with judgment and end with judgment. (p. 4)

With regard to the relative roles of judgment and statistics in detecting item bias, William H. Angoff (1982) is particularly instructive: "statistical methods are only supplemental to human judgment, certainly no substitute for it" (p. 96). Angoff also declares: "It should be understood that the presence or absence of bias is unavoidably a matter for human judgment, for which the statistical analysis is only a useful tool" (p. 114). Angoff suggests that we reserve the term *bias* for its important social usage and that we refer to the statistical methods under consideration here as *item discrepancy methods* rather than *item-bias methods*. He concludes with the judgment: "These methods are, after all, only item discrepancy methods; they should not be credited with a higher function than they are capable of serving" (Angoff, 1982, p. 114).

Most of the item-discrepancy procedures described in Berk are intended to "flag an item as operating in a suspicious manner with regard to different population subgroups, but they will give us relatively little guidance about what caused this suspicious outcome," (Scheuneman, 1982, pp. 181–182).

Studies of Effects of Wording Changes

There is little research of any sort to guide test-writers in the wording of prompts. What information there is tends to be anecdotal and is mentioned in passing in the context of a larger focus of research interest.

Problem Words and Phrases.

Harpin (1976) and his 50 collaborating teachers devised writing situations during a 2-year study of the writing of 300 English children ages 7.0 to 9.11. Harpin (1976) comments on the significance of wording changes in creating writing situations:

> Where intention and outcome failed to match . . . teachers had to shoulder much of the responsibility. Substituting one word for another, though apparently a trivial change, may profoundly affect the way a child interprets the task—"Describe what you saw as you walked through the fog" gave very different results from "Describe what you felt as you walked through the fog." A similar effect is caused by the change from "What does this music make you think of?" to "What does this music make you feel?" (p. 109)

Karen Greenberg comments on the problem of misinterpretation:

> The opportunities for lexical and syntactic misinterpretations of test topics are numerous. For example, last semester, one of the topics asked about "vigilante groups that patrol our city's streets and subways." (We assumed that most students knew about groups like the "Guardian Angels.") . . . We got responses about the "villian groups," the "vigorous groups," the "Garden Angels," and so on. (K. Greenberg, letter, March, 1981)

There is always a potential problem with presumptions about prior knowledge. The famous "tennis shoes" exercise administered to 9-year-olds in the 1974 National Assessment of Educational Progress offers a case in point. The text of the topic follows:

> Some people write just for the fun of it. This is a chance for you to have some fun writing.

> Pretend that you are a pair of tennis shoes. You've done all kinds of things with your owner in all kinds of weather. Now you are being picked up again by your owner. Tell what you, as the tennis shoes, think about what's going to happen to you. Tell how you feel about your owner. Space is provided below and on the next two pages. (p. 17)

This subject is susceptible to problems of comprehension in different regions of the country. The familiar footwear are known to 9-year-olds as "sneakers" in some parts of the country. Others may know neither of these terms but recognize "gym shoes." And some may know the object only by a trade name like "Keds" or "Adidas."

Some other examples of wording problems appear in NAEP's account of its early exercise development procedures (Finley & Berdie, 1970). During one of the first large-scale tryouts of exercises, the investigators established that

> the major problems with the exercises were directions that were too complex or involved and use of vocabulary that was so difficult that low achieving students had difficulty understanding the task or the question. Post-test interviews were particularly productive in identifying specific words, phrases and directions that were incomprehensible. (Finley & Berdie, 1970, pp. 61–63)

Two examples follow:

Literature Exercise (9-year-olds)
(Quoted in part)

Directions: This is not a test; we would like your opinion. Read the following selection carefully and then answer the question about it. Mark the *one* answer you think best.

Today is cold; the snow is falling. The only noise is a pheasant calling.

Question: Which of the following is closest to what you think about the selection?

_____ (A) It belongs in a poem because it rhymes.

_____ (D) It belongs in a poem because it does not move regularly. (Finley & Berdie, 1970, p. 62)

The interviewer found that a number of words could not be read by the third graders: *selection, pheasant, regularly, opinion. Opinion* caused the most difficulty because, even after it was pronounced, many students could not understand the word. The interviewer recommended asking 9-year-olds "what they think" instead of calling for "an opinion."

In other exercises administered to 9-year-olds, students did not know the meaning of directives such as "arrange in order," but they could do the exercise when told to put the smallest number in the blank next to the first word, and so on.[5] Substituting the word *song* for *melody* solved a vocabulary problem in a music exercise. In another music exercise administered to young adults, the respondents were asked if they *recognized* a piece of music. Some respondents construed *recognize* as *know the name of* and said that they had heard the piece but could not identify it. The interviews concluded that much editing of the exercises was needed for tone, clarity of instructions, and vocabulary. Clearly, there is considerable evidence to show that both the subject as well as any small changes made in the wording of that subject have an impact on writing performance, at least at the individual level.

[5]See Cole and Means (1981, pp. 47–57) for further examples of problems of wording task instructions for children participating in cognitive experiments.

Cognitive and Experiential Demands of "Agree–Disagree" Topics. In an effort to better understand the effects of wording essay questions one way or another, Greenberg (1981a) set up a well-designed, theory-based experimental study which she hoped would answer questions about the "agree/disagree" format and the impersonal nature of the essay question format used in the City University of New York Writing Skills Assessment Test administered to entering freshmen.

Greenberg (1981a) studied the effects of varying the "cognitive" and "experiential" demands of essay questions on the writing of entering freshmen at CUNY. For the purpose of the study, she designed four versions of one topic (see examples of each version):

1) high cognitive/low experiential demands (HCD/LED);
2) high cognitive/high experiential demands (HCD/HED);
3) low cognitive/low experiential demands (LCD/LED);
4) low cognitive/high experiential demands (LCD/HED). (Greenberg, 1981a, pp. 4–5)

The questions were presented in uniform formats consisting essentially of two parts:

1. A short passage (20–60 words) which introduced the subject to be written upon.
2. The instructions. The evaluative questions (high cognitive) asked the question: Do you agree or disagree with this statement? And they also requested supporting explanation and illustration in detail. The interpretive question (low cognitive) asked for a discussion of the opening statement, proposed at least three strategies for accomplishing the task, and requested reasons for the interpretations. (Greenberg, 1981a, pp. 10–11)

The HCD questions called for an *evaluation* of an issue and required the use of evidence as well as an ability to distinguish among facts, opinions, and values. The question format called for the writer to "agree or disagree"—to *judge* the issue—and defend his or her position with logical reasons. The LCD question called for an *interpretation* of an issue, to *relate* issues rather than to judge them, and it provided generalizations and criteria for making judgments. This question format called for the writer to "discuss" ideas and provided a number of options for structuring the response.

Greenberg also sought to control the "experiential" demands of these essay questions, and thus she formulated questions with "high experiential demands" (HED) and "low experiential demands" (LED). The HED questions invited writers to relate personal experiences in response to solicitations cued with the second-person personal pronoun "you." The LED questions encouraged students to respond in a less personal way with factual data and abstract generalizations.

The four versions of one of the topics used in the experiment are now presented:

Version 1: High Cognitive/Low Experiential Demands

The traditional grading system used by most colleges includes A, B, C, D, and F grades. This should be changed to a Pass/Fail system for all courses because the traditional grading system forces most students to compete for good grades rather than to strive for knowledge and learning.

Do you agree or disagree with this statement? In an essay of about 300 words, explain and illustrate your answer in detail.

Version 2: High Cognitive/High Experiential Demands

The traditional grading system used by most colleges includes A, B, C, D, and F grades. This should be changed to a Pass/Fail system for all of your courses because the traditional grading system forces you to compete for good grades rather than to strive for your own knowledge and learning.

Do you agree or disagree with this statement? In an essay of about 300 words, explain and illustrate your answer in detail.

Version 3: Low Cognitive/Low Experiential Demands

The traditional grading system used by most colleges includes A, B, C, D, and F grades. Some colleges, however, use a Pass/Fail system for all courses in order to move the focus of an education away from getting a certain grade to striving for knowledge and learning.

In an essay of about 300 words, discuss the traditional grading system (A–F). In your essay, you might wish to choose one of the following strategies: contrast the traditional grading system to a different type of grading system *or* explain some reasons for keeping the traditional grading system, *or* suggest some changes in the traditional grading system and give reasons for these changes.

Version 4: Low Cognitive/High Experiential Demands

The traditional grading system used by most colleges includes A, B, C, D, and F grades. Some colleges, however, use a Pass/Fail system for all courses in order to move the focus of your education away from getting a certain grade to striving for knowledge and learning in your classes.

In an essay of about 300 words, discuss the traditional grading system (A–F). In your essay, you might wish to choose one of the following strategies: contrast the traditional grading system to a different type that you have experienced, *or* explain some reasons for keeping the traditional grading system, or suggest some changes based on your experiences. (Greenberg, 1981a, pp. 94–97)

Greenberg attempted to control the rhetorical, propositional, and syntactic difficulty of the experimental questions in order to determine the effects of the two main variables, the cognitive and experiential demands. She also took great care in selecting subjects to avoid tasks that might be boring or threatening or outside the experience of the writer. Greenberg was aware of the confounding effects of controversial subjects such as abortion upon both writers and readers, and so she chose education as an area of shared personal experience that could best be shaped into the experimental questions. Greenberg piloted sixteen questions with four instructors and 29 students, and eventually eight questions in four sets of two each were judged to meet the specifications for the four conditions. Forty-eight students wrote essays under each of the four conditions, thus producing 192 essays for the experiment.

Greenberg hypothesized that there would be a significant interaction between the cognitive and experiential demand levels of the essay questions, with the low cognitive/high experiential demands eliciting higher overall quality of writing as measured by holistic scores. Greenberg expected that the relative ease of the structured interpretive question (low cognitive) combined with the interest and accessibility factors of personal experiences (high experiential) would sustain better writing performances than the more abstract, less personal question (high cognitive, low experiential).

For the purposes of this study, a question that asked for an evaluation was considered to be making a high cognitive demand, while a question that asked for an interpretation was considered to be making a low cognitive demand. Greenberg's conception of the relative level of complexity of evaluative and interpretive questions was based on Sanders's (1966) interpretation of these questions in Bloom's (1956) *Taxonomy of Educational Objectives: Cognitive Domain*. The high-experiential-demand questions were those which "asked students to respond with personal experiences and which used the second person pronoun, 'you' in order to do this" (Greenberg, 1981a, p. 14). Her low-experiential-demand category "consisted of questions which encouraged students to respond in a less personal way, with factual data and abstract generalizations" (Greenberg, 1981a, p. 14).

Greenberg's (1981a) hypotheses were not confirmed: "None of the four types of questions elicited a substantially superior measure of rhetorical, syntactic, or lexical performance" (p. 58). The types of changes made in the content and structure of the questions used in this experiment did not have any statistically significant effect on the students' quality or fluency of performance as measured by holistic score or as determined by supplementary analyses such as scorings for syntactic complexity, sentence control errors, word form errors, and essay length. Interestingly, the personalized forms of questions which used the second-personal pronoun "you" as a cue to elicit personal experiences did not produce better writing or even a higher frequency of first person "I's" in the responses. Greenberg speculates that this latter finding might have resulted from the students' belief that the first-person pronoun was inappropriate in an essay produced for academic purposes. If so, this response would have to be considered an unexpected effect of the testing condition. Greenberg also states that the students might have had little faith in themselves as "reliable authorities" (p. 59). Greenberg mentions, among other reasons for the results, the possibility that test anxiety might have constrained students from comprehending the instructions and taking full advantage of suggested strategies. She also concludes that the fact that so many of the students in the sample were "inexperienced" writers in remedial courses might have affected the way these students attended to variations in question wording (p. 60).

It may also be the case that these students simply never perceived the so-called "variables" in the same way the test-maker did. Greenberg (1981b) recognizes this possibility, too, for in a paper related to this study, she comments

> The most important thing I learned from my research is that the relationship between any writing task and students' writing performance in response to that task is profoundly influenced by the nature of the encompassing situation. The effects of writing task variables differ depending on the nature of the encompassing situation. The effects of writing task variables differ depending on the nature of the student and the nature of the setting. (p. 8)

In interviews with some of the students participating in her study, Greenberg (1981b) found that "many had not even read the entire question—they simply read half-way through and then began writing the standard five-paragraph essay that their English teachers had always required of them. . ." (p. 8). It would seem that the students were "reading" the context of the school testing *situation* more closely than they were reading the *test instrument* itself. They may have thus responded automatically with what Lanham (1979) calls the "school style." The practical wisdom of meeting the demands of a test situation—writing for a supposedly traditionally oriented evaluator-reader and avoiding grammatical or ideological offense—may itself beget the bland strings of unqualified assertions that so many observers find in the persuasive discourse of students at all levels. The effects of testing contexts are described more fully at the end of Chapter 5.

After a close analysis of the Greenberg study, Hoetker (1982) concludes that the experimental topics "resemble one another very closely . . . all are rather lengthy and set forth in the same formal 'voice,' . . . and all the verbs in the charge to the writer imply a knowledge of rhetorical tradition—'agree' or 'disagree' . . . 'explain' and 'illustrate . . . discuss . . . contrast' " (p. 384). Hoetker also suggests that the topic versions which were intended to make low cognitive demands might actually have made higher demands because they required selecting among alternatives.

The Inconclusive Nature of Experimental Studies

The Greenberg study may demonstrate just how difficult it is to attempt to measure the impact of relatively small wording changes. We encountered a similar problem in our Writing Assessment Project, when we conducted an experiment (described in Chapter 8) in which we asked students to write on two versions of the same topic. We thought we were manipulating only *one* variable—degree of audience specification—in the two topic versions, and we were employing wording changes to do so. Yet we, too, found "no significant difference" in performance on the two topic versions as measured by holistic score. We began to wonder if the experimental method were the appropriate one to use in studying effects of changes in wording, for we saw how problematic is the manipulation of variables in experimental research with human subjects. We became convinced that the current state of understanding about the performance of students on timed writing tests is sufficiently primitive to warrant a wider range of observations. To counteract the limitations of the experimental method, we turned to other methodologies (described in detail in Chapter 7). We were attracted particularly to the idea of *triangulation* which has been described by Cohen and Manion (1980):

> Triangulation may be defined as the use of two or more methods of data collection in the study of some aspect of human behavior. It is a technique of research to which many subscribe in principle, but which only a minority use in practice. The use of multiple methods, or the multimethod approach as it is sometimes called, contrasts with the ubiquitous but generally more vulnerable single-method approach that characterizes so much of research in the social sciences . . . triangular techniques in the social sciences attempt to map out, or explain more fully, the richness and complexity of human behavior by studying it from more than one standpoint and, in so doing, *by making use of both quantitative and qualitative data.* (emphasis added, p. 208)

By the time we undertook our Central High School study of the participants, the processes, and the products of a writing assessment episode, we had developed a multimethod approach which is described in Chapter 7.

FIVE

Knowledge from Scholarship and Research on Writing: Task Instructions

Specifying Rhetorical Context

"Circle of Readers"

Of all principles espoused for designing the writing assignment, specification of a full rhetorical context is the one that seems to be most strongly established in the canons of practice. The lineage of this notion can be traced back to classic rhetoric, and it has found vivid restatement at various times in the history of writing instruction. P.B. Ballard (1939) enunciates the principle in his chapter on "The Hartog Method," based on the work of Sir Philip Hartog as it appeared in *The Writing of English* in 1907. Ballard sets forth the first principle in Hartog's method:

> A pupil should never be required to write a composition without his having clearly in mind the audience for whom it is intended, and the object he has in view in writing it. This principle is flagrantly violated not only in school exercises but also in the essays set at public examinations. Current practice is neatly summed up by Sir Philip Hartog in the formula: "Write anything about something for anybody." Nobody does this in ordinary life. To quote Samuel Butler: "It takes two people to say a thing—a sayee as well as a sayer. The one is as essential to any true saying as the other." He might have added that something else is essential: a motive for saying it . . . . Nobody writes for the mere fun of expressing himself on paper: he addresses himself to somebody whom he wants to influence; he wants to question him, to inform him, to persuade him, or to convince him. He has always at the back of his mind this possible reader or circle of readers—a friend, a coterie, or the world at large. Without this recipient and responsive factor the business of writing resembles an attempt to work a battery with only one terminal. Whatever else you may get, you will get no electricity. (pp. 79–80)

"Task Environment"

Flower and Hayes' (1979) process model of composing provides a contemporary view of the nature and significance of the rhetorical context in the act of writing. Their model begins with the definition of the "task environment" ("the world outside the writer's skin") which consists of "the rhetorical situation" ("the specifications of topic and audience to which a writer must respond") and "the text which the writer has produced so far" (Flowers & Hayes, 1979, pp. 90–91). Flower and Hayes (1980) discuss "the rhetorical situation" in terms of "the demands of the rhetorical problem":

> Whatever writers choose to say must ultimately conform to the structures posed by their *purpose* in writing, their sense of *audience,* and their *projected selves* or imagined roles. In essence writing is also a speech act and therefore subject to all the constraints of any interpersonal performance. (p. 40)

Flower and Hayes view the rhetorical problem as the most important element in beginning the act of composing because writers solve only the problem that they represent to themselves. Consequently, discovering how the rhetorical problem works to affect the writer is an important goal for research. Flower and Hayes (1980) describe the strategies that writers use to solve the problem of excessive constraints: They "throw a constraint away," "partition the problem," "draw on a routine or well-learned procedure," and "plan" (pp. 41–44). According to Flower and Hayes (1980), "Writers inevitably set such priorities in the way they define their Rhetorical Problem (e.g., this is a letter to Aunt Tilly, so you can safely ignore run-on sentences and fragments; she won't mind)" (p. 42).

It is doubtless true that Aunt Tilly doesn't mind a few grammatical lapses, but the relentless evaluator usually does mind. Given the usual evaluative function of a writing test, the designer of tests needs to be cautious in specifying audience, for an injudicious specification may have syntactic consequences that will affect an assessment rating. Crowhurst (1978) found that a tenth-grade boy, writing in the argument mode, produced a substantially longer mean T-unit length when writing for a teacher audience than he did when writing for a best friend audience. The identification of an audience for a writing assignment is tricky, as Steinberg (1980) notes:

> Posing reasonable audiences is not as simple as it sounds. On the one hand, the audience should be specific enough to govern what facts the writer uses and what the tone and thrust of the written statements should be. On the other, the audience should not be so exotic as to invite laughter or irritation. I can remember a period here at Carnegie-Mellon University when, in our zeal for teaching problem solving in writing courses, we posited such bizarre audiences that we annoyed our students instead of motivating them. In one assignment, for example, we asked students to write an explanation of the use of the toothbrush for a native of the Canadian Arctic region who had never seen one. . . . it was clear that the students were moving from amusement to annoyance when one day about midsemester I came into the room at the beginning of the hour and saw on the board something like the following: "Write an explanation for a one-armed paper hanger who is allergic to paste about how he can paper this room while standing on one foot without harming the newly shellacked floor." (p. 166)

Effects of Full Rhetorical Specification

When Hoetker (1982) concluded his first review of the literature on development of essay topics, he was convinced that full rhetorical specification was desirable. Hence, he recommended in that original version that topics for

Florida's Teacher Certification Examination "should take the form of scenarios simulating writing tasks likely to come up in the course of a teacher's work" (Hoetker, 1982, p. 387). But the results of Brossell's (1983) study of the "information load" of topics caused Hoetker to change his recommendation to favor briefer, less fully specified topics instead.

In 1980, Gordon Brossell, Hoetker's colleague at Florida State University, conducted an experiment to test the hypothesis that essay questions that specify a full rhetorical context are superior to less complete versions of the same questions. Brossell used six topics written on three information levels to generate writing samples to evaluate, by holistic scoring procedures, the effects of information level and subject. Topic six, quoted here, presents the subject of "violence in the schools" at three levels of specification:

Levels of Specification on Topics
(From Brossell, 1983)

Level 1, *low information load,* presented the topic in a brief phrase. Decisions about audience, purpose, form, mode of discourse, voice were left to the writer with no guidance provided.

Topic: Violence in the schools.

Level 2, *moderate information load,* presented a topic containing a general introductory statement. It then posed a what or a why question asking for expression of personal opinion.

Topic: According to recent reports in the news media, there has been a marked increase in incidents of violence in public schools. Why, in your view, does such violence occur?

Level 3, *high information load,* presented a hypothetical situation and requested the expression of personal opinion as in level 2. But this version also specified role, audience, purpose and form or mode.

Topic: You are a member of a local school council made up of teachers and citizens. A recent increase in incidents of violence in the schools has gotten widespread coverage in the local media. As a teacher, you are aware of the problem, though you have not been personally involved in an incident. At its next meeting, the council elects to take some action. It asks each member to draft a statement setting forth his or her view on why such violence occurs. The statements will be published in the local newspaper. Write that statement expressing your own personal views on the causes of violence in the schools. (p. 166)

The other five topics dealt with what were assumed to be familiar subjects: (a) the "basics" of education, (b) teaching as a career, (c) discipline in the classroom, (d) the four-day work week, and (e) American wastefulness.

The six topics, each in three versions, were randomly administered to a sample of 360 undergraduate education majors at Florida State University and at the University of South Florida. A panel of three raters read and holistically rated the essays on a scale of 1–4 according to criteria developed for the examination. The score assigned was the sum of the three ratings (3–12). Interrater reliability was .828.

The statistical analysis was designed to determine the effect of subject matter, information load of topic, and length of essay on holistic score. Subject matter of topics did not make a significant difference. Information level effects, though not statistically significant, were much stronger, and essay length was significantly correlated with score. Level 3 essays–those from fully specified topics–received the lowest mean score and had the shortest mean length. Brossell (1983) was careful to note that "the differences between these means and those of the other two information levels are not large" [or statistically significant]. But "they are strikingly contrary to what one would expect if one assumed the superiority of topics containing full rhetorical specification" (p. 168).

Brossell discusses the results, noting that level 1 required the writer to focus the subject and find an organizational scheme while level 2 offered a definite beginning focus and even something of an organizational strategy. Although level 3 provided a full rhetorical context, it did not provide direct aid for organizing or focusing the actual writing. Brossell (1983) reports that "many writers failed to go beyond a purposeless rehash of the information in a given scenario," and it often seemed to act "as a hindrance rather than as the facilitator it was meant to be" (p. 172).

Brossell's results led his colleague James Hoetker (1982) to wonder about the reading burden of the longer scenario type of writing prompt. Hoetker (1982) points out certain difficulties in reading this type of prompt:

> First, such a scenario introduces into the testing situation all the problems of varying individual interpretations and responses that are associated with the reading of any work of fiction. Second, the sheer amount of language that students must process is increased. Opportunities for confusion, misinterpretation, and creative misreadings are proportionately increased. Third, the more language and information students are given the more difficult it seems to be for them to get beyond the language of the topic to discover what they may themselves have to say, so that examiners find themselves receiving, not "original responses," but their "own prose back in copy speech." (pp. 386–387)

Derek Rowntree (1977) provides a different insight into what might be happening to a writer as the level of specification is increased in a given essay question. Whereas Hoetker suggested that there would be *more* "opportunities for misinterpretation and creative misreadings," Rowntree claims that the effect would be less variation. As Rowntree (1977) makes the following set of essay questions progressively more specific, we see that with each added constraint there is an increasing likelihood of eliciting more convergent responses with a corresponding loss of opportunity for divergent responses:

1. What aspects of the political system of modern Sweden seem to you most worthy of comment?
2. Comment on the political *stability* of modern Sweden.
3. *Explain* the political stability of modern Sweden.
4. Identify and discuss *three factors* that might help explain modern Sweden's political stability.
5. Identify and discuss three factors that might help explain the emergence of a stable political system in Sweden *despite the massive social and economic changes engendered by processes of modernization.* (p. 155)

Rountree shows that each successive version restricts the student's scope of response. With this restriction comes a gain in uniformity of response and comparability of answers, but there is also a loss of information about the possible range of variability. Since the question and the criteria for answering are preformulated, the question can no longer measure how the student could have formulated the task and decided the relevant criteria unaided. Rowntree (1977) concludes:

> In an attempt to ensure comparability and make the grading more accurate, we may have ended up comparing and grading less significant abilities in the student. [We may have committed] Macnamara's Fallacy, perhaps—making the measurable important rather than the important measurable. (p. 156)

Concepts of Audience

In the last 10 years there has been a marked increase of interest in the study of the concept of audience. The new scholarship in literary theory points to subtle and complex features of the writer–reader relation which have implications for developing writing tasks. Two scholars who are seeking to define the concept of audience more sharply are Long (1980) and Park (1982). Long (1980) argues that the traditional ways of specifying audience in writing exercises by listing observable physical or occupational characteristics (white male university administrator) rests on the false assumption that "people sharing certain superficial qualities are alike in all other respects" (p. 233). It is a practice that he thinks would be called "stereotyping" in any other context. Long, therefore, calls for a redefinition of audience and the application of literary theory to a refinement of the concept.

It is in Walter Ong's (1977) concept of "the audience as a fiction" that Long finds his new model. He follows Ong who said "the writer must construct in his imagination, clearly or vaguely, an audience cast in some sort of role—entertainment seekers, reflective sharers of experience, . . . and so on . . . A reader has to play the role in which the author has cast him, which seldom coincides with his role in the rest of life" (pp. 60–61). Ong's conception of the audience as a "created fiction" requires the writer to posit a new set of questions such as these asked by Long (1980):

> Rather than beginning with the traditional question, "who *is* my audience?" we now begin with, "who do I *want* my audience to be?" Rather than encouraging

a superficial, stereotyped view of the reader, we are asking the student to begin with a statement about the audience she wants to create . . . This leads directly to question of method: what distance between reader and subject should be established? What of diction and the creation of tone? What pieces of information do I want the reader to take for granted?, etc. (p. 225)

Douglas Park (1982) identifies a number of conceptual traps in the way audience is usually specified. Writers attend to a number of different issues when they think about audience. According to Park the meanings of audience tend to move in two directions: one movement is toward actual people external to the text; the other movement is toward the text itself and the audience implied therein. But however real the readers may be outside the text, "the writer must create a context into which readers may enter and to varying degrees become the audience that is implied there" (Park, 1982, p. 249).

Park (1982) divides the two general conceptions of audience into four more specific audiences:

1. *Anyone who happens to listen to or read a given discourse:* "The audience applauded."
2. *External readers or listeners as they are involved in the rhetorical situation:* "The writer misjudged his audience."
3. *The set of conceptions or awareness in the writer's consciousness that shapes the discourse as something to be read or heard:* "What audience do you have in mind?" represents the shorthand version of this set of awarenesses.
4. *An ideal conception shadowed forth in the way the discourse itself defines and creates contexts for readers:* "What does this paragraph suggest about audience?" (p. 240)

The latter two conceptions are particularly important for teachers or others interested in designing writing tasks. Park explains the implications of his analysis for the creation of writing assignments. Like Long, he thinks teachers depend too heavily on the concrete image of audience as readers external to the text, and he identifies problems in the strategy of designating members of the class or the teacher as the audience for student papers:

The former strategy, of course, means that students write knowing that their papers will be "published" in the classroom. This practice has obvious powerful effects on how students see the act of writing, but it can be said to provide an audience only in the commonly used sense of external to listener or readers. Students' reading of one another's writing does not provide that crucial ingredient, people rhetorically involved. The student writing for members of the class still has the problem of finding or inventing appropriate rhetorical contexts. In fact, useful as this strategy is, it may also create problems. (Park, 1982, p. 256)

The awareness of specific critical readers, whether they be students or the teacher, may inhibit and complicate rather than simplify the problems of dealing with audience. Park states, "the fact is that most of the time we want students to learn to write for a 'general' audience. That is to say we want them to write in relatively unstructured situations where little is given in the way of context and much remains to be invented by the writer" (p. 256).

These two analyses of the "meanings" of the term "audience" by Long and Park show how conceptually complex this rhetorical construct is. Two other recent articles, Ede (1984) and Ede and Lunsford (1984), provide further clarification of the tasks of writers in relation to the "audience addressed" and the "audience invoked." Ede and Lunsford (1984) define these concepts:

> The "addressed" audience refers to those actual or real-life people who read a discourse, while the "invoked" audience refers to the audience called up or imagined by the writer. (p. 156)

Ede and Lunsford (1984) present a model that seeks to unify these two perspectives:

> It is the writer, who, as writer and reader of his or her own text, one guided by a sense of purpose and by the particularities of a specific rhetorical situation, establishes the range of potential roles an audience may play. (Readers may, of course, accept or reject the role or roles the writer wishes them to adopt in responding to a text.) (p. 166)

The addressed audience (existing outside the text) appears in particular roles: future audience, mass audience, critic, colleague, friend, self. The invoked audience emerges in the creation of the text through the deployment of language which subtly cues readers to adopt particular roles: self, friend, colleague, critic, mass audience, future audience, past audience, anomalous audience.

Perhaps the notion of audience can be simplified conceptually, as Linda Flower (1981) has proposed, by understanding the distinction between what she calls "writer-based" prose and "reader-based" prose. As she states, "Good writers know how to transform writer-based prose (which works well for them) into reader-based prose (which works for their readers as well)" (p. 144). Flower (1981) is concerned with developing process strategies "to create a momentary common ground between the reader and the writer" (p. 122). She thinks that the writer who is composing reader-based prose needs to develop a critical awareness of his intended reader—his knowledge, attitudes, needs. But, the writer needs an even larger frame of reference, for contemporary reading theory posits that the writer's text will meet a "creative" reader who actively makes personal meanings; yet this reader has certain limitations of short-term memory and certain expectations for the structural pattern of the text being read affecting the potential range of meanings he can create. Thus, a writer needs not only to *know* his reader, but he also needs to aid him by providing a context for new ideas (Flower, 1981).

A Definition of Audience in School Writing

Harold Rosen (Britton, et al., 1975) reconceptualized the idea of *sense of audience* and its relation to writing in a school situation as part of the Schools Council Writing Project (1971–1974), a British study of development of writing ability in the age group 11 to 18. Rosen's audience categories are related to a general model of the functions for writing developed by James Britton.

Rosen looked at writing in the school setting and asked, What is unique to this situation? In school a student is required to perform a variety of writing tasks—notetaking, summarizing, outlining, composing essays, and completing exercises that call for filling in gaps in sentences with one word. Unlike the situation outside school where people have their own reasons for writing and thus define their own audiences, inside school it is usually the teacher who "initiates the writing and who does so by defining a writing task with more or less explicitness. Not only does he define the task, but he also nominates himself as audience" (Britton, Burgess, Martin, McLeod, & Rosen, 1975, p. 64). So the "teacher-as-audience" dominates school writing. Rosen describes the teacher in this role:

> Teachers often attempt to direct the sense of audience away from themselves by a variety of means. They may *specify another audience* . . . . They may simply urge the pupil to *represent to himself* a general reader's difficulties with understanding of flow of sympathies or capacities for response. They may offer *stylistic advice or rhetorical precepts* which have a more general reader in mind, but this advice is not made explicit. But whatever strategy the teacher adopts it is difficult for him to elude the stubborn reality of himself as audience. Thus many pupils-writers have to operate a double-audience system which may give rise to particular tensions. Behind one audience stands the spectre of another . . . a distinction should be made between the feigning required for some specific fictionalized audience, and the gradual development both of the desire to reach out beyond the teacher and an awareness of how to do so. In other words the development of the pupil may be seen in terms of the move from "the internalized other" (the teacher) to the "generalized other" (the writer's unknown public). (Britton et al., 1975, pp. 64–65)

Category System for Sense of Audience
in School Writing
(from Rosen in Britton, et al., 1975)

Definition: the sense of audience is revealed by the manner in which the *writer* expresses a *relationship* with the *reader* in respect to his (the writer's) *undertaking*. The main divisions are self, teacher, wider known audience and unknown audience.

   1. *Self*
      1.1 Child (or adolescent self) to self

2. *Teacher*
    2.1 Child (or adolescent) to trusted adult
    2.2 Pupil to teacher, general (teacher-learner dialogue)
    2.3 Pupil to teacher, particular relationship
    2.4 Pupil to examiner
3. *Wider audience (known)*
    3.1 Expert to known layman (any non-expert in area of chosen topic)
    3.2 Child (or adolescent) to peer group
    3.3 Group member to working group (known audience which may include teacher)
4. *Unknown audience*
    4.1 Writer to his readers (or his public)
5. *Additional categories*
    5.1 Virtual named audience (e.g., letter to named person)
    5.2 No discernible audience (pp. 65–66)

Applebee's (1984) recent studies of writing in secondary schools in the United States indicate that writing for the *teacher-as-examiner* dominates here as well as in England. The percentages ranged from a low of 64% for social science papers to 98% for science writing. Opportunities in school-sponsored writing to write for oneself were limited (about 4%) as were opportunities to write for a wider audience (about 6%) (Applebee, 1984, p. 36).

The Effects of Audience Specification in School Writing

At the end of a dissertation on writing, Brooke Neilson (1979) made a trenchant observation about the problems that writers encounter in shifting from a known to an unknown audience:

> Especially interesting is the hierarchy of difficulty associated with audience (or tenor). It appears that writers, when changing from a known audience to an unknown audience, often misconstrue the presuppositions shared by writer and reader, and thus misunderstand the kind or degree of explicitness required of them. While research on audience and presupposition is a text-level, and not a sentence-level, sort of study, it is possible that such text-level considerations affect sentence-level performance. (p. 154)

This kind of misunderstanding is illustrated in the research of Collins and Williamson (1984) who investigated *inexplicit meaning* in the kind of writing that suggests but does not state the meaning adequately. The following tenth grader's sentence is an example of the kind of inexplicit meaning studied:

> One kid have a bag of candy and this boy took the bag and eatin a piece of his candy he hit him on the arm. (p. 285)

Its meaning was judged inexplicit because the sentence requires the reader to complete its meaning by sorting out the references and inferring a causal relationship between the acts portrayed in it. Borrowing a term from Vygotsky, the researchers call this phenomenon *semantic abbreviation.*

Collins and Williamson analyzed samples of writing from grades 8 and 12 where the writers had been given three tasks for three audiences: (a) a description of place for a peer audience, (b) a persuasive letter to a parent audience, and (c) a persuasive letter to the editor of *TV Guide.* The 120 writing samples that were analyzed were distributed as follows: 60 in each of two ability groups, 60 at each of two grade levels, and 40 in each of three rhetorical context categories. Two measures of semantic abbreviation were used to analyze the samples: (a) personal and demonstrative exophora (reference to things/people outside the text (Halliday & Hasan, 1976); and (b) formulaic expressions (Ong, 1979), (Collins and Williamson, 1984, p. 289).

The results revealed that semantic abbreviation as a measure of inexplicit meaning in student writing varied with assigned purpose and audience and with writing ability and grade level. In twelfth-grade samples judged to be strong, semantic abbreviation decreased according to the audience addressed, in this order: parent, peer, editor. In eighth-grade samples and in twelfth-grade samples judged weak, the rate of semantic abbreviation was nearly the same for parent and editor audiences and increased for peer audiences. Collins and Williamson (1984) concluded:

> The rate of semantic abbreviation varies for both weak and strong writers, and it varies more for strong writers. Strong writers, according to intimacy with an assigned audience, are more able to vary the extent to which their writing includes the situational and cultural contexts of their language. Weak writers are less able to do this. It is not simply a higher rate of semantic abbreviation that characterized weak writing. Rather, it is a rate of semantic abbreviation that is inappropriate for the assigned audience. (p. 292)

Neilson's speculations about the problems of misconstruing the nature of shared knowledge when writers shift from known to unknown audiences seems to be confirmed in the Collins and Williamson study.

Specifying Mode

The Problem of Discourse Classification

The problem of discourse classification—of what to call different kinds of writing—will be dealt with in Chapter 6 where we explore the features of several theories of discourse and the terms they bring with them. Here it is only necessary to make a few preliminary distinctions. There is no uniformity in the approaches to the classification of mode in the research studies to be discussed, so we will use the traditional categories—narration, description, exposition, and argument—because they provide a familiar system from which to diverge in discussing more radical, new classifications.

Effects of Mode or Type

Of the several variables in the expression of writing tasks, there is one that has received considerable research attention: the specification of mode. After Braddock et al. (1963) called attention to the neglect of control of the mode of discourse variable by people doing research in composition, a number of studies were conducted (Crowhurst, 1978; Crowhurst & Piche, 1979; Perron, 1977; Whale & Robinson, 1978; Rosen, 1969).

Marion Crowhurst and associates have found in their series of studies that syntactic complexity is affected by such writing task variables as the specification of mode and audience. When Crowhurst and Piche (1979) had sixth and tenth graders write in the modes of argument, description, and narration, they found that both groups wrote longer T-units and clauses in the argumentative mode. They also found that in varying the audience, only the tenth graders responded to the difference in the task with longer clauses. The sixth-grade students responded syntactically to the change in mode but not to the change in audience.

In another study Crowhurst (1978) found argument papers more syntactically complex than narrative papers at grades 6, 10, and 12. Since her findings were in agreement with Perron (1977), Rosen (1969), and San Jose (1972), Crowhurst (1978) concluded:

> It may be regarded as well established by research that (a) differences in syntactic complexity are associated with differences in mode of discourse, and (b) narrative writing is generally less syntactically complex than argument. (p. 8)

Still another study of the influence of discourse type on syntax is that of Cooper and Watson (1980). These researchers designed a study of fourth graders to find out whether 9-year-old writers adapt their syntax to different discourse purposes—to explain, to persuade, to express feelings—and if they do, which syntactic features they vary. As a regular part of their fourth-grade curriculum, students from 6 different teachers in 6 different elementary schools (in Michigan, New York, and Illinois) wrote 18 essays for the study, 6 in each discourse type: expression, persuasion, and explanation. The topics strongly emphasized the discourse purpose. Papers were scored holistically, and then the first ten T-units of each paper were analyzed syntactically for 17 different features. The average 9-year-olds in this sample showed no greater differences in their ability to control any of the syntactic features than did the superior members of the sample. But many of the syntactic features were used quite differently by the writers in the three discourse types. Thus, the study confirmed the influence of "the writing situation" or topic on writers as early as age nine. The authors noted that "paralleling our findings, San Jose (1972), Perron (1977), and Crowhurst and Piche (1979) found among the modes they examined that argumentative writing was syntactically the most complex" (Cooper & Watson, 1980, p. 41). They concluded:

> Our main finding about the effect of writing situation on syntax provides direct empirical support for a current discourse theory like James Kinneavy's (1971). Kinneavy argues that the major discourse types—explanation, persuasion, expression—require different thinking and planning strategies and are organized and patterned differently. Our findings demonstrate that difference at the sentence level. (Cooper & Watson, 1980, p. 44)

A further implication of Cooper and Watson's research is that instruction and assessment of fourth graders that aim at sentence-level issues aim too low, and therefore, are "clearly a disservice to these students" (Cooper & Watson, 1980, p. 49). Instruction and assessment should be aimed at guiding them through the patterns of higher-level discourse structure.

The Texas statewide writing assessment results offered further evidence of effect of mode on performance. In Texas, when writing prompts are designed, they must reflect the objectives to be measured and the demands of the Kinneavy model of discourse (Sachse, 1984, p. 22). Testing authorities in Texas have selected three purposes for writing—expressive, informative, and persuasive—and three modes of writing—narrative, descriptive, and classificatory—as eligible for testing. Thus, Texas writing tasks attempt to focus on a dominant mode, and these purpose/mode combinations are varied periodically to "ensure that all elements of the model will be taught" (Sachse, 1984, p. 22). A consequence of this practice has been fluctuation in the percentages of passing scores at fifth grade and ninth grade based on variation in mode. In fact, fifth-grade scores have varied for each year of the assessment.

In 1980 and 1983, when the same type of writing (expressive/narrative) was measured, the percentages of passing scores were equally high: in 1980, 94% of fifth graders received passing scores of 2, 3, or 4 on a 0–4 scale; in 1983, 97% received the same passing scores. But in 1981 and 1982, when different types of writing (types not reported) were measured, the percentages of passing scores dropped to 81% in 1981 and 69% in 1982. Texas ninth graders were ill-prepared for the persuasive/descriptive writing measured in 1980 when only 60% received passing scores of 2, 3, or 4. But with practice in the persuasive/descriptive mode, ninth-grade passing scores rose to 83% in 1981 and 90% in 1983.

Difficulty Level of Modes

There seems to be little doubt that writing in the argument mode is difficult for students through early college levels. Freedman and Pringle (1981) shed some light on possible causes of the difficulty in a study of the ability of 12- and 13-year-old students to compose arguments as opposed to narratives.

The researchers found that these students were far more successful in realizing the conventional schema for story structure than for the structure of an argument (98% of the students could embody narrative structure in their stories, but only 12.5% could use the classical argument patterns). In discussing their findings, Freedman and Pringle declare that it is too simplistic to attribute this failure to create well-wrought arguments to "lack of organization" or "lack of a sense of form or structure," because these students demonstrate extraordinary deftness in organizing narrative material. Thus, they concluded that while students have multiple opportunities to internalize narrative schemas, no such parallel opportunity exists to internalize argument patterns. Freedman and Pringle also discussed the developmental aspect of written argument—that it requires cognitive maturation. To be able to write argument, students must have had sufficient exposure to the genre through reading and through direct instruction in its patterns. In addition, they must have attained a level of cognitive maturity which would enable them to cope with complexities of the form.

In his doctoral dissertation, Harold Rosen (1969) also asked, "How far do differences in the nature and formulation of composition topics lead to significant differences in performance?" Rosen sampled fifth-year pupils in a variety of schools on the O-level Examination (Ordinary Level in English Language in the General Certificate of Education) in response to a series of writing tasks. According to Pearce's (1974) authorized account of Rosen's unpublished dissertation, Rosen found "a clear difference in the order of difficulty of different kinds of essay writing. Narrative/descriptive writing is least difficult, discussion/speculative writing is the most difficult" (p. 55). Rosen also found that

> differences between an individual pupil's performances on different kinds of writing could be very great . . . The most satisfactory measures of linguistic maturity appear to be of limited validity and correlate more strongly with the kind of writing being attempted than with the overall competence of the writer . . . One-word essay titles, instead of allowing for flexible, imaginative treatment, yield uniformly less good results than others. (Quoted in Pearce, 1974, pp. 55–56).

Rosen found the best writing was generated by open-ended literary or poetic stimuli which encouraged commitment without requiring self-exposure. He also found that students in the fifth form were not yet prepared to meet the examiners' model of "good writing"—discursive prose which adopts a detached, speculative treatment of a general or public issue. Pearce (1974) noted the implications of Rosen's findings for conducting examinations:

> The kind of writing which the candidate is asked to do, or allowed to choose, may exert more influence on his performance, and hence on his result, than any other variable such as linguistic competence, intelligence, or age. (p. 57)

After considering his findings along with "the unknowns in the problem of formulating topics for essays," Rosen concluded that "the strongest possible reservations with regard to the matter of single-sample testing" are in order (Quoted in Pearce, 1974, p. 56).

Dixon and Stratta (1980a&b) also have been attempting to determine what range of written tasks can be tackled successfully by students at ages 14 to 16 as part of the Schools Council Project for Improving the Examination System. Their reports deal with achievement in the following modes of writing: (a) narrative based on personal experience; (b) narrative based on imagined experience; and (c) argument. (See Chap. 12 for an extended discussion of their work.)

Research focusing on process also suggests that composing processes of writers may differ when they are involved in different kinds of writing tasks. For example, Matsuhashi (1981, 1982) demonstrated that the planning requirements in the composing process of a writer varied for the two different discourse purposes of *reporting* and *generalizing.* Matsuhashi's observational data (pause time and hand movement) suggest that students can report more efficiently than they can generalize. In discussing her findings, Matsuhashi (1982) concluded that reporting required less mental effort than generalizing because a "schema for the reporting task is well-practiced and readily available," and because the organizing of content for a reporting task is more linear, "something like the step-by-step progress of following a road map" (pp. 284–285). Matsuhashi's research suggests that different writing tasks may tap different cognitive skills, and that some tasks may be more difficult than others. Evidence in the research literature suggests that narrative forms are mastered earlier and are acquired more easily than more abstract forms (Freedman & Pringle, 1980a; Matsuhashi, 1981; Keech, 1982b).

The issue of task variation in the *evaluation* of writing performance has been addressed in a study by Quellmalz, Capell, and Chou (1982) which compared writing profiles derived by tests differing in discourse mode. Analyses of the data showed that levels of performance varied according to the purpose of the writing task. The researchers pointed out that their findings have important implications for practices in evaluating writing competency, noting that "many current writing assessment programs fail to consider the validity of test data that do not distinguish among the demands of writing tasks" (Quellmalz, et al., 1982, p. 255).

Taken together, the findings in these studies should be viewed with concern by the designers of writing tests. Although these studies have dealt with a limited number of comparisons among the diverse kinds of writing tasks that could possibly be examined, the evidence provides sufficient grounds for questioning the assumption that any single writing task can be considered an adequate measure of writing competence. A single writing task measures only one of many kinds of functional writing skills. Different skills are likely to be associated with different tasks.

Research on Influences from Testing Contexts

We are just beginning to understand the nature of context as an encompassing framework around the process of writing and assessment. According to Staton (1981), "there is research to suggest that the greatest failure of writing instruction and assessment comes in not creating conditions under which students would have reason to compose a text (Graves, 1978, 1979)" (p. vii). Roger Shuy (1981) who also raised a number of questions about assessment and the constraining conditions imposed upon the writer concluded:

> What we are assessing is not the writers' ability to think, organize, sequence, explain, persuade, narrate, or describe, but rather their ability to do these things under the special set of circumstances created for the writing assessment. (p. 170)

Shuy created a metaphor to convey the idea that writing under assessment conditions constitutes an unnatural act, measuring only what the writer can do with a specific task under severely constraining conditions. It is as if walking ability were to be determined by assessing "the ability to walk on a slippery pavement with a broken toe and high-heeled shoes" (Shuy, 1981, p. 171). We would not necessarily learn anything about the ability to write or to walk in this approach to assessment.

Michael Clark (1980) has analyzed the power relation in effect among the participants in an assessment situation. To portray this condition, he drew on the famous work of William Labov who had examined the interviewing techniques of some researchers whose results led to classification of their subjects as "linguistically deprived." Clark quoted two key passages from Labov which he thinks speak equally well to the situation in writing assessment, although Labov's observations applied specifically to an interview. First, Labov (1969) pointed out the origins of a subject's defensive maneuvers in an interview situation:

> The child is in an asymmetrical situation where anything he says can literally be held against him. He has learned a number of devices to avoid saying anything in the situation, and he works very hard to achieve this end . . . If one takes this interview as a measure of the verbal capacity of the child, it must be as his capacity to defend himself in a hostile and threatening situation. (Quoted in Clark, 1980, p. 130)

Even when the actual stimulus question is the same for each respondent, virtually all of the other variables of the communication context may differ from respondent to respondent. Consequently, says M. Clark (1980), "To judge all the samples elicited from the interviews by the same criteria is therefore to render the evaluations meaningless" (p. 131).

M. Clark (1980) declared that

any evaluation of speech or writing that ignores the extraverbal "sociolinguistic" feature of the context in which the language was elicited is irrelevant as a measure of communicative competence. Furthermore, any assessment of language that purports to measure verbal capacity outside of a specific context—"Good Writing"—is therefore either deliberately misleading its users or is looking for something that is precluded by the test itself: Our assignments and evaluations often proceed from the same false assumptions about the context-free nature of language acts. (p. 131)

M. Clark describes an approach to the "assessment examinations" for the placement of incoming students in one of several freshman English options at the University of Michigan. Clark believes that these examinations are structured to avoid the problems already summarized. He considers the Michigan examination to be "program-specific"—that is, used in a particular context with a defined group of students to direct them to appropriate courses. The examination specifies the audience and the "ostensible purpose" of the essay. Students are even given a

> choice of tones and styles to use through a pair of sentences given to them to begin the essay. These sentences differ in tone, diction, and approach to the problem (statistical vs. affective, for example) and are designed to establish a rather narrow set of constraints for the essay in order to limit the number of choices the writers have to make. In other words a role is created for the writers in which many of the variables they would encounter in a real situation are fixed, and the essay can be evaluated precisely according to their ability to determine the features of the given information salient to the communicative context and to match those features in their own writing (M. Clark, 1980, p. 132).

M. Clark (1983) provided a sample of the Michigan type of topic in another article:

> Write a letter to the parents of a young child advocating a particular policy of television watching for their child. Explain to them why you advocate such a policy.

> Begin your letter with the following sentence (which you should copy into your bluebook):

> By the time the average person in North America graduates from high school, she or he will have seen 18,000 hours of television.

> Now select *one* of the following as your second sentence and copy it into your bluebook.

> The present generation of preschoolers watches an average of 42 hours of television a week.

> Since real experience is the primary source of learning, children are growing up addicted to television and ignorant of life.

According to a well-known critic, television is giving the present generation "an extraordinary exposure to standard adult English and an opportunity to see many things."

Now complete your letter developing the argument that follows from the first two sentences. Do your best to make your argument convincing to the parents who are your readers. (pp. 61–62)

It is difficult to see just how the University of Michigan assessment procedure escapes the decontextualizing processes of other examinations. One has to wonder how the students in the Michigan test escape "the role established for them by the context of the test" any more readily than the participants in any other test situation. If anything, Michigan seems to impose more constraints on the writer than one tends to find in other examinations.

Pianko's (1979) study of the writing processes of college freshmen confirms the existence of some of the "sociolinguistic" variables operating in a testing context. Pianko found a number of "interesting paradoxes" in the methods currently used for teaching and testing writing:

In the first instance, students do not view writing which has the context specifically set by the teacher and which must be completed within the constraints of a class meeting as an activity that is worth committing themselves to. The limitations placed by the typical school writing activity negate the possibility for greater elaboration, commitment, and concern. Yet many instructors insist that the most effective way to evaluate students' writing abilities is to have the writing controlled for topic, place, and time. According to the students in this study, such a writing activity does not permit sufficient time for them to regroup their energies and thoughts; therefore, they merely attempt to complete the assignment in some expedient fashion and "give the teachers what they want." So, in fact, what writing teachers are actually evaluating is how well students follow instructions, not how well they write. (p. 18)

In 1979–1980 Clark and Florio (1982) undertook a naturalistic study of schooling and the acquisition of literacy. They sought to document how two teachers and their respective students produce occasions for writing by means of interaction. Clark and Florio also sought to describe the process of teacher planning for writing instruction, to develop a typology of the diverse occasions for writing in each classroom, and to examine these occasions as contexts for writing that may make differing cognitive and social demands on the students as writers. It is the latter purpose of this study which is of interest here. Clark and Florio (1982) identified four broad functions of writing in a second/third-grade classroom and in a sixth-grade classroom:

1. Writing to participate in community,
2. writing to know oneself and others,
3. writing to occupy free time, and
4. writing to demonstrate academic competence. (p. 159)

We will consider here only the last category, because this seems to be a clear case of what Labov called the "display function" of an assessment. Clark and Florio (1982) describe "writing to demonstrate academic competence" in the classrooms they studied as "a teacher-initiated activity" and as "the only type of writing that received formal evaluation from the teacher":

> It is the only type of writing that was typically both composed and formatted by an outside third party—the publisher. This fact, so commonplace in classrooms in our culture, was at first taken for granted by the researcher. However, when students were asked to sort and talk about their written work, they consistently grouped worksheets and workbook pages together because they were produced "by machine." (p. 165)

These "academic performance" writing activities engaged students in a variety of discourse functions, including explanation and description, but these activities were not generated or ultimately controlled by the students:

> The topic was constrained, the format of the writing was limited, and the function of the writing was predetermined by others. (Clark & Florio, 1982, p. 166)

Clark and Florio describe an interesting example of how a teacher-imposed task that is intended to stimulate private, free writing (fulfilling the writing-to-know-oneself function) is actually interpreted by the students in a way unintended by the teacher. It becomes, in effect, writing to display competence. One teacher set up an activity called "Diary Time" which was intended to be mainly private. Students were to be free of concerns about audience and form; they were to write their own thoughts. But in actual practice, Diary Time had some features that made it similar to more formal types of school writing. Clark and Florio (1982) describe this situation:

> The fact that Diary Time was a teacher-imposed task, that the teacher knew and taught about "the rules" of diary keeping, that the teacher read aloud a part of her own first journal entry, and that the teacher collected and stored the diaries in her filing cabinet all supported the idea of the "teacher as audience." Student concerns about accurate spelling, questions about how the teacher "will correct them," and teacher assistance for those who could not think of what to write constitute additional evidence of teacher as audience. (p. 65)

The authors found this to be an instance of an assignment that sent a "mixed message" to the students and thereby caused confusion in their efforts to accomplish it. Clark and Florio (1982) observed three types of student response:

1. Some treated the Diary Time as "just another school writing task" and wrote what they thought would please the teacher.
2. Some treated the Diary Time as a reflective writing task where the usual "rules" of school writing were suspended.

3. Some wrote nothing and waited for the teacher to help them think of what to write and thereby remove the ambiguity from this new type of writing task. (pp. 66–67)

Clark and Florio (1982) concluded that "ambiguity about the audience of a student writing activity can affect both the interpretation of the task and the students' performance of the writing in diverse ways" (p. 67). Clark and Florio's work illustrates how difficult it is for teachers and assessors to overcome the constraints of writing in a school context. No matter how ingenious the teacher or assessor may be in creating fictional rhetorical contexts, behind the invented context of the assessment task stands the real audience—a teacher-as-evaluator.

SIX

Knowledge from Theories and Models

Discourse Theory

Discourse theory, which deals with the development of full texts in speech or writing (Kinneavy, 1971), provides another source of knowledge that influences the design of writing assignments for both instructional and testing occasions. Discourse theory, with roots and traditions reaching back to antiquity, attempts to describe the varieties of discourse and the elements which contribute to the making of texts, whether spoken or written. Various schools of thought have emphasized one or another element such as the *writer*, the *subject*, or the *audience*, either individually or taken together. A fourth element, *function* (also called *purpose* or *aim*) arises from the interaction of writer, subject, and audience. Related to all of these is the concept of *form* (called *genre* or *type* or *kind of writing*). Another concept related to all of these is *mode* (also called *method of development*). The basic problem in dealing with this field is the richness of the area and the problems attendant upon selecting from among competing theories. It is outside the scope of this review to present in depth each of the leading discourse theories introduced in this chapter, but it is important to consider briefly the kinds of organizing principles each one provides for instruction in writing. These various discourse schemes are a source of the rhetorical specifications and constraints appearing in writing tasks.

Discourse theory has proceeded in two directions: (a) traditionally, discourse theorists have looked at the *products* of writing and sought to classify what they found; (b) more recently, theorists have attempted to describe the *processes* of writing as well. We shall examine the first set of theories as *categorical systems* and the second set as *relational systems*.

Categorical Systems

Bain's Classical System

D'Angelo (1976) credits Alexander Bain with having established in 1890 the traditional forms of discourse which have dominated the organization of writing curricula and testing even to this day. The traditional forms are *description, narration, exposition,* and *argumentation,* although Bain's original set also included a fifth form, *poetry*. According to D'Angelo's (1976) account of Bain's theory:

> Each form is assumed to have its own function, its own subject matter, its own organizational patterns, and its own language . . .

The mind can be divided into three faculties: the understanding, the will, and the feelings. The aims of discourse (to inform, to persuade, and to please) correspond to these three faculties. The forms of discourse are the kinds of composition that relate to the faculties of the mind, the aims of discourse, and the laws of thought. Thus, description, narration, and exposition relate to the faculty of understanding, persuasion relates to the will, and poetry to the feelings. (pp. 115–116)

Bain's system characterized and categorized the products of writing. The following graph derived from D'Angelo's (1976, p. 115) account summarizes the main forms and their distinctive characteristics. (See Table 6.1.)

Table 6.1.
Bain's Forms of Discourse (Derived from D'Angelo, 1976)

	Function	Subject	Organization	Language
Description	Evoke sense experience	Objects of senses	Space/time	Denotative and connotative, figurative, literal, impressionistic, objective
Narration	Tell a story, narrate an event	People and events	Space/time	As above
Exposition	Inform, instruct, present ideas	Ideas, generalizations	Logical analysis and classi-fication	Denotative and factual
Argument	Convince, persuade, defend, refute	Issues	Deduction and induction	Factual and emotive, depending on appeal

Rockas's Concrete and Abstract Modes

A contemporary approach to the classification of kinds of discourse has been developed by Leo Rockas (1964), who attempted to combine the literary modes identified by Plato and Aristotle with the rhetorical modes identified by Bain:

My analysis has suggested that these poetical and rhetorical modes extend themselves naturally and elegantly to the concrete modes, description, narration, drama, and reverie; and to the abstract or plagal modes, definition, process, dialogue, and persuasion. These are also classified by means of procedure as the static modes, description and definition; the temporal modes, narration and process; the mimetic modes, drama and dialogue; and the mental modes, reverie and persuasion. Though the modes may be modulated and mixed, I consider them to be exclusive of each other, and together inclusive of whatever can happen in discourse, at least at the simplest level of rhetorical analysis (p. ix.)

D'Angelo's Conceptual Rhetoric

Frank D'Angelo (1980) finds in mental processes the theoretical base for his rhetorical forms. "Principles of composition such as analysis, classification, comparison and contrast, and cause and effect are *ways of thinking*" (p. 42). In other words, these conceptual patterns in discourse reflect the underlying processes of thought. Because D'Angelo (1980) based his college-level composition textbook on his earlier theoretical work, *A Conceptual Theory of Rhetoric* (1975), the textbook provides a convenient synopsis of his theory as it unfolds chapter-by-chapter through practical exercises. Only that part of his theory that seems most relevant to the creation of topics for assessment is included here.

D'Angelo (1980, pp.19–20) begins with the *writing situation* which must take into account the elements shown in Table 6.2. D'Angelo (1980, pp. 25–26) then classifies kinds of writing according to *purposes* and *aims* of writing as presented in Table 6.3. *Aims of writing,* taken as broad general categories in D'Angelo's system are separate from *specific intentions* of individual writers. *The writer's intention* is the *response* that he or she expects to get from the *reader* or *audience.*

After a writer determines the subject, the purpose, the audience, then comes the need to decide on the *methods or modes of development.*

Table 6.2.
The Writing Situation (Adapted from D'Angelo, 1980)

1. The writer	The writer's attitude toward his/her subject
2. The writer's purpose	The change the writer wants to bring about in the reader
3. The reader/audience	Parents, friends, others
4. The occasion	The circumstance (event, question, problem, idea) that moved the person to write

Table 6.3.
Aims and Purposes of Writing (Adapted from D'Angelo, 1980)

Aims	Purposes
1. Informative discourse	1. To inform or instruct
2. Persuasive discourse	2. To convince or persuade
3. Literary discourse	3. To entertain or please with an aesthetic purpose
4. Expressive discourse	4. To express strong feeling and emotion

D'Angelo regards the term *mode* as synonymous with the term *topic* as it is used in classical rhetoric. Instead of using *topic* in its contemporary sense of referring to the subject for discussion or writing, D'Angelo (1980) restricts its meaning to refer to *"categories that can be used to direct the search for ideas or the arrangements of these ideas into orderly patterns"* (p. 42). Hence, he categorizes a number of familiar rhetorical terms as *topics of invention,* using the term "topic" in its classical Aristotelian sense of *topoi,* meaning not a list of topics but a set of ways in which arguments relating to any subject matter can be discovered. The choice of the mode or topic depends on the subject, purpose, and audience for the discourse. D'Angelo (1980, p. 43) provides a partial listing of topics of invention. (See Table 6.4.)

The hierarchical arrangement of the system signifies that each category, "static" or "progressive," controls a range of "topics of invention." Most discourse involves more than one of these methods of development or "topics." A writer uses the "topics" to explore a subject to find out what he has to say about it.

Table 6.4.
Topics of Invention or Methods of Development
(Adapted from D'Angelo, 1980)

Logical	
Static	Progressive
1. identification	narration
2. analysis	process
3. description	cause and effect
4. classification	
5. exemplification	
6. definition	
7. comparison and contrast	

Kinneavy's Aims of Discourse

Another influential system for classifying the modes and aims of discourse was proposed by Kinneavy (1971) in a comprehensive, multidisciplinary examination of the contributions of classical and contemporary rhetoric. Kinneavy's system begins with the *communication triangle* formulated in communication theory. He divides the universe of language into three fields of study (syntactics, semantics, and pragmatics) which are related to the terms of the communication triangle. The communication triangle is depicted on the next page.

The area most closely tied to discourse in Kinneavy's (1971) scheme is pragmatics, which concerns the study of the *use* of language in actual spoken (or written) situations (p. 22). According to Kinneavy the *aims* of discourse are based on the four elements of the triangle. When the focus of

Figure 6.1.
The Communication Triangle
(Based on Kinneavy, 1971)

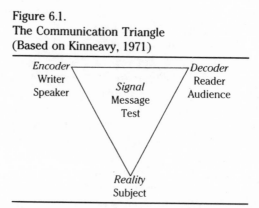

communication is primarily on the speaker-writer and the aim or purpose is self-expression, the resulting text is *expressive* discourse. When the focus is on the reader-audience and the speaker-writer's aim or purpose is to persuade, the resulting text is *persuasive* discourse. When the focus is upon the subject or reality under consideration and the speaker-writer's aim is to explain the world clearly and logically, the result is *referential* discourse. When the focus is upon the text and the speaker-writer's aim or purpose is to give pleasure, the result is *literary* discourse.

Kinneavy views the modes of discourse as "grounded in certain philosophic concepts of the nature of reality considered as being or becoming" (p. 36). Thus, the modes refer to classifications of "kinds" of realities. But Kinneavy (1971) altered Bain's traditional quartet, keeping description and narration but substituting *evaluation* and *classification* for *argument* and *exposition*. Kinneavy (1971) rejected *exposition* and *argument* as modes because he considers them aims of discourse. In other words, Kinneavy uses the term *mode* to cover *what* is being talked about, and *aim* to cover the *why* or the purpose or function of what is being talked about.

Relational Systems

Moffett's Realm of Discourse

Moffett (1968) grounded his discourse model on the Piagetian theory of intellectual development where cognitive growth corresponds with achieving control over increasing degrees of abstraction:

> The concept that I believe will most likely permit us to think at once about mental development and the structure of discourse is the concept of abstraction which can apply equally well to thought and to language. (p. 18)

Moffett proposed a naturally structured theory of discourse which analyzes the subject into increasing degrees of abstraction following a progres-

Table 6.5.
Schema of Discourse

Progression of Speaker-Audience Relationship (From Moffett, 1981)	
Thinking to oneself	Inner verbalization
Speaking to another person face to face	Outer vocalization
Writing to a known party	Informal writing
Writing to a mass, anonymous audience	Publication

Table 6.6.
Progression of Speaker-Subject Relationship (From Moffett, 1981)

Recording what is happening	Drama	The chronologic of ongoing perceptual selection
Reporting what happened	Narrative	The chronologic of memory selection
Generalizing what happens	Exposition	The analogic of class inclusion and exclusion
Inferring what will, may, or could be true	Logical Argumentation	The tautologic of transformation and combination

sion of speaker-audience relationships, subjects, logical sequences and literary forms. The most recent presentation of Moffett's schema appears in *Active Voice: A Writing Program Across the Curriculum* (1981) where the main lines of progression are listed (p. 13). (See Table 6.5 and 6.6.)

On one dimension, Moffett displays the kinds of discourse in a continuum of time abstractions: *drama* records *what is happening, narrative* reports *what happened, exposition* generalizes about *what happens,* and *argument* theorizes about *what may happen.* The temporal movement is from present to past to future. On another dimension Moffett orders discourse in a continuum of distance (space) between participants, moving in abstractive range from *I–you* in relation to readers and from *I–it* in relation to the subject.

The audience (reader) relation is a movement from self as audience for introspection and reverie to an immediate audience and then to a mass audience removed in time and space. The relation to the subject moves from a personal, subjective response to an impersonal, objective analysis.

Writing assignments that conform to Moffett's (1981) theory of discourse ask the student to:

draw subjects from actual personal observation and to abstract this material in ways that entail increasingly sophisticated and artful decisions; assume a more and more remote audience; lead from vernacular style to literary style, from improvisation to composition; and open up for the student progressively higher realms of abstraction. (p. 6)

Britton's Functions, Roles, Audience

At the University of London, James Britton and his associates developed a comprehensive multidimensional model of discourse derived during a 5-year Schools Council Project (1966–1971) to study the written language of 11–18-year-olds. This British research team found that the traditional discourse categories from the "predominantly Scottish tradition of rhetoric" were lacking in a number of respects:

> They are derived from an examination of the finished products of professional writers, from whose work come both the categories and the rules for producing instances of them. The tradition is profoundly prescriptive and shows little inclination to observe the writing process: its concern is with how people *should* write rather than how they do. It can scarcely, therefore, be helpful in studying the emergence of mature writers from young writers. (Britton et al., 1975, p. 4)

Even in the very early stages of their work, Britton et al. took a searching look at the nature of the writing process, beginning with the writing task. Instead of following the traditional rhetorical categories, Britton's research team developed a two-dimensional model which on one plane classifies writing according to the predominant *function* that it performs. On another plane it addresses the audience dimension in somewhat the same manner as does Moffett's scheme. The audience scale developed by Rosen (Britton, et al., 1975) moves from the self to the teacher to an unknown audience. The main categories in Britton et al.'s (1975, p. 83) scheme of the functions of written utterances are displayed in a diagram:

Figure 6.2.
Functions of Writing (From Britton, 1975)

Mature Writer	TRANSACTION----EXPRESSIVE----POETIC
↑	↖ ↑ ↗
Learner	EXPRESSIVE

Britton, et al. (1975) see the expressive form of writing as "a kind of matrix from which different forms of mature writing are developed" (p. 83). They define the *expressive* form as "language close to the self, revealing the speaker, verbalizing his consciousness, displaying his close relationship with the reader" (p. 88). They define the *transactional* form as "language to get things done, i.e., it is concerned with an end outside itself" (p. 88).

Britton, et al., (1975) define the *poetic* form as "a verbal construct, patterned verbalization of the writer's feeling and ideas . . . . not restricted to poems but . . . includ[ing] such writings as a short story, a play, a shaped autobiographical episode" (p. 90). Neither the expressive nor the poetic forms are further subdivided, but the transactional is divided into *informative* and *instructive (conative),* and each of these has further subdivisions. The instructive (conative) is divided into the *regulative* and the *persuasive* functions. The informative is divided into categories following Moffett's categories of *record, report, generalized narrative* or *descriptive information, analogic* with a low level of generalization, through higher levels of generalization and *speculative (tautological)* forms. The informative category at the lowest level records concrete experience and moves progressively to generalize, abstract, speculate, and theorize at the highest levels.

Psychological Models

Emig's Composing Process

Janet Emig (1971) was the first to attempt to study the process of composing systematically. She studied the composing processes of twelfth graders, basing her analysis on think-aloud protocols and tape-recorded pre- and postwriting sessions. From her investigation, Emig developed an "Outline of Dimensions of the Composing Process Among Twelfth-Grade Writers." Since we are interested here in the place where writing begins—the writing task—we will limit this account of Emig's important pioneer work to that part of her model that deals with the "nature of the stimulus." Emig (1971) regards "The first dimension of the composing process [to be] the *nature of the stimulus* that activates the process and keeps it going" (pp. 33–39). The features of the writing stimulus are outlined in Table 6.7 on p. 96.

Emig's model also displays the other dimensions of the composing process that she identified: (a) the context of composing; (b) the nature of the stimulus; (c) prewriting; (d) planning; (e) starting; (f) composing aloud; (g) reformulation; (h) stopping; (i) contemplation of product; and (j) the teacher influence on the piece.

Flower and Hayes's Rhetorical Problem

Flower and Hayes studied writing as a problem-solving, cognitive process. They wanted to find out what happened at the very beginning of the process in the act of finding or defining the problem to be solved. So Flower and Hayes asked both expert and novice writers to "think aloud" as they responded to the following problem: "Write about your job for the readers of *Seventeen* magazine, 13–14-year-old girls." The resulting protocols became

Table 6.7.
Nature of the Writing Stimulus (Derived from Emig, 1971)

The stimulus can evoke the appropriate registers, the varieties of language from which the writer can make choices: (1) area of experience, (2) mode of discourse, (3) tenor of discourse.

Registers

1. Fields of discourse or areas of experience provide the stimulus.
   a. Encounters with the natural environment
   b. Human relationships
   c. Encounters with induced environments or artifacts
   d. Self
2.   Modes of Student Writing

Expressive

field
of
Reflexive   <discourse>   Extensive

3. Tenor of discourse
   Distance between self and experience
   expressed by
   Degree of formality in the writing

Origin of Stimulus

1. Self-encountered stimulus
2. Other-initiated stimulus
   a. Assignment by teacher
      Context of relationships
         With peers
         With teacher
         With general curriculum
         With English curriculum
         With other composition assignments
      Assignment's internal specifications
         Registers
         Formulation of assignment
         Length
         Purpose
         Deadline
         Amenities of spelling, punctuation
         Treatment of outcome
   b. Reception by student
      Nature of task
      Comprehension of task
      Ability to enact task
      Motivation to enact task

the material for analysis. From these protocols Flower and Hayes (1980) developed a model of the *rhetorical problem* (p. 24).

Figure 6.3. The Rhetorical Problem (From Flower & Hayes, 1980)

The Rhetorical Problem	
Elements of the Problem	Examples
THE RHETORICAL SITUATION	
Exigency or Assignment	"Write for Seventeen magazine; this is impossible."
Audience	"Someone like myself, but adjusted for twenty years."
THE WRITER'S OWN GOALS involving the	
Reader	"I'll change their notion of English teachers . . ."
Persona or Self	"I'll look like an idiot if I say . . ."
Meaning	"So if I compare those two attitudes . . ."
Text	"First we'll want an introduction."

The *rhetorical problem* falls into two main parts: (a) the *rhetorical situation,* and (b) the *writer's own goals.* Thus, writers represent to themselves these two kinds of information. Information about the rhetorical situation includes the "exigency" or assignment, an audience, and a set of constraints. Information about the writer's goals include the effect the writer wants to have on the reader; the self, persona, or voice the writer wants to project; an attempt to create meaning; and selection of a genre or particular kind of text.

Flower and Hayes found that good writers *respond* to all aspects of the rhetorical problem. Poor writers, by comparison, are concerned primarily with features and conventions of written texts. Good writers construct their problem representation with readers in mind. They represent the problem with more breadth and depth, and as they write they continue to develop their image of the reader. Flower and Hayes (1980) concluded that

> good writers are simply solving a different problem than poor writers. People only solve the problem they represent to themselves. Our guess is that the poor writers we studied possess verbal and rhetorical skill which they fail to use because of their underdeveloped image of their rhetorical problem. . . . their representation of the problem doesn't call on abilities they may well have . . . there is much we could learn about how people define their rhetorical problems as they write and why they make some of the choices they do. (p 31)

Bereiter and Scardamalia's
Cognitive Processes in Writing

Carl Bereiter at the Ontario Institute of Studies in Education and Marlene Scardamalia at York University in Canada are cognitive psychologists engaged in a long-term Toronto research project involving a number of carefully designed studies of writing aimed at developing an account of the thinking and planning of elementary and secondary students. Bereiter and Scardamalia want to teach students to become aware of how they think during the writing process: They want students to recognize the specific operations that are involved and to know when they are working on intention, strategy, content, language, and revision of any of these elements. (Scardamalia, Bereiter, and Fillion, 1981). Their cognitive approach

> acknowledges that different mental processes can be identified and made the focus of instruction. In this regard it is compatible with a subskills approach. But it recognizes that these mental processes must function together as part of a cognitive system and that instructional activities must preserve this system intact . . . In this way it reflects a holistic approach. . . . The activities in this book provide for a focus on problem-solving, on strategies, and on goal-directedness that tends to be missed in the other approaches. (pp. X–XI)

There are rather obvious implications for the conduct of instruction and assessment and the development of writing tasks if one follows Bereiter and Scardamalia's cognitive approach. Bereiter and Scardamalia are not so much concerned with the broad purpose in writing and a general orientation to the reader as with solving the specific problems of more narrowly defined "consequential" assignments. To illustrate the Bereiter-Scardamalia perspective, we will use an example of one of their typical writing tasks described by Freedman, Pringle, and Yalden (1983):

> Pupils were asked to write a story that would conclude as follows: *And so, after considering the reasons for it and the reasons against it, the duke decided to rent his castle to the vampires after all, in spite of the rumor he had heard.* (p. 6)

Instead of just assigning a topic for a short story, Bereiter and Scardamalia build into the task structure a number of constraints which challenge students to develop particular strategies associated with the genre such as writing a narrative from a particular point of view and establishing credibility with the reader.

Bruce's Cognitive Science Model

Bruce, Collins, Rubin, and Gentner (1978) have developed a cognitive science view of the process of writing from three perspectives: (a) as a communicative act; (b) as an act in the context of a taxonomy of communicative acts; and (c) as an act made up of various subprocesses. Theirs is not a unified theory, and they regard their work as just the first step in a more comprehensive theory. They are attempting to explicate the nature of the writing process by introducing formalisms from theoretical linguistics and artificial intelligence. This approach has led them to build on such notions as "debugging," "successive refinement," and "constraint satisfaction."

The work of this research team is of interest because in adopting a communicative perspective toward writing, they are compelled to take the reader into account. Their attention to the active role of the reader has led them to emphasize audience: "Knowing that the reader is an active participant should and does suggest to the good writer a concern for how the text will be read, not just how it is written" (Bruce et al., 1978, p. 5). Given this perspective, the authors have formulated four principles that form the tacit objectives of any communicative act: comprehensibility, enticingness, persuasiveness, memorability.

Once they have explored the various dimensions of writing as a communicative act, Bruce et al. introduce a preliminary process model of writing, which shows how a written text is constructed. This model represents the process as one of satisfying a variety of constraints coming from three sources: text structure, content, and purpose. Integral to the text production is idea production, or the generation of what goes into the text. Idea production involves collecting, manipulating, and discovering ideas to produce text structure. The model takes into account the devices of text structuring, and most importantly, various means of overcoming constraints.

One way to ease the number of constraints that have to be satisfied at any one time, according to Bruce et al., is to "fractionate" the main task into intermediate ones. For example, the "production of text task" can be modified to an intermediate form where the student does not have the responsibility for generating the full text. In this procedure the student, given a set of ideas, puts them into one of several structural forms, say, the pyramid form of a newspaper article.

> Next, the filled-out form is judged by peers in terms of, not its correctness, but its comprehensibility, memorability, enticingness, and persuasiveness. Such a task allows the beginning writer to focus on text structure as a skill to be learned, but does not destroy the communicative purpose of writing. (Bruce et al., 1978, p. 38)

The model developed by Bruce, Collins, Rubin, and Gentner offers an interesting if not fully developed picture of how "ideas necessarily evolve with the production of text."

The Domain of Writing and the Specification of Competence

Before we can assess writing, we must define what we mean by competence in writing, and we must decide what range of tasks constitutes the domain of writing that we wish to examine. But when Linda Polin (1980) reviewed re search and theory in writing, she characterized the field as "somewhat disordered" with ". . . little consensus among professionals about what constitutes 'good' or even 'adequate' writing performance, or even about what knowledge and subskills it subsumes" (p. 1). As she examined the field, she found three main types of information sources:

1) studies of writing structure where evidence of competence is based on the linguistic features of the writing produced;
2) studies of writing function where evidence of competence is based on ability to adapt to a variety of audiences and rhetorical purposes; and
3) studies of writing as a cognitive process where evidence of competence is found in ability to cope with task demands.

In the unification of these three perspectives, Polin conceived a means of explaining the "complex domain of writing" (p. 2). Three other scholars (Mellon, 1977; Odell, 1981; Purves et al., 1982, 1984) have also attempted to define competence in writing and the means of assessing it. In the following sections we will describe each of these approaches in turn.

Polin on the Assessment of the Writing Process

Many observers, including Polin (1980), have noticed that much of present practice in writing assessment is incongruous with the accounts we have of the real world writing process. Current assessments often elicit an impromptu written product based upon an imposed topic within a time frame that seldom allows adequate opportunity for the natural unfolding of a process of conception, development, revision and editing. Evaluators get what is essentially a rough draft which they proceed to rate and rank in relation to other papers received, or in relation to an arbitrary rating scale or rubric. Polin points out that this practice raises questions about the validity of procedures which don't allow the prewriting and revision activities which, as research suggests, distinguish between skilled and unskilled writers (p. 2).

Polin proceeds to argue for "adopting a process orientation that [does] recognize the developmental quality of component skills and subprocesses, the interrelationships among those skills, and the behaviors or outcomes that demonstrate competence" (p. 8). Thus, because she wants the domain of writing to include what happens before, during, and after the drafting of the written text, she discusses the subskills involved in planning, drafting, and reworking a paper. Yet, in the end, she acknowledges that "we must wait for further research and refinement of theory to help us decide upon defensible, valid task analyses and competence markers" (p. 12) before we can actually assess what happens during these various stages in the process of writing.

Mellon's Taxonomy of Compositional Competencies

Mellon (1977) looked at indications of writing competence from a different perspective. He used research in writing as a base from which to extract a

taxonomy of writing competencies. It is impractical to repeat Mellon's
(1977) entire taxonomy here; it is sufficient to note its existence and some of
its general dimensions, and to recommend that it be consulted by test-
makers. The taxonomy is organized in five general categories that are subdivided as follows (pp. 257–264). (See Table 6.8.)

The taxonomy ends with eight recommendations for teachers and curriculum coordinators: These deal with (a) establishing a base for writing
through wide reading and vocabulary learning; (b) developing an assignment sequence; (c) developing pre-writing worksheets to be used with the
assignments; (d) preparing booklets of model writing; (e) preparing instructional manuals for peer readership and peer response; (f) preparing writing
checklists to accompany the manuals for peer readers; (g) engaging students in sentence-combining practice; and (h) designating a "special

---

Table 6.8.
Taxonomy of Compositional Competencies (Adapted from Mellon, 1977)

    I.   Lexical and Sentential Competencies
         A.   Vocabulary content
         B.   Vocabulary fluency
         C.   Syntactic fluency
   II. Discourse Competencies
         A.   Recognition that the structure of meaning is integrative and
             hierarchical
         B.   Recognition of logico-semantic relations
             1. Elementary statements
                 a. Relations of case category
                 b. Relations of attribution
                 c. Relations of modality
                 d. Relations of implication
             2. Inter-sentential conjunctive relations
             3. Supra-sentential relations among hierarchically structured
                discourse chunks
         C.   Recognition of organizational unity as governed by dominant
             purpose
             1. Informational writing
             2. Conative writing
             3. Expressive writing
             4. Literary writing
         D.   Recognition that intention may be expressed implicitly as well as
             explicitly
  III. Psychological Competencies
         A.   The ability to discover (invent in one's own mind or collect from
             external sources . . .)
         B.   The ability to cast ideas creatively . . .
         C.   The ability to think bi-channelly [to inscribe what is being written
             while simultaneously storing in memory what has not yet been
             said] . . .
         D.   The ability to prevent, control, or overcome writing apprehension. . .

Table 6.8. (cont.)

IV. Competence in Conforming to the "Rules of the Writing Game"
    A. Knowing how to introduce a topic . . .
    B. Knowing how to employ the many transitional/referential locutions essentially unique to writing
    C. Knowing how to draw to a close any piece of writing . . .
    D. Knowing which words of the spoken language . . . are barred from formal registers of transactional writing . . .
    E. Knowing how to achieve a particular writing style or styles . . .
    F. Knowing how to recognize and meet the informational needs of a general and undifferentiated reading audience as distinct from a known correspondent . . .
    G. Knowing how to conform to the mechanical conventions
V. Habit Structures and Self-Governance
    A. Pre-writing
    B. Decenteredness
    C. Reflectiveness
    D. Effort and staying power
    E. Criticism and revision
    F. Risk-taking
VI. Accidental Problems Requiring Special Instruction or Therapy
    A. First-language intrusions
    B. Spoken-dialect intrusions
    C. Spelling dyslexia and other biological dysfunctions

teacher" status for persons trained in the diagnosis of compositional dysfunctions. The writing activities embraced under this program would focus on expressive writing in the upper elementary and middle school years with transactional writing (expository composition) postponed until the secondary grades (pp. 265–268).

Odell on Defining and Assessing Competence in Writing

Lee Odell (1981) has examined at length the issues in defining and assessing writing competence. He has developed a more complex definition of competence than the common textbook standard which equates competence with the ability to follow the practice of "educated people." Odell defines competence in writing as *"the ability to discover what one wishes to say and to convey one's message through language, syntax, and content appropriate for one's audience and purpose"* (p. 103).

Defining further the global term *writing*, Odell includes a great many kinds of writing, ranging from diary entries and memos to formal reports, and involving diverse purposes and speaker-audience relationships (p. 103). These different forms, audiences, and purposes require writers to use various *registers* to develop different organizational strategies and to provide different kinds and amounts of information.

Odell (1981) then makes a number of suggestions for measuring competence in writing. A condensed version of these suggestions follows (pp. 113–118):

Suggestions for Measuring Competence in Writing
(Adapted from Odell, 1981)

1. To obtain an adequate sample of students' writing, we need to:
    a. Have students write under circumstances that approximate the conditions under which important writing is done
    b. Ask them to do more than one kind of writing; that is, have them write for more than one audience and purpose
    c. Provide them with information about the audience and purpose for which a given piece of writing is intended
    d. Assess the demands of our writing assignments, especially when we create more than one assignment
    e. Base our judgments on an adequate amount of students' writing.
2. To establish appropriate conditions for writing, we need to:
    a. Allow time to engage in the process of discovery
    b. Help students understand the purpose for the assignment
    c. Allow time for planning, drafting, and revising.
3. To evaluate writing we need to evaluate several different kinds of writing performance.
4. To design clear assignments, we need to:
    a. Let students see what their purpose is—to persuade, inform, express
    b. Help students understand that they need to consider such questions as the following about audience *even when writing for a teacher*:
        • How much does my audience know about this subject?
        • What is my reader's attitude toward me? Is he or she sympathetic? Hostile? Interested in my personal feelings or conclusions?
        • Does my reader have values, preconceptions, or feelings that might influence his or her response to the subject or to what I say about the subject?
    c. Identify the form: journal entry, letter, memo, editorial, essay, summary, short story, etc.
5. To assess the demands of writing tasks, we need to study the results of administrations, asking such questions as:
    a. Do students consistently choose some topics and ignore others?
    b. Do students who choose topic X consistently receive a higher grade than do students who choose topic Y?
    c. Do different topics require writers to draw upon different sources of information?

d. Does one topic require writers to be particularly conscious of their own or someone else's assumptions?

e. Does one topic invite chronological development, whereas another requires analogical development?

6. To obtain an adequate sample of a student's ability to perform more than one kind of writing task, we must have at least two writing samples of the student's writing for *each kind of writing*.

Odell identifies three types of questions addressed by writing assessments, each of which requires a different procedure and set of writing tasks:

1. Are individual students improving as writers?
2. Is our language program helping large groups of students?
3. Are students attaining minimum competence—that is, skill in communicating effectively?

According to Odell, the procedures required in an assessment vary somewhat with the assessment questions we seek to answer. To answer question 1, keep a writing folder for a student for a year; periodically during the year, evaluate the pieces of writing according to criteria discussed in class, and then each time share observations with the student for diagnostic purposes. To adopt a more rigorous procedure, take two pieces of writing from the beginning of the year and two from the end. Give to each of two trained judges a pair of essays (one early, one late) to determine which is better (p. 131).

To answer question 2, decide in advance, either as a grade level committee, as an English department, or as a school district what kinds of writing to stress during the year. Create four assignments, two for each of the two kinds of writing we are interested in. Give two of these assignments at the beginning of the school year as a pretest; give the other two at the end of the year as a post-test after instruction in the desired features has been conducted. Each assignment specifies topic, audience, and purpose. The procedures of administration allow two periods for each assignment, one period for the first draft and one period to revise and edit. Teachers of students being assessed meet to discuss the demands of the assignment, read some sample essays, and agree on a profile of the primary traits needed for success on the assignment. Then stress these characteristics in assignments given during the academic year, and then give the post-test. (pp. 133–134).

To answer question 3, agree on a definition of "minimum" competence. This is no easy task. Resist the tendency to equate minimum competency with simple mastery of mechanics (spelling, punctuation) and basic knowledge about grammar and usage as measured by standardized, multiple-choice test formats without writing samples. Answers to question 3 will vary from place to place, for as Odell says:

. . . we have no ready-made answers . . . ; there is no existing set of criteria that would let us make satisfactory, reliable decisions as to what would be minimally acceptable for students in every school district or state in the nation. Lacking such criteria, we will need to proceed as we would in doing any rank ordering of student writing. In following such a procedure, it seems very likely that the definition of "minimum competency" may vary from school district to school district or from state to state. (p. 133)

To sum up, according to Odell, we can describe and evaluate our students' writing performance when we have defined what we mean by competence in writing, when we know what our purpose is in evaluating students' writing, and when we understand the nature and limitations of existing procedures for measuring writing ability. Odell's advice applies in both local and national evaluation contexts.

Purves's and Vähäpassi's Specification of the Domain of School Writing

Acting on a charge from the International Association for the Evaluation of Educational Achievement, a group of educators from Finland, the Netherlands, Hungary, and the United States met to develop plans for the international study of achievement in written composition (Purves & Takala, 1982). Purves and his international associates began to explore the domain of school-based writing as a basis for classifying composition assignments. Eventually they developed a system (Purves, Söter, Takala, and Vähäpassi, 1984) which they consider to be a type of criterion-referenced procedure for designing a test in which the interpretability of the test result is the primary concern. Purves, et al. have contrasted this domain-referenced measurement goal with that of the norm-referenced test. In the latter the aim is to produce scores that rank examinees against each other, but in a domain-referenced test, the aim is to acquire information about what and how much has been mastered with respect to the domain-specifications.

Vähäpassi (1982) developed the initial general model of school-based writing. The features of this model appear in the form of a grid that can be tested empirically as a classification system by placing different types of writing products within its cells. The model provides an unusually comprehensive depiction of the domain of school-writing tasks as shown in Figure 6.4. (Purves, et al., 1984, pp. 394–395).

This model has proved useful for several purposes at a fairly high level of generality, but the two dimensions of the model did not cover all the variables that the researchers found in actual assignments. After looking at a number of composition assignments, they developed an expanded classification system (Purves et al., 1984). Only the major categories of their elaborated system can be listed here. The reader is referred to the source for a full

Figure 6.4. Tasks in Relation to the Domain of School Writing (From Purves, et al., 1984, Reprinted by permission of the National Council of Teachers of English)

Dominant Intention/Purpose	Cognitive Processing: Primary Content / Primary Audience	REPRODUCE — Facts	REPRODUCE — Ideas	ORGANIZE/REORGANIZE — Events	ORGANIZE/REORGANIZE — Visual images, facts, mental states, ideas	INVENT/GENERATE — Ideas, mental states alternative worlds
To learn (metalingual)	Self	Copying; Taking Dictation		Retell a story (heard or read)	Note; Resume; Summary; Outline; Paraphrasing	Comments on book margins; Metaphors; Analogies
To convey emotions, feelings (emotive)	Self; Others	Stream of consciousness		Personal story; Personal diary; Personal letter	Portrayal	Reflective writing –Personal essays
To inform (referential)	Others	Quote; Fill in a form; Message		Narrative report; News; Instruction; Telegram; Announcement; Circular; Message	Directions; Description; Technical description; Biography; Science report/experiment	Expository writing –Definition –Academic essay/article –Book review –Commentary

The traditional literary genres and modes can be placed under one or more of these four purposes.

Figure 6.4. (Continued)

Cognitive Processing		REPRODUCE	ORGANIZE/REORGANIZE	INVENT/GENERATE

To convince/persuade (connative)	Others	Citation from authority/expert	Letter of application Advertisement
			                Letter of advice
			Statement of personal
			    views, opinions
				Argumentative/persuasive writing
				-Editorial
				-Critical essay/article

To entertain, delight, please (poetic)	Others	Quote poetry and prose	Given an ending, create a story Create an ending Retell a story Word portrait or sketch Causerie	Entertainment writing -Parody -Rhymes
PRIMARY MODE OF DISCOURSE		DOCU-MENTATIVE DISCOURSE	CONSTATIVE DISCOURSE Narrative Descriptive Explanatory	EXPLORATORY DISCOURSE Interpretive Literary (Expository/ Argumentative)

annotation of each category and illustrative applications (pp. 396–416). (See Table 6.9.)

Table 6.9.
Dimensions of a Writing Assignment
(Main Categories only)
(Adapted from A. Purves, A. Söter, S. Takala, A. Vähäpassi, 1984)

A. Instruction	I. Tone, style
B. Stimulus	J. Advance preparation
C. Cognitive demand	K. Length
D. Purpose	L. Format
E. Role	M. Time
F. Audience	N. Draft
G. Content	O. Criteria
H. Rhetorical specification	

Theory and Research-Based Assessment Models: Special Cases

Skills Models and Discrete Point Measures

All of the discourse models that we have just described stand in sharp contrast to the skills model of the learning-to-write process. Advocates of the skills model view writing as the sum of separately taught sub-skills. In the world of practice, this conception leads to a series of separate activities or skills, each to be practiced, mastered, and tested in turn by multiple-choice tests. The skills pattern often includes a minutely detailed definition of objectives with the class exercises and tests matched to these objectives. Under this skills model, teachers, texts, and test designers all focus on the mastery of discrete points for learning the essentials of good writing—e.g., grammar, spelling, punctuation, capitalization, topic sentences instead of a holistic approach. This model may have originated in some early day common sense analysis of surface features of written products, but whatever its origin, it evolved and became sanctified by a behavioral psychology and a positivistic philosophy which placed a premium on observable, measurable knowledge.

Much of the traditional teaching of writing in academic courses in secondary schools has relied on the skills model. A national study (Applebee, 1980) of writing in the secondary school revealed the consequences of this practice. This study showed that an average of 44% of the lesson time observed was involved with writing activities. But mechanical uses of writing (short-answer, fill-in-the-blank tests) occurred 24% of the time, and note taking occurred just 17% of the time. Writing that was a paragraph in length or longer occurred only 3% of the observed time, and homework assignments of at least a paragraph in length also occurred only 3% of the time. Writing that was a paragraph in length occurred most frequently in English classes, averaging 10% of lesson time. The most prevalent writing task was classified as requiring informational writing; imaginative uses were, for the most part, limited to English classes.

The consequences of this emphasis on the more mechanical forms of writing across the secondary curriculum are described by Applebee (1980):

> One of the major problems with an overemphasis on mechanical writing tasks is that the students may never learn to use . . . resources on their own, relying instead upon the structure or scaffold that the teacher has provided.

> Because the emphasis is on specific items of information, rather than on the way those items are integrated and presented in coherent prose, such writing situations provide little opportunity for instruction that might help students to develop specific writing skills. For learning to write well, the most effective writing situation will be one in which the effectiveness of the writing matters— where the student can savor the success of having presented a convincing argument, or struggle with the problems of having failed to do so. (pp. 143–144)

What emerged from the Applebee (1981) study is a recognition that students function in a classroom setting that offers little opportunity to *practice* the writing skills on which they may be formally *assessed.* Much of the classroom writing that students do is assigned in a testing context rather than in an instructional one. Moreover, the testing situation itself tends to be undemanding of integrative compositional processes because the dominant test forms require only the "slotting-in" of information or short answers which do not test the student's ability to actually structure an idea.

Tasks, prestructured by the teacher-as-examiner, would seem to constitute scant preparation for the types of writing that subsequent large-scale assessment tasks frequently demand. Such teacher-prepared texts, with their gaps to be filled in, seem to call for a different sort of cognitive ability than is required for creating and monitoring the development of one's own text, especially the sort of impromptu text that is required for many writing tests (Bartlett, 1981). Since the teacher's own writing assignments constitute the student's only practice for later assessments, whether at the school level or as part of a national sample, logic suggests that there should be prior work on what is to be assessed. The post-course examination itself should not constitute the student's only practice of particular task demands and discourse forms.

The discrete activities and the mechanical slotting in of information that occur in the name of skill development are antithetical to all of the discourse models presented above. Kinneavy (1980), on reviewing the theoretical stances of Moffett, Britton, and D'Angelo alongside his own, noted that he and his fellow discourse theorists each believe

> that composition is best taught with examples of full discourse. The concerns with mechanics, sentence structure, style, even invention and arrangement are best seen in the act of handling a full discourse. (p. 38)

Assumptions about the nature of writing and models of the writing process have consequences for the design of assessment instruments. If writing is conceived of as a loose aggregation of skills, we may be satisfied with discrete point, mutliple-choice measures; however, if writing is conceived of as a complex, purposeful, cognitive act, we must demand writing tasks that draw on these communicative and cognitive processes.

The Primary Trait Model

The discourse theories of Kinneavy (1971), Moffett (1968), Britton (1975), and D'Angelo (1975) have all been tested in some measure in classrooms, and elements of these theories already underlie some local, state, and national programs of assessment. We have seen earlier how Kinneavy's discourse theories guide the Texas assessment. Now we shall present the discourse theory underlying the National Assessment of Educational Progress.

Lloyd-Jones (1977) explained why he and Carl Klaus selected a discourse model to guide the procedures of the National Assessment of Educational Progress:

> In order to report precisely how people manage different types of discourse, one must have a model of discourse which permits the identification of limited types of discourse and the creation of exercises which stimulate writing in the appropriate range but not beyond it. (p. 37)

Consequently Lloyd-Jones and Klaus selected a three-part model after rejecting several others as being either too simple or too complicated. For example, they rejected the model shown in Figure 6.5. as too complicated for the purposes of the national assessment (p. 40). Even so it remained a useful explanatory model.

Although they acknowledge that there is a blend of purposes and associated forms in actual discourse, Lloyd-Jones and Klaus settled on a tri-polar scheme from which they expected to derive the *primary rhetorical traits* associated with each type of writing represented. The model they finally developed (p. 39) has guided the design of exercises for NAEP since 1974. It is depicted in Figure 6.6.

A Research-Based Model of Writing Task Development from E.T.S.

Currently, the Test of English as a Foreign Language (TOEFL) program at Educational Testing Service (ETS) uses an indirect, or multiple-choice, measure of writing, but no direct measure or writing sample. Bridgeman and

Figure 6.5.   Model of Discourse (From Lloyd-Jones, 1977)

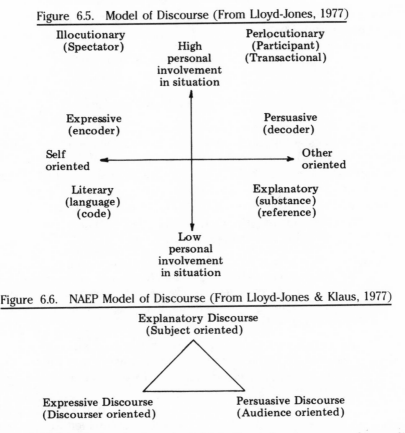

Figure 6.6.   NAEP Model of Discourse (From Lloyd-Jones & Klaus, 1977)

Carlson (1984) have reported on the initial steps taken to prepare for a validation study of a new TOEFL which might include a direct measure of writing. Before such a study could be conducted, however, the academic writing skills required of beginning undergraduates and graduate students had to be defined. In their attempt to develop this definition and appropriate writing tasks, Bridgeman and Carlson worked out procedures that may well serve other groups interested in writing task development.

Bridgeman and Carlson (1984) surveyed faculty in 190 academic departments at 34 U.S. and Canadian universities with high foreign student enrollments. Their findings are of particular interest to anyone using either the TOEFL or locally developed examinations for non-native writers, but what is unique and generalizable about this survey is their questionnaire development strategy and the questionnaire's content.

The researchers used three primary sources of data: a literature review which suggested the areas of concern that needed to be addressed, an advisory committee made up of experts in the area of writing assessment, and interviews with faculty at nearby institutions. Bridgeman and Carlson (1984) then developed a comprehensive questionnaire with six major sections:

I.   Asked for background information about the academic department
II. Surveyed writing task demands
III. Investigated criteria used to evaluate written assignments
IV. Obtained data on problems of native and non-native students
V.   Solicited information on potential use of a writing sample in the admissions process
VI. Asked for acceptability ratings on ten specific topic types

The development of these topic types and the method of collecting acceptability ratings are of most interest to us here. It is common practice to have review panels rate the importance of features of writing tasks presented as abstract elements in lists. But because Bridgeman and Carlson assumed that concrete examples of tasks would enable respondents to appraise task demands more realistically, they diverged from common practice by putting actual writing tasks exemplifying ten different task demands into section VI of their questionnaire. In reacting to topic types,

> respondents were instructed to respond to the writing communication demands and the skills likely to be elicited by a type of task, rather than to the specific wording or subject matter of an example. The topic types were structured to demonstrate how a stimulus for a writing sample might elicit particular writing skills. (p. 254)

Two specific examples were provided for each topic type.

The ten topic types, with commentaries on some of the assumptions underlying each type, were presented in an extensive report published by ETS (Bridgeman & Carlson, 1983). Space limitations allow us only to identify the topic types without summarizing the commentaries. For the details of these commentaries and the actual topics, the reader is directed to this useful, well written report. The ten topic types as listed in the report are as follows (1984, p. 271):

Ten Basic Topic Types (From Bridgeman & Carlson, 1984)

A. personal essay
B. sequential or chronological description
C. spatial or functional description
D. compare and contrast
E. compare and contrast plus take a position
F. extrapolation
G. argumentation with audience designation
H. describe and interpret a graph or chart
I. summarize a passage
J. summarize a passage and analyze/assess the point of view

The Bridgeman and Carlson (1983) findings about the preferences of different academic departments for particular topic types are of interest. Topic H was a favorite of engineering and science departments, but it was considered inappropriate by a majority of undergraduate English faculty. Topic G was a favorite among MBA programs. Type E was also reviewed positively by the MBA programs and was the favorite among undergraduate English programs. Bridgeman and Carlson (1983) report:

> The survey data distinctly indicate that different disciplines do not uniformly agree on the writing task demands and on a single preferred mode of discourse for evaluating entering undergraduate and graduate students. The extent to which essays written in different discourse modes produce different rank ordering of students remains to be seen. (p. 56)

It would be interesting to conduct a parallel survey to determine what academic writing tasks would be deemed important for all students by the participating faculty members.

Models of Large-Scale Assessment

We have already taken note of the large-scale International Study of Achievement in Written Composition (Purves & Takala, 1982) and its approach to writing assignment classification. But there are additional insights into topic development to be gained from other models of large-scale writing assessment, notably from projects conducted by England's Assessment of Performance Unit (APU), Assessment of Writing; and Canada's Ontario Institute of Studies in Education, Writing Evaluation Project. These two writing assessment projects are worthy of more attention than our limited space allows. We aim in this account merely to identify them and direct the reader to the excellent reports that describe their procedures and findings.

An English Model: The Assessment of Performance Unit

The Assessment of Performance Unit (APU) was created in 1975 within the Department of Education and Science to provide information about general levels of performance among children and young people in the schools in England, Wales, and Northern Ireland. The APU is similar in function to the National Assessment of Educational Progress in the United States, and for that reason, it is interesting to examine this agency's procedures as reported in the primary survey (Gorman, White, Orchard, Tate & Sexton, 1981) and the secondary survey (Gorman, White, Orchard, Tate & Sexton, 1982).

The primary survey aimed to assess the writing of 11 year olds. A representative national sample of about 4600 pupils drawn from about 300 schools was asked to complete a booklet which contained four parts—two writing tasks, an editing task, and short questions about attitudes toward writing. Ten booklets were used. Students were asked to produce writing in relation to three tasks, two of which were common to all booklets—the explanation of a viewpoint and the editing of a short composition/report written by a pupil of the same age.

These surveys take into account the social context in which writing usually takes place. Accordingly, they are not conducted under "traditional" test conditions. That is, the teachers are encouraged to introduce the writing tasks before the group of pupils begins writing, but a particular focus for the composition is not necessarily given by the teacher. Pieces selected by the teacher from writing produced in the normal course of classwork are also gathered for evaluation as part of the survey.

All papers relating to the topics to be released in the public report are re-read so that detailed comments on the problems encountered and the nature of the writing achievement can be described. Three of the writing tasks used in the survey—a report based on an eyewitness account, a story, and an informal letter to a friend—are included in the public report so that specific features of the writing of 11-year-olds can be explicitly illustrated and discussed in detail (Gorman et al., *Primary Survey Report, No. 1,* 1981).

The secondary survey was planned to assess the language performance of 15-year-olds. A representative national survey of 3,100 students completed the tests in writing and 700 took tests which linked reading and writing. As in the primary survey, ten booklets were used. These booklets were constructed so that each contained the same short writing task, together with one of ten other writing tasks (involving, for example, description, narration, instruction, explanation, reporting, persuasion, and the expression of feeling), a passage to be edited, and three short questions on attitudes toward writing. Three of the writing tasks used in the survey are illustrated and described in the public report—one required a persuasive argument to be constructed on the basis of strong personal opinion; one involved giving a detailed explanation of how to perform a chosen skill for the benefit of a novice; and the third involved a letter of application for a summer job. Some of the results from the editing tasks are also briefly noted (Gorman, et al., *Secondary Survey Report, No. 1,* 1982).

A Canadian Model: Ontario Writing Assessment Projects

Peter Evans (1979) provides a Canadian perspective on the evaluation of writing at grades 8, 12, and 13 in his monograph reporting the results of a two-year study based on a careful sampling of schools and students in the province of Ontario. Since the aim of the monograph is to provide incentive and guidelines for school systems to conduct their own assessment programs, there is an especially useful final chapter on "A Program for Writing Evaluation Within a School System" (pp. 67–83). The model presented in this chapter derives from the two-year research study described in earlier chapters. In brief, Evans's evaluation model incorporates program planning and setting the expectations of writing performance, a "good sampling of writing over the term reflective of program emphasis, and means of improved dialogue between teacher and student, together with the *summative* evaluation through the final pair of assignments holistically scored and subsequent analyses of a sample representing the full score range" (p. 67). Evans's (1979) own summary is the most succinct means of giving an account of his proposed evaluation model:

Evaluation Model for a School System
(From Evans, 1979)

The first and critical step for the planned evaluation of writing within a school or a system is the establishment of reasonable consensus of expectations concerning the writing program at the grade levels concerned: these expectations include careful identification of the *modes* of writing reasonable for the grade and of a number of criteria reasonably applicable to these modes.

I strongly recommend that teachers draw on available published resources to a considerable extent in defining criteria so the task of specifying criteria will not be too burdensome.

The second step is a reasonable standardization of the manner in which the student's writing is kept on file together with appropriate records. For this, I recommend the writing folder and frequent use of analytic scoring by teacher and student.

The third step, assuming one wishes to include a reasonable sample of writing over the term, is to achieve some agreement about the frequency, modes, and scoring treatment of formal assignments over the school year, with the understanding that scores on these will form a substantial portion of the final mark.

The fourth step is a decision concerning the final pair of assignments for holistic scoring and the conditions under which they will be written and scored. Mode and topic must be controlled.

This decision should be made early in the school year and all information except the specific topics shared with the students.

At this stage also a number of organizational matters—type of paper, time and locations for writing, student coding, distribution of essays for scoring, reasonable concessions to scorers, and compilation of data—should be dealt with. The plan should permit students to receive their scores before the end of the school year.

The fifth step is the analysis of a random sample of the writing by a small trained team. The dimensions of that analysis should be agreed to early in the project with consideration of the value of certain kinds of information to different audiences or "clients" and very particular consideration of the value of the information in making program decisions and assessing the effectiveness of program change (pp. 82–83).

With regard to the two topics for holistic scoring, Evans recommends *two* assignments on different days, in different but important modes, with control of the topic [subject] variable. Students and staff should have complete information about the final pair of assignments—only the subject is not given in advance. "Students also should have adequate time to write, revise, and recopy, and have access to dictionaries, a thesaurus, and other such resources. In short, the situation should be normalized as far as possible" (p. 74).

The Ontario Ministry of Education (1979, 1982) provides packages of assessment materials related to the writing components of the Ministry of Education curriculum guideline, *English I Intermediate Division, 1979*. These materials from the Ontario Assessment Instrument Pool are available to local systems who desire to conduct their own assessments. The original assessment package (1979) and its supplement (1982) contain field-tested topics with commentaries from the OISE Evaluation Project (1977, 1979) and from the New Brunswick Evaluation Project (1977, 1978). In introducing these topics, the guidelines assert: "The selection of effective stimuli should receive a great deal more attention than it frequently does" (p. W-29). The packet also contains sample papers representing different scoring levels. The packet also presents information on maintaining a writing folder and various scoring systems.

The Ontario Ministry materials emphasize the point that "a single piece of writing cannot be truly representative of the range of a student's ability" (p. W-2). Thus, the Ministry takes the position that there is "need for a number of assessment schemes to serve different purposes in different contexts" (p. W-3). The Ministry also asserts that "two or three pieces of work form an inadequate basis for evaluating the student's performance in writing. Any fair assessment must include samples of the student's writing over time, and this implies a writing folder, or portfolio, with records concerning performance (p. W-3)."

SEVEN

The Writing Assessment Episode: A Model for Investigation

Foundations of the Model

Introduction

> When children fail, I wondered, why do they fail? What is it they cannot do? To try to find out I sat down with some children between the ages of nine and thirteen and got them to tackle a selection of typical questions and talk to me about what they were doing. I asked them to "think aloud" as far as possible.
>
> Margaret Donaldson,
> *Children's Minds*, 1978, p. 78

How does a writer read the topic that initiates the act of writing? This was the pivotal question that we had in mind when we began in the fall of 1980 to develop our model of the writing assessment episode. Our review of the literature had drawn a blank when it came to locating research dealing directly with the processes of interpreting the texts of writing tasks. We had found a few scattered reports of research where the investigators had asked students to interpret items in objective tests (Cicourel, et al., 1974; Meier, 1973; Fillmore & Kay, 1980), but nothing pertaining to writing tasks. Meanwhile, James Hoetker had conducted an extensive review of the literature on essay examination topics in 1979 on behalf of the Florida State Department of Education, which was preparing to launch the Florida Teacher Certification Examination. In a version of that report later published in 1982, Hoetker observed:

> Since there are no studies of how students read essay topics, we know little about how the structure or the rhetoric or the vocabulary of a topic affects students' interpretations of it or their affective responses to it. (p. 380)

Meanwhile, in the late spring of 1980, the Bay Area Writing Project, with funding by the National Institute of Education, had begun a Writing Assessment Project to conduct several related studies. The final report of that project, *Properties of Writing Tasks: A Study of Alternative Procedures for Holistic Writing Assessment* (Gray & Ruth) was completed in November 1982.

This chapter describes the development of our model of *the writing assessment episode,* and several studies conducted by the research team of the BAWP Writing Assessment Project. The results and the issues brought to light in these studies will be presented in Chapters 8 through 11.

Problems of Meaning in Topics

The act of writing in an assessment actually begins with an act of *reading comprehension*. We have usually assumed that each writer receives the same message to direct the writing performance. In fact, the very stability of our writing measurement rests on this underlying psychometric assumption that the stimulus properties of a topic affect all students uniformly. But this is a questionable assumption. The intentions of test makers often "misfire," to borrow the apt term used by J.L. Austin (1965) to describe those occasions when an act of communication is "botched," when responses fail to meet expectations. If a "misfire" occurs in a *classroom writing context*, we can assist in repairing the breakdown. We can reconnect the circuits, so to speak, when the initial attempts to engage students with a classroom writing assignment fail. But much current practice within *testing contexts* requires the writing prompt to function autonomously. That is, the writer must read and respond to the topic without aid because conditions for the writers must be carefully controlled, formal, depersonalized—in other words, standardized.

Theories of testing need to be aligned with theories of language and cognition if the process of interpreting questions and topics is to be well understood (Ruth 1980). Recent cognitive theory accounts for the types of "misfires" exemplified in the two following anecdotes, which illustrate how meaning resides neither in the questions per se nor necessarily in the respondents' perception and reasoning, but rather in the *transaction* between the question and its receiver. The *Interviewer's Manual* (1969) from the Michigan Survey Research Center tells how a particular question had been answered as expected in its field trial, but in its actual use, an unanticipated meaning emerged. When the interviewer asked, "Do you think the government should control profits or not?" one respondent replied, "Certainly not. Only Heaven should control prophets (p. 6)."

Another example of a mismatch occurred when a school inspector visited a rural village school in England. The inspector intended to restrict his questions to ones that he imagined would be within the limits of the rural students' world knowledge. He held up a picture of a common rural animal and said, "What is this?" and both he and the teacher were astounded when no one answered. They both presumed that of course these children could certainly identify a sheep. Later the teacher asked the children why no one had answered. One child said, "Well, Miss, we didn't know whether he wanted to know if the sheep was a pure Cheviot or a Crossbreed (Reynolds & Skilbeck, 1976, p. 89)."

The unexpected responses in these two anecdotes illustrate that although investigators and examiners may assume that a common linguistic and social frame of reference is shared by the questioner and the respondent, in fact, variable acts of cognition and interpretation are occurring. This phenomenon of variation in response is recognized in the field of survey research as "response error" (Cannell & Robinson, 1971). Response errors are further sub-categorized according to the source of error; hence, there are *instrument errors, respondent errors,* and *contextual errors.* These concepts from survey research that are applied to various types of question instruments seem useful in considering the potential sources of "error" in interpreting writing assessment tasks. Thus, we might analyze topics for *instrument errors* that derive from linguistic features of the writing task; *respondent errors* that emerge from mis-readings of the writing task by the student-writers and teacher-raters; and *contextual errors* arising from students' failures to understand how rules of normal discourse may be suspended in a writing test. For example, the "friendly letter" requested in a writing test requires a higher level of performance than one might normally accomplish when casually writing a real letter to a friend. The student who confuses the purposes of the two types of letter-writing will risk penalties for composing a genuine, casual letter in a test even though the task instructions literally cue informal writing, e.g. "Write a letter to a friend. . . "

Current Theories of Comprehension
Applied to Topic Interpretation

Our BAWP Writing Assessment Project attempted to understand better the language and structure of writing tasks, their author's intentions and the responses that these tasks evoked in student writers and teacher raters. To account theoretically for the variability in the interpretations of writing tasks, we turned to the constructivist theories of the reading process and to reader-response theories in literary criticism which together illuminate the real nature of the so-called "response error." (Ruth, 1980)

Models of reading comprehension have been changing within the last few years as a result of theoretical and experimental work in fields such as psycholinguistics, cognitive psychology, artificial intelligence, literary critical theory, and other disciplines. We are learning from cognitive psychologists how the meanings of texts, spoken and written, are constructed in the minds of their hearers or readers through active, participative processes. We saw in the text processing models (Flower & Hayes, 1979; Bruce et al., 1978) described in Chapter 6 how readers and listeners take a received "text" into consciousness and make it their own.

In 1938, from the perspective of aesthetics, Rosenblatt conceived of readers as "creators" or "evokers" of texts long before the cognitive psychologists had begun to adopt similar positions in the early seventies. Her landmark work, *Literature As Exploration* ([1938] 1976), along with her most recent work, *The Reader, The Text, The Poem* (1978), together provide an account of the early development and later extension of her *transactional theory* of the reading process. Rosenblatt depicts the reader's role in the transactional process as it occurs in the reading of a poem. (Note: Rosenb-latt uses "poem" as a generic term for all members of the category, "literary work of art.")

> The reader's attention to the text activates certain elements in his past experi-ence—external reference, internal response—that have become linked with the verbal symbols. Meaning will emerge from a network of relationships among the things symbolized *as he senses them.* The symbols point to these sensations, images, objects, ideas, relationships, with the particular associa-tion or feeling-tones created by his past experiences with them in actual life or in literature. The selection and organization of responses to some degree hinge on the assumptions, the expectations, or sense of possible structures, that he brings out of the stream of his life. Thus, built into the raw material of the literary process itself is the particular world of the reader. (1978, p. 11)

But, it is very important to note that "the world of the reader" connects with a text. Even as the reader brings meanings *to* the text, the text simultaneously *returns* meanings that may lead the reader to alter his initial stance:

> The text may also lead him to be critical of those prior assumptions and asso-ciations. . . . He may discover that he had projected on the text elements of his past experience not relevant to it, and which are not susceptible of coherent incorporation into it.

> "Transaction" designates, then, an ongoing process in which elements or fac-tors are, one might say, aspects of a total situation, each conditioned by and conditioning the other. (1978, pp. 11 & 17)

The meaning of a text achieves its final significance only when an active reader is both responsive and responsible to it—when he takes possession of it in his own frame of knowledge. It is not, however, a matter of readers creating just any meaning. The author expresses his intentions directly or indirectly through his selection of linguistic elements to convey those inten-tions. Texts do set limits to possible ranges of meaning, but for various rea-sons the reader does not always re-create the intended meanings (Ruth, 1980).

The act of "knowing" is what occurs in the transaction between a reader and a text. Rosenblatt ([1936] 1976) calls this process a "transaction" be-cause she believes this term preserves a sense of the complexity and whole-ness of the performance that is not conveyed in "interaction," (Rumelhart, 1978) the term more often favored in cognitive psychology to label what hap-pens between a reader and a text. Rosenblatt (1985) recognizes in the us-ages of "transaction" and "interaction" reflections of different scientific par-adigms. She associates "interaction" with Newtonian dualism and the behavioristic stimulus-response model of research, and she links "transac-tion" with Dewey and his holistic view of a total situation or experience in-volving the whole personal, social, and cultural matrix (pp. 99–100).

Recent approaches to the study of comprehension adopted in cognitive psychology, psycholinguistics, artificial intelligence, and generative semantics also have provided fresh insights into the reading process (Ruth 1980). Reading, viewed from the perspective of these sciences, is seen as a specific application of a general cognitive processing skill. In a sense, it is akin to reasoning. Cognitive science focuses on the non-aesthetic side of reading, or what Louise Rosenblatt (1985) calls the "efferent" function of reading. When one reads "efferently," he focuses on what he can take away from the reading—the "facts" of the story, the genre information, the logical solution to a problem, the directions or actions to be undertaken. In contrast, an "aesthetic" reader focuses on what happens as he "lives" through the reading (1985, pp. 24–25). Of course, even aesthetic texts may be given efferent readings ("What facts does this poem teach?" is a favorite Rosenblatt example of a misapplied question leading to an efferent reading of a poem). When an aesthetic text is placed in a testing context, the questions posed usually require an efferent reading. The very nature and purpose of the text of a writing prompt require an efferent reading, for embedded in the writing task is a set of instructions (explicit and implicit) to be carried into the writing performance to guide and shape it.

Efforts to connect reader-response criticism, contemporary reading theory, and composition theory into a unified theory of reading, interpretation, and composition are a fairly recent development (Peterson, 1982). The application of "post-structural" literary criticism to the reading of student writing is an even later development (E.M. White, 1984). Edward White has stated an obvious connection that seems to have escaped notice until now:

> Responding to texts, whether they are artistic or naive . . . is the business that unites us as teachers of literature and of writing. Theories of reading lie behind the ways we respond to all texts, even though we tend, because of the nature of our training, to be much more aware of these theories when we read literature than when we grade papers. (p. 186)

The theories of Wolfgang Iser, Stanley Fish, David Bleich, Norman Holland, and others that White cites all deal with ways readers "interact" with text. White notes that although each of these critics takes a different stance toward the role of the reader, they all do oppose the approach of New Criticism which assumes that "meaning resides in a text." Their response-oriented theories introduce the issue of the "misreading of literary texts," and White extends this concept to the reading of student papers. White believes that acceptance of the idea of the "necessity of misreading" in the post-structuralist sense will make us as teachers "less sure of the objectivity of our reading and more ready to grant to the student possible intentions or insights not yet present on the page" (p. 191). The cultivation of this sensitivity in the classroom, may lead to the refinement of drafts. But what does this post-structuralist notion of "misreading" mean for concepts of reliability in the reading of student papers in a testing context? The notion of allowable variant readings will surely complicate scoring procedures in both holistic and primary trait types of writing assessments. (See E.M. White, 1985, for further discussion of these points.)

According to Peter H. Johnson's (1983) monograph on the implications of using a cognitive basis to assess reading comprehension the constructivist position renders an account of comprehension as a complex process that depends on extra-sentence as well as inter-sentence context. The constructive process incorporates information presented in text structures, the context of that information, and the existing knowledge framework of the reader. Johnson explains how a reader using different levels of strategies, including problem-solving strategies, constructs a model of meaning which he assumes that the writer has intended. The reader uses various knowledge structures and cuing systems in the text to construct his own model of the meaning of the text.

Johnson (1983) provides a valuable synthesis of basic research on four variables which influence reading comprehension and hence the quality of an assessment. These factors, which would need to be taken into account in designing any assessment instrument, including, in our view, writing assessment tasks, are:

1. the *text:* its content, structure, and language;
2. the appropriateness of the text to the student's prior knowledge;
3. the sources of answers to questions;
4. the task demands of the assessment procedures. (p. 20)

Although Johnson deals exclusively with objective test items, the writer of essay topics has much to gain from his monograph.

Fillmore and Kay's (1980) text semantic analysis of reading comprehension tests also provided us with particularly useful insights into the process of understanding texts. Fillmore and Kay designed a research project that enabled them to observe readers constructing an understanding of the text of individual items gleaned from a variety of standardized, objective reading tests, with the majority of items coming from the Gates-MacGintie Test. The test was administered to a third grade class. Several weeks later each child was interviewed on selected items from this test using various types of probes to discover "the way the child sees or 'envisions' the content of the text as it may or may not affect his/her ability to answer the test item question" (p. 8). The researchers looked at the ways these third graders assigned meanings to unknown words and drew upon their "scriptal" knowledge (detailed world knowledge held prior to the test event), and used other strategies to build up their meanings of the texts of the reading test items presented to them. The researchers aimed to collect reader/test interaction data that would prove helpful to designers of tests and teachers in the construction and evaluation of future tests.

Our initial constructivist model for interpreting writing tasks hypothesized that the readers of the topic (both the student writers and the teacher raters) choose among cues embedded in the text of the task, both honoring and ignoring elements which may enable them, with varying degrees of success, to match the test maker's intentions and expectations. Our investigations later confirmed that the "meaning potential" of any given task for a student writer or a teacher rater is relative to the linguistic, cognitive, and social re-verberations set off in the respondents. What meanings the properties of a writing task may elicit are contingent on the language of the topic, the world knowledge of all the participants in a writing test, and their awareness of the special language conventions governing participation in a test.

Social Interaction in Testing Contexts

As a research team, we considered a test to be a socially anchored event, so we were interested in the field-based perspectives in sociology as applied to investigations of contextual aspects of testing. Aaron Cicourel, et al. (1974), a cognitive sociologist, provides further evidence of the validity of constructivist theories through his investigations of practices in classroom testing:

> Our observation of teacher, tester, and children's performances in testing and classroom situations suggests that children do not always share the teacher's or tester's idea of what the lesson or test is about . . . the informational content of lessons and tests influence both the child's performance and the teacher's, tester's, and researcher's inferences about the child's underlying competence.

> Our research shows that what could be called "errors" in responding to standardized curricula and tests may be the result of misunderstanding on the part of the teachers, testers, and children, which are created by the interactional activities they are engaged in. . . . Treating errors and misunderstandings as natural aspects of educational encounters would enable participants to have access to them and become less preoccupied with a rigid notion of what is right and what is wrong. Our materials show that the problem of what is right and wrong cannot be resolved by some absolute notion of a correct answer. (pp. 5–6)

Cicourel, et al. (1974) concluded that it is necessary to understand the complexity of the intermingling of information processing, differential aspects of attention, and the social interactional aspects that are all involved in those situations defined by adults as testing occasions. Otherwise, we cannot make adequate judgments of the students' performance.

Methodological Concerns

Many researchers doing studies to investigate the effects of particular variables on performance in writing tests have depended on the strategy of creating different versions of topics in an attempt to keep certain variables constant while manipulating others e.g., Brossell (1983), Greenberg (1981a), Leu, Keech, Murphy, Kinzer (1982). But the results of any study which depends on the strategy of creating different versions of topics, must be greeted with caution. In studies of this kind, it may be particularly difficult to create topic versions which accurately reflect the distinctions one wishes to make. Rhetorical elements operate in a dynamic relationship to one another; in changing one element, the researcher may inadvertently be affecting the others in unknown or unpredictable ways. Ultimately, experimental manipulation of topic variables may have limited utility, because this approach fails to account for still another and very important source of variation—the student reader, and the possibility that there may be different "readings" of the same topic among a given group of students. Hoetker raised this issue in his review of research on essay examination topics with regard to the problem of reliably classifying "modes" of writing. He pointed out that "the 'mode' of writing called for by any essay topic is precisely that mode that any particular student interprets it as calling for" (Hoetker, 1982, p. 379). Hoetker cited a number of cases where topics failed to elicit the "mode" of writing intended. He concluded that this phenomenon of variant readings, a "commonplace of contemporary literary criticism" has received insufficient attention in the research on the characteristics of different kinds of written compositions (e.g. narrative vs. argument). Hoetker's criticism of the researchers who avoid the problem of classification by assuming that the " 'mode' of an essay is determined by the intentions of the author of the stimulus topic" (p. 379) is apt, but he may not have carried the implications of this problem far enough. The assumption that each reader receives the same message from any particular topic to direct his subsequent writing performance underlies not only research in which different topics are employed to elicit different kinds of writing, but also research which attempts to isolate variables by creating different versions of the same topic. Studies of topic effects which classify and attempt to manipulate particular variables suffer from the same limitation. Until we know more about *how* students read topics, construct rhetorical tasks for themselves, and make choices in composing responses, we cannot form valid conclusions about the effects of varying the texts of topics.

During our research for the Writing Assessment Project, we became increasingly aware of the limitations of any approach which relies on the assumption that each reader is receiving the same message to direct his subsequent performance as a writer. Thus, we recognized a need to develop new modes of inquiry, but we also were aware that there are certain risks involved in designing new research methods. Researchers who deliberately depart from conventional approaches in a conservative educational research world where the dominant model is still an experimental design may risk later reproachful evaluations of their work. Cases in point are the recent "reassessment" of Janet Emig's study of the composing processes of twelfth graders (Voss, 1983) and the substantive attack on protocol analysis and model building as practiced by Flower and Hayes (Cooper & Holzman, 1983) where they are charged with practicing "introspection" (p. 284) and building a model "too underspecified to be testable" (p. 287). Therefore, to counter the view that there is only one right way to do "scientific" research and develop models in educational settings, we think it is useful to review here some recent trends in scientific research and how these led us to develop procedures that empiricist philosophers of science would classify as "unconventional" modes of investigation and model development.

The dominant versions of scientific explanation that are applied in educational research are well-known and codified in classic texts, Kerlinger (1964), Campbell and Stanley (1966), Travers (1973), Gage (1972), and others. But these long-favored experimental methods, patterned after the research models of the physical sciences, have themselves been the object of increasingly severe criticism. More and more researchers in the social sciences and in certain humanities areas (e.g. composition research) have concluded that human behavior is far more subtle and complex than the narrowly conceived, tightly controlled experimental models can take into account. For example, the cognitive psychologists, P. N. Johnson-Laird and P.C. Wason (1977) in the Preface to their recent collection of readings in cognitive science commented on the traditional research models that are characterized by

> an empiricist obsession with experiments—with designing, executing, analyzing, reporting, and criticizing them. In psychology, one experiment is worth a thousand theories. . . . It is no surprise that psychology is not noted for its theoretical expertise. Unfortunately, an understanding of human mentality is not to be achieved by merely carrying out experiments—no matter how exemplary they are. . . . (p. 2)

Mitroff and Kilmann (1978), who have analyzed the new styles of inquiry that have been emerging in the social sciences, acknowledge the existence of a "crisis of scientific belief." They note a "growing disillusionment and disenchantment with the nature of the scientific enterprise." They believe that the academic world is "on the edge of a revolution with regard to . . . thinking about the character of science" (pp. 2–3).

Of late, there also has been a call for new modes of inquiry in educational settings. Certain commentators have questioned the overuse of a narrow range of research methods, and they have endorsed efforts to create novel research approaches. The Seventy-First Yearbook of the National Society for the Study of Education, *Philosophical Redirection of Educational Research* (Thomas, 1972), as its title suggests, has called for new models and paradigms to guide the important practice of educational research. Against this background of growing concern about the restricted range of problems amenable to formal procedures of experimental research, Sutherland (1973) suggested that it is the subject of inquiry that should dictate research method, rather than the converse (p. 16). Sutherland also argued that the approach to a problem should be "dictated by emergent properties of the phenomenon itself not by *a prioristic* or axiological predicates which serve to artificially constrain the reality at hand or which predetermine the results of analysis . . ." (p. 16). Thus, dissatisfied with the limitations of conventional methodologies in educational research, we decided to develop contextually-based, holistic modes of inquiry and analysis to use in our study of how students read topics.

The importance of conducting research in natural settings and using multiple sources of data in observing a single phenomenon is emphasized in the work of Cicourel (1974) who argues that when

> a strong educational psychology bias demands that only certain research strategies be used to ensure presumed 'rigorous' controls, sampling conditions, and 'objective' measurements of the activities studied[,] most of these 'rigorous' studies miss their intended goal because they are so inflexible vis-a-vis what is called data and how these data are collected. (p. 10)

Cicourel describes an alternative research method that he calls "indefinite triangulation." This procedure requires the researcher to interview the teacher and the children at several points in a classroom investigation. The researchers make videotaped records of the lessons observed and then use them in various ways as a basis for further investigation in talks with the students and their teacher. Cicourel (1974) explained:

> This research strategy has been called "indefinite triangulation" because it provides details on how various interpretations of "what happened" are assembled from different physical, temporal, and biographically provided perspectives of a situation. Comparing the teacher's accounts of the lesson before and after it was presented, and comparing the teacher's version with those of the children produced different accounts of the "same" scene. *It was sometimes difficult to recognize that the children and the teacher witnessed the same event.* (Italics added) (p. 4)

The Nature of Models

A method is a procedure used to arrive at the solution to a problem. A solution to a problem offers an explanation. Since we adopted the method of developing a model as part of our research procedure, it is important to clarify how a theoretical model counts as explanation. Ruth (1980) summarizes the work of several theoreticians on the development of models. Scriven (1972) distinguishes two forms of explanation: one kind produces predictions; the other type produces information. Because the predictive model of explanation is valued as the more desirable, scientific model, the other type of explanation is judged to be weak. The predictive model of explanation has not been achieved nor can it be achieved in complex open systems such as the social sciences. So runs Scriven's (1972) main argument, where he speaks on behalf of the second type of explanation:

> This permissive view of explanation . . . focuses attention on the development of just the kind of theory that will produce explanations of a legitimate informative kind instead of the kind that must also produce predictions, and since the search for the latter in complex open systems is largely (not entirely) chimerical, this is a constructive overdue step. (pp. 124–125)

In his definitive article on theory construction in the *Second Handbook on Research on Teaching,* Snow (1973) describes the usefulness of models: "Building theories and models is not only respectable, but extremely useful, perhaps even indispensable in pursuing research on teaching" (p. 77). Snow recommends an eclectic approach to the construction of models and theories (p. 85), an approach that we followed in developing our own model of the writing assessment episode. We drew upon different disciplines for the elements of our model, including reading research, literary critical theory, psycholinguistics, cognitive psychology, artificial intelligence, and sociology.

Model-building as a form of explanation functions also as a method of condensing information. For example, Kaplan (1964) has spoken about the "systematizing" function of theory to bring order to "congeries of fact," "to make sense of what would otherwise be inscrutable or unmeaning empirical findings" (p. 302). Thus we used the model-making process to bring order to our concepts. Model making is essentially a re-constructive process. Our model, in essence, is then a construction that combines intuitive knowledge possessed by competent practitioners with formal knowledge tested and assembled through the disciplined procedures of the various fields contributing concepts to the model. But in the final evaluation, models are only as good as the evidence behind them. Although we have put great effort into our search for evidence to support this model, we know that our work is only a beginning. We present our model of the *writing assessment episode,* hoping that it will be useful in developing more contextually sensitive, holistic explorations of the assessment of writing than we have had under the long dominant psychometric models.

A Model of the Writing Assessment Episode

In thinking about the occasion called a "writing test," we found it helpful to keep in mind the idealized model of an entire writing assessment episode, depicted in Figure 7.1. Some features of this model may seem self-evident if

Figure 7.1. A Model of the Writing Assessment Episode: Participants, Processes, and Texts (From Ruth & Murphy, 1985, p. 414)

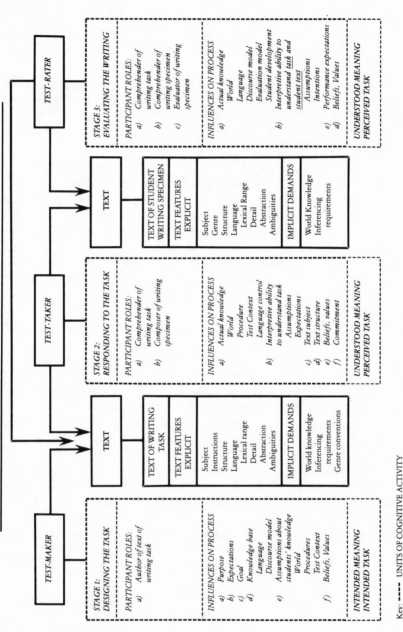

considered in isolation, but we wanted to conceptualize the unity of the elements of the writing assessment event and to investigate the dynamic, interactive relationships of the participants, processes, and texts which comprise the total event.

This model directs attention to the principal actors during the assessment episode—the test maker, the test taker, and the test rater, each performing at particular moments during the assessment episode. The model identifies three stages of cognitive activity in an assessment episode: first, the creation of a writing topic; second the reading/writing response to the topic by the student; and third, the evaluation of the student's response. Our model emphasizes the reading role each actor must play at successive stages, interpreting and making sense of the two focal texts created in a writing episode: (1) the text of the writing topic and/or (2) the text of the writing specimen generated during the episode. Each text has specific properties. Each reader interacts with each of the given texts to make meaning and to accomplish the communicative goals of that assessment episode—as *those goals are understood by each participant.*

The first stage of a writing assessment episode begins when the test makers assemble to create a writing test made up of topics, questions, or other types of stimuli. As the first box made of broken lines indicates, test makers are subject to various sorts of influences during this process—their understanding of the purpose of the particular assessment; their own knowledge, including their notions about language and the act of writing; their implicit theories of rhetoric, discourse structure, and student development; their assumptions about the students' knowledge of the world; their own beliefs and values about the nature of the world and about the contexts in which tests are taken. The outcome of this first stage of the assessment episode is a highly specialized form of discourse—a test item, a topic, or some other type of prompt which aims to establish a context for assessment.

The second box, made of solid lines, encloses descriptors of the writing topic considered as a text. This specialized text carries various explicit features, such as the information and instructions conveyed by the words and sentences. But there are also implicit features, both intended and unintended, which require the test taker to employ capacities for inference, memory, and problem solving in reading and interpreting the topic. Underlying the given cues are the test-maker's assumptions about the test taker's knowledge of the world, knowledge of language, and knowledge of test-taking procedures.

The second stage of the writing assessment episode, indicated in the model by the second box made of broken lines, occurs when the student test taker encounters the text of the given assessment topic. The act of writing actually begins in the act of reading the assessment topic, during which the test taker must make sense of the topic and understand the task intended by the test maker. This initial act of reading comprehension and subsequent re-readings at any stage of composing call into play all of the forces operative in making a text meaningful: activation of memory schemata or frameworks, inferential interpretation of the test maker's expectations and assumptions, and determination of the relative importance of text elements essential to understanding and carrying out the task proposed. The outcome of this act of reading comprehension is the *understood meaning,* the test taker's perception of the writing task. The degree of congruence between the author's *intended meaning* and the test taker's *understood meaning* will depend upon characteristics both of the text and of the reader. The communicative intent of the author of the assessment topic may be thwarted by the reader's faulty *constructions of meaning,* leading to ambiguous, mixed messages or various unintended interpretations. The communicative intent of even a well-designed text may be misconstrued because of limitations in the processing capacities of its readers, such as inadequate control of linguistic and semantic knowledge, inadequate world knowledge, weak commitment to succeeding on the test, or inexperience with testing contexts and conventions.

Within the time constraint and the social context of a particular assessment event, the test taker reads and re-reads a writing prompt as he composes a writing specimen, which itself also displays explicit as well as implicit features producing intended as well as unintended effects during subsequent readings by judges or raters. The test taker's fundamental task is to produce a text which will become the object of analysis and assessment at the next stage in the writing assessment episode.

The third stage of the assessment episode, designated in the model by a third box made of broken lines, occurs when the test rater receives the writing specimen for evaluation and ranking. Actually, the test rater receives *two* texts requiring reading and interpretation: the text of the writing task itself and the text of the writing specimen. The reading of these two texts is governed by all the constructive processes of interpretation and creation of meanings that are integral to the reading act. Adoption of an evaluator's frame of reference by the test rater is of course fundamental to accomplishing the purpose of this reading. Nevertheless, a host of other underlying forces converges to shape the evaluator's emerging *understood meaning,* both of the writing task and of the writing specimen that it elicited. These constructions of meaning are dependent upon the reader's assumptions, expectations, preferred rhetorical models, world knowledge, biases, notions of correctness, and various other conditions.

General Description of the Studies

The Main Research Questions

The stages of the writing assessment that we have described in the model—the construction of the writing text, the reading of the prompt and the writing of a response by the student, and the evaluation of the student's composition by the test rater—all involve interactions between texts and participants in the assessment episode. These interactions are represented in the model (Figure 7.1) by lines with arrows indicating particular points of interaction. Key points of interaction where "misfires" may occur are in the interpretation of the writing task by the student and in the interpretation of the student's writing specimen by the rater. Our concern about what happens at these points of interaction led us to propose these research questions (Gray & Ruth, 1982):

1. What practical knowledge is available to guide the design of writing tasks? What theory and research are available?
2. How do subject and topic wording affect response? Which of the test-maker's cues does the writer recognize, understand, and use?
3. How do students read topics? How do students construct an understanding of a writing task? What is the nature of the interaction between topic and composed text?
4. How do different communities of raters interpret the same topic? What happens to judgments of quality when high school students, novice teachers, and expert teachers rate papers on the same topic?
5. How do students define writing tasks in "open" topics that allow variation by subject and mode? Does the nature of the student's task construction vary with the student's grade level?

Sources of Knowledge Studies

We recognized a need to review thoroughly not only what researchers have to say about the assessment of writing skills, but also to report what skilled practitioners have to say about testing from years of direct experience, so in order to examine assumptions, raise and answer questions, and identify the best practices in the assessment of writing we moved in two directions: a) We conducted as thorough a literature review as possible, pulling together existing research from a variety of disciplines (Ruth, 1982). Chapters 2 through 6 contain an expanded, updated version of that review. b) We also developed a trial version of a guide for designing topics and submitted it for review to a panel consisting of 8 veteran writing instructors and 10 professional researchers and test experts. We made subsequent revisions for our final report on the basis of panel recommendations (Keech, 1982a). A newly written, updated and expanded version appears in Chapter 12.

Subject and Wording Effect Studies

To investigate the effects of varying the degree of audience specification and the nature of the rhetorical purpose, we designed an experiment in which 114 high school students from one teacher's four classes were randomly assigned one of two versions of the same writing task. In each version the students were asked to write for 30 minutes about an occasion in which they had experienced something for the first time. The main difference between the two versions of the topic was the more explicit specification of audience and rhetorical purpose in one version. Essays were scored holistically. The day after the writing, students completed a questionnaire about their attitude toward the writing prompt, their recollections of the writing process, and their attitude about other aspects of writing (Leu, Keech, Murphy, and Kinzer, 1982). The results of this study are presented and discussed in Chapter 9.

A second investigation of subject and wording effects was based on an analysis of two personal experience prompts that were selected from a set of eight that had been piloted for use in a county assessment program and classified as equivalent. These two prompts had significantly different mean scores, whereas the scores for the other six topics had remained within predicted ranges. A representative sample of 40 papers (20 related to each prompt) was chosen for task analysis. A task analysis system was devised to identify the demands of the prompt, and then papers were read by two raters to determine how the demands of the task were reflected in the student writing. (Kinzer & Murphy, 1982). This study attempted to relate salient aspects of the topic with the student responses in their essays. Post hoc analyses of students' papers allowed only limited possibilities for making inferences about the processes that may have produced them. Our conclusions were also limited by the fact that students may *interpret* a task one way initially, but then do something else when they actually compose a response. Because we were examining only the student essays, we had no way of knowing which was the case.

A Study of How Students Read Topics

During our first year of work we conducted the two preliminary studies mentioned above using conventional methodologies. In what came to be known as the Central High School Study, we undertook during our second year an investigation of the whole writing assessment episode depicted in Figure 7.1. Although we made observations during each of the three stages of the assessment episode, we focused particularly on stage 2, students reading topics. We did as Margaret Donaldson reported doing in the quotation at the beginning of this chapter, and as Piaget had done before her: We asked students to tell us what the text of the writing task meant to them. It is surprising how infrequently designers of tests ask students what they think the questions mean. In the early days of National Assessment, some post-test interviews were conducted (Finley & Berdie, 1970, p. 61, pp. 94–97), but we have not determined whether this step was carried on as a standard procedure in all subsequent exercise development at NAEP. Apparently the idea of asking students to tell how they interpret test questions is not widely practiced apart from those few instances we have already noted. Voss's (1983) observation matches our impression: ". . . relatively few researchers have sought to . . . interview students while they are dealing or immediately after they have dealt with assignments generated by their teachers . . ." (p. 282). However, in the Central High Study, we interviewed students about their interpretation of the writing task both before they wrote and immediately afterwards. But, we did not have students do "think-aloud" protocols while writing.

Because we recognized that the problem of variability in interpretation was not confined to "student" task interpretations, that more than one group of "readers" is involved in the interpretation of a topic, and that variability can also occur during the reading of the writing samples produced in response to a topic, we designed a study to provide an in-depth analysis of the various points of interaction between readers and writers and the texts they encounter and produce within each stage of a single writing assessment episode (Murphy, Carroll, Kinzer & Robyns, 1982). Various kinds of data were collected during the three stages in the writing assessment episode we studied. For example, from our experience with the study on rhetorical specification, we saw the value in obtaining questionnaire data. Questionnaire data had the potential for providing more direct evidence about students' perceptions of their task, their attitudes toward it, their knowledge of the subject of the topic, and their interpretations of what the topic was asking them to do, than any post hoc examination of compositions could provide in isolation from other data.

We also considered the limitations of this sort of data. Questionnaire data collected after a test, for example, might be influenced by the students' intervening experience of actually writing the essay. That is, students' responses to questionnaire items might have more to do with what they actually accomplished than with their initial interpretations of the topic and their task. To obtain more direct evidence about how students and teachers interpreted the topic, we conducted interviews with a subsample of students immediately prior to the time they actually wrote their essays, and with the raters prior to the time they scored the essays. We also monitored and tape recorded the teachers who created the topic during the process of its development so that we would have information about the intentions of the topic authors. Using these multiple data sources, we were able to compare the intended effects of the topic with both the initial interpretations of the subsample of student writers and with what they actually accomplished in their written compositions. We were also able to compare the interpretations of these student writers with the interpretations of the teachers who scored the essays. Both descriptive and statistical methods were employed, depending upon the nature of the data. The findings in this study are discussed in chapters 8 and 9, along with findings from other Writing Assessment Project studies related to the following questions: 1) How do students read topics for writing? 2) What are the sources of variation in interpretation? 3) Do students read topics in the same way as teachers? and 4) What affects the way teachers rate papers?

Variations Among Communities of Readers

Though it had been introduced earlier by Wayne Booth (1961), the notion of "interpretive communities" really began to take hold in academic circles with the publication of Fish's (1980) collection of essays, *Is There a Text in This Class?* Here Fish moved away from an earlier position he had taken which placed the reader at the center of authority in creating texts to a new position which now made the reader a member of an interpretive community that produces the meanings (1980, pp. 13–14). According to Fish, interpretive communities are

> made up of those who share interpretive strategies not for reading (in the conventional sense) but for writing texts, for constituting their properties and assigning their intentions. In other words these strategies exist prior to the act of reading and therefore determine the shape of what is read rather than, as is usually assumed, the other way around. (1980, p. 171)

Fish chronicles the evolution of his idea in his introductory essay where he also presents the latest stage of his thinking about the nature of the experience of the reader:

> What I finally came to see was that the identification of what was real and normative occurred within interpretive communities and what was normative for the members of one community would be seen as strange (if it could be seen at all) by the members of another. In other words there is no single way of reading that is correct or natural, only "ways of reading" that are extensions of community perspectives. (1980, pp. 15–16)

We have introduced Fish's theory here, not because it particularly influenced us at the time we conducted our study of differences between groups of students and teachers in their "ways of reading" the same student papers, but because it seems to explain the differences between the communities of readers that we observed. In subsidiary phases of two studies, the "first time" topic variation study and the Central High School Study, we collected data that contrasted teacher and student readings of the same topic (Keech & McNelly, 1982; Murphy et al., 1982). The divergent responses of the different "interpretive communities" of readers to two topics are presented and analyzed in Chapter 10.

Student Rhetorical Task Construction
Across Grade Levels

Chapter 11 offers an account of the Project's attempt to deal with defining and measuring progress in writing. Although designers of tests may be able to control the set of constraints and options expressed or implied in the text of a writing assignment and thus create parallel task demands on subsequent occasions, they are less able to control the way the student construes the task. As students mature, as they learn about different forms of discourse, they may, from any given topic, set a more complicated rhetorical task for themselves before they have full control of the required form. Thus, as they tackle something more difficult, their scores may actually drop, thereby masking the real cognitive advance in writing ability that is being made and that assessors may be attempting to measure. During the course of our investigations, Keech (1982b) developed a preliminary theoretical model as an attempt to account for this phenomenon. This study (Warantz & Keech, 1982) is discussed in Chapter 11.

EIGHT

How Topic Wording and Testing Context Affect Response

Introduction

Although theorists may not agree on the optimal system for categorizing writing tasks, they generally do agree that writing includes different modes with diverse purposes and audiences requiring different organizational structures. Recognizing that writing tasks vary along several dimensions, writing researchers have begun to examine the effects that wording differences in writing tasks can have on writing performance. In some cases, researchers have been primarily concerned with effects on the composing process. In others, the focus has been on features of written texts that may vary according to the kind of writing attempted. Recently, research has also begun to examine how measures of the quality of performance may vary according to the kind of writing attempted. All three of these approaches have tended to confirm what many teachers of writing would assume to be true: Differences in the wording of writing tasks can influence performance.

Investigations of written products suggest that *differences* in writing tasks do produce *differences* in performance. Each rhetorical element introduced into a writing task can affect the performance of the writer. The evidence presented in Chapter 5 suggests that designers of tests will need to take into account these elements when they evaluate topics for their comparability. Within the context of any single assessment, they will have to make decisions about what kind of mode, subject, or purpose will best suit the aims of that assessment. However, the designer's problems do not end here. He not only has to decide which of each of these elements to specify, but also how much information is needed to convey adequately his intent. The continuum of rhetorical specifications could hypothetically extend from a topic with a subject and the directive, "Write!", to a topic which specifies subject, purpose, mode, audience, and the identity and role of the speaker. An additional problem looms for the test designer if he attempts to control the *degree* of specification for any single variable. The complexity of these variables and their potential to interact in unpredictable ways is likely to create problems also for researchers who wish to conduct tightly controlled experimental studies. These issues require attention because various unexamined assumptions about rhetorical specifications and other procedural matters have been guiding the design or the selection of test topics.

In this chapter we examine two rhetorical elements—audience and purpose—in studies where different versions of the same topic were employed. We explore a common assumption—that the identification of audience and rhetorical purpose will enhance student performance. In the light of the results of these studies and others, we observe that the evidence about the nature of topic effects is inconclusive. However, given the limitations of these and other recent studies with similar aims, we propose considerations for further research that avoid the problems identified.

Effects of Rhetorical Specification on Performance

Woodworth and Keech (1980) conducted an early study examining the effects of rhetorical specification on performance. The authors employed three "audience" conditions. The subject of the student essay, *an occasion when the writer experienced something for the first time,* was held constant across the three versions. The writer was directed to:

"Think of an experience in which you did something for the first time."

In one condition, the audience was unspecified. The writer was simply directed to:

"Describe this experience."

In a second condition, an imaginary audience was specified when the writer was further instructed to:

"Imagine you are writing this description for someone who is about to experience this activity for the first time."

In a third condition a "real" audience was specified when the writer was further instructed to:

"Write about this experience for a particular person (brother, sister, friend, etc.) who has not had such an experience. After this person has read your description, he or she should be prepared to undergo the experience himself (or herself).

For this last condition, writers were also advised that:

"Sometime between now and Christmas, after this paper has been returned to you, plan to deliver your paper to your reader so that he or she may respond. Be sure to tell who your reader is on the back of your paper (e.g. brother, age 12)."

Additional procedural specifications for all three conditions informed writers that they were free to select the form for their writing.

"You may write a story, a letter, a journal entry or any other form of your choice."

The topic versions were randomly distributed within one teacher's six classes—three 9th-grade and three 12th-grade classes. The authors found no significant differences in the mean holistic scores awarded under the three audience conditions. The findings in this study thus appear to contradict the commonly held assumption that specification of audience and rhetorical purpose will enhance the quality of student performance, at least as measured by holistic scoring.

This assumption was also investigated in a study conducted by the Writing Assessment Project research team (Leu, Keech, Murphy & Kinzer, 1982). This study also employed two versions of the "first time" topic which varied in specification of audience and purpose. The two topic versions follow:

Topic Version A:

Think of an occasion when you experienced something for the FIRST TIME. It may have been something you later came to do more easily or something you now take for granted; but, for some reason, your *first time* was memorable. Write about this "first time" experience so that your reader can understand your feelings and why this memory has stayed with you.

You may write an essay, a short story, a letter, or a journal entry as a way of retelling your experience.

Topic Version B:

Think of an occasion when you experienced something for the FIRST TIME. It may have been something you later came to do more easily or something you now take for granted; but, for some reason, your *first time* was memorable. Imagine that you are writing to someone who has *just had* a similar experience, OR to someone who is *about to have* such an experience. Your writing might help prepare your reader for the experience, or it might help your reader understand that other people have gone through the same kind of thing.

You may write an essay, a short story, a letter, or a journal entry as a way of retelling your experience.

The major difference between the two versions of the topic is the more explicit specification of audience and rhetorical purpose in version B. In version B, the instruction specifies an imaginary audience, "someone" who has shared or will share whatever "first time experience" the student chooses to write about. In version A, specification of audience is less restricted and refers simply to "your reader."

The students in the school where the study was conducted were tracked into accelerated and non-accelerated English programs according to ability level. Tracking decisions were based on teacher recommendations and the student's performance on a test consisting of a structured-response examination and a writing sample collected by the English department. The structured-response examination covered usage, mechanics, vocabulary and spelling. The writing sample was evaluated on the basis of form and content.

The 114 students who comprised the population for this study came from one section of advanced composition juniors and seniors ($n = 22$), two sections of college-track English literature juniors ($n = 65$), and one section of general English, average ability sophomores ($n = 27$). The juniors and seniors in advanced composition and English literature were in the accelerated program at the school; the sophomores were in the non-accelerated program; and classes were all taught by the same teacher. The two topic versions were randomly distributed within each class and the students were allowed thirty minutes to write.

The results were similar to those found in the Woodworth and Keech study. There was no association evident between the assigned topic and the holistic performance score among the 114 students who completed the writing test: The mean ranks of total holistic scores were not significantly different for the two versions (M/rank A$'$ = 54.97, M/rank B$'$ = 60.03, $p > .05$). The mean score for version A was 6.09; the mean for version B was 6.28. Thus, the findings in this second study also would appear to contradict the commonly held assumption that specification of the rhetorical context will enhance the quality of student performance, at least as measured by the holistic score in a timed writing test.

However, several limitations to these studies should cause us to reserve final judgment. Several alternative explanations for the results of both studies are possible. For example, a possible explanation for the failure to find a difference in the case of our own study can be found in the fact that the sample population differed in certain respects from what would be expected in a fully representative sample of high school students. Most of the students who participated in the study came from accelerated courses. Moreover, the distribution of holistic scores was skewed toward the high end of the scale. For example 31.5% of the papers received one of the two highest holistic scores (7–8). Only 5.4% of the papers received one of the two lowest scores (2–3). Because scores on the performance measure were skewed high, a topping-out effect may have minimized the range of differences and therefore limited the likelihood of finding a significant difference between the mean ranks of the holistic scores for the two versions. As Hoetker (1982) has pointed out, holistic scoring may have limited usefulness as a research tool for examining such topic effects. Typically, scores tend to cluster around the average score, and distribution is often sharply peaked. In the Writing Assessment Project study, the scores were skewed high. In either case, however, applications of parametric statistical procedures would be inappropriate because the distributions are not normal. Less powerful non-parametric procedures, such as those used in this project study, must then be employed, limiting the likelihood of finding statistically significant differences. A student population in which holistic scores are distributed normally, or perhaps a rating using Diedrich's (1974) method of forced quartile distribution, might be more likely to produce significant differences in topic effects.

Given these cautions about interpretation, we will now examine further some results of the project study.

The Nature of the Topic and the Degree of Specification

Possible explanations for the failure to find significant differences can also be attributed to characteristics of the two versions of the topic and even to the nature of the topic itself. For example, in version A in the project study, the audience, (i.e. "your reader") though general, is nevertheless mentioned. Including a clearly specified communicative purpose ("Write about this 'first time' so that your reader understands how you felt and why this experience stayed in your memory") is likely to constrain the set of possible audiences and the sense of rhetorical purpose. Moreover, saying "your reader" serves to *remind* the student that *someone* is going to read this, and the student may him/herself *mentally specify* a reader—much like the possible readers suggested in version B— although some students will think only of "the teacher" as the reader. In version B, the audience is only vaguely specified (i.e., "Imagine that you are writing to someone who has just had a similar experience, or to someone who is about to have a similar experience.") The writer does know something about the reader; he or she has had or will have a similar experience, but no more than that. Thus, the failure to find differences in the quality of compositions written in response to these two versions may have occurred because they both represent middle range examples on a continuum of specification. That is, there wasn't a sufficiently noticeable difference in the way the two versions specified "audience" in the first place.

The nature of the topic itself should also be considered apart from the issue of degree of specification, because implicit in this task (writing about a first-time experience) is the idea that one should write to an audience that *can* understand and appreciate the writer's particular first-time experience. In this sense then, writing about a first-time experience does, in fact, provide an audience. For this kind of assignment, writers may assume that their readers will be interested in an entertaining anecdote, whether a particular audience is specified or not. Some topics may have naturally occurring implicit audiences. Introducing audience specifications into such topics may introduce further constraints.

The Interaction of Variables

Finally, the possibility of interactions between the specified rhetorical elements should also be considered. It should be noted that in the two studies, both audience and rhetorical purpose were manipulated in such a way that it is impossible to determine the individual effects of either variable. This issue has only recently received attention in research. In a study by Witte, et al. cited in Brossell (1986), the researchers created a series of twelve versions of a single topic in order to represent three levels of audience specification, two levels of purpose, and two levels of content. The essays written in response to these topic versions were scored by three groups of raters under three different training conditions. Significant main effects were found for audience and purpose. As audience specification increased, the quality of writing increased as well, but as purpose specification increased the reverse occurred—the quality of writing decreased. The results of this latter study thus suggest the possibility that the effects of one variable may counterbalance the effects of another. In contrast to the other two studies, the findings in the Witte study would seem to confirm the assumption that specification of audience, but not purpose, enhances the student performance. However, before definitive answers can be given to questions about specification of audience and rhetorical purpose, findings such as these need to be replicated and research conducted on a wider variety of subjects and modes. Under some conditions, particular kinds of specification may have an effect, and under others, they may not.

Problems in Comparing Versions of a Topic

To recapitulate, no statistically significant differences were found between different versions of the "first time" topic in two related studies. However, the results of these studies should not be taken as an indication that specification of the rhetorical context will *not* enhance student performance. Rather, these two studies should serve to illustrate the complexities of the issues that will have to be addressed if valid answers to basic questions about what to specify and when are to become possible. The matter of degree of specification should also be studied further. Topics which vary the degree of specification only slightly may not show the score differences which might appear under more extreme variations, and findings that hold true for one mode, subject or purpose may not hold true for another. The nature of the subject also deserves attention because particular subjects may imply a kind of audience whether or not audience is literally specified, as was the case in the studies discussed here. Interactions of rhetorical elements will also need to be investigated further, with a variety of subjects calling for different modes of discourse. New scoring methods will have to be investigated to provide more fine-grained alternatives to current holistic scoring procedures (Hoetker, 1982). And, finally, to avoid the pitfalls of previous research, the applicability of the experimental research model will need to be examined, and new models from cognitive research may need to be adopted.

Effects of Topic Wording Not Measured by Score

Although two task constraints were experimentally manipulated in the Writing Assessment Project study of rhetorical specification, several other variables also were investigated through a questionnaire. If the study as a whole can be viewed more as a descriptive and explanatory investigation rather than as an exactingly controlled experiment, it offers a number of provocative leads for further investigation. For example, two questions are being addressed in this chapter: (1) Can variations in wording influence students' choice of a form for writing? and (2) Can variations in wording influence students' composing strategies? In both cases, evidence from the questionnaire data in the project study suggests that they can, and it also provides data on the issue of allowing the students a choice of form for writing. For the complete account of the study, the reader may wish to consult the original technical report (Leu et al., 1982).

Data collected in the study included student responses to a questionnaire[1] designed to elicit information about their attitudes toward the topic versions, their recollections of the writing process during the timed writing test, and their descriptions of their other writing behaviors, both in and out of school. The questionnaire was distributed the day after the students had been given the writing test. Ninety-nine of the 114 students doing the writing test also completed the questionnaire.

A proficiency level was assigned to each student according to his or her course placement; that is, the juniors and seniors in the advanced composition class and the juniors in the two sections of English literature came from the accelerated track and were, therefore, considered to be relatively proficient writers. The sophomores in the general English class who came from the non-accelerated college-prep track were also a year behind the junior sections in their academic program, and could, therefore, be classified as less proficient writers. The validity of this classification was supported by a comparison of the median rankings of the two groups' total holistic scores. A Mann-Whitney U Test revealed that juniors and seniors in the accelerated track performed significantly better on the timed writing test than sophomore students who were in the non-accelerated track ($U = 520.00, Z = 4.56$, p<.05). The mean rank of the proficient students was 65.02 compared to the mean rank of the less proficient students which was 33.26. The means and standard deviations of proficient and less proficient writers' total holistic scores can be seen in Table 8.1.

The Influence of Wording on Choice of Form
A preliminary examination of the students' papers showed that different forms were used in responding to the two versions of the prompt (e.g., story, letter, journal entry, essay). An analysis was then performed to find out whether or not the prompt itself had any effect on selection of the form of writing. The story form was the dominant choice of writers on both tasks.

[1]See original technical report (Leu et al., 1982) for the text of the questionnaire.

Table 8.1.
Means and Standard Deviations of Proficient Students' and Less Proficient
Students' Total Holistic Scores by Class, Section and Grade Level

	Proficient Students				Less Proficient Students
	Advanced Comp. Section 1 Jrs. & Srs.	English Lit. Section 1 Jrs.	Section 2 Jrs.	Total	General English Section 1 Soph.
M	6.64	6.49	6.41	6.50	5.19
SD	1.049	1.25	1.13	1.21	1.11
n	22	33	32	87	27

Even so, a total of 27 students selected alternative forms. Although 76.3% of the students responded with a story, 18.4% responded with a letter, 4.4% with a journal entry, and 0.8% with an essay. Table 8.2 summarizes the frequencies of the different forms selected by the students.

The effects of the topics are clearly associated with the student's choice of form. Although equal numbers of students wrote on each version, more version B students produced alternative forms of writing. Students who wrote on version A produced 7 alternative form papers (5 letters and 2 journal entries) while students who wrote on version B produced 20 alternative form papers (16 letters, 3 journal entries, and 1 essay). Almost three times as many alternative form papers were produced by students writing on version B. Most of the alternative form papers (96.3% or 26 of 27) exhibited personal forms of writing such as letters or journal entries and most of these more personal forms occurred in response to version B, which directed students to "imagine you are writing to someone . . . ." There was no significant differ-

Table 8.2.
Frequencies for the Different Forms of Writing Produced by Topic Version A
and Topic Version B

		Alternative Forms			Raw Total
	Story	Letter	Journal	Essay	
Topic A					
%	87.7	8.8	3.5	0.0	50.0
n	(50)	(5)	(2)	(0)	(57)
Topic B					
%	54.9	28.1	5.3	1.8	50.0
n	(37)	(16)	(3)	(1)	(57)
Total					
%	76.3	18.4	4.4	0.9	100.0
n	(87)	(21)	(5)	(1)	(114)

ence in the mean ranking of holistic scores for story and alternative form papers (story = 56.40, alternative forms 61.06, $p > .05$). The mean total holistic score for stories was 6.13, while for alternatives it was 6.40. Finally, there was no apparent interaction between selection of form (story and alternative forms) and proficiency when total holistic score was used as the dependent measure. Table 8.3 indicates that both proficient and less proficient students performed similarly whether they chose to write a story or employed an alternative form.

Table 8.3.
Mean Total Holistic Scores by Proficiency and Form Selection

	Proficient Ss	Less Proficient Ss
Narratives		
M	6.48	5.09
SD	1.11	1.19
n	65	22
Alternative Forms		
M	6.55	5.60
SD	1.30	0.55
n	22	5

Because we wanted to employ topics and procedures that were actually being used by local districts, we included the procedural specification which allowed a choice of form for writing in the two topic versions. The findings in the study seem to suggest that choice of form did not affect the score a student received. However, given the small number of alternative form papers, it would be erroneous to conclude that choice of form would make no difference in the ways students are evaluated. On the contrary, other evidence from this study suggests that the selection of particular alternatives may have been disadvantageous. Students and teachers who participated in the study tended to evaluate writing in the form of letters to friends or parents and entries to personal diaries differently during the rating training sessions conducted for both student raters and teacher raters. The students tended to value more the pieces sounding like "real letters" than those sounding like "English themes." Teachers, on the hand, paid less attention to the distinction between simulated life-like communicative writing and school writing. In some cases, the raters penalized students for features of their writing which could be justified by the characteristics of a particular form (e.g. lack of detail in a letter to parents who could be presumed to share knowledge of such details). For further discussion of this aspect of the study, see Chapter 10. Given the weight of evidence cited in this and in previous chapters which indicates that level of performance is highly task specific, one has to question the advisability of allowing a choice of form in an assessment. This practice introduces even more variability into a situation which is already fraught with complex and interacting factors. Raters are likely to find it difficult to make valid comparisons between compositions which differ in both form and function.

The Effects of Wording Variation on Composing Strategies

Although many of the responses to the items were similar for both versions, differences which suggest an interesting effect of the wording of prompts on the writing process did appear. More students who wrote on Version A, for example, reported that they spent at least 5–10 minutes thinking about what they wanted to write (Version A = 79.6%, Version B = 62.9%, item 6). More students who wrote on Version A also reported that they had difficulty choosing which of several possible experiences to write about (Version A = 75.5%, Version B = 46.0%, item 4.) The apparent discrepancy in amount of planning time between prompt versions is also supported by students' response to item 7. More students who wrote on Version A felt rushed when they actually started writing (Version A = 40.8%, Version B = 28%).

Questionnaire Item Responses, Related to Effects
of Topic Variation on Composing Strategies

4. I had a hard time choosing *which one* of several possible experiences I should write about.
6. I spent a lot of time (at least 5 or 10 minutes) thinking about what I wanted to write before I started.
7. Because I spent so much time planning, I felt rushed when I actually started writing.

The questionnaire items relevant to the effects of variation in wording are given in Table 8.4 which summarizes the results of the questionnaire data by topic version.

In general, more of the students who wrote for a less specified audience (version A) spent a substantial amount of time planning what they were going to write. Students who wrote for a more specified audience (version B)

Table 8.4.
Results of Questionnaire Data by Topic Version

Item No.	Version A (n = 49)		Version B (n = 50)	
	Disagree	Agree	Disagree	Agree
4.	24.5	75.5	54.0	46.0
6.	20.4	79.6	38.0	62.0
7.	59.2	40.8	72.0	28.0

less frequently spent a substantial amount of time planning. This difference is illustrated in Figure 8.1.

Figure 8.1.
A Diagram of the Differences in Planning and Writing Time for Versions A and B

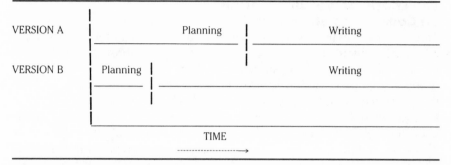

It is important to note, however, that despite these process differences, there was no significant difference in the final quality of the product as measured by total holistic score (Mann-Whitney $U = 1480.5$, $z = -.85$, $p > .05$). Of the 99 students who completed both the writing test and the questionnaire, the mean holistic score for version A students was 6.09 ($n = 49$); for version B students, the mean holistic score was 6.28 ($n = 50$). On the surface, at least, these versions appear to be similar with respect to the holistic scores that they produce.

In addition to an analysis of the main effects, an analysis of the interaction between topic version and planning time was conducted. Table 8.5 indicates that students who wrote on different versions performed similarly. In addition to this two-way analysis between topic version and planning time, a three-way analysis was conducted between topic version, planning time, and re-reading. Table 8.6 shows the eight possible combinations of these three variables, the means and variances of the holistic scores for each combination, and the number of students in each group.

In the writing performance of version A students, re-reading seemed to interact with planning time. Version A students in Group 4 who re-read their papers and spent 5–10 minutes planning had a higher mean holistic score ($M = 6.42$) than students in Group 2 who re-read their papers but did not plan ($M = 5.67$). Apparently, re-reading had an effect for version A students, only if, in addition, they had spent 5–10 minutes planning.

Taking no time for re-reading, among version A students, also interacted with planning but in the opposite direction. That is, version A students in Group 1 who did not re-read their papers and who did not spend 5–10 minutes planning had higher mean holistic scores ($M = 6.43$) than students in Group 3 who did not re-read and did plan ($M = 5.93$). Not re-reading, for

Table 8.5.
Total Holistic Score Means, Standard Deviations and
Numbers of Students by Topic Version and Planning Time

		Version A	Version B
Spent 5–10 Minutes Planning			
	M	6.08	6.39
	SD	1.31	1.28
	n	39	31
Did Not Spend 5–10 Minutes Planning			
	M	6.20	6.26
	SD	1.23	1.20
	n	10	19

version A students, was associated with higher holistic scores only for those students who also did not plan.

Among version B students, re-reading also interacted with planning time. Students in Group 6 who re-read and did not plan had higher mean holistic scores ($M = 6.29$) than students in Group 8 who both re-read and planned ($M = 6.00$). Apparently, re-reading had a positive effect for Version B students only if, in addition, they did not plan.

Not re-reading, among Version B students, also interacted with planning time. Version B students in Group 7 who planned but did not re-read had

Table 8.6.
Total Holistic Score Means and Standard Deviations
by Topic Version, Planning Time, and Re-Reading

Version A	Group 1	Group 2	Group 3	Group 4
Greater Audience Constraint	No	No	No	No
Spend 5–10 Minutes Planning	No	No	Yes	Yes
Finished and Re-read	No	Yes	No	Yes
M	6.43	5.67	5.93	6.42
SD	1.13	1.53	1.24	1.44
n	7	3	27	12

Version B	Group 5	Group 6	Group 7	Group 8
Greater Audience Constraint	Yes	Yes	Yes	Yes
Spent 5–10 Minutes Planning	No	No	Yes	Yes
Finished and Re-Read	No	Yes	No	Yes
M	6.25	6.29	6.55	6.00
SD	1.10	1.50	1.18	1.50
n	12	7	22	9

higher mean holistic scores ($M = 6.55$) than students in Group 5 who neither planned nor re-read ($M = 6.25$).

Variations in the Planning Process

To summarize, although mean holistic scores did not significantly differ between the topic versions, there were clear differences in the planning process. Decreasing the audience specification seemed to produce an increase in planning time. It may be that a topic lacking both implicit and explicit audience specification would produce even greater differences in planning time, at least among writers who are willing and able to use time to plan during a test requiring impromptu writing. Finding complex interactions between various composing strategies, including planning and re-reading, suggests an additional explanation for equivalent mean scores for two prompt versions. These complex interactions may have generated similar mean scores for the two versions, although in fact, the topic versions may have differentially affected the product quality of particular individuals. With further research it should be possible to determine whether students' composing processes are influenced by different topic versions, whether or not these processes are natural to the students who adopt them, and whether or not these processes are optimal for successful performance. Observing the same students over several writing tasks would reveal whether or not some kinds of tasks consistently elicit or require more planning time than others, at least among students who plan, and whether planning consistently produces better writing.

We may also speculate on the observation that version A, because of fewer constraints, seems less likely to *quickly* provide students with a good subject to write about. Students who are serious about their writing—and who therefore seek subjects they care about—may be required to spend more time searching when faced with version A. (Less serious, more perfunctory writers faced with version A may begin writing quickly, having fewer resources for scanning and selecting appropriate subjects—hence the association of lower scores with version A non-planners). Version B, on the other hand, while allowing such a search, seemed to trigger more instant responses in a wider range of students. Students quickly chose a subject which usually engendered successful writing within the given time limit. However, the search for meaningful, appropriate subject matter engaged in by version A students may have contributed something to the composing process that raised these papers to the highest level of quality—a level less available to version B students who selected their subjects more quickly. If such a finding were to be confirmed by more precise observations of the composing process and analysis of the written products, the implications would be important for the evaluation of instructional programs and for research measures which seek to assess differences in the performance of both able and less able student writers.

The differences in the frequency with which different rhetorical forms were selected in response to the two topic versions is also of interest. The version with the greatest audience constraint (B) produced far more papers in journal entry or letter form. This version may thus encourage students to adopt more informal registers and to select more personalized forms. It would be useful to know if this is due solely to increased audience specification or if it is also a function of the particular communicative purpose implied in version B. Further research might also be directed toward determining the effects of specifying different audiences. It would be interesting to know, for example, if more personalized forms are also produced when the audience specified excludes peers: "Explain this first-time experience to a prospective employee who has just has or is about to have a similar experience."

Effects of the Testing Context

In the studies described above, no statistically significant differences were found between scores awarded to compositions written in response to topics varying on the dimension of specification of the rhetorical context, either in degree or in kind (e.g. imaginary or "real" audiences). Several explanations for this lack were discussed. Below, the effects of another powerful variable—the testing context—are discussed. Two issues are addressed: (1) possible effects of the testing context on students' conceptions of the writing task they were being asked to perform, and (2) possible effects of the time allowed for writing on student performance. The evidence suggests that the effects of the testing context influenced students' conception of the writing task in such a way that any possible effects of the differences between the versions were minimized. The evidence further suggests that short, timed writing tests do not give an accurate picture of students' abilities.

The Influence of Testing Context on the Student's Conception of Task

In the studies described above, students wrote under various conditions, where audiences, either "real" or "imaginary" were specified to different degrees. And, as we have already suggested, whether or not an audience is specified, since writers may assume that their readers would appreciate an interesting anecdote about a first-time experience, the nature of the task itself implies some kind of audience. Another kind of "audience" must also be considered if one asks: Who is the *real* audience for these students' compositions? What is the *real* purpose for writing? That is, what is the *real* rhetorical context?

For a classroom assignment or test, the students' audience is most often their teacher. For assessments of larger populations, however, the ultimate audience is a group of judges. In a testing context, moreover, the real purpose for writing is to display writing competency and students are well aware of this. As Hoetker has pointed out, their ideas about the real reader-ship of the test may be stereotyped: "Most students, regardless of what role they are asked to assume or what audience they are asked to imagine, write for what they imagine is their real audience—hypercritical English teachers" (Hoetker, 1982, p. 387.) The possibility should be considered, then, that in the studies discussed above, the influence of the testing context had its own effect on students' conceptions of the task they were being asked to perform.

Woodworth and Keech (1980) made an attempt in their study to provide a "real" audience—not just the test-readers—in one of the topic versions, e.g. "Write about this experience for a particular person (brother, sister, friend, etc.) who has not had such an experience." However, as the researchers noted, many of the students who wrote in response to this topic version re-ported they had difficulty thinking of an actual person with whom they could share their composition. Only 16 of the 30 students in that group indicated that they had been thinking of anyone in particular when they wrote. Thus, the task for almost half of the students in that group was more similar to the other tasks in the study than the researchers had originally intended.

The original idea for the study had arisen out of Woodworth's observation that his students wrote much more successfully when they were producing student handbooks that would actually be read by other students. Wood-worth commented: "Not only were students willing to revise and edit their writing, but even early drafts were longer, richer in detail and voice than any other classroom writing" (Woodworth & Keech, 1982, p. 11). Apparently, however, the effects of writing to a "real" audience (in addition to the teacher) for a "real" functional purpose (other than demonstrating writing competency) could not be simulated in a testing situation. Rosen (Britton, et al., 1975) reminds us that behind any school assignment designating a "real" or "imagined" audience stands "the spectre" of the actual audience, the teacher-as-evaluator (p. 64). An interesting variation of this study would be to compare writing done actually for peers under classroom sponsorship such as Woodworth described with writing that is done for testers or re-searchers. A finding of a significant difference in that case would substanti-ate the opinion of many teachers: that test results should not form the sole basis for evaluating a student's writing competency and that writing per-formed under other conditions should also be accumulated for review.

A study of this kind would, of course, create additional design problems. One would have to consider, for example, the relative effects of time limits on writing and revising as well as the effects of having or not having a real audience and purpose. The situation is complicated even further by the fact that, for individual students, the testing situation itself may have either posi-tive *or* negative effects. Woodworth raised this issue in reflective comments made after he had had the opportunity to evaluate his students' writing for several months after the test had been given. Woodworth observed:

> I came to the conclusion that the test had had the quality of a special occasion for many students and that, furthermore, many of them had written better pieces on this occasion, regardless of which form of writing task they had been given. (p. 37)

For this testing occasion, then, the testing context may have had positive effects on student performance. However, as Woodworth also pointed out, the effects of the testing context may not always be positive. For some students, the special occasion of the writing test may serve as a "boost to motivation," but it may cause other students to "labor over their work, complain they haven't enough time, even give up" (Woodworth & Keech, 1980 p. 38). The influence of the testing context can thus be seen as an important factor in research design, not only because it may minimize the effects of differences in topic versions, but also because it may have either positive or negative effects on particular individuals' motivation and consequently their performance. Under other conditions, specifying an audience, especially a real one, might very well enhance students' performance.

The Effects of Time Limits on Performance

In the Writing Assessment Project study, when questionnaire data were examined in terms of the proficiency level of the students, several very striking and consistent patterns appeared. First, there were significant associations between proficiency level and responses to several questionnaire items. These associations seem to suggest that proficient writers (1) used a substantial amount of planning time, (2) felt rushed when they actually started writing, (3) felt they didn't have enough time to write, and (4) did not have time to re-read their papers.

There was a significant relationship ($\chi^2 = 4.51$, $p < .05$) between proficiency and response to the statement: "I spent a lot of time (at least 5 or 10 minutes) thinking about what I wanted to write before I started." A majority of the proficient writers (77.0%) agreed with this statement compared to 52.0% of the less proficient writers. At least part of the additional planning time that proficient writers seemed to spend was taken up in deciding which of several possible experiences they should write about. For example, 67.6% of the proficient writers, compared to 40.0% of the less proficient writers, agreed with the statement: "I had a hard time choosing *which one* of several possible experiences I should write about." ($\chi^2 = 4.85$, $p < .05$). In this study, writing proficiency appeared to be associated with taking time to consider a range of alternatives accessible in memory before selecting a specific experience to write about.

Because proficient writers took so much time to plan their composition, they often felt rushed when they finally began writing. Proficiency and agreement with item 7, "Because I spent so much time planning, I felt rushed when I actually started writing." were significantly associated. ($\chi^2 = 8.79$, $p<.05$). Only 8.0% of the less proficient writers agreed with this statement compared to 43.2% of the proficient writers.

The extended planning time typical among the proficient writers may also have contributed to their feeling about the amount of time necessary to complete the assignment adequately. Proficiency and agreement with item 3: "I did not have enough time to write." were also significantly associated ($\chi^2 = 8.79$, $p<.05$). Proficient writers agreed more frequently with item 3 (Proficient $= 43.2\%$, Less Proficient $= 8.0\%$).

Finally, the extended planning time typical of proficient writers may have prevented many of them from re-reading or proofreading their papers. There was a significant association between proficiency and agreement with item 8: "I did not have time to re-read or proofread my paper." ($\chi^2 = 8.03$, $p<.05$). Some 59.5% of proficient writers agreed with this statement compared to 24.0% of less proficient writers.

There is also some indication that less proficient writers may be less likely to re-read their papers. For example, 52.0% of the less proficient writers agreed with item 9: "Although I finished before the time was up, I did not re-read my paper," compared with only 23.0% of the proficient writers ($\chi^2 = 6.14$, $p<.05$). This association, however, may be due to the greater number of less proficient writers who had sufficient time to re-read their papers (less proficient $= 76.0\%$, proficient $= 40.5\%$).

In addition to the associations that exist between proficiency, planning time, and the consequences of taking 5–10 minutes to plan one's composition during a 30-minute test period, there is an association between proficiency and students' attitudes about how additional time to write would have influenced their writing performance. Proficiency was positively associated ($\chi^2 = 5.91$, $p<.05$) with the belief that the final product would have been very different if they had had several days to complete the task. Of the proficient writers, 79.7% agreed with this statement (item 10) compared to only 18.1% of the less proficient writers. Proficiency was similarly associated ($\chi^2 = 18.75$, $p<.05$) with the belief that the final product would have been better if students had had an hour to write, rather than just thirty minutes. Of the proficient writers, 83.8% agreed with this statement (item 11) compared to 36.0% of the less proficient writers. Proficient writers believed that additional time would have changed and benefited their writing performance.

The pattern of results from investigating the relationships between proficiency and questionnaire items suggests that a 30-minute timed writing test may not adequately measure the ability of proficient writers. Placing a very short time limit on the writing task may create a ceiling effect on students' performance. Even though their writing was generally superior, proficient writers reported that they could have done even better if they had had more time. The fact that proficient writers more frequently reported that they didn't have time to (1) complete the task or (2) re-read their papers seems to support this interpretation. Additional research would be necessary in order to establish the exact effects of limited versus unlimited amounts of time on the writing performance of various types of students.

Several of the questionnaire items relevant to this issue were significantly correlated with performance on the timed writing test as measured by holistic score. First, as holistic scores increased, there was significantly greater agreement with item 3: "I didn't have enough time to write." Students with higher holistic scores more frequently felt a need for greater writing time (Tau$_c$ = .16, $p<.05$).

Second, as holistic scores increased, there was significantly greater agreement with item 7: "Because I spent so much time planning, I felt rushed when I actually started writing." (Tau$_c$ = .19, $p<.05$). Although most of the students did not feel rushed as a result of taking time to plan, those who did feel rushed were among the top scorers.

Third, while most students felt they would have done a better job if they had been given an hour to write, this appeared to be especially true for those students with high holistic scores (Tau$_c$ = .20, $p<.05$). Students who indicated they would have written differently if they could have taken the assignment home also tended to score higher, although this association was not statistically significant.

In general, then, the more successful writers were students who had a complex view of the task (or who had set high expectations for their writing); they wished they had had more time to write and felt that their performance would have been enhanced by this additional time. Further empirical support for these findings in additional studies would suggest that short, timed writing tests are likely to truncate severely the range of performance elicited during the assessment, although good writers will still receive top scores on a short test. This raises questions about the validity of using holistic scores from a single sample as an assessment measure. It suggests that students' performance on a short, timed writing test may differ substantially from the conditions more typically associated with regular classroom writing assignments. It would be useful to understand how performance differs as the amount of available writing time increases: Does the quality of writing differ substantially? What type of student seems to revise the most when greater time is available? How is the writing process different when greater time is available? Which individual differences (grade, sex, verbal ability, attitude, etc.) seem to interact with differences in the amount of available writing time to produce changes in the quality of writing?

In general, students who are likely to receive top scores on longer tests will probably also receive top scores on short tests. Short, timed tests, then, may be adequate in a gross way to identify proficient students or to predict success at longer tasks. However, they may be inadequate to distinguish among various levels of proficiency and hence may be poor measures for evaluating writing programs which aim to move writers toward greater proficiency.

If the purpose of an assessment is merely to measure minimum proficiency, short tests may provide a sufficient range of performance among most populations. But since short tests may reveal only the more gross differences in ability among homogeneous populations, improvements in writing ability over a semester or a year as a result of certain instructional practices may be totally obscured, with students appearing to make little or no improvement. Hence, short tests may actually be poor evaluation measures for evaluating the effects of instruction.

We must keep in mind, of course, that many of the above observations are based on reports by students of their own writing processes. Thus, these results should be viewed only as suggesting questions which might best be answered not by questionnaire, but by direct observation of individual students during the act of composing. Many such observations will be needed to determine the significance of the trend noted here and its implications for both test design and for our understanding of the writing process during impromptu timed writing tests. The findings do, however, raise an important issue with regard to the comparability of test results. For example, it would not be valid to compare test results from occasions allowing different amounts of writing time, not only because performance might vary according to the amounts of writing time allowed, but also because different amounts of time might have different effects for individuals at different levels of proficiency. Additional research is clearly needed to determine how individuals of various abilities perform under a variety of test conditions, and in addition to specifying time for actual writing, time for pre-writing activities and time for revising should be considered. Since we are *teaching* students the value of pre-writing and revising, we shouldn't deprive them of the opportunity to do the same when we are *testing* them.

NINE

How Students Read Topics

Central High Study of the Construction of Meanings of a Topic

In our study of a writing assessment episode (Murphy, Carroll, Kinzer & Robyns, 1982) we selected a subsample of twelve students for interviews about their interpretations of a topic which would be used for the regular writing assessment of the sophomores at a Northern California high school that we will call Central High School. The students were recommended by their teachers as average writers who would not be uncomfortable in an oral interview situation. The primary question of interest in this part of the overall project study was whether or not there would be substantial variation in the ways students read the topic. We also wanted to determine the sources of that variation, should it occur. The topic used in the assessment follows:

> Many different suggestions for improvement of Central High School have recently been made. Describe one problem or situation at Central which you feel needs correction or improvement, giving reasons for your choice and suggesting one or more solutions.

We interviewed students individually, twice, both before and immediately after they had written their essays for the assessment. The interviews were tape-recorded. During the first interview, the interviewer employed a "think-aloud" procedure, where students were encouraged to express orally and point by point their interpretation of the topic and their plans for composing. Prior to encountering the actual topic for the assessment, the students practiced the procedure with a different topic so that they would become comfortable with the idea of "thinking aloud." The interviewer then solicited initial responses to the actual assessment topic by asking general questions such as, "What does this bring to mind?", and prompted the students to continue until they had chosen the content and focus for their compositions. Immediately after this first interview, the students wrote compositions as part of the school's regular assessment procedure. After writing, they returned for the second interview in which they were asked about differences between their initial plans for composing and the compositions they had actually written. One student was later eliminated from the sample because of problems in the tape recording of her pre-writing interview. The final subsample of students thus consisted of 11 students.

By considering three sources of information, e.g. (1) the topic itself, (2) the initial interpretation/response, and (3) the written compositions, we were able to identify various interpretive and composing strategies used by the students in responding to the topic. Although these three sources of information are discussed below in sequence, our analysis was non-linear.

Each source of data served to shed light on the others. At times, student responses focused attention on problematic features of the topic. Conversely, certain features of the topic, which were recognized as being ambiguous, suggested where we might look for potential areas of confusion within student responses. Finally, by comparing what students said their understandings were with what they actually did in their compositions, we were able to obtain a rough idea of how much the students' initial interpretation influenced what they actually wrote.

Sources of Information in the Study

The Topic and Alternative Interpretations

In this section, we will discuss several paths of interpretation that readers might take through the text of the Central High School writing assessment prompt. Our aim is to display several different potential constructions of meaning which all make sense and may at least partially account for variations in the way the topic is interpreted. The text of the prompt is repeated verbatim here for reference throughout the discussion below.

> Many different suggestions for improvement of Central High School have recently been made. Describe one problem or situation which you feel needs correction or improvement, giving reasons for your choice, and suggesting one or more solutions.

The First Sentence.   There are at least two ways in which the first sentence *could* be read. If the reader knows, for example, about "suggestions recently made," then the first sentence could function as a reference to the context of a familiar discussion. On the other hand, if the reader considers the first sentence to be *new* information being introduced for the first time, then it functions to inform the reader of an existing state of affairs of which he is yet unaware. In this case, the reader would expect this piece of "news" to be qualified, illustrated or expanded in the sentence that follows. However, the second sentence does not provide additional information about either *what* the suggestions are, or *who* made them. This lack of specific links between the first sentence and the second was viewed as a potential source of difficulty for students in the assessment, at least for those students who did not have prior knowledge of any suggestions that had been made for school improvement. These readers might find it difficult to form a coherent interpretation of the text. They might, for example, be forced either to re-examine their initial interpretation or to try to imagine a plausible presupposed context for the first sentence.

Several possible imagined contexts for the first sentence are possible given its passive construction. For example, if the reader associates the plural marker "s" and the qualifiers "many" and "different" with either the *process* of making suggestions or the *source* of the suggestions in addition to or instead of the *result* of the suggestion-making process, several alternative meanings arise.

1. many different sources of opinion are engaged in one process;
2. one source of opinion is engaged in many different processes; or
3. many different sources are engaged in many different processes.

Prior experience with "suggestion-making" situations might guide the reader toward a prototypical "scenario." For example, one such scenario might involve multiple sources of opinion offering many different suggestions in a group context on one or several occasions. For the reader who is forced to search for a plausible context for interpreting the first sentence, many different interpretations are possible.

We should also consider that whether or not the reader has knowledge of "suggestions recently made," he or she might still question the purpose the first sentence serves. The reader might ask, "Is this the subject of the composition I am about to write, or is it intended to be merely an introduction to what follows?" Thus, in either case, whether the reader treats the information in the first sentence as *new* or as *old* information, he or she may be forced to search for a unifying purpose with which to relate the two parts of the text.

The Second Sentence.   The potential for different interpretations of the topic can be illustrated further by examining the elements of the second sentence in light of the first two possible initial interpretations of the first sentence discussed above (i.e., as old or as new information). For example, in the second sentence, the modifier "one" is posed as a quantitative constraint on the number of "problems" or "situations" to be described. It can also be interpreted as a kind of link with the first sentence, especially if the first sentence is interpreted as old information and if the reader equates the phrase "suggestions for improvement" with "problems" or "situations." If the reader bases his or her interpretation on the presupposition that many different opinions already exist as to what constitutes a "solution or improvement," and, in addition, what constitutes a valid "suggestion," the reader may conclude that he or she is required to describe "a" suggestion for improvement, i.e., "one" from a defined set of different "things that need to be improved."

The reader is also faced with a choice of describing either a "problem" or a "situation." The presence of imperfective processes in both sentences may lead some readers to make the latter choice. In the first sentence, an incomplete process is presupposed in the definition of the word "suggestion" itself. For example, a "suggestion" is not the same as a "solution" since a suggestion involves only the beginnings of a solution (or resolution). In the second sentence, this incomplete process (making a suggestion) is reinforced by the progressive participial constructions "giving" and "suggesting."

The distinction between the tasks of describing a perfective vs. an imperfective process can be illustrated by examining two hypothetical cases of readers. In one case, the repeated words or derivatives with common roots ("improvement," "suggestions," "suggesting") may lead the reader to conclude that he should describe a "situation" (a state of affairs or combination of circumstances) and propose a *process* which will provide partial resolution ("improvement") to the "situation." In a second case, the reader may see his task as defining a problem, a definitely negative or problematic single circumstance, and posing a definitive "solution" for an absolute "correction" of that problem.

Relations Between the Two Sentences.   For readers who either fail to synthesize the two sentences or who simply choose to ignore the first, a somewhat different interpretation is possible. The imperative "describe" presupposes the goal of the task to be a *description,* which is a product of personal observation. The single instance of the imperative form indicates that the readers' observations are being elicited as the central feature of the task they are being asked to perform. The importance of the *personal* nature of these observations is implied by the phrase "which you feel." Thus readers might conclude that their task is to describe their observations, propose "solutions" to what they *personally* consider problematic, and to develop or illustrate "reasons" why they found their choice of subject matter personally problematic, as per the segment "giving reasons for *your* choice."

However, if a reader has interpreted the first sentence as old information, the segment "giving reasons for your choice," could be interpreted as *giving reasons for why the reader chose to discuss a particular problem or situation (suggestion for improvement) above all others established in a set of precedents*. In other words, readers may be reminded that they are to be held accountable for a background of shared knowledge, against which they are to justify their choices of problems to discuss. These readers may conclude that they have to explain why the problems they chose to discuss are more important than others. On the other hand, readers may also conclude that they must justify their choices against a background of opinions as to what constitutes a "valid" suggestion. In this case, "giving reasons for your choice" might also be interpreted as *giving reasons for why the problem should be considered a problem*.

Essentially, what we are suggesting here is that elements in the topic may pull readers in different directions. Evidence from the student interviews indicates that the various interpretive possibilities described above did indeed occur.

The Interviews and Patterns of Interpretation

The "Idea Unit" as a Unit of Analysis.
In order to analyze the data systematically, we adopted a unit of analysis that would allow us to compare segments of the students' responses with particular topic segments and with segments of their compositions. Several systems of text analysis and descriptions of discourse structure offered possibilities, but because we were studying processes of interpretation and composition, systems of analysis which were based on (and derived from) actual language phenomena held the most appeal. For this reason, we transcribed the tape-recorded pre-writing interviews and then coded these transcripts for oral idea units according to criteria for oral language analysis developed by Dr. Wallace Chafe of the Department of Linguistics at the University of California, Berkeley (Chafe, 1979, 1980). An idea unit is basically a number of words bounded by a measurable pause and/or a change in intonation which serve as indications that the speaker is treating the word group as a conceptual unit. Each idea unit expresses a focus of attention in consciousness through a composite of lexical information corresponding roughly to a simple clause, or syntactically, to one verb and its associated noun phrases. Later, we segmented the written compositions of our subsample of students into units based on Chafe's adaptation of his oral discourse analysis techniques for use with written discourse (Chafe & Danielewicz, personal communications, 1981). Thus our data consists of two sets of protocols: one oral, one written. *Dots denote pauses in oral data.*

Topic Plus Comment Pattern.
In the interview data, references to the topic were frequently followed by references to personal experience, references to shared knowledge, or statements of opinion. The most typical *topic + comment* pattern involved a mention of a phrase from the topic followed by related commentary.

Katie		
Reference to topic:	(4)	"Describe one problem or situation at Central which you feel needs correction or improvement."
Comment:	(5)	. . . I can think of one (laughs).
	(6)	. . . The lunch lines are horrible.
Reference to topic:	(10)	. . . And "suggest one or more solutions."
Comment:	(11)	. . . Well . . . I would think they just . . . they should make a bigger cafeteria.

		Martin
Reference	(17)	And . . about a solution to the problem,
to topic:	(18)	. . . I guess the . . the solution to my
		problem would be . . . peer pressure,
Comment:	(19)	and you'd have to . . . get . . get kids
		involved in wanting the school to look nice,

In examining the interview protocols, we found that many of the idea units incorporated words or groups of words from the topic. Reference to the topic was generally accomplished in one of three ways:

1. by the mention of the exact wording of segments of the prompt,
2. by a paraphrase of segments of the topic, resulting in the reconstruction of the wording or the syntax of the topic and,
3. by reference to the topic as a whole.

In all cases, reference to the topic often acted as a point of departure which resulted in idea units performing multiple functions to suit the purpose of the student at any given instance in the interview. In referring to the prompt, students borrowed and paraphrased units of different sizes. Sometimes single words from the prompt appeared in student comments; often entire phrases or sentences were adopted. The idea units in the examples below are numbered according to their location in each interview.

Exact Wording Pattern.   The student reiterated the exact wording of the topic or a segment of the topic and might incorporate it into his or her own statements.

Kim:	(2)	Ok (laughing, long pause) . . . 'kay, describe one problem, (cf. "Describe one problem")
Katie:	(4)	. . . Describe one problem or situation at Central which you feel needs correction or improvement. (cf. "Describe one problem or situation at Central which you feel needs correction or improvement.")
Don:	(7)	And I don't know an . . of any . . . suggestions of . . . for improvement. (cf. "suggestions for improvement")

Paraphrase Pattern.   Paraphrase involved the reconstruction of the wording or the syntax of the prompt through substitution, deletion, and reordering of word groups of varying size.

| Kim: | (41) | just describing my problem, (cf. "Describe one problem" . . .) |
| Kim: | (23) | Um. . . ok, student apathy is a problem at Central. (cf. "one problem . . . at Central") |

Katie:	(10)	. . . and suggest one or more solutions.
	(11)	. . . Well . . . I would think they just
		. . . they should make a bigger cafeteria.
		(c.f. "suggesting one or more solutions")
Martin:	(17)	And . . about a solution to the problem
	(18)	. . . I guess the . . the solution to my problem would
		be . . . peer pressure,
		(cf. "Describe one problem . . . giving . . . one or more solutions.")
Jay:	(33)	. . . there really isn't any solution to . . the problem. (cf. "Describe one problem . . . giving . . . one or more solutions.")

Reference to Whole Topic Pattern. Some of the writers make reference to the topic as a whole.

Carla:	(2)	. . . Um . . . I feel this . . um . . is asking me to
	(3)	. . . you know . . tell . . the problems of Central.
Joe:	(9)	It just . . . it just . . bring Central to me.

Reference to Topic Segment Pattern: First Sentence. Examination of the responses associated with particular topic segments revealed that students did, in fact, interpret the first sentence of the topic in a variety of ways. As the examples below illustrate, some students treated the first sentence as old information and were able to access relevant details in memory. Other students failed in the attempt. Still other students were apparently attempting to imagine, or construct a plausible context for interpreting the sentence.

Alice:	(2)	Um . . that comes to mind how everybody's always talking about: "All we need is grass?"
	(3)	You know, "There should be a swimming pool!"
	(4)	Cause we were supposed to have a like uh a football stadium.
	(5)	We were supposed to have . . . a swimming pool, bowling alleys
Carla:	(70)	. . . Okay . . it says 'Many different suggestions for improvements . . of Central . . have recently been made,'
	(71)	. . . so . . like . . you mean just from students.
Martin:	(4)	They are thinking about . . um
	(5)	. . . giving money for . . to make the school look a little better
	(6)	And the—
	(7)	. . . they've . . they've got a big grant,

	(8)	. . . state or federal or something,
	(9)	. . . to improve the curriculum
	(10)	. . . of the school.
Don:	(7)	. . . And I don't know an . . or any suggestions of . . for improvement.
	(8)	. . . That've been made recently.
Jay:	(2)	. . . uh—. . . the improvements of Central.
	(3)	. . . Well one thing has been the landscaping.
	(4)	. . . It . . like it used to be mud all over and they started to put trees,
	(7)	. . . Um . . . they've painted the doors down there.
	(8)	. . . and they've kind of just changed the way they've uh—
	(9)	. . . taught the . . uh . . students from last year.
	(10)	. . . Last year was a different . . method they taught.

Some of the students in our subsample indicated they were aware of suggestions that had been made (e.g., Alice). Among these students, however, the suggestions were attributed to various sources, (cf. Carla, Martin). Among the students who had some knowledge of suggestions, two knew about *specific* suggestions which fitted the temporal constraints specified in the first sentence ("recently been made"). These suggestions had been given detailed coverage in a school newspaper article discussing the tentative plans which school personnel were considering for the use of recently acquired grant funds for school improvement projects (e.g., Martin).

In contrast to students who claimed to have some knowledge of what the first sentence could refer to, other students indicated a lack of such knowledge (e.g. Don). Another student, who had ignored the first sentence altogether in his first interview, made the following comment when he was questioned about what he didn't like about the topic:

Interview:	Just the way it's put together . . . . . . um . . . cause I haven't heard very many of the s . . Central High School's suggestions . . for improvement. I wouldn't know much about what to write about.

The students' comments clearly showed different degrees of familiarity with the debates about specific suggestions for school improvement. As a result, they made various interpretations of the first sentence of the topic. However, in providing these particular examples, we are not intending to suggest that topic authors should necessarily attempt to insure that everyone who is being assessed shares exactly the same knowledge. Clearly that would be an impossible task. Student always will bring different background knowledge to each writing task; thus, responses to any writing topic will reflect the diversity of students' personal knowledge and past experiences. Yet, it was appropriate for the authors of this topic to assume that all of the students would have something to write about because the subject draws on knowledge of conditions at the school. In the context of this particular assessment, however, there was an unusual complication. Specific suggestions *had* been made for school improvement and the first sentence of the topic could be interpreted as a reference to previously made "suggestions"—even by students who had no apparent prior knowledge of this fact.

Reference to Topic Segment Pattern: Second Sentence.

Examination of response patterns also revealed that various interpretations were given to other segments of the prompt. Some students in our subsample justified their choice of a problem in relation to other problems:

Martin:	(42)	. . . that I would single that out, (attitude)
	(44)	. . . the grounds,
	(45)	. . . the . . landscaping and stuff,
	(46)	. . . that's not so important.

Other students justified their choice in terms of personal relevance:

Jay:	(24)	. . . And—the reason I chose it was because in the beginning it was really bothering me when I was studying.

Other students appeared to interpret the phrase "giving reasons for your choice" as a directive to *give reasons why a solution is needed* (i.e. why the problem should be considered a problem):

Bob:	(8)	. . . Um . . . the reasons for my choice would be . . . because
	(9)	. . . the school,
	(10)	. . . It doesn't look good this way.

Student responses also revealed that some students chose to ignore certain segments of the topic. One student said:

Interview:	The way I interpreted that [the first sentence] was just as an introduction . . . I figured they were just saying this so they could tell you to describe one problem . . . I didn't think that was important . . The most important part was [the beginning of the second sentence.]

Awareness of Alternative Interpretations.

Our examination of the students' responses in the interviews revealed that they did in fact form various interpretations of the task they were to perform, and further, that most students read selectively, focusing on some elements of the topic and ignoring others to form their interpretations. However, our examination also revealed that some of the students were aware of more than one possible interpretation of the writing task implied by the topic. Carla, for example, demonstrated that she was aware of two possible ways to approach the task. In her pre-writing interview Carla said:

Carla: First I'd talk about all the suggestions that were made to im-
          prove Central, and then narrow it down to the best few and
          then [to] the main thing that needs improving.

Subsequently, in her post-writing interview, Carla indicated that she rejected her initial interpretation before writing:

Carla: I was thinking of doing that but then I read the topic again . . .
          I just thought it'd be best to start right in [on one problem.]

Thus, the data from the interviews revealed that some of the students in our sub-sample changed their minds about their interpretations of the topic. In the written compositions we also found additional indications that some students were aware of more than one possible interpretation of the topic and its segments.

The Interview and the Essay Compared

The excerpts from the student essay quoted below illustrate how Jay attempted to accomplish two of the different tasks implied by the phrase "giving reasons for your choice."

Jay   The reason I *think* that open classrooms are a problem in
Essay: Central is because when the classrooms are open the way
         they are there is (sic) a lot of disturbances around you.
         The reason I *choose* (sic) this problem is because when I first
         started high school my grades dropped really fast.

In the first sentence above, "the reason I think" is followed by a conditional or logical causal relation signaled by "when," "there is," which is generalized by the use of the generic pronoun "you." Thus the sentence is an attempt to account for the general relevance of the problem which the student selected. In the second sentence, the phrase "the reason I choose" is linked to a recounting of personal experience. Thus it expresses the personal relevance of the chosen problem.

Although a few of the students did change their plans for composing after making their initial interpretation, there is a striking similarity between the content of most of the students' interviews and the content of their essays.

An underlying assumption in our analysis is that the student accesses possible content in memory in the process of reading a topic which he or she can then decide whether or not to use in composing a written response. For this topic, the reader was selecting the subject of his or her essay (e.g. lunch lines, open classrooms) and details which would support whatever argument fitted his or her particular interpretation of the task. As the examples below illustrate, many of the ideas for content expressed in the oral interviews also appeared in the compositions. However, the examples also clearly show that the students formed different interpretations of particular topic segments.

Variations in Oral and Written Texts. One of the students in our subsample, Martin, justified his choice of a problem in relation to other problems and expressed his justification in both his oral interview and his written essay:

Interview:	. . . that I would single that out, (attitude)
	. . . and . . . and ah . . . the ah . . . the grounds,
	. . . the . . landscaping and stuff,
	. . . that's not so important.
Essay:	And what is landscaping
	just a superficial cover that would be
	destroy (sic) by student with bad additude (sic).

In contrast, another student, Jay, justified his choice in terms of personal relevance:

Interview:	. . . And—the reason I chose it was because in the beginning it was really bothering me when I was studying.

In his written essay, Jay examined the same idea to include a consequence, as well as a reason for that consequence.

Essay:	The reason I choose (sic) this problem is because when I first started high school my grades dropped really fast. . . . I could not concentrate because there was always a commotion or noise that distracted my attention from the classroom.

Still another student, Bob, explained why the problem should be considered a problem.

Interview:	. . . Um . . . the reasons for my choice would be . . . because . . . the school . . It doesn't look good this way.

In his written essay, Bob stated this same idea more formally:

Essay: The "unlandscaped" look the west side of the school currently has detracts from the school in many ways.

Our comparison of students' oral and written protocols indicated that students employed information that they remembered while reading the prompt; however, the rhetorical function of particular segments and the language used tended to differ markedly.

Differences between oral and written language have received much attention in the past decade by linguists working in the field of text analysis (Ochs, 1979; Chafe, 1979; Tannen, 1984). Much of this work has focused on the ways in which the same ideas, concepts, or events are expressed differently in written and spoken language in terms of the characteristics of the language used. Tannen has noted, for example, that ". . . planned written discourse makes use of complex syntactic structures, formal cohesive devices, and topic sentences. In general it is more compact" (Tannen, 1978). Chafe has also commented on this characteristic of written language, describing it as "integrated." Spoken language, in contrast, is often loosely strung together with coordinating conjunctions or with no overt marking whatsoever of the relationships between propositions (Chafe, 1979). The result is that ideas, and descriptions of characters and/or events which are typically expressed in several loosely joined clauses in oral language may often be expressed in fewer words in written language because of the greater degree of integration that can be achieved in writing through processes of subordination and subject deletion.

In our data, oral and written units reflected similar content. However, differences were both a result of the transformations which occur between oral and written styles *and* a result of the necessity to perform within two different situations. One situation involved the student interacting with both the prompt and the interviewer. The other situation involved writing an essay in response to the prompt which would be evaluated by the teachers at the school. Consequently, some of the ideas that were expressed in several idea units in the oral interviews were compressed into single sentences in the written compositions while other ideas were expanded.

An example of the sort of compression that occurred follows. The student's oral comments are his initial responses upon reading the prompt.

Martin   (2)   . . . Ah . . . the first thing about improvements,
Interview: (3)   Y'know like, that I like, ah . . landscaping,
             (4)   they are thinking about . .um
             (5)   . . . giving money for . . to make the school look a little
                    better.
             (6)   And the—
             (7)   . . . they've . . they've got a big grant
             (8)   . . . state or federal or something,

   (9)   . . . to improve the curriculum
   (10) . . . of the school.
   (11) . . . I know, the thing about a . . . situation or . . prob-
           lem,
   (12) I think the . . students here have a . . kind of an attitude
           problem.

In Martin's written composition, the same topics (landscaping, the grant for improving the curriculum, and the student attitude problem) are framed as suggestions and are covered in a single sentence—the opening sentence of his essay.

Martin Essay:	(1)	The many suggestion (sic) for improvement have been made (sic) landscaping, the C.I.P. grant, and the additeud (sic) of the students.

The differences between the two excerpts can largely be accounted for by the fact that the actual audiences for the oral interview and the written composition were different. In the oral interview, Martin's comments are addressed to an outsider, one who doesn't know, presumably, about recurring problems, recent suggestions, or about the recent acquisition of grant monies at the school. Accordingly, his comments serve to supply background information for the interviewer about proposals which had previously been considered by others (they). His comments also introduce his own idea for a problem to discuss, the "attitude problem" of the students. In contrast, the topics in the written composition are introduced in a simple list which is treated as old information which could be assumed to be shared by the teachers at the school who would be reading his essay. Moreover, it is interesting to note that Martin includes his own idea for a problem to discuss within the list. By framing his own subject within the list, Martin may have been hoping to validate his own choice immediately as one of an established set of issues that others have raised. Thus, although the same ideas are expressed, the purpose for their expression differs.

As mentioned above, oral versions of ideas that occurred to the student during the process of reading and interpreting the topic were not always longer than their written counterparts. In many cases, ideas were expanded and elaborated upon in the written compositions. In addition, different interpretations of the topic appeared to encourage disparate rhetorical strategies. In contrast to Martin, for example, Katie never referred to any previous suggestions that had been made about ways to improve the school in her oral interview. She immediately identified lunch lines as a problem at the school:

Katie Interview:	(2)	Many different . . suggestions for improvement at Central High School have recently been made. (reading)

(3)   . . . OK
(4)   . . . Describe one problem or situation at Central which you feel needs correction or improvement. (reading)
(5)   . . . I can think of one (laughs).
(6)   . . . The lunch lines are horrible.

Later, she made the following comments when describing how she planned to write her paper.

Katie	(18)	. . Like we're um . . . just rushing out of fourth period.
Interview:	(19)	. . . and . . you've gotten all your books.
	(12)	. . . For your next class.
	(21)	. . . Run down the halls.
	(22)	. . . And . . to stand in a big mile long line
	(23)	. . I'm exaggerating a little bit.
	(24)	. . . but . . you know . . to get the point across.
	(25)	. . . That's how I'd write it.
	(26)	. And then . . standing there,
	(27)	. . for half the . . lunch period
	(28)	. . wait for your lunch
	(29)	. . . (laughs) And then you finally get your lunch go outside and eat it.
	(30)	. . . And then . . the period'd be over while you're still eating your lunch.
	(31)	. . . s . . . And then . . . you could finish your lunch and then go to class—,
	(32)	. . like P.E. (laughs) . . . It's not nice to go to class when you've just hurried up and eaten your lunch.

In her written version, Katie elaborated upon the ideas that occurred to her during the "think aloud" procedure. What is originally treated in 14 idea units in the oral interview is expanded to 25 segments in the written.

Katie	(1)	Buzzz.
Essay:	(2)	The five minute bell rang.
	(3)	My fourth period teacher had finished his lecture
	(4)	and we had the rest of the period for ourselves.
	(5)	I scrawled out one last math problem before closing my books.
	(6)	"How much time, Kirsten?"
	(7)	I asked.
	(8)	"Two minutes"
	(9)	Kirsten said after looking at her watch.
	(10)	I put my homework paper into my binder,
	(11)	and stacked my books in my arms.
	(12)	Bzzz.

(13)   I jumped up

(14)   and raced out of the room emerging into the traffic of other students hurrying to lunch,

(15)   I ran to my locker,

(16)   shoved in my books

(17)   and sprinted to the cafeteria.

(18)   There I was met by a gigantic line.

(19)   My stomach growling I waited in line for fifteen minutes.

(20)   With a sigh of relief I got my lunch

(21)   and went out side (sic) to eat.

(22)   Half way (sic) through my lunch the bell rang signaling (sic) for the end of lunch.

(23)   This time my stomach didnt (sic) growl,

(24)   I did!

(25)   This situation is a slightly exaggerated example of one of the main problems at Central High.

The different rhetorical strategies in Katie's oral and written segments are related to differences in the tasks she was performing (i.e., responding to an interview situation vs. composing a written text). In the oral version Katie gives only a sketchy outline of her plan, but in the written version she must actually implement it. In the oral version, she makes use of the generic pronoun "you" to imply that the experience is typical, one that happens every day to anyone at the school. Her use of the generic expands the scope of a personal frame of reference or experience, and the experience serves as an illustration for the interviewer. In the written version, she uses different rhetorical strategies. She dramatizes the event as "real," having taken place sometime in the past. She assumes the role of protagonist, and the narrative proceeds from her own perspective. Dialogue and an additional character are introduced. Much of the expansion occurs in lines 1 through 12 in the written text, where Katie is presenting new elements of detail to create a context for the episode she wishes to dramatize. However, although elements are added and different rhetorical strategies are adopted, the underlying structure of the event is the same in the oral and written segments. The "same" event sequences occur between lines 13 through 18 in her written text, and between lines 18 through 22 in the interview. Comparable sequences also occur between lines 19 through 22 in her written text and lines 26 through 30 in the interview.

Like Martin, Katie's written composition is clearly tied to the way she interpreted the topic, but unlike Martin, she ignores the first sentence. That is, she does not treat it as a reference to old information, but merely as an introduction to the real topic. She begins her composition by embarking immediately on a personal experience, complete with sounds, actions, and feelings described in sequence. Once this experience is described, it serves as her argument. The result is that her essay gives the impression of a strong voice while she provides a "narrative" illustration of her argument. And just in case her reader doesn't get the point, she explains it:

Katie Essay:	(25)	This situation is a slightly exaggerated example of one of the main problems at Central High School.

However, none of the other students were as successful as Katie in developing an argument. One could surmise that their lack of success depended to some degree on their interpretation of the topic. In contrast to Katie, Martin is an example of a student who felt that it was necessary to justify his choice of a problem based on what he knew had already been suggested for school improvement. This is reflected in the fact that he lists those suggestions in the beginning of his essay, and compares the worth of his choice of subject matter to the other suggestions that had been made at several points in his essay:

Martin Essay:	(9)	If the student gave so (sic) respect to the school
	(10)	it would do more than anything else could.
	(12)	By bettering their out look (sic) on this school it would improve it.
	(13)	Improve it more than C.I.P.
	(16)	And what is landscaping
	(17)	just a superfical (sic) cover that would be destroy (sic) by student (sic) with bad additude.(sic)
	(22)	Then if you do this
	(23)	you would improve the school more than landscaping, more than C.I.P.
	(24)	These other thing (sic) could only be fully appeacated (sic) by student (sic) who care about their school.

Because Martin interpreted his task as requiring him to justify his choice, he was forced to discuss more than one problem, and was perhaps unable to provide vivid descriptions, in the allotted time, of the problems he mentioned. In any case, he resorts to rather empty generalizations in his effort to justify his choice.

Martin was not the only student in the subsample to adopt an ineffective strategy for developing his essay. On the contrary, many of the students relied on strategies which suggest that they didn't have much confidence in the relevance or appropriateness of their own opinions, both in the interviews and in their essays. For example, many of the students relied on indirect methods to bolster their arguments. These strategies are discussed below.

Methods of Developing an Argument

Narrative and Evaluative Elements

Previous research on evaluative strategies has dealt with evaluative comments embedded within narrative (e.g. Chafe, 1980; Labov, 1972). Although our data are similar to that of Chafe and Labov insofar as the respective tasks involved the recall of personal experience, the overall function of evaluative elements in our data differ. To clarify our use of terminology, the overall *evaluative* task in the narrative situation is to establish that a given narrative is worth telling, or that a given fact or event within a narrative is indeed remarkable. The "burden of proof" that the story is a good one lies with the person telling the story. Hence, the narrator uses evaluative comments— that is, comments which illustrate the point or worth of the narrative. However, the "burden of proof" in the case of our students required something more than evaluating an experience to show what the point is or whether it is interesting.

The topic in this assessment ultimately required the student to produce a persuasive argument. In particular, it asked the student to frame an argument in such a way as to answer one or more of the following questions: (1) why did the student choose a particular problem above other possible choices, (2) why is the problem *generally* relevant (i.e. why is the problem a problem), and/or (3) why is the problem *personally* relevant. This topic required the student to adopt an evaluative frame for the purpose of developing an argument which could draw on personal experience for supporting data. Loosely coherent groups of idea units, in the form of a discussion of a series of events or observations, more or less in order of occurrence, appeared frequently in our data. But in general, these groups of idea units served to illustrate, through the recounting of actions, one or several points within a larger evaluative structure. Although these groups resembled narratives in structure, they were used to make a point within that larger structure. Thus, while evaluative text was frequently embedded in narrative text in the data analyzed by Labov, in our own data the reverse occurred: Narrative text was most often embedded in evaluative text.

For example, in the following excerpt from an oral interview, the student evaluates the topic he is considering, and then proceeds to relate a series of events as an illustration of his point. In the process, he fills in necessary information for the interviewer, and his experience is recounted as a series of temporally ordered events. The effort to use these events to illustrate a point requires that the student link his past experience to his present task.

Don	(25)	. . . but . . oh I know, ok, I know one that's good
Interview:		heres,
	(26)	. . . that I ca . . I came here in the beginning of the year
	(27)	. . . and I had a ca . . I had my schedule,

	(28)	. . . we got to pick our schedules.
	(29)	. . . And so I had my schedule.
	(30)	. . . And . . . the geometry class I was in was too big.
	(31)	. . . So they took . . they took me out,
	(32)	. . transferred me out of my geometry class,
	(33)	and put me in with the sixth period,
	(33)	. . . which means . . which meant I had to change my English class too.

Narrative-like segments were also embedded within the evaluations of plans for composing, as can be seen in the following example:

Katie	(15)	. . . How would I go about writing it. (laughs)
Interview:	(16)	. . . Probably . . . act like,
	(17)	. . . um . . write it more like a story.
	(18)	. . . Like we're um . . . just rushing out of fourth period
	(19)	. . . and . . you've gotten all your books.
	(20)	. . . For your next class.
	(21)	. . . Run down the halls.
	(22)	. . . And . . to stand in a big mile long line.
	(23)	. . . I'm exaggerating a little bit,
	(24)	. . but . . you know . . to get the point across.

In addition to the overtly evaluative comments such as the one in idea unit (23) above, we also found that students adopted a number of more indirect evaluative strategies. These strategies appeared in both the oral and the written data, and are outlined below.

Attribution

The protocols revealed that many of the students attributed opinions and/or experiences to others in order to provide additional support for their own points of view. For example, the students below created consensus groups to support the development of their arguments.

Chip	(49-51)	Cause my friend he always says . . . it's a pain. You never get what you want or anything.
Interview:		
Carla	(18)	A friend and I were discussing another way of solving the litter problem,
Essay:		
	(19)	and we came up with this suggestion
Don	(13)	A lot easier for me and my friends,
Interview:	(14)	And . . well, I guess my friends are annoyed too.
Jay	(15)	One other reason I chose this subject was because my brother also had problems with the open classroom.
Essay:		

Generalized Attribution

In the examples above, experiences and/or opinions are attributed to specific individuals or particular groups of individuals. In other cases, students attributed opinions and/or experiences to larger groups, signaled by the use of mass or plural nouns—kids, students, people, plural pronouns (they, we), indefinite pronouns (everybody, everyone), and the generic pronouns (you, one).

In some cases, the use of this strategy aligned students with positive consensus groups and placed them in opposition to negative groups. In the following excerpt from her interview, Carla aligns herself with a positive consensus group, one with an authoritative, decision-making role, at the same time that she places herself outside of the group that is responsible for the problem.

Carla Interview:	(52)	We've tried a lot of things—and . . nothing seems to get through their heads.

In an example from his interview, Martin attributes to "students here" an "attitude problem" which, he claims, is at the root of all the problems he has learned about in connection with planned improvements at the school.

Martin Interview	(13)	. . Like the way they're above everything else,

In other cases, students used the generalized attribution strategy to generate the impression of universal agreement with their own position. This variation of the strategy was most often marked by the use of the generic pronouns (you, one) and the indefinite pronouns (everyone, everybody) which served to signal the speaker or writer's assumption that, within the particular conditions being described, all people would react the same way.

Joe Interview:	(24)	. . . and then . . you sort of . . lose friends.
Carla Interview:	(18-19)	. . At home you wouldn't have people . . . you know . . . throwing things on the ground and—,
Jay Essay:	(6-7)	When you are distracted from the classroom, you will end up in trouble and your grades will drop drastically.
Jay Interview:	(82)	. . . Because that seems to give the most problem to everybody.

Still another variation of this general type of strategy involved the introduction of a hypothetical individual representing all students within the same set of circumstances.

Don	(21)	By changing *a student's* class and teacher it
Essay:		first makes it hard for *the student* to adjust to new teaching methods.
Kim	(17)	One would think that *a student* would be
Essay:		interested in how his school functions.

In this last example, this hypothetical individual became the main strategic vehicle adopted by the student in developing her argument.

Generalization

Students also used the strategy we have called *generalization* in contexts where opinions were not overtly being attributed to others. In these cases, their use of the strategy again allowed them to avoid direct statements of their own opinions. This type of generalization sometime appeared in the form of dummy subjects or objects (e.g. "it").

Carla	(3)	*It* is really incredible how its(sic) so
Essay:		difficult to pick up a piece of paper and put *it* into the garbage can.

In addition, students frequently transformed descriptions of actions into states or conditions where the action is constant and ongoing:

Don	(21)	All the people *are coming* here
Interview:	(22)	. . and *crowding* other schools up.

In this second example, the strategy works to bolster the student's argument by implying that the problem chosen is indeed serious and deserves immediate attention.

Comparators

The students also frequently used *comparators* (Labov, 1972) which according to Labov, include negatives, futures, questions, or-clauses, superlatives and comparatives (e.g. "more"). Such constructions provide a way of evaluating events by placing them against the background of other events that could happen or might have happened. Negatives, for example, provide a way of evaluating certain events by highlighting them against the background of other events which might have happened, but which did not occur. (Labov, 1972).

Our data indicated that students used negative constructions frequently:

Joe	(31-32)	. . . you know . . people sit here, . . . and
Interview:		there . . . you can't sit with them.

Joe	(6)	Unfortunately, many students and teachers
Essay:		don't feel as fortunate as I do.
Carla	(9)	. . because um . . . litter seems to be a big
Interview:		problem when it really shouldn't be.
Carla	(18)	. . . At home you wouldn't have people, . . . you
Interview:		know . . . throwing things on the ground and—,
Kim	(48)	and kids just don't show up.
Interview:		
Bob	(25)	. . it wasn't landscaped then,
Interview:	(26)	. . and every time I've been at school it's never been landscaped.
Don	(41)	. . . My grades haven't been too well.
Interview:		
Alice	(28)	They won't let us do it.
Interview:		

The following is a particularly plaintive case of defeated expectation:

Joe	(16)	I have firmly believed that many teachers
Essay:		don't like helping the students. . . .

Students also frequently used conditionals as frames for suggested solutions to the problems they chose to discuss.

Carla	(11)	I think if we had an enclosed cafeteria
Essay:		
Carla	(85)	. . . if . . you know . . we could get more—. . student
Interview:		participation,
	(86)	. . we could probably . . solve most of these problems—
Martin	(22)	Then if you do this
Essay:	(23)	you would improve the school more than landscaping, more than C.I.P.

These if-then and comparable when-then constructions appeared in several essays, and some students also used this framing device to qualify the proposed institution of the student's suggestion:

Joe	(2)	The suggestion that I would make
Essay:	(3)	if I was asked
	(4)	would be the attitudes of people at Central.
Joe	(14)	The basic goal that I would have is trying to
Essay:		work together and get everything pulled together.

Sources of Variation in Interpretation

The Nature of the Topic

These latter two examples provide particularly telling illustrations of the students' general lack of confidence in the relevance of their own opinions. Occurring throughout the data are numerous examples of indirect kinds of strategies, which attribute opinions to others, magnify the importance of the problem in indirect ways, and reflect the students' lack of control over their ability to institute a suggestion. One could argue that these strategies depended in part on the nature of the topic. That is, describing a problem at the school is a potentially controversial subject, at least from the student's point of view. The topic requires students to criticize their school, which may lead some students to adopt ineffective strategies and/or to select safe subjects they may think their evaluators will agree with (e.g. the problem with student attitudes selected by Martin).

The Context of the Writing Performance

It has been customary for linguists to view a text, such as the topic used in this study, within the situation in which it was presented. In the context of the *test*, then, the topic represents a piece of a larger set of assumptions and presuppositions about what is expected for adequate performance. One could then argue that students may have been encouraged to adopt these sorts of strategies by the context of their writing performance. In this case, the context was a test, and because this was an assessment situation, students may have interpreted the topic as carrying an implicit directive: conform to the *correct* development of the topic in form, content, *and* context.

The context of this social situation then, because it was a test, may have placed a certain amount of pressure on the students to come up with the correct answer, i.e. the single most important problem. Students who are test-wise may be more able to disregard this pressure because of an intuitive sense of what evaluators will be looking for. That is, test-wise students may rightly conclude that evaluators will be less concerned about *which* problem the student chooses to discuss than *how well* the student develops the essay. Moreover, because such students have a well-developed sense of what is required in a testing situation, they may also be more aware that certain kinds of signals (e.g. "Describe *one* problem,") are implicit cues for certain kinds of development (e.g. a focus on one problem). Other students who are not so test-wise or who lack confidence in their own opinions may struggle to find the correct answer and adopt less effective rhetorical strategies for developing their arguments.

Learned/Taught Writing Strategies

Learned strategies for writing also influenced the ways students constructed their tasks. For example, the student who described her experience with lunch lines (Katie) adapted a rhetorical strategy she had learned from instruction in the "show and not tell" method of writing to fit the constraints of the topic and the task as she perceived it, producing in the end an essay that had a "show and then tell" kind of development. Not all students were as successful as Katie, however, in adapting learned strategies to their interpretations of the topic and task. One student, for example, attempted to use a particular learned strategy for writing a five-paragraph theme—a strategy in which the writer gives a thesis statement and introduces three supporting details in the first paragraph, develops the three details in the following three paragraphs, and then summarizes (restates) the thesis statement in the final paragraph. When the student tried to apply this strategy to what he perceived to be the implicit three-part structure of the task (describe a problem, give reasons, suggest a solution) he ran into trouble. In the end, he produced an incoherent and poorly organized essay which vacillates between two strategies for development, one based on his learned strategy, and one based on the implicit three part structure of the topic:

> One problem at Central which I feel needs improvement or correction is the placement of students. The system is good from the students point of view but sometimes classes end up too full. The system either needs to be modified or replaced.
>
> The system of placement of students at Central is held in a way to let the students pick their own classes, teachers and periods. At the end of the summer, students go to school and get a number for walkthrough. At walkthrough you go in order according to your number and pick your classes.
>
> The system is well liked by the students because they are able to have teachers that they are compatible with or are good academically. It also lets them have the period they would like to have, so as not to interfere with sports or something of that sort. Although the students like this way better, it has its flaws. Classes end up too large and kids have to be moved to different classes different periods, which defeats the whole purpose of the system in the first place. The system should be so that the classes are not going to be too big, than (sic) they wouldn't have to be changed. By changing a student's class and teacher it first makes it hard for the student to ajust (sic) to new teaching methods. Other problems are also present such as the transfer of grades from one teacher to another. If the transfer is not completed the student could end up with a worse grade than they deserve or an incomplete in the class.
>
> This system needs to be modified or replaced. The best way I can think of to modify it would be to limit the amount of students to each class. Instead of changing the classes when they are already settled, don't let them get too big in the first place.
>
> Although the students like the system and it lets them pick their teachers and periods, it often makes classes too full resulting in class changes for many people. The problem needs to be modified or the system replaced. This is the biggest problem I can think of at Central.

Selective Reading Versus Misinterpretation

As we have demonstrated, the topic in this study offered the potential for several different and arguably valid interpretations, depending, of course, on which elements (or elements in combination) the students focused on. Researchers may have the time and motivation to speculate about various possible interpretations of a text, but real readers, including the students in this study, read selectively in order to form a coherent interpretation, or merely to get on with the task at hand. However, in addition to the potential for more than one valid interpretation, the problem of misinterpretation must also be considered. For example, one student's initial interpretation of the topic could be seen as a clear case of misinterpretation in the sense that it would not be considered even potentially valid by the general community of language users. This student focused on a fragment of the topic, and in the process, treated "improvements" as the subject of the first sentence, i.e., he treated the first sentence as a declaration that many different *improvements* had already been made (cf. "Many different *suggestions* for improvement of Central High School have recently been made"). Subsequently the student began a search in memory for an "improvement" which he could use as the subject of his essay.

Interview: . . . uh— . . . the improvements of Central. . . . well one thing has been the landscaping. . . . it . . like it used to be mud all over and they started to put trees—, . . um . . . they've painted the doors down there. . . . and they've kind of just changed the way they've uh— . . . taught the . . uh . . students from last year. . . . last year was a different . . method they taught.

This student corrected his intepretation later in the interview, and proceeded to write an essay about the problem/situation of open classrooms. Not all students, however, may be so fortunate as to catch their own reading errors; the problem of reading ability might represent a serious disadvantage for some students.

The Text of the Topic

We have argued that this topic offered the potential for several valid interpretations. However, it should also be noted that the wording of this topic may also have contributed to the range of variation in interpretation. For example, assuming one does not consider "problem" and "situation" to be synonymous, the topic appears to offer students the opportunity to select either of these *alternatives*. In other words, students who read "or" as an indicator of alternatives would be faced with a choice of a "problem" that needed to be *solved* or a "situation" that needed to be *improved*. On the other hand, "or" could also be interpreted as if it indicated that a "situation" was just another way of saying a "problem" (as in the sense of a problematic situation). Thus, the addition of "situation" to the original version of the topic may have broadened the possible range of interpretations of the topic.

The lack of explicit links between the two sentences of the topic may also have encouraged a variety of interpretations, depending on which elements were seen as most important by the students. As we have noted above, some students tried to synthesize the two sentences into a single coherent interpretation. Subsequently, some of them defined their task in a way that required them either to justify their choice of a problem, or to defend its general importance. Other students chose to ignore the first sentence altogether, viewing it as merely an introduction to what they were really being asked to do—e.g. describe a problem relevant to them, and offer a solution. Thus the selective way students read the topic also figured as an important source of variation in the ways students construed their task. However, it is also fair to say that the wording of this topic created problems for those students who recognized that the first sentence could be interpreted as a reference to old information and then worried because they didn't know about "any suggestions that had been made." Variation in interpretation was thus partly the result of the wording of the topic itself.

Summary

To summarize, in interpreting the topic, in constructing writing tasks for themselves, and in accomplishing (or failing to accomplish) whatever tasks they set out to accomplish, students drew on several sources of meaning. One major source was the students' own prior knowledge, including personal experiences, their knowledge of learned strategies for writing, and their knowledge of language and how it operates in different kinds of texts. Prior knowledge was clearly a source of variation in the ways students construed their task. But knowledge of language and how it operates and learned strategies for writing also influenced the ways students construed this task.

Another major source of meaning was represented by the text itself, i.e. the source represented by a particular combination of subject matter, instructions, structure and language that the students were interpreting while they were defining their writing task. The nature of the topic subject in the study played a role because it required students to criticize their school. For some students, this meant selecting safe subjects they could assume the evaluators would agree with. The wording of the Central High School topic itself also affected the ways students construed their task, and may have contributed to the wide range of interpretations we identified.

A third major source of meaning was the testing context. As we have argued, the testing context may have also influenced the ways the Central

High School students construed their task as well as their success or failure at what they set out to accomplish. For some students the testing context appeared to provoke a "search" for the single "correct" answer. For others, the testing context appeared to trigger a kind of pre-programmed performance. Thus the social situation may have figured directly in the way students interpreted the topic and in the way they defined their task. Finally, it should also be noted that these sources of meaning did not operate in isolation, but that they operated together to produce each student's own individual and unique interpretation of the task.

TEN

How Different Communities of Readers Interpret Topics

In Chapter 9, we described how students differed in their interpretations of a topic that they had received as part of the annual end-of-year school assessment. The topic and the oral and written responses to it provided us with the data we used to study the nature of a writing assessment episode. The analysis of the student interview data and the written compositions produced in response to this topic suggested that the students were reading selectively and had focused on particular elements of the topic. They had drawn on several sources of meaning as they interpreted the topic and wrote their essays. The nature of the testing event, the text of the topic, and prior knowledge—including knowledge of the subject, conventions of language use, and strategies for writing—all supplied meanings used by the students as they interpreted the topic and wrote their essays. We demonstrated that these sources of meaning are potential sources of variation in interpretation, all of which should be taken into account in future studies of direct measures of writing competence.

In this chapter, we will address two other questions: (1) Do teachers read topics the same way students do? and (2) Do teachers evaluate papers the same way students do? It is important, for designers of tests, students, and test scorers to all agree on what the topic is asking the writer to do. Otherwise the scoring rubric may not reflect the designer's original criteria. In addition, students might interpret the task differently from the way the test-makers intended and perhaps even be penalized for their interpretations if their task interpretations do not match those of the evaluators. It is important for students to have a clear idea of what a successful completion of a task entails. Thus, the success of students' performance may depend not only on their ability to match their evaluators' *interpretations* of the task elicited by the topic, but also on their ability to match their evaluators' expectations about what a *successful completion* of the task would entail. Additional evidence from our in-depth study of a writing assessment episode, as well as evidence from other studies conducted for the Writing Assessment Project, indicates that test makers, writers, and raters do not always have the same perception of what the task is, that some task interpretations may generate weaker writing than others, and that writers and raters do not always have the same perception of what constitutes successful completion of a task.

Divergence in the Interpretation of Topics by Students and Teachers: Data from the Central High Study

During the Central High Study, we collected data while the topic was being developed so that we could compare the students' interpretations of the topic with the original intentions of the designers of the test. The three teachers who created the topic had substantial experience in topic development and holistic assessment. All three had acted as consultants for the Bay Area Writing Project, had taught English for several years, and one was a consultant for a professional testing agency. During a 2½-hour session, several topics were considered, partially developed, critiqued, and ultimately rejected in favor of the one used for this particular tenth grade assessment. As they developed the final topic, the teachers talked about what they expected to find in the students' responses. We made an audio-tape recording of the session, and one member of the project research team took notes on the issues and the topics discussed but did not participate in the discussion.

The original version of the topic that we used was brought to the topic design session in the following form:

> There are currently plans being formed for improvements to Central High School as a result of a State of California grant for School Improvement. There are many committees working on plans for school improvement. Identify three improvements you would like to see made at Central, telling why you feel each improvement needs to be made and what you would like done.

The final version of the topic is provided here again for comparison:

> Many different suggestions for improvement of Central High School have recently been made. Describe one problem or situation which you feel needs correction or improvement, giving reasons for your choice, and suggesting one or more solutions.

In a subsequent communication to researchers, the author of the topic explained why the original wording of the topic was changed:

> It struck me, as I began to read it as being unnecessarily formal and wordy (Did kids really need to know all the background in order to write? If they did, could it be put in simpler form?).

During the session, the topic developers ultimately dropped all references to outside information (e.g. "State of California grant") in favor of what they regarded as a more general statement. They hoped that students would understand that there is no single right answer to the directives in the second sentence of the final version. It is important to emphasize that the authors of the topic began by describing a very specific context, but attempted to move toward a simpler version of the topic. The result of this effort was the first sentence containing a residual core of information removed from the specific facts and circumstances surrounding it:

> Many different suggestions for improvement of Central High School have recently been made.

Teachers often construct topics that include initial contextualizing or background material even though they may view these contextualizing statements as merely introductory and subsidiary to the main task called for by the topic. As shown in Chapter 9, however, some students do not always view these contextualizing statements as intended.

In Chapter 9, we emphasized that the topic contained the basis for students' misconceptions of what the task actually required. But the students' interpretations can be described as *misconceived* only insofar as they did not meet the expectations of the topic authors: the students' seemingly errant interpretations of the topic should not be considered *misunderstandings*. Rather, they should be viewed as variant plausible interpretations cued by elements of the topic.

The Interview Data from the Teachers

Throughout the topic development session, the topic authors were obviously concerned with the implications of every word in the topic. The topic had originally asked for *three* suggested improvements to the school, but this was regarded as "too structured," and the teachers then asked instead for a description of *one* problem or situation. They wanted to "force a choice" between possible school improvements. Although it was not explicitly stated in the topic, the topic authors also expected the "solution" to the "problem" to be expressed in terms of something that "money can buy." At one point, the phrase "money is no object" was written into the topic, but it was later deleted. In effect, students who related their problem choices and solutions to monetary factors conformed more closely to what the topic authors expected than the students who did not.

The topic authors also indicated through their discussion that it was not enough for the writer to simply *describe* the problem. They expected the responses to include reasons *why* the problem was thought to be significant. The authors also expected the responses to show that the problem was related to the writer, that the solution would benefit the writer, and that the writer felt the problem needed correction.

Key words in the topic also elicited specific expectations on the part of the topic authors. For example, during this session, the authors added "situation" to "problem" because they felt that a problem could be "corrected," but not "improved." They expected the word "describe" to invite writers to begin with strong detail and to create a strong setting. They expected "many" to give the writer an indication that there was no single "right" answer to the topic. The phrase "at Central" replaced the original "at the school," because the authors felt the latter excluded problems external to the school curriculum such as landscaping. Thus it appears that the topic authors thought that each word in the topic should have a particular meaning for the writer. However, as shown in Chapter 9 students actually ignored some segments and interpreted other segments in unexpected ways. The word "many", for example, did not prevent some students from searching for the one "right" answer.

Although the authors intended each segment in the topic to cue the writer about what he or she should include in the response, certain parts of the topic appeared to assume more significance for the authors than other parts. For example, the authors agreed that the word "one" would cue the student to focus on one issue. The importance of this particular cue was also evident to the teachers who evaluated the papers but who had not participated in the topic development session. When these evaluators were asked to discuss what they thought a good response to the topic would consist of, several commented that "the structure of the paper is there in the topic." Several of these evaluators also said that they felt the main problem that student writers might encounter was one of "narrowing down the focus." The following statements are representative of these evaluators' responses upon reading the topic:

> He (the writer) will have to declare a focus. Then he has to describe *the** problem and give reasons for the choice.

> If he manages to avoid the list and does decide on *one* problem . . . he'll have a good paper.

> I guess the key is finding *that one problem.*

> The two pitfalls may be the list . . . and the very general description of *the* problem.

> It has to be negative . . . they have to persuade you . . . they have to argue (that *it's* a problem). This calls for an argument . . . to convince someone . . . that *it* needs correction.

> The response needs *one problem,* concrete examples and specifics beyond general statements.

> *(emphasis ours in each one)

The above statements illustrate that the evaluators who did not participate in the development of the topic had expectations similar to those expressed by the topic authors. Although there was no unanimous agreement on what a good response should contain, there was general agreement among the teachers on the need for a focus on "one" issue. These evaluators also agreed that those essays that were well-grounded in students' own personal experiences at the school would be the strongest and most credible.

Not all students, however, recognized the significance of the word "one" as a cue for a focus on a single problem or situation, nor the importance of providing details from personal experience. One student (see Martin in Chapter 9), discussed the relative merits of several problems in his attempt to justify his own choice, but failed to describe any single problem in detail.

The Questionnaire Data from the Students and Teachers

Evidence of divergence between teachers' and students' interpretations of the writing task appeared in the questionnaire data as well as in the interview data. The questionnaire, which students completed on the day following the assessment, provided a record of their attitudes toward writing and an evaluation of both the topic and of the task demands suggested by the topic. Twelve of the questionnaire items—those focusing on evaluation of the topic and judgments about the task demands—were also presented to the teachers in the study. Differences among teachers' and students' perceptions of these demands are discussed below.

Responses to the items on the questionnaire were recorded on a scale of 1 to 5, with 1 signifying agreement with a positive statement and 5 signifying agreement with a corresponding negative statement. Participants' responses shown in Table 10.1 are collapsed into 3 categories. The table shows student-writer responses compared to the responses of the combined group of evaluators. The student writers disagreed with the other participants across many of the areas discussed.

The figures for items 1-4 reflect responses to general evaluative state-

Table 10.1.
Responses by Students and Topic Authors/Raters
to Selected Questionnaire Items*

	Evaluation of the Topic			
	Agree	Neutral	Agree	
1. The topic is more pleasing to write about than most others given in school.	31 70	37 20	31 10	The topic is less pleasing to write about than most others given in school.
2. The topic is easy to read and understand.	78 80	18 20	3 0	The topic is difficult to read and understand.
3. The topic is easy to write about.	60 60	23 20	17 20	The topic is difficult to write about.

Table 10.1. (*continued*)

	Evaluation of the Topic			
	Agree	Neutral	Agree	
4. I think the topic will give a good indication of my [the student's] writing ability.	21 70	37 20	42 10	I think the topic will not give a good indication of my [the student's] writing ability.
5. It is important to describe only one problem.	35 90	42 0	21 10	It is not important to describe only one problem.
6. It is important to explain why the subject is a problem.	82 90	13 10	3 0	It is not important to explain why the subject is a problem.
7. It is important to suggest a solution to the problem or situation.	84 80	13 20	2 0	It is not important to suggest a solution to the problem or situation.
8. It is important to suggest more than one solution to the problem.	69 10	22 20	7 70	It is not important to suggest more than one solution to the problem.
9. It is important to point out that many suggestions for improving the school have been made.	53 0	38 10	9 90	It is not important to point out that many suggestions for improving the school have been made.
10. It is important to relate the problem to everyone in the school.	71 10	22 20	7 80	It is not important to relate the problem to everyone in the school.
11. It is important to show how the problem affects the writer.	51 20	36 20	12 60	It is not important to show how the problem affects the writer.
12. It is important to explain how the solution will improve the school.	77 40	19 40	2 20	It is not important to explain how the solution will improve the school.

Note. The top row of numbers in each case refers to the students ($n = 302$), the bottom row to topic authors/raters ($n = 10$). Some rows do not total 100% due to rounding error and/or missing responses.

ments about the topic. In general, the students found the topic far less pleasing, compared to other topics given in school than did teacher authors and raters. Also, the students were less likely than teachers to agree with the statement that the writing produced by the topic would give a good indication of student writing ability. The combined group of authors and raters, therefore, appeared to have a different idea of the relevance or quality of the prompt than did the student writers.

Only one evaluator felt strongly that the topic would not give a good indication of writing ability because, as she argued, topics need to be relevant to the writer and the situations discussed must be perceived as being within the writer's control. She pointed out that students may be tired of writing about school problems which they cannot directly influence and which must be solved by adults. In fact, she felt that students might realize that no one with decision-making power would read their suggestions, and that the students might resent having to spend their time providing solutions which no one would implement. One of the student's comments from the interviews supports her thesis:

> The only way we can solve this problem is . . . have our parents speak for us. They (the school board) should listen to them because they (the parents) are the ones who pay taxes.

Responses by the two groups to statements about the importance of including certain elements in these compositions are reported in items 5 through 12 in the table. More than 80% of both groups agreed to both of the following statements:

> 6. It is important to explain why the subject is a problem.
> 7. It is important to suggest a solution to the problem or situation.

One of the most dramatic differences between teacher and student responses was their opposing views on the need to mention the actual suggestions which had been debated at the school in the months preceding the assessment. Fifty-three percent of the students but *none* of the teachers agreed with the following statement:

> 8. It is important to point out that many suggestions for improving Central High School have been made.

In other words, a majority of the students thought they *should* refer to those suggestions, while all of the teachers considered this sentence to contain only background information.

Another difference across the groups can be noted in responses to the statement:

> 5. It is important to describe only one problem.

Ninety percent of the evaluators felt that a focus on one problem would be a vital part of a response to this prompt. Yet, only 35% of the student writers agreed that this was important.

The disagreement on the number of problems to include in the composition was consistent with the disagreement on the number of solutions to suggest. Sixty-nine percent of the students agreed with the statement: "It is important to suggest more than one solution" while only 10% of the teachers thought this was necessary.

One could easily argue that because many students found it necessary to discuss more than one problem, they might also have found it necessary to suggest more than one solution. On the other hand, it should also be noted that this may have simply been a reflection of the students' responses to the phrase segment "suggesting one or more solutions." But, for whatever reason, whether students discussed more than one solution because they discussed more than one problem, or even whether they were merely padding their essays by providing more than one solution, teachers and students obviously disagreed on the importance of this aspect of the task.

The Questionnaire Responses and Holistic Scores

The topic directs the responses of all participants in a writing assessment episode from authors to writers to raters. In order for a topic to function as intended, it must, first of all be comprehensible, and second, it must be capable of triggering an appropriate written response. Thus, certain aspects of knowledge and intention must be communicated from the testmaker to the writers and the evaluators. A writer can produce successful writing in response to a given topic when he or she can understand and match the testmaker's expectations of what a "good" response will contain. Furthermore, if we measure success in terms of grade or score, the expectations of the evaluator must be satisfied by the writer's written product as well. The evaluators' expectations about student performance are guided by reading the topic. If the students' reading similarly guides their understanding of the topic, they will be more likely to produce an acceptable response. To investigate this issue, we employed Kendall's coefficient of correlation. This coefficient, symbolized by the letter tau, is a method of determining the relationship between two sets of ranks. A value of 1 indicates perfect agreement, while a value of -1 indicates disagreement. Correlation coefficients were computed for the students' total holistic scores and their responses to each of the items in Table 10.1 for both the group of students who were interviewed ($n = 11$) and for the entire group of students who were assessed ($n = 302$) including the eleven who were interviewed. The results are shown in Table 10.2. Given the small number of students in the interview group, it is not surprising that statistically significant results were not found. However, for the larger group of students, several items were in fact statistically significant.

Table 10.2.
Kendall's Correlation Coefficients: Responses to Selected Questionnaire Items with Total Holistic Score

Item	Students ($n = 302$) Whole Group		Students ($n = 11$) Interview Group	
1. The topic is more pleasing to write about than most others given in school.	.07	.035	.06	.411
2. The topic is easy to read and understand.	−.196	.001*	−.09	.340
3. The topic is easy to write about.	−.02	.297	−.05	.410
4. I think the topic will give a good indication of my [the student's] writing ability.	.01	.478	−.12	.303
5. It is important to describe only one problem.	−.02	.289	.43	.032
6. It is important to explain why the subject is a problem.	−.16	.001*	−.29	.105
7. It is important to suggest a solution to the problem or situation.	−.13	.001*	−.28	.118
8. It is important to suggest more than one solution to the problem.	.03	.238	−.05	.417
9. It is important to point out that many suggestions for improving the school have been made.	.02	.321	.05	.417
10. It is important to relate the problem to everyone in the school.	−.09	.012	−.25	.146
11. It is important to show how the problem affects the writer.	−.02	.243	−.27	.123
12. It is important to explain how the solution will improve the school.	−.11	.002*	−.59	.006

Note. *Alpha = .05/12

In the larger group of students surveyed, significant associations were found between total holistic score and four of the items. Before we discuss these results, however, it is important to point out that although some of the measures of association are significant, they are very low. But if one considers that many factors influence the evaluative judgments that teachers make in reacting to a written composition, including factors which are not related to features of the topic—such as legibility, mechanical errors, and spelling—the low correlations should not be surprising. Given this qualification, the results do support the viewpoint that there is an important connection between reading and writing in a writing test situation.

In the present study, students who found the prompt "easy to read" received higher scores. In his review of the literature on topic effects, Hoetker (1982) suggests that readability and students' reading skills are factors that should be considered in topic design and test evaluation. The results for item 2 above support the notion that students with "reading" problems are also likely to have difficulty in making an appropriate response in a writing assessment.

However, it should also be noted that task demands which were *not* stated explicitly in the topic were also significantly correlated with holistic score. Agreement with the statements "It is important to explain *why* the subject is a problem," and "It is important to explain how the solution will *improve* the school," were significantly correlated with holistic score. Students who agreed that these task demands were important were awarded higher scores. Yet explaining *why* the subject is a problem is not precisely equivalent either to "Describe one problem," or to "giving reasons for your choice." Similarly, explaining how the solution will improve Central High is not explicitly stated as a demand of the task. Students who consider these tasks to be unnecessary elaborations and/or students who interpret the task differently may be evaluated in part on the basis of their interpretation of the topic. Thus the problem for student writers is not simply a matter of whether or not they can read the words of the text and form plausible interpretations, but whether they can form interpretations that will match the unstated expectations of the evaluators.

One would expect that those task demands that are stated explicitly in the prompt would be correlated with score. Thus it is not surprising that students who agreed with the statement "It is important to suggest a solution to the problem or situation" received higher scores. However, the fact that higher scores were awarded to students who recognized the importance of *unstated* task demands suggests that students whose task interpretation matched the intention of the evaluators in this regard were more likely to satisfy their expectations and thus to perform well in the assessment.

How students actually interpreted the topic in different ways was discussed in detail in Chapter 9. Briefly, however, students interpreted the phrase, "giving reasons for your choice," variously as meaning: (1) giving reasons why the problem should be considered a problem, (2) giving reasons why the problem was chosen above others, and/or (3) giving reasons why the problem was personally relevant. Because higher scores were awarded to students who agreed that it was important to explain why the subject chosen *was* a problem, it appears that the first interpretation may have been favored by the evaluators. For students to recognize the importance of including this explanation, they had to go beyond the explicitly stated requirements of the topic. The data presented here thus clearly indicate that implicit task demands affected the way students were evaluated, and that students do not always "read" or understand topics the same way teachers do.

The Evaluation of Papers by Students and Teachers: Data from the Rhetorical Specification Study

Evidence of disagreement among participant groups in assessment situations appeared in other studies conducted for the project as well. Keech and McNelly (1982) compared the ways different groups of evaluators rated the compositions that had been collected for the rhetorical specification study described in Chapter 8. In that first study, two topic versions were employed. Both versions asked students to write about a "first time" experience, but they varied in the degree to which rhetorical context was specified. Subsequently, Keech and McNelly made comparisons among the ways students and different groups of teachers—including *novice* teachers who had had little previous experience with holistic assessment and *expert* teachers who had had substantial experience—evaluated the compositions written in response to the two topic versions.

During the training session for holistic scoring and the scoring session itself, Keech and McNelly (1982) gathered information about the evaluative criteria employed by three groups of raters. By comparing student rater evaluations to those of the two teacher groups who had evaluated the same essays, this study uncovered several sources of variation which may affect scores in unpredictable ways in any assessment situation. Again, evidence from this study suggests that teachers and students do not always have the same perception of 1) what the task is, and 2) what constitutes a successful completion of the task.

In the Keech and McNelly study, four statistical comparisons were reported. In addition, qualitative comparisons were made based on the researchers' observations of the training and scoring processes. The findings of the study will be briefly summarized here. For a more complete discussion, the reader is referred to the original technical report (Keech & McNelly, 1982, pp. 260–315).

The Raters as Subjects

The subjects in this study were three groups of raters, all of whom were evaluating the same set of papers. The 87 *student raters* were drawn from three of the four classes of students who had taken the writing test in the original study. One class (27 sophomore, nonaccelerated) was excluded from scoring because it was considered to be potentially less accurate and consistent. Training and scoring took place during regular 50-minute class periods over 2 days. During training, the high school students were given a brief introduction to holistic scoring, and then sets of anchor papers were distributed to the students in each class. The anchor papers had been selected by Catharine Keech, the researcher-trainer, after she had read the entire set of 114 essays. During training, the high school students were asked to read quickly through several of the anchor papers to form an impression of the range of quality in the set. After establishing the outer boundaries of the scoring range (1–4), students were asked to rank the papers. Discussion of the anchor papers followed this initial rating. Then the essays were distributed randomly to the class, two to each student. Scores given on the first reading were concealed before the students passed the papers along to other students for a second reading. On the second day, students from the two largest classes completed scoring the essays after being retrained with the remaining anchor papers.

The 15 *novice teacher raters* were teacher trainees in the Bay Area Writing Project Teacher Credential Program at the University of California at Berkeley. For these novice teachers training was conducted as part of a general workshop on holistic scoring and followed an introduction to assessment theory not given to the student raters. Apart from this, however, the same training procedures described above were employed, with the researcher/trainer eliciting and tallying the novice teachers' initial responses to each anchor paper before attempting to summarize and achieve a consensus. Twenty-three student teachers participated in the first training session, but they tended to use the session as a "forum for exploring and shaping their own criteria for evaluating writing," (Keech & McNelly, 1982, p. 268) and thus consensus was not achieved, necessitating a second training session which was held a week later and included 15 student teachers from the original group. These 15 then proceeded to score the entire sample.

The 4 *expert teacher raters* were teacher consultants from the Bay Area Writing Project with previous experience in holistic scoring, not only for their own school districts but also for the Educational Testing Service. Having taught English 20 years or more each, the 4 teachers were clearly experts in their field. For these teachers, similar training procedures were employed, with the researcher/trainer tallying initial responses to the anchor papers. Each expert teacher rater evaluated approximately one fourth of the entire sample during the scoring.

Agreement Within and Among
Three Groups of Raters

In this section, the amount of agreement among raters within each of the individual groups and among different groups is reported.

Interrater Reliability Estimates

Two sets of figures given in Table 10.3 describe the amount of agreement among raters within each of the three groups of evaluators. The first set of figures simply involves a report of the percentages of essays receiving discrepant scores, i.e. scores from two raters with more than a one-point difference. For example, when raters use a scale of 1 to 4, paired scores of 1 and 3 or 2 and 4, would be reported as having received discrepant scores. These percentages in Table 10.3 are entered as, for example, .078 or (7.8%). For purposes of comparison, Keech and McNelly (1982) reported that local holistic assessments in California typically find discrepancy percentages of less than 10%.

The second set of figures consists of the correlations between the scores of the first and second raters on all papers for each of the three groups of raters. The measure used here is Pearson's r. A perfect correlation would be represented by 1.00, meaning that all first and second readers agreed exactly on the scores assigned to each paper. In contrast, a finding of no correlation would be represented by 0.00, meaning that no first and second readers agreed exactly on the score of any paper. Values for Pearson's r ranging between .01 and .35 are considered to be low, while correlations between .35 and .69 are considered to be moderate. Correlations of more than .70 are considered to be fairly strong rates of agreement.

The correlations of inter-rater reliability show that the student raters achieved a statistically significant correlation of $r = .68$ ($p = <.01$), an acceptable rate of agreement. The novice teachers, in contrast, achieved only a moderate correlation, $r = .55$ ($p = <.01$). The expert raters achieved a

Table 10.3.
Reliability Data for Three Groups of Raters

Groups	Discrepancy Percentage	Pearson's r	Papers
Student Raters (87)	.078	.68*	109
Novice teacher raters (15)	.150	.55*	106
Expert teacher raters (4)	.044	.71*	114

Note. Discrepancy percentage = proportion of total papers requiring a third reading.
*$p = <.01$

fairly strong correlation, $r = .71$ ($p = <.01$), clearly an acceptable rate of agreement, but lower than the researchers expected. Keech and McNelly reported that recent testing programs have been finding "raw, unadjusted correlations between readers of .70, .80, and in some instances of better than .90" (Keech & McNelly, 1982, p. 271).

Agreement Among Groups

Each essay received two scores from readers in each of the three different groups. The combined total of these two scores was used for making comparisons among the groups. Pearson's r was used to report correlations between the total holistic scores awarded by each group. The results in Table 10.4 indicate that the lowest rate of agreement was between the students and the novice teacher raters ($r = .47, p = <.01$). A moderate rate of agreement was found between the students and the expert teacher raters ($r = .50$, $p = <.01$). The strongest rate of agreement was between the novice teacher raters and the expert teacher raters ($r = .62, p = <.01$). As the authors noted, these correlations should alert us to potential discrepancies in the ways disparate groups of raters evaluate papers (Keech and McNelly, 1982, p. 274). Raters with varying amounts of experience in evaluating writing may approach the task differently and employ dissimilar criteria. Table 10.4 compares the scoring agreement between groups reading the same sample set of papers.

Table 10.4.
Agreement Between Groups of Raters

Rating Group's Scoring Same Samples	Pearson's r	Papers
Student raters with novice teacher raters	.47*	105
Student raters with expert teacher raters	.50*	114
Novice teacher with expert teacher raters	.62*	105

$*p = <.01$

Score Distributions for Three Groups of Raters

Table 10.5 reports the means and standard deviations of the scores awarded to the essays by the different groups of raters. Student raters produced a mean score for the entire set of essays of 5.66. Novice teachers provided a more positive estimate of the writers' performance, with a mean of 5.95. Expert teacher raters produced an even more positive estimate of the writers' abilities than did the students, with a mean score of 6.18. Keech and McNelly point out that the difference between the means of the expert teacher raters and the student raters is .52, or about half of a scoring point,

Table 10.5.
Scoring Distributions for Three Groups of Raters

		Full Sample	Version A	Version B
Student Raters (87)	M	5.66	5.65	5.67
	SD	1.49	1.64	1.33
Papers		114	57	57
Novice Teacher Raters (15)	M	5.95	5.67	6.26
	SD	1.33	1.40	1.20
Papers		106	55	51
Expert Teacher Raters (4)	M	6.18	6.09	6.28
	SD	1.27	1.29	1.25
Papers		114	57	57

and that the difference is statistically significant ($p < .05$). In other words, student evaluations of the papers in this set are significantly lower than teacher evaluations of the same set.

Figure 10.1 shows the distribution of scores awarded by the three groups of raters. Clearly—and perhaps surprisingly—the students came closest to providing the sort of normal distribution of scores that would be desirable in a large-scale holistic assessment. Apparently the students were more willing

Figure 10.1.   Distributions of Scores Awarded by 3 Groups of Raters

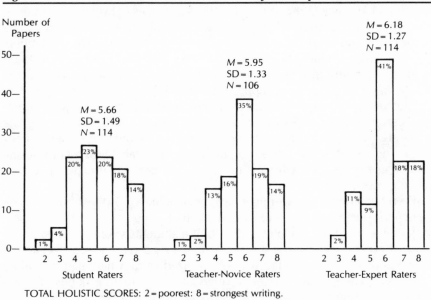

TOTAL HOLISTIC SCORES: 2 = poorest: 8 = strongest writing.

to use the low end of the scoring range. Six of the papers scored by this group received a score of 1 from at least one reader (Note that the total scores of these papers would be either a 2 or a 3, depending upon the second rating). Novice teachers, on the other hand, awarded a 1 to only three papers. Expert teachers used the lowest category twice, but even then, both of the papers received a score of 2 from the second reader. None of the papers scored by the experts received a minimum total score of two (2 scores of 1). This result was especially surprising since the expert teacher raters, as a group, assigned one of the anchor papers a score of 1, indicating that this was typical of that score category. But when the same paper was rated again during the formal reading, at least one expert teacher gave it a score of 2.

Apparently students also had a broader sense of the score category 2, because they distributed papers in the middle range (papers with scores of 2 or 3) equally across both score categories. Novice teacher raters, in contrast, awarded a score of 2 to fewer papers, and a score of 3 to more. The expert teacher raters were even more generous. Forty-seven papers received total scores of 6 (two scores of 3) with only 10 papers receiving total scores of 5 and only 13 receiving total scores of 4. Clearly, the student raters seemed willing to judge the work of student writers more harshly than did the teachers. Possible explanations for the differences among these distributions are explored more fully below.

The Data from the Training Sessions

Keech and McNelly (1982) argue that the differences between the groups in the inter-rater reliability achieved are not surprising given the backgrounds of the groups and their experiences in the training sessions. The researchers point out that the students were eager to cooperate and to "learn how to do it right," resulting in a fairly strong rate of agreement of .68. The novice teachers, on the other hand, appeared less willing to reach consensus during the training session. Because the novice teachers tended to use the training session as a forum for exploring their criteria for evaluating writing, the inter-rater reliability correlation for this group was only moderate to poor (.55). The expert teacher raters, on the other hand, achieved a fairly strong rate of agreement (.71) which is not surprising given their experience with holistic scoring.

Even higher correlations might have been achieved by the groups, the researchers suggest, if the readers had not had to compare, in some cases, very different modes of writing. Most of the students wrote personal narratives. However, some of the students who responded to the topic version in which audience specification was emphasized wrote what might be called "process" papers—that is, papers which give "how to do it" kinds of directions. One of these, Sample D, used as an anchor paper, follows:

Sample D

So I hear that your (sic) going to play a guitar for the first time. I know that at first you'll probibly (sic) think that you're never going to be able to play the guitar successfully but don't let this discourage you. I felt the same way when I started but I kept on practicing and now it's easy for me. At first you may find that changing from chord to chord is the most difficult (sic) your fingers will tie up in knots running around themselves. The best way to overcome this problem is to use a very simple two or three finger chord and just strum the strings as you move each finger in unison up and down the six strings on the same fret and then do the same thing on different frets over the fret board; put your fingers in an A position on the second fret, strum a couple times, move your three fingers up to the fifth, forth, and third strings, strum a couple more times, move back down to the A position, strum, and then move your whole hand up to the fifth fret and repeat. Soon you'll find playing the guitar just as comfortable as it is fun. (p. 292)

Keech and McNelly (1982) point out that raters may have difficulty in comparing two very different types of writing in a single rank-ordering based on overall quality. Thus, the differences between these "process" papers and the personal narratives may have accounted for some of the differences between the ratings. The researchers report that some raters responded more positively to the process papers than did others, "believing that giving directions is a more difficult task than narrating an event" (Keech & McNelly, 1982, p. 276). These raters may have over-rewarded writers who attempted the more difficult task. Other raters may have found the process papers dull in comparison to personal narratives. Initial scores by each group collected during the training sessions for this paper are shown in Table 10.6. The scores indicate that the students responded less favorably to the above paper during the training sessions than did either the novice teachers or the experts.

Another factor which may have contributed to disagreement among raters

Table 10.6.
Scores Awarded to Sample D During Training

Scores	Students		Teacher Novices		Experts		Researcher	
	n	%	n	%	n	%	n	%
1	4	7	2	13	0	0	0	0
2	30	57	5	33	1	25	0	0
3	22	39	8	53	3	75	1	100
4	1	2	0	0	0	0	0	0
N	57		15		4		1	
Consensus Score	2/3		3		3		3	

was the instruction which allowed students to select a form for writing: "You may write an essay, short story, letter, etc." Letters and diaries present special problems to raters who may have to deal with (or ignore) very casual language and organization, lack of development, and/or lack of vivid concrete details, all of which features may accurately reflect the tone and style of a real letter or diary entry. During training sessions, there was substantial disagreement about anchor papers that were written in these two forms. An example is provided in Sample E along with the initial scores awarded by each of the rater groups, as well as the researcher-trainer's comments about the raters' reactions (Keech & McNelly, 1982).

Sample E

Mom,

We are leaving here in about four hours. I had the most exciting vacation. This is the first time I have ever been away from the family alone. Even though my friend came with me, it's still different. You add so much security when we're in foreign places. I run into a distant stranger every second. I miss you and Dad because I never had to worry about a thing when your're (sic) near. I have learned alot (sic) this trip because I've had to worry about money, my car and eating. Don't misunderstand me, I need to do this. I feel as though I am just beginning to grow up. It's like a young sparrow leaving his mothers (sic) nest to go out into the world and defend his own life. It's a very scarey (sic) feeling but a good one. I have enjoyed myself very much and it's been a great experience. Thanks for keeping me under your wing till I was ready to take flight. I look at this as one step towards independence. Thanks also for trusting me to be alone and being so understanding.

your daughter

Researcher/Trainer Response. In spite of the apparent cliche, "like a young sparrow leaving his mother's nest," and the general lack of specificity in the writing, I tentatively scored this paper a 3 rather than a 2 because I regarded it

Table 10.7.
Scores Awarded to Sample E During Training

Scores	Students		Teacher Novices		Experts		Researcher	
	n	%	n	%	n	%	n	%
1	2	3	0	0	0	0	0	0
2	14	23	4	27	3	75	0	0
3	29	49	8	53	1	25	1	100
4	15	25	3	20	0	0	0	0
N	60		15		4		1	
Consensus Score	3		3		2		3	

as doing effectively what it set out to do. This writer creates an absolutely believable letter—one which might be written at the end of a journey, after other letters which were more like travelogues. This one would be intended to sum up the meaning of this extended "first time" experience. After hearing the experts discuss this paper, I became more aware of its weaknesses and see that, had we scored this paper 2 . . . we might have made a broader distribution of papers and been more precise in our use of 2 and 3 as scoring categories. Nevertheless, it is clear that this paper presents evaluation problems in comparison with other papers because it deals with a so-called first experience which was actually a series of experiences, and it deals with that experience on an abstract level.

Student Rater Response. Students were divided fairly evenly over three scoring categories, with the bulk (49%) concentrating on a score of 3 for this paper, but with a strong minority (23%) giving it a 2 and an equally large group (25%) giving it a 4. Lower scoring students didn't have much to say about this paper: "I didn't like it. I don't believe she did that (traveled alone). There aren't enough details—she ought to tell something about a time when she wished her parents were there, but managed to get herself out anyway." The latter comment is, of course, a strong and valid criticism of this paper. Higher scoring students defended this paper as being a believable letter, answering the primary criticism of lack of details by saying, "That's not the kind of letter it is. She's writing at the end of the trip—she wrote that other stuff before." This view reflected my own view [Keech] in choosing to give this paper a score of 3. Students had little difficulty in seeing that the paper was not strong enough for a top score, reaching consensus at 3. One interesting comment in favor of the paper was a compliment paid by one student in response to the metaphor of the sparrow leaving its mother's nest—reminding me again that what are cliches to adults may be fresh images for students.

Expert Teacher Rater Response. This group surprised me with 3 out of 4 readers giving this paper a 2 after having used the 3 category so freely. I asked them to defend their low scoring in this case. Line by line they pointed out the rather empty generalization, some awkwardnesses. They were put off by the sparrow. They were not interested in considering the letter format or the special voice of the writer which might be assumed to result from the context of writing a letter to a parent. Given that context, they felt the student could or should have written more effectively.

Novice Teacher Rater Response. The low raters in this group expressed the feeling that this entire paper was a cliche. They felt superior to this student's struggling effort to express emerging feelings of independence. Fortunately, a high rater pointed out what I had learned from the student responders: what seems trite to us may be very effective and new to students at this age. These readers agreed, however, that this writer is not giving any reader new or deeper insights into what it means to gain independence: at best, we have a small portrait of how one adolescent responded with gratitude to being given responsibility. Certainly not a 4 paper, but the group was happy to agree on 3 instead of 2. (p. 294)

In addition to the differences in evaluative criteria among the rater groups, the researchers point out that some of the disagreement revealed by the low correlations between groups and by differences in the scoring distributions may be attributed to differences in the training procedures in general and particularly in the procedures for defining initial scoring categories. The expert raters quickly reached a high rate of agreement. However, they defined the three categories more broadly than the researcher/trainer had expected. During the initial training session, the researcher/trainer decided not to intervene because she believed that "letting them determine the scoring boundaries, which seemed clear to them, would increase the reliability of their scoring." She also notes that:

> Having initially defined the score categories in something approaching a normal curve (albeit skewed by the population) the researcher-trainer withdrew from the discussion of the experts, who seemed to be drawing on a common experience and making reference to outside criteria to determine the scale point intervals in terms of quality of writing. (Keech & McNelly, p. 269)

During the reading, the expert teachers recognized that they may have defined the 3 category too broadly, attributing to it "high threes" and "low threes," and remarking that none of the other categories got broken up this way. They agreed that a five-point scale was needed for these papers "to deal with their feeling that too large a range of papers received a score of 3." (p. 269). Thus the experts were dealing with what may be an inherent problem in setting the scale in an assessment:

> a conflict between the practice of trying to distribute students in a fairly normal distribution across scoring points and the practice of trying to arrive at scoring points that are equal intervals apart in terms of the quality of the essays, rather than in terms of the number or percentage of essays that fall in each interval. (Keech & McNelly, 1982, p. 269)

In contrast to the expert teachers, the student writers were amenable to training, and thus were likely to divide the sample in a way that more closely matched the researcher-trainer's original intentions. More directive procedures for training the expert teacher raters might, therefore, have yielded different results. Or instead of the researcher choosing the anchors, if expert teachers had read the entire sample themselves before pulling anchors, the distribution of scores might have resembled the students' distribution more closely.

The possibility also exists that the expert teachers were drawing on external criteria and redefining their scoring categories during the reading itself, and this represents an important potential source of variation in the ways students are evaluated in an assessment situation. The researchers note that the expert teachers may have been influenced by their familiarity with the score categories and the quality of the essays drawn from the general high school population that they encounter when scoring the California High School Proficiency Exam (CHSPE). In general, the student writers in this study performed better than might be expected in a larger school or state population. The fact that the expert teacher raters rated few papers in the low score categories suggests that they may have been employing criteria based on their experience with a much larger and more normally distributed assessment population.

An interesting phenomenon which occurred with the expert teacher raters suggests that this was the case. As mentioned above, during the training session, the expert teachers did agree to assign a score of 1 to at least one anchor. But during the actual reading, they failed to give that same paper a score of 1 on both of its readings. If the teachers were, in fact, employing criteria drawn from their previous assessment experiences about the kind of writing which typically falls in the lowest scoring category, then it is not so surprising that the paper was not given a score of 1 during the reading. Scores of 1 in the CHSPE, as well as in many local high school assessments, are reserved for very poor, very short papers, that are also severely flawed with spelling and punctuation errors. Given the generally higher level of ability of the students assessed in this study, raters would not expect to encounter such severely flawed papers. The paper in question is provided below, along with data on the scores awarded during training.

Sample I

When I was about five years old I put some insect poison in my mouth not knowing that it was poison. I later found out that it was poison, and became very scared. I rember (sic) hiding by myself wondering if I was going to die. After a while I was still feeling allright so I came inside, went about my normal routine, and soon after forgot the incident. It embarassed (sic) me so much that I never told anyone about it, and I think this is why I still remenber (sic) it so well.

Table 10.8.
Scores Awarded to Sample I During Training

Scores	Students		Teacher Novices		Experts		Researcher	
	n	%	n	%	n	%	n	%
1	31	59	10	67	4	100	1	100
2	18	35	4	27	0	0	0	0
3	3	6	1	5	0	0	0	0
4	0	0	0	0	0	0	0	0
N	52		15		4		1	
Consensus Score	1		1		1		1	

One widely recognized problem in holistic assessment is the maintaining of consistent standards, which require that the same scoring criteria be employed from one assessment to the next. Given the expert teachers' long experience with the criteria employed in other, more typical assessment situations, it is reasonable to suggest that the expert teachers in this study were using different criteria for scoring categories. This explanation is consistent with the fact that the expert teachers almost never employed the lowest scoring category during the actual reading.

Summary

To summarize, several important sources of variation in the ways students are evaluated were found in this study. Students and teachers tended to differ in the criteria they employed for deciding what constituted a successful completion of the task and in the criteria they employed for ranking the essays according to scoring categories. The three groups of raters were, in fact, working within three distinctly different frames of reference for judging the essays. The students' frame of reference was most likely derived from their familiarity with their teacher's expectations and the standards set forth in their own classroom as well as the scoring categories defined by the researcher-trainer. The novice teachers' frame of reference was most likely derived from their rather limited experience of evaluating writing and the training process may have had little effect. They may have depended largely on their own idiosyncratic definitions of what constitutes good writing. The expert teachers, on the other hand, were drawing on years of experience as well as pre-existing notions about the characteristics of papers at particular score categories. The results of the study also suggest that raters found it difficult to make reliable comparisons among different forms and modes of writing. Finally, in this study, differences in the training process among the three groups may also have influenced the ways raters evaluated the papers.

ELEVEN

How We Assess Development in Writing

Introduction

The developmental history of written language . . . poses enormous difficulties for research. As far as we can judge from the available material, it does not follow in a single direct line in which something like a clear continuity of forms is maintained. Instead, it offers the most unexpected metamorphoses, that is, transformations of particular forms of written language into others. . . . This means that, together with processes of development, forward motion, and the appearance of new forms, we can discern processes of curtailment, disappearance, and reverse development of old forms at each step. The developmental history of written language among children is full of such discontinuities. Its line of development seems to disappear altogether; then suddenly, as if from nowhere, a new line begins, and at first it seems that there is absolutely no continuity between the old and the new. But only a naive view of development as a purely evolutionary process involving nothing but the gradual accumulation of small changes and the gradual conversion of one form into another can conceal from us the true nature of these processes.

L.S. Vygotsky,
Mind in Society 1978

Parents, teachers, and evaluators, taking what Vygotsky calls "a naive view of development," often expect students to evolve steadily in their ability to produce a successful piece of writing on a test, as measured by a holistic, analytic, or primary trait scoring system. Many expect smooth progression toward mastery of whatever criteria have been established. Instead, some students—even able ones—perform inconsistently on writing tests, earning high scores one semester and lower ones the next. Or the scores remain the same. Either condition is dismaying, for the evidence of the score seems to indicate either that no development has taken place or that the students have gotten worse. However, it is necessary to look beyond the score to determine what is happening.

We can see how problems in the interpretation of the meaning of scores originate: 1) tasks in successive assessments may not be of equivalent difficulty; 2) the rating standards may vary with different sets of readers from assessment to assessment; 3) the student writers themselves may be "off" in their performance for a variety of individual and contextual reasons. Any single one of these conditions may cause an apparent—but misleading— discrepancy in the score comparisons from one assessment to the next. In fact, in every form of measurement of educational progress, there are potential sources of error in the test situation. This is why every responsible evaluator insists on using several indicators of development, with formal tests of any type being only one of these.

Aside from the fallibility of the tests we use to measure development, there is the complexity of the human beings that we are trying to describe by our simple measures of performance. For example, when looking at pieces of writing from two students addressing the same writing task, one may see marked differences in accomplishment. One student's writing could be well-organized, fluent, and technically perfect, but utterly bland, unoriginal, and inconsequential in its handling of the subject. The other paper could show some organizational problems, some odd losses of fluency, and several types of mechanical errors, but it could also offer imaginative flashes in use of language and a fresh perspective on the subject. What may have happened is that the first student adopted a low-risk strategy, interpreting or *constructing* the task in such a way as to set for himself an easier job to accomplish than the other student who may have set for himself a much more complex task. The student writer, to a large extent, defines the difficulty level of the writing task he undertakes regardless of the test maker's intention.

Some students, such as the second of our examples, seem to adopt strategies that put them at risk in an assessment situation where surface fluency is prized. In attempting a more difficult *task construction*, the student may actually be striving to achieve a new level of communicative competence, to achieve more than he has heretofore attempted. So a holistic score, which records a general impression of overall achievement, may seem to indicate no improvement or even retrogression, masking the real advances the student is making. A closer analysis of the student's vocabulary, conceptual design, and level of abstraction might reveal that he had actually progressed from an easier to a more difficult form of writing.

We come then to several questions about the measurement of progress in writing:

1. How do we define progress? What approaches toward the definition of progress are currently in use?
2. How do test makers and raters define task complexity?
3. How do students define writing tasks? How do we classify student "task constructions," particularly with respect to "open" topics?
4. Are changes in student task constructions at different grade levels reflected in holistic scores?

Definitions of Progress in Writing

If we are to assess progress in writing, we must have some notion of what constitutes progress. But the minute we begin to attempt to identify specific indicators, we are caught up in a welter of confusing theories and counter claims. The field lacks consensus on what terms to use to describe the various dimensions of development in writing.

Linguistic Definitions

A favorite means of measuring the growth of "maturity" in writing has been to use a quantitative approach—that is, to report gains in clause length, and T-unit length over a period of time. Lester Faigley (1980) claims that descriptions of *growth* of *fluency* and *complexity*, as derived from these syntactic measures, are highly problematic because they are indefinite, imprecise terms that obscure a number of subtle and complicated issues. For example, *length*, considered apart from content or complexity, is a misleading criterion. Faigley observes that excessive clause length is one characteristic of the bureaucratic style and that it is easy to turn a virtue into an absurdity. He quotes Kinneavy as warning that "we should sense when syntactic maturity becomes syntactic senility" (p. 294). As Faigley reminds us,

> Counts of T-unit length and clause length tell us nothing about a writer's skill in executing rhetorical strategies. These measures are based on concepts from grammars designed to study one sentence at a time. Sentence grammars are capable of yielding cumulative data characterizing an individual text, making possible certain relative stylistic judgments such as Hunt's normative scale of syntactic maturity. But many features of written discourse remain that sentence grammars cannot describe. (p. 298)

A basic problem of the T-unit measure of maturity in writing is that it is insufficiently complex because it neglects to take meaning into account as it is conveyed through propositional structures appropriate to a particular communicative context. Faigley also considers it necessary to account for the effect of discourse type (e.g. a technical report) on the structure of discourse before we can really devise an adequate notion of "maturity."

When we write, we use a great variety of identifiable structures. When we move beyond individual words to patterns, we are in the realm of grammar. We can then note such units of structure as paragraphs, sentences, clauses, phrases. When such elements are identified, we can perform a number of calculations, beginning with counting the number of words in the structure, the number of particular types of clauses, and so forth. The problem is to determine which features signal growth. Because the practice of using the sentence as a unit of analysis creates problems, Hunt (1965) and Loban (1963) devised the T-unit and the index of subordination to measure the development of student ability to control the writing system.

Although findings from these earlier studies are still important and influential, they did not take into account the full context of communication nor the effect of discourse mode on text type. Several more recent studies—San Jose (1972), Perron (1977), Crowhurst and Piche (1979)—found that mode of discourse affects syntactic density and complexity, with argumentation producing longer clauses and T-units. The studies of Faigley (1980) and of Cooper and Watson (1980) have called attention to the fact that knowledge about increase in T-unit length or clause length is not enough. We need to know more about the kinds of structures that make up these units in order to create an adequate description of development of competence at the level of syntax. There are differences in the ways fourth graders, twelfth graders, and college level students use various sentence features. For example, Cooper and Watson (1980, pp. 43–44) found that although there were similarities in the use of structures within sentences, there also were some differences, most notably in the use of free modifiers in all positions—initial, medial, and final.

Cognitive Definitions

Psychologists such as Piaget, Vygotsky, and Bruner have all made substantial and enduring contributions to our understanding of the general course of human intellectual development. Writing theorists such as Moffett and Britton have made important additions to these psychological theories in their accounts of the development of writing. We have already presented some features of their theories in Chapter 6, but a few additional details are relevant here.

Moffett's Progression of Writing Development.　In *Active Voice* (1981), James Moffett provides a series of assignments arranged "according to basic communication structure and principles of verbal and conceptual growth" (p. 11). This framework should prove useful both to teachers and evaluators in designing assignments appropriate to different types of students at their various stages of development. The main progressions of development in writing are as follows:

Main Progression of Development in Writing
(From Moffett, 1981)

1. From vocal speech and unuttered speech to private writing to public writing.
2. From dialogues and monologues to letters and diaries to first-person narratives to third-person narratives to essays of generalization to essays of logical operation.
3. From an intimate to a remote audience.
4. From vernacular improvisation to literary composition.
5. From immediate subject of small time-space scope to remote subjects far flung in time and space.
6. From recording (drama) to reporting (narrative) to generalizing (exposition) to theorizing (argumentation).
7. From perception to memory to ratiocination.
8. From present to past to potential.
9. From chronology to analogy to tautology. (pp. 11–12)

In presenting his assignments, Moffett makes clear that the sequence is not linear, but spiral. He comments on how easy it is to say that "growth goes from informal to formal, personal to impersonal, and lower to higher abstraction, but it is not easy to know what these progressions really mean . . ." (p. 12). Moffett is careful to explain that this progression does not necessarily mean that formal or more impersonal or more abstract writing is better.

> The goal of writing through such a spectrum is not to "come out on top" but to be able to play the whole range. As applied to abstraction, "higher" and "lower" are not value terms but refer, rather, to stages of symbolizing that people progress through as they become *able,* but not *obliged,* to discourse at further removes from the here-and-now. I've tried to show that every stage of writing has its own value and that writers of whatever maturity return to earlier stages over and over. (p. 12)

Britton's Model of Writing Development.   In Chapter 6, we also presented Britton's model of writing development which describes a progression from immature *expressive* forms to the mature *transactional* and *poetic* functions. Britton subdivides transactional writing into the *informative* and the *conative.* The later is further subdivided into *regulative* and *persuasive* discourse. Britton acknowledges Moffett's scheme as the origin of his more elaborate informative category, which accounts for increasing levels of abstraction, beginning with *record* at the lowest level. The next stages follow as *report, generalized narrative, low-level analogic, analogic, speculative, tautologic.*

Writing is of different kinds and it serves different functions in Britton's view. And each of these functions is a different stance adopted by a writer to address a specific purpose before a particular audience. Britton (1975) says,

> We found it unsatisfactory, certainly, that studies of development could be undertaken which paid no attention to differences in writing tasks; or that examination papers could be set which assessed the performance of writers without distinguishing between the framing of argument or the recounting of an anecdote. (p. 138)

Thus, writing tasks should be set for real purposes and real readers. Growth in writing, according to Britton's scheme, means searching for personal meanings through the opportunity to confront a full range of functions and purposes in school writing.

Freedman and Pringle's Study of Writing Development in College.   Freedman and Pringle (1980b) undertook a long-term project to study development in writing in the college years. They collected papers written in the last year of high school (grade 13 in Ontario) and in the third year of the university in four disciplines: English literature, history, geography, and biology. To analyze their collection of papers, Freedman and

Pringle used three instruments to determine growth: a syntactic measure, a rhetorical scale, and a cognitive measure. The rhetorical instrument was

> based, broadly, on the well-known Diederich instrument of evaluation and is similar to many other such measures widely used. . . . In our study, this 'current-traditional rhetorical' instrument was used primarily to reveal how closely students were able to accommodate their writing to the norms of formal expository prose and to indicate whether there was a growth in such rhetorical ability over the years.

> The criteria specified on the rhetorical instrument included, originally, the following: unity, organization, development (that is, use of supporting detail), overall stylistic effectiveness, register (degree of formality), vocabulary range, vividness, economy, and coherence. (pp. 315–316)

On the cognitive scale, an index of levels of abstracting, Freedman and Pringle (1980b) attempted to characterize elements of composition usually omitted from accounts of development in writing: ". . . those features relating to the complexity of the task undertaken and indicating thus the nature of the intellectual processes of the writer" (p. 316).

Freedman and Pringle's (1980b) scale is applied to the discourse as a whole, not just to sentences or T-units. Their scale was based on Britton's modification of Moffett's scale of progression in abstraction (record, report, generalizing narrative, low-level analogic, analogic, speculative tautologic). Freedman and Pringle dropped the first level, *record*, that appears in the other two scales because they could find no instances of it in their own sample. So their scale begins with *report* and then moves up the scale to *commentary*, a mid-level category they had to add between the report and generalizing categories in the original Moffett/Britton versions. The next levels up are *first-level generalization* and then *second-level generalization*. A summary of the characteristics of Freedman and Pringle's (1980b, 318–319) levels of abstracting follows in Table 11.1.

Freedman and Pringle (1980b) found: (1) Rhetorical criteria are most important in determining the grade on the essay, if other criteria are held constant. (2) Of rhetorical criteria, development and use of supporting detail were the most important. (3) There was no significant relationship between level of abstraction and grade. (4) Rhetorical criteria did not correlate with level of schooling. (5) Level of abstraction did correlate significantly with level of schooling.

The authors explained these findings by suggesting that in the traditional model of composition teaching, rewards by grades are distributed on the basis of the rhetorical criteria of development: organization, unity, coherence, appropriate language. This model seems to ignore the cognitive features of the writing as reflected in the levels of abstraction attempted by the writer. Freedman and Pringle noted that the university essays gave substantial evidence of higher level cognitive processes, yet they were not better

Table 11.1.
Cognitive Scale: Index of Levels of Abstracting
(Based on Freedman & Pringle, 1980b)

Level	Characteristics
Second-Level Generalization	Includes classifications of classifications; generalizations about generalizations; conceptual units ordered under a larger framework.
First-Level Generalization	Generalizations organize the body of data. Has logical or argumentative structure.
Commentary	Has organizational structure of the report but also has occasional or frequent generalizations.
Report (based on données or given material)*	Retrospective presentation of scenes, events, data, but no generalization. Organization is chronological, or spatial, not logical. Related to base material.*

*The données, or given base material, for reports in the study were experience (including experience as structured in a biology lab), a literary object (which has its own internal order that is not the order of discursive thought), and classifications (whose internal order is the order of logic and discursive thought). The authors note that differences in the nature of the primary data for writing may itself be an index of the cognitive difficulty of the task, but that we do not yet have the evidence to tell whether, for example, it is more difficult to abstract from unstructured experience than from classification with established logical orders. (pp. 318–319)

than the high school essays with respect to rhetorical strategies such as organization, development, coherence, and the like. Freedman and Pringle observed that this seeming lack of rhetorical control in the university essays might be related to the fact that a cognitively more difficult task was undertaken. They commented: "The breakdown of rhetorical and grammatical skills that accompanies attempts at more complex tasks has been noted by a number of researchers and theorists" (p. 321). They further noted: "The fact that there has been no growth in rhetorical skills thus relates directly to the increasing complexity of the writing tasks engaging these students. It is quite simply more difficult to write when the task is more intellectually taxing" (p. 322).

With respect to teachers' evaluation of essays, Freedman and Pringle (1980b) later concluded:

. . . teachers seem to be looking horizontally across the grade without a vertical sense of each student's development, and certainly without a sense of the complex nature of such development, in which growth in one dimension may entail momentary awkwardness in others. The growing awareness of how writing abilities develop had not yet been assimilated into the evaluative structures of at least that body of teachers taking part in our study (p. 322).

Intellectual Processes as Measures of Development.

Another important effort to define cognitive indicators in the development of writing is Odell's (1977) scheme of measuring changes in intellectual processes. Odell believes that the identification of intellectual processes enables the evaluator to achieve three objectives: "making qualitative distinctions between pieces of writing done in the same mode and for the same audience; diagnosing writing problems; measuring growth in writing" (p. 121). In identifying and using intellectual processes as measures of progress in writing, Odell (1977) makes three assumptions:

1. A relatively small number of intellectual processes involved in thinking will allow us to describe much of what goes on.
2. We can identify linguistic cues in the surface structure of language that will help us identify what processes are in use.
3. To improve the writing of students we need to know how they are currently functioning and what processes they are currently using. (p. 108)

Odell presents an elaboration of the mental processes identified by Pike along with examples of the linguistic markers of these processes. The six processes are *focus, contrast, classification, change, physical context,* and *sequence.* As recounted by Odell, Pike's argument for selecting these particular mental processes proceeds as follows: In order to think and respond to any phenomenon, we must *focus* on distinct units of experience. After focusing on some chunk of experience, we must then perform certain operations to understand it. One of these operations is *contrast,* knowing what a thing is and is not. As we think of differences between two entities, so must we think of likenesses—what goes with what—or *classifications.* We must also have an understanding of the nature of changes these things undergo and of how *physical context* influences our awareness and our feelings. And finally, because order also gives meaning to things, we need to know their *sequence* (pp. 108–120).

Odell (1972) provides a theoretical procedure for describing growth and applies it to two pieces of writing in which quality seems directly related to the number of intellectual processes that are employed by the writer. Odell's scheme is too complex to report in full detail here, so we will cite only one example of his procedure—the mental process of making a *contrast* (pp. 111–113), which operates when we make distinctions signalled by such linguistic cues as

(1) *Connectors* (or, nor, but, instead, however, etc.);
(2) *Comparative* and *Superlative Forms* (more/most, -er/-est);
(3) *Negatives* (no, not, without, none, etc.);
(4) *Negative affixes* (anti-, -il, -less, a-, un-, etc.);
(5) *Lexicon* (noun, verb, adjective, and adverb forms of such words as "contrast, paradox, distinction, difference," and their synonyms). (Abridged from p. 112)

In examining a piece of student writing, Odell sorts through it to identify all the linguistic markers of the mental process of *contrast*. Then, in turn, he lists the markers of the other five mental processes. Progressing from *focus* to *contrast* to *classification* and so on, Odell develops a profile of the mental processes that are evident on the basis of his specific markers. For the two essays he analyzed in this fashion, Odell claimed that "the quality of the essay seemed to be directly related to the number of intellectual processes reflected in the essay" (p. 130). Odell's goal is to be able to make accurate and useful descriptive statements about the students' present writing with the intent that these observations would have import for appraising students' later writings.

Odell's Features of Mature Writing.   In a later article, Odell (1983) associates maturity in writing with maturity in thinking. He suggests that mature thought, "decentered" thought, is reflected in writing when the writer recognizes the difference between the audience and himself. Drawing on the psychological theories of Piaget and William Perry (see the last section of this Chapter), Odell describes how this recognition is manifested in writing when the writer:

1. provides an appropriate context for his/her statements;
2. bases his/her arguments on values the audience is likely to share. (p. 104)

Some other features of mature writing might show an author trying to:

1. anticipate and respond to objections/questions the audience is likely to have;
2. recognize the legitimacy as well as the limitations of other points of view on a given subject;
3. acknowledge, where appropriate, the limitations of his/her own point of view;
4. recognize the complexity of the subject at hand, attending to more than one feature of an experience. (p. 105)

In defining maturity in writing, Odell (1983) emphasizes how risky it is to draw conclusions from a single piece of writing. He says, ". . . a writer's performance can vary widely from task to task. People who think and write with some maturity in one context may not do so in other contexts" (p. 105). He points out another difficulty: recognizing egocentrism in writing is not as straightforward as marking T-units, and our definition may have to vary according to the kind of writing one is doing (pp. 106–107). But whatever the difficulties, Odell suggests we need to continue to devise studies that help us to refine our definitions of cognitive maturity in writing.

Bereiter and Scardamalia's Conception of Levels of Progress in Writing.   In Chapter 6, we described Bereiter and Scardamalia's (1981) theory of the process of writing and their strategies for aiding students to generate content suitable for their own purposes. Here we consider Bereiter and Scardamalia's (1983) developmental theory of learning to write. This theory distinguishes between two levels of progress in writing: the "high road" and the "low road" to development and use of mental capacity in writing. They based their generalizations on their four-year study of how children acquire the abilities to handle the complexities of prose composition. They have analyzed the problems of learning to write as problems of learning how to convert the collaborative language production system of conversation into the self-sustaining language production system of writing.

Bereiter and Scardamalia (1983) asked, "Does learning to write have to be so difficult?" They suggest the answer lies in which road the writer takes, the "high road" or the "low road" toward competence. On the high road, writing is always difficult because the writer sets goals just beyond present levels. Bereiter and Scardamalia state,

> The task of writing is not fixed but is very much what the writer makes it. People for whom writing keeps getting harder are people who keep reformulating the task into one of increasingly complex demands. . . . The high road is characterized by struggling to master the art of writing in all its complexities . . ., [while] the low road is characterized by striving to avoid or minimize the burden of these same complexities. (pp. 22–23)

The high road requires different allocations of energy and mental capacities. Bereiter and Scardamalia (1983) believe that children on the high road start to think about what they are writing down as related to other things in their minds. Therefore,

> attending to this relationship . . . in a very important sense reconstitutes the whole task. Writing becomes a task of representing meaning rather than a task of transcribing language. . . . To focus on this relationship is to use writing as a way of advancing one's own thinking and this transforms the task radically . . . Individual children on the high road keep incorporating new relational considerations into the writing task and thus keep re-constituting the task at a higher, more complex level. (pp. 25–26)

Bereiter and Scardamalia (1983) characterize the students on the low road to writing competence as initially having their mental energy taken up with the mechanics of the process—that is, all of the lower level skills involved in transcribing. But eventually, transcription becomes less of a problem, and the next obstacle to fluent writing—the generation of content—looms large. During this period in the middle years, students seize on any device that aids them in generating content. When this problem has been overcome, the next one—rambling—emerges, which is symptomatic of lack of overall rhetorical purpose and plan. Other obstacles also continue to hamper low road students. It should be noted that high road students encounter many of the same obstacles also—audience, organization, purpose—but they handle them differently, usually unifying them into a coherent task construction. Bereiter and Scardamalia (1983) identify a common low road strategy as "knowledge telling:" "Executing a writing task, then, consists essentially of selecting a [mental] file appropriate to the task and telling what is in it" (p. 29). The procedure consists mainly of providing a string of items drawn from the "file" and commenting on them. In contrast, the high road strategy begins with analysis and elaboration of the rhetorical problem; and, from a variety of "files," the writer draws knowledge that is reported in such a way as to accomplish the rhetorical purpose.

Bereiter and Scardamalia (1983) consider low road writing to be limiting, even though it doesn't necessarily produce bad writers:

> Low road writing is used to communicate thoughts and knowledge, but it serves at most a clerical role in the development of thought and knowledge. High road writing, on the other hand, plays a central role in mental life. Because it is such a massive integrative process and because its dimensions reflect the dimensionality of intellect itself, writing becomes for many people the organizing force in their mental development. (p. 31)

In concluding their analysis of the two roads of development in writing, Bereiter and Scardamalia "guess" that over 90% of students are on the low road. They aver that success in shifting students to the high road would require radical reforms in teaching, along lines developed by Donald Graves (1983), especially his use of "conferencing" (pp. 32–33).

Affective and Moral Definitions.   Writing theorists and researchers generally have not attempted to study the development of feeling and moral stance in writing. Wilkinson, et al. (1980) is one investigator who has looked at these elements through his multi-dimensional study of development. Recently other scholars (Newkirk, 1983; Hays, 1983; Bizzell, 1984) have taken an interest in applying Perry's (1968) model of intellectual and ethical development in the college years to college level writing. The work of these scholars is summarized in the following sections.

The Crediton Project Multi-Dimension Model of Writing Development.   The Crediton Project, an important multi-dimensional study of the development of writing, was conducted by Wilkinson, Barnsley, Hanna, & Swan (1980) in Crediton, Devon (U.K.), 1978–1980. Wilkinson and his associates studied the development of written language of children 7–14 on four planes–cognitive, affective, moral, and stylistic. Four compositions–narrative, autobiographical, explanatory, and argumentative–were requested from three classes of about 30 children each at ages 7, 10, and 13 in the context of their usual lessons over a period of three months. The cooperating teachers set no time limits and responded to questions during the writing session as they normally did. The same four writing tasks were given to each group and the results were compared according to models for the analysis of writing—representing each of the four planes. We will summarize some of the main points which the researchers used to describe the stages of development reached by many of the 13-year-olds.

Because so many analyses of development consider linguistic features and do not take into account the developing child, the Crediton Project researchers decided to encompass other dimensions. They were interested in the nature of thought (cognition), feeling (affect), moral stance, and style. Hence they constructed four models of these areas to guide analysis. The project report (Wilkinson, et al., 1980) presents lengthy descriptions of each model along with examples, but space limits us to present only the brief version given in the Introduction to the Project:

Crediton Project Models of Development
(From Wilkinson, et al., 1980)

Cognitive. The basis of this model is a movement from an undifferentiated world to a world characterized by mind, from a world of instances to a world related by generalities and abstractions.

Affective. Development is seen as being in three movements—one towards a greater awareness of self, a second towards a greater awareness of neighbor as self [This occurs when the sense of others increases and combines with a good self-image to enable one to love others, e.g, Christ's vision of "loving thy neighbor as thyself"]; a third towards an inter-engagement of reality and imagination.

Moral. "Anomy" or lawlessness gives way to "heteronomy" or rule by fear of punishment, which in turn gives way to "socionomy" or rule by a sense of reciprocity with others which finally leads to the emergence of "autonomy" or self-rule.

Stylistic. Development is seen as the making of choices in relation to a norm of the simple, literal, affirmative sentence which characterizes children's early writing. Features such as structure, cohesion, verbal competence, syntax, reader awareness, sense of appropriateness, undergo modification. (pp. 2–3)

Wilkinson et al. (1980) discussed the complexity of selecting writing tasks to elicit a broad sample of abilities. They recognized the necessity of sampling more than one type of writing because "Language performance is to some extent situation specific" (p. 84). These researchers also were aware of the problems of specifying audience and decided that the "well-worn 'Write a letter to a friend' invitation fools nobody, least of all the child who knows that what he would write for a real friend is not for teacher's eyes" (p. 85). They decided that there could be only four audience conditions that are "real" to a child in the classroom: child to teacher as trusted adult; child to peer group; child as an "expert" (on how to . . .) to known layman, and child to a wider public of children, teachers, parents and so on. Yet they were also aware that ". . . the younger children might simply ignore the signals and write for 'self' or 'teacher as trusted adult' on all four tasks. When the researcher or teacher specifies fully how a topic is to be dealt with, leaving little for the writer to decide, it is difficult to know what the writer's actual sense of audience might be. Therefore, the researchers left both content and purpose in at least two of the topics provided.

Wilkinson and his associates are quite definite about the impossibility of comparing writing elicited by different tasks:

> If the question of what constitutes development in writing is to be answered, it is important that children at different age levels be presented with the same tasks: an autobiographical anecdote by a thirteen year old cannot be compared with an explanation for a process from an eleven year old: the tasks tap different types of linguistic, stylistic, cognitive, moral and affective considerations on the part of the writer. . . . The language acts have to be directly comparable. Research in this area is needed. (p. 90)

Wilkinson (1983) presents a selection of the findings of the project with regard to development in the biographical-narrative and explanatory modes, but he cautions about generalizing from these data:

Crediton Project Findings
(Abridged from Wilkinson, 1983)

Seven-year-olds.

Style. Short compositions with an additive structure, often incomplete. Traditional story openings like "Once upon a time." Chronological organization. Locational markers often omitted. Cohesive devices limited to *and, so, then.* Mode spoken rather than written.

Affective mode. Does not express feelings directly but emotional states may be inferred. Often egocentric, though *he* or *she* may be used instead of *I.* May have insufficient language control to realize what they wish to say.

Ten-year-olds

Style. May write coherent compositions organized on a temporal principle with more audience awareness. Have become fond of details but insufficiently selective. A variety of openings and endings observed. More confident use of pronouns rather than repeated nouns.

Affective mode. May express more feeling but doesn't show high level of awareness of feeling. Can assess dispositions of other people and represent these in dialog. Can choose elements of environment for significance in stimulating emotional impulse. Moves easily into fantasy or wish fulfillment.

Thirteen-year-olds

Style. Significant stylistic development showing deliberate organization. Can insert flashbacks or glances forward into chronological order. Increased verbal competence showing an awareness of connotations of words in contexts. Cohesive devices more sophisticated.

Affective mode. Show marked development over ten-year-olds. Many show awareness of complexity of emotions in selves and empathy for feelings of others. Can characterize people in terms of speech and actions. Beginning to show environmental factors, social and physical, that are significant in stimulating emotion. Beginning to know own feelings, and to come to terms with world of reality and world of imagination. (pp. 83–84)

According to the cognitive model devised by these researchers, two dimensions of development emerge. One dimension encompasses the amount of information children can handle as they move from partial accounts to full details, e.g., an explanation of the rule system for a game. In the other dimension they move toward greater objectivity. While younger writers may place themselves in a game, seeing it from the viewpoint of, say, the goal keeper, older ones can stand back, taking a more comprehensive view. They see the game as a system rather than as a single instance of behavior (Wilkinson, 1983, pp. 84–85).

Wilkinson, et al., (1980) offer their models of development only tentatively. However, they feel that their multidimensional model is an advance over the Britton model, which is largely cognitive and does not take into account either affective and moral development or style. Wilkinson, et al., (1980) are seeking ways of making more comprehensive appraisals of progress toward maturity that are more fully descriptive than those models of development in writing which attend to fewer dimensions of growth.

Perry's Forms of Intellectual and Ethical Development in College.   Our account of the literature on the study of writing development would be incomplete without at least brief mention of the interest just now emerging in applying Perry's *Forms of Intellectual and Ethical Development in the College Years: A Scheme* (1968) to composition research (Newkirk, 1983; Hays, 1983; Bizzell, 1984).

William G. Perry, Jr. was head of the Harvard Bureau of Study Counsel when he conducted a four-year, longitudinal study which showed how undergraduate Harvard men progressed through nine intellectual/philosophical stages (1968). His study, based on annual interviews, suggests that the college experience elicits new kinds of cognitive development in a regular, identifiable sequence. Perry's developmental model, expressed in terms of the student's attitude toward schoolwork, describes movement through three major "world views," each with three substages. These three world views are—*Dualism, Relativism,* and *Commitment in Relativism.* The foling composite account draws on Newkirk (1983), Hays (1983), and Bizzell (1984) in its summary of the three main positions along Perry's developmental scale.

Scale of Intellectual and Ethical Development
(Based on Newkirk (1983), Hays (1983) and Bizzell (1984))

Duality. In this first stage, the student views the world in terms of absolutes, either/or terms. The student Dualist works hard and is obedient. Education is a process of finding right answers with the help of the teacher as authority. Knowing the world means memorizing the absolutes and applying them in individual instances. The Dualist doesn't know whether he has learned something until the test is returned. The Dualist resists exploring problems without one right solution and prefers disciplines which supply quantified answers.

Relativism. In the second major stage, Dualism gives way to Relativism. Absolutes are either unknowable or they no longer exist. Dualism cannot account for the pluralism of the university where students differ in beliefs, authorities disagree, and professors even occasionally admit confusion. Since right answers do not exist, education for the Relativist is a process of devising persuasive answers. The Relativist discovers "qualitative contextual relativistic reasoning." The Relativist now insists there are a number of sides to every issue, or even that everyone has a right to his own opinion. The Relativist prefers courses where problems abound and where teachers do not stand on their authority.

Commitment in Relativism. In the third major stage, Relativism extends to include Commitment. The world is still without absolutes and authority, but it does have order and one can take responsibility for making choices in contexts. Commitments derived from knowing one's world of family, friends, religious and ethnic traditions, and intellectual interests guide the choices of values that will order one's life. The Committed Relativist makes judgments about what is better or worse for himself while realizing other people who have sufficiently examined their own values may employ different but valid standards of judgment. For the Committed Relativist, education is now a process of discovering, with a mentor teacher, the contingent knowledge necessary for making commitments.

These are the basic developing world views resulting from exposure to the multiple perspectives of a four-year liberal-arts education. Students typically pass through the cycle in this order, sometimes pausing or backtracking. Each world view shapes value judgments about family, politics, religion, intellectual interest and so forth.

In a very thoughtful analysis of Perry's scheme Patricia Bizzell (1984) reminds us that it

charts the creation of not just any intellectually and ethically mature adult, but precisely "the liberally educated man," a man (or woman) "who has learned to think about even his own thoughts, to examine the way he orders his data and the assumptions he is making, and to compare these with other thoughts that other men might have". (p. 450)

Essentially this is the educated man that emerges from Harvard's pedagogy of pluralism. Bizzell says Perry acknowledges this as a conditioning factor in his results and that he does not claim universality for them. But according to Bizzell, Perry does argue in favor of "this particular education-induced development," and he implies that other colleges ought to follow suit (p. 450).

Bizzell (1984) notes how easy it is to match typical kinds of student essays to positions in Perry's scheme. But she believes that much more research is needed before we can use Perry's scheme to classify student writing:

> We do not know to what extent Perry's scheme can extend its explanatory power across a variety of student abilities, academic preparation, and college experiences. . . . Perry provides no timetable for progress through his scheme. . . . The existence of these gaps in our knowledge of the scheme's application to student writing argues against using the scheme to classify student writing in any detailed way. (p. 451)

Newkirk (1983) does not share Bizzell's concern about the limits of applicability of Perry's scheme. A professor of English at the University of New Hampshire, Newkirk says that Perry's model defines the effect of a liberal education on many of the students who attend a state university even more closely than on students who attend Harvard: "the ones in Willie Morris' words, 'with good minds and small-town high school diplomas' " (Newkirk, 1983, p. 11). Newkirk says that Perry helps locate the writing course at the center of liberal education. Bizzell might agree with this point, since she does consider Perry's work useful in helping college writing teachers understand why differences occur in student writing, provided they do not apply his classification scheme too rigidly:

> Perry's greatest use to writing teachers is to provide us with a sort of philosophical map of the changes liberal education seeks to induce in our students. Such a map can help us understand that certain typical problems students have with writing in college should be regarded as problems with accepting the academic community's preferred world view, and not necessarily as problems of achieving 'normal' cognition. (p. 452)

What Perry does, essentially, is provide a picture of the kind of "cultural literacy" required in a liberal arts college, showing the ways of thinking that one must master to participate in this kind of community. In the college community, learning to write means passing through stages of abstracting and distancing, such as those portrayed by Moffett, until one can learn to think about one's own thinking.

Janice N. Hays (1983) sees Perry's model as tracing "the moves from simple and concrete to complex, abstract thinking, the ability to 'conceptualize about concepts' " (p 130). She thinks that if Perry's scheme has validity, it ought to be evident in the development of student writing. And if it is evident, it has "profound implications for the sequences and methods with which we teach writing" (p. 130). To test the applicability of Perry's scheme to writing, Hays collected the papers from most of the students enrolled in freshman writing seminars at Skidmore College, New York, in the spring of 1978. She also collected the papers of a smaller number of advanced students (at junior, senior, and graduate levels). For the purposes of her discussion, she selected 12 excerpts, "each typical of the student's entire paper and also representative of numbers of student responses. . . . All papers were written upon one of two topics [texts not given] involving identical rhetorical situations" (p. 130).

Hays (1983) discusses each of the 12 excerpts selected to sample freshman level to graduate level writing. Comparing early and late papers in this academic sequence for T-unit length, discourse structure, elaboration of argument, and sophistication of diction, Hays (1983) finds an identifiable sequence:

> Writers first construct "arguments" using flat, simplistic and unsupported assertions. They next . . . justify them and . . . begin slightly to qualify them and to acknowledge . . . other points of view. At the next stage . . . writers display a reasonably full recognition of multiple perspectives and some elaboration of these perspectives but lack the ability to deal with and resolve their implications. Students in this stage either simply state differing points of view or else fall back on earlier strategies. . . .

> In terms of Perry's scheme, the transition from Stage Four to Stage Five [Hays refers to sub-divisions of the main divisions given above.], from multiplicity to relativism, appears to be the most difficult shift for these student writers. Once they have made it, their writing becomes more elaborated, more qualified, more concessionary, and yet at the same time more committed to a position. Seemingly they now have the ability to work through complex realities and make judgments about them. These more mature writers can also enter into points of view other than their own and fully engage them, and they develop the ability to shape their discourse to an audience's needs. (pp. 140–141)

In her analysis of a sophomore paper, Hays commented as follows: "This ability accurately to project oneself into an imaginary situation in writing, to present ideas in ways that will be effective with one's audience, is virtually lacking in younger writers" (p. 137). What Hays may have observed here is an example of the difficulty of projecting oneself into particular types of hypothetical situations, ones that may either be too remote from the experience of the writer, or too close, too personal. For example, one topic in this study required the students to prepare a statement for an abortion panel that included a Catholic priest. To anticipate and take into account the potential response of "a Catholic priest on an abortion panel" will surely pose problems for the person without the appropriate prior knowledge to supply the expected response. It may also pose too complex a problem to grapple with under the constraints of an essay exam for the well-informed person who knows all too well the subtleties of the opinions of priests on abortion. (See Chapter 5 on the complexities of specifying audience.)

Hays thinks that the value of taking a developmental perspective is that it helps the instructor realize that "freshmen are not simply recalcitrant or stupid when they write in ways that seem so puerile and simplistic. They really are struggling to achieve a new perspective on reality." (p. 142).

Students' Definitions of Writing Tasks

At several points in our review of research, particular researchers—Bruce et al., (1978); Flower and Hayes (1980); Bereiter and Scardamalia (1983)—have described in general terms the phenomenon of the student's construction of the writing task. These researchers have suggested that some children and youths keep re-constituting the writing tasks they are given. Students do indeed interpret topics in ways not intended by topic writers, and even when they do interpret topics in the way the tester intended, they may be unable to accomplish the task for a variety of reasons: They may find the task too complex, they may be unfamiliar with the necessary rhetorical strategies for accomplishing the task, or they may simply choose to do something different. All of these factors point to the need for researchers to examine just what tasks students are, in fact, setting for themselves as they read and interpret the topic, since students' re-definition of the given rhetorical task can contribute to an apparent developmental unevenness from test to test. Consequently, it is also necessary to devise a way to define and classify students' own *task constructions*—or re-constructions—and the effects of these constructions on the discourse they ultimately produce. A closely related issue in the area of topic effects is the basic problem of classifying topics and/or the discourse they are intended to elicit. The complexities involved in attempting to produce such a description are displayed in Harpin's (1976) survey of classification systems.[1]

Systems for Classifying Writing Tasks
(Based on Harpin, 1976)

1. by content, subject matter
   (what it is about, e.g., the Dewey Decimal System of classification);
2. by form
   (poetry, prose, essay, report, etc.);

[1]See also Purves et al. (1984) for a recently developed comprehensive system for classifying writing assignments.

3. by audience
    (learned, popular, the distinctions of rhetoric);
4. by writer-audience relationship
    (Joos's account of the interrelation of language, style, and speech events and
    Moffett's schema of distance progressing from thinking to oneself to writing for
    a mass, anonymous audience);
5. by writer and task
    (creative, free, intensive, imaginative, practical, factual, recording);
6. by function, purpose, intention
    (expressive, poetic, transactional (as in Britton above); or to tell a story, to de-
    scribe a thing, to produce an emotional effect (as in Herbert Read and Bonamy
    Dobree); or the order of phenomena in space in *descriptive* writing, the order
    of phenomena in time in *historical* writing, real or fictitious; the order of
    thoughts in the mind in *expository* writing (as in H.J.C. Grierson). (pp. 38–44)

Ultimately, Harpin (1976) concluded that an almost endless series of classifications is possible: "Writing will refuse to fit into a cut and dried scheme of labels, no matter how cunningly or patiently constructed" (p. 37). What is important, Harpin says, is to select the scheme that is of greatest value in teaching—and, we might add, in assessment and research.

Part of the problem in our failure to establish reliable and useful ways of classifying writing tasks, however, may stem from the nature of traditional systems of classification themselves. Keech (1982b) argues, that most avail-able discourse classifying systems

> represent what might be called ideal text types, the products of accomplished
> adult writers rather than of students who may be only approximating these dis-
> course forms. Further, existing typologies offer three to four global categories
> which perforce must obscure almost as many differences between texts as
> they are able to identify. (p. 483)

Problems of Classifying Responses to Open Topics

Some of the problems of classifying responses to "open" topics were ad-dressed in the first phase of a developmental study (Keech, 1982b; Warantz & Keech, 1982) conducted for the Writing Assessment Project by Catharine Lucas Keech, who developed a system for classifying student texts based on an analysis of a sample of student papers collected during six years of an annual writing assessment program at a local high school in Northern Cali-fornia. The topics for the sample appear below.

Topics used in Six Years of Writing Assessment
at a High School in California

1973   Write about an event you wish you had witnessed or could
witness. The event can be real or imagined; the time of the event
can be past, present or future. Make it clear why the event is
significant to you. You may write a journal entry, letter, dialogue,
monologue, essay, story, autobiography, or other form.

1974   If you had to choose to be something other than a human being, what plant or animal or other form would you choose? In your writing, give your reader some idea of what you think it would be like to be that form, and of why you chose it. You may do this writing as a journal entry, a letter, a dialogue, a story, an autobiography, an essay, a poem, etc.

1975   If you could change places with someone else, who would it be? The person you write about can be living, dead, drawn from past or present, from books, films etc., or from your own imagination. In your writing give your reader some idea of what it would be like to be that person, and of why that life appeals to you. You may do this writing as a journal entry, character sketch, dialogue, letter, story, autobiographical essay, argument, poem, or other form.

1976   Not all inventions have been good for all humanity. Name one invention we would be better off without, and make it clear why. You may do this writing as an essay, journal, letter, story or other form.

1977   Imagine that a small group of people will be sent to colonize a new planet. Food, clothing, shelter and transportation have been provided for. You are among those asked to select a few additional things to be sent along in the limited space available in the ship. What one item would you recommend, and why? You may write your recommendation in the form of a story, a dialogue, a letter, a speech, an essay or other form.

1978   Write about some way in which your life has been, or might be influenced. You might write about the influence of another person, a book or film, an idea, or an event such as a triumph or defeat, or a sudden gain or loss. Make it clear just what or who influenced you, and what the effect was upon you, or what the effect could be upon you. You may do this writing as a journal entry, character sketch, dialogue, letter, story, autobiographical essay, or other form.

The reader will note that this assessment program used what we might call "open" topics. That is, both subject and form were left to the student's option. No attempt was made to control the nature of the response to the assignment. Each year, the instructions included a phrase which indicated that students were free to select a form for writing, and each year the specific subject was left relatively open within a general subject framework.

Additionally, the type of writing task implied by the topics varied from year to year. For example, the 1976 topic appears to call for persuasive writing, regardless of the form selected, while the 1973 topic appears to call for some sort of narrative, i.e. a recounting of an event. This effort to use a variety of open writing tasks reflects the commendable commitment of the teachers to sample performance on a range of discourse types in the curriculum, but from a measurement perspective, this degree of variability within topic and between topics would now be questioned by researchers and teachers who recognize that different writing tasks are difficult to compare in a single scoring session, and that different tasks should not be used to compare student ability from year to year. However, the sample did provide a rich source of data for the purpose of developing a taxonomy based on the diverse kinds of texts students actually create when they write in response to open topics. As they examined the papers in the sample, Warantz and Keech (1982) noted that existing classification schemes did not adequately preserve distinctions in the sample:

> Some writers chose to use a narrative "schema" (telling a story) in order to dramatize an idea. Other writers were able to express the same or similar idea, equally successfully, by using expository prose (i.e. a hierarchical arrangement of arguments in an explicit discussion). Similarly, some writers chose to reveal a character "they would like to be" by narrating a key event in that character's life. Others chose to describe the character in terms of its habitual actions. (p 518)

Thus, Keech set out to develop a new approach to task definition and classification of writing.

A Taxonomy of Student Text-Types

In order to capture the complexity of the student texts in the sample, Keech distinguished between two ways of describing a text, one in terms of its function and the other in terms of its form. In the typology that Keech developed, this distinction is expressed as "rhetorical function" and "discourse strategy."

> By rhetorical function, we mean "What does the *text* do?" How does it function for the reader?" . . . By discourse strategy, we mean "How is the text structured? What are the *means* through which a rhetorical function is achieved? What is the form of the text?" (p. 519)

Three distinct functions were identified in the sample of texts studied:

1) to "tell a story" (e.g. describe a sequence of events)
2) to "reveal an entity" (e.g. disclose the nature of an object, person or place, etc.) and
3) to "express an idea" (e.g. discuss "an idea, an abstraction, or a classification scheme"). (p. 520)

In addition, three distinct strategies were identified:

A) narration,
B) description, and
C) evaluation (commentary). (p. 520)

The researchers (Warantz & Keech, 1982) defined these three strategies as follows:

> For example, strategy A (narration) is composed of a chronological linking of "events" which form the spine of the text and through which the text is developed. Events thus serve as the "core propositions" of narrative strategy. In addition, a narration may contain a great many incidental or supportive commentary and descriptive propositions, but these are linked to individual core propositions and not to one another. Similarly, in strategy B (description), the core propositions are descriptive; commentary and event propositions provide support for the individual descriptive propositions. In strategy C (evaluation), the core propositions are commentaries; event and descriptive propositions are supportive. (p. 521)

Thus organized, the typology allowed for a distinction to be made between the purpose or aim of the text as a whole, and the strategies used to accomplish that goal.

As one would expect, certain strategies tended to occur with certain functions, e.g. function 1 (tell a story) with strategy A (narration). However, the typology also allowed the researchers to categorize essays which used different strategies to serve the same function:

> It is equally possible to reveal an entity (a character) through a dramatization of that character's life (or a key episode in that character's life) as it is to straightforwardly describe that character. Similarly, one may express an idea by "showing" that idea (through narration) or by "telling" that idea (through commentary) . . . (p. 521)

By making the distinction between function (purpose) and strategy, the researchers were able to account for a variety of ways different strategies may be used to accomplish the same purposes. It is important to note, however, that not all combinations of strategies and functions are possible in this typology. For example, as the researchers point out, it is impossible to use any strategy other than narration to accomplish the purpose of telling a story. Moreover, they indicate that there is a general pattern of co-occurrence such that more concrete strategies (e.g. narration) may be used to fulfill more abstract functions (e.g. evaluation), but that the reverse does not occur. That is, more abstract strategies are not used to fulfill less abstract functions. The commentary strategy, for example, cannot be used to fulfill any function in the typology other than to express an idea.

The researchers also report that the sample included papers which appeared to contain mixes of more than one function. Some of the texts fulfilled dual functions, such as when a story was used to reveal an entity, while in other papers, dual functions were combined with dual strategies. For example,

> Strategies can be mixed through *framing* (e.g. an evaluative introduction and code surrounding a narrative body), *shifting* (a sharp transition from one strat-

egy to another within the body of the the text), *merging* (a subtle transition, back and forth, between two strategies within the body of a text), and *integration* (where core propositions of two strategies are linked to one another, so that the text is structured in terms of the simultaneous development of the two strategies, e.g. narrative and evaluation). (p. 524)

The approach to text classification adopted by Keech et al.(1982) offers a very promising approach for future research. Categorization systems based on ideal text types generally fail to characterize adequately what students actually accomplish when they write. In this case, the categorization system was based on an examination of actual student writing. In addition, the system provided a way of describing combinations of text characteristics, a problem that is largely ignored in those systems of classification that describe prototypical texts, or those systems which categorize texts along only one dimension, e.g. form or mode, as opposed to function. Actual texts may not fit neatly into prototypical categories and they may contain a mixture of classifiable structural characteristics.

Measuring Development of Writing Ability Over Time

Earlier in this chapter and in previous chapters, we have discussed project studies which examine the issue of variability in task interpretation and execution among individual students and among different groups of participants in writing assessment episodes. In the project study now being discussed, task construction by writers at different stages in the development of their writing abilities was investigated by Keech and other project researchers. Although the data base for the study is problematic in that the attributes of the topics varied from year to year, the study, nonetheless, suggests some further confirmation of the phenomenon that various scholars (Vygotsky, 1978; Freedman & Pringle 1980b; Hayes, 1983) have observed, namely, that as writers attempt new rhetorical functions and use new strategies for structuring texts, unexpected regressions may occur at certain points in the development of their writing abilities.

We have already described the development of the typology of student texts, the first phase in the developmental study. A brief summary of the second phase of the study is provided below. For the complete report of both phases of the study, the reader is referred to the original technical reports (Keech, 1982; Warantz & Keech, 1982). A refined and expanded version of the typology and additional analyses of the data are also presented in Keech, 1984, along with case studies of several of the student writers in the sample.

The Nature of the Sample

The overall sample was drawn from papers written in response to the topics given above. Thirty papers for each grade level and year were drawn, for a total of 720 papers. Smaller sets of papers (10–12) were used for application of the typology because analysis and coding of large numbers of papers was not possible. For this aspect of the study, papers were selected from students who had been assessed during all four of their high school years. Papers were selected if the student's scores failed to progress in sequence as indicated by an adjusted quality ranking which was obtained by combining three different ratings—the original score assigned by the teachers at the times of the assessments, a second rating obtained during a pooled re-scoring of all the essays in the sample drawn for the study, and the results of a "forced-choice" ranking of the four papers produced by each student. Problematical cases were eliminated, such as particularly capable students whose performance was consistently high (whose papers were difficult to rank order) and very low ability writers (whose papers exhibited scribal difficulties or contained very little text), and other problematical cases such as students who had written poetry. The sub-sample to which the typology was applied consisted of 240 papers. Further details about the sample selection procedures are available in the original technical report.

The Limitations of the Sample

The researchers formulated their research questions on the basis of available data, which consisted of an extensive series of papers that had been collected over a six-year period. The six-year series of topics in the available data had been developed without the strict controls for unexpected topic effects that must be applied in the topic design stage in order to be able to compare student performance on *different* topics. Thus, although it was possible to make comparisons among the four different grade levels in any *one* year—because the topic for that year was the same for all grade levels—or to make comparisons among the grade levels for all six years combined, it was not possible to draw definitive conclusions about changes in student task construction over time because the topics differed from year to year. The conclusions that could be drawn from this study were limited also because parts of the analysis were based on very small numbers of coded papers for each yearly topic and each grade level (10–12), and for some parts of the analysis, papers were not randomly drawn.

Coding the Papers in the Sample

Training readers to code the papers in the reduced sub-sample followed typical procedures used in holistic scoring sessions: raters were trained through the discussion of anchor papers chosen as representative types. Papers from the sub-samples were then coded independently by two raters, who assigned separate codes for function and strategy. Agreement was assessed according to a minimal criterion: If raters agreed on at least one element (of strategy or function) for a given paper, then they were considered to be in agreement on that element. This method was adopted in order to make a distinction between the most salient text functions and strategies and the least salient text characteristics. For example, if one rater coded a particular paper as having dual functions (e.g. to "tell a story" and to "reveal an entity") while another rater coded it as having a single function (e.g. to "tell a story,") then the function "tell a story" was considered the primary function of that paper. In cases of disagreement between the two raters, papers were assigned to a third independent rater for coding. When discrepancies could not be resolved by the third raters, such papers were assigned a code to indicate that they were unclassifiable according to the typology for either function or strategy or both. Sixty discrepancies occurred in coding for function and/or strategy. Of these, 49 were resolved by a third reader, and 11 were coded as unclassifiable for either function or strategy or both. The reported results for analyses of the reduced sub-sample are based on coded papers where raters were in agreement.

Analyses of the Data

Warantz and Keech (1982) report that preferred task constructions reflect the primary types of combinations of function and strategy described above, combinations that would be expected to co-occur. The primary types were:

1) the use of the strategy of narration to "tell a story,"
2) the use of the strategy of description to "reveal an entity," and
3) the use of the strategy of evaluation (commentary) to "express an idea."

Preferred task constructions for each topic/year of the study are summarized in Table 11.2.

Although there appeared to be preferred task constructions for each of the topics, it should also be noted that each of the topics produced a variety of response combinations. In 1973, for example, while 43% of the students responded with the narrative primary type combination of function and strategy, 34% responded with primary type 3, i.e. the combination of the function "to express an idea" with the strategy of evaluation. Other responses to this topic were distributed over nine different categories representing other po-

Table 11.2.
Preferred Task Constructions By Topic/Year

Year	Topic	Primary Type	% of Responses
1973	"Event"	1	43
1974	"Be a non-human thing"	2	26
1975	"Be another person"	3	27
1976	"Invention"	3	60
1977	"Space object"	3	47
1978	"Influence"	3	29

Note. This table is based on data reported in Warantz & Keech (1982, p. 535).

tential combinations of functions and strategies. Thus it is apparent that students constructed their writing task in very different ways in responding to the 1973 topic. Some students treated the demand to "Write about an event you wish you had witnessed or could witness" as a directive to *identify* an event and comment on it. Other students seem to understand the topic as a directive to *recount* the event, and still other students employed different combinations of functions and strategies (Warantz & Keech, 1982, p. 532).

Variability in task interpretation existed for each of the topics above, as the figures suggest. However, it should also be noted that some topics appeared to produce fewer dominant preferences for task interpretation than others. For example, 26% of the responses to the 1974 "Be a non-human thing" topic employed the strategy of *description* to fulfill the function of "revealing an entity" while 74% of the responses contained some other combination of function and strategy. In contrast, the 1976 "Invention" topic elicited the strategy of *evaluation* (commentary) to fulfill the function of "expressing an idea" in 60% of the cases. Thus, while there was variability in the ways students constructed their tasks in responding to any particular topic, some topics appeared to produce more uniform task constructions than others.

The study also provided interesting cross-sectional and longitudinal data. Figure 11.1 plots the mean scores received by each of three longitudinal sub-sample groups from their freshman to their senior years as well as the overall mean for each topic/year. The means are based on the new scores received during the pooled rescoring mentioned above, as opposed to the old scores originally given during each assessment. Figure 11.1 provides a graphic illustration of unexpected directions of change in scores. For example, the reader may note that students in group 2 produced lower scores as seniors than as freshmen, that scores declined for group 1 between their sophomore and junior years, and that scores for group 3 declined between their junior and senior years. These drops in score are unexpected in the sense that one would ordinarily expect improvement from year to year. School administrators who equate quality ratings with the improvement of writing abilities would find such a record distressing and perhaps question the efficacy of their writing program. However, several factors may contribute to such unexpected scores apart from the quality of instruction.

One factor is the effect of the topics themselves: Some topics may elicit better writing than others, and some may be more difficult than others. Note, for example, that the lowest mean score earned by group 2 occurs in topic/year 1977, when the lowest mean score in the overall sample was also produced. This suggests that the topic itself was problematical. A similar parallel drop in score between the overall mean and the performance of a particular group occurs with group 1, between their sophomore and junior

Figure 11.1. New Score Means for Overall Sample and Individual Groups

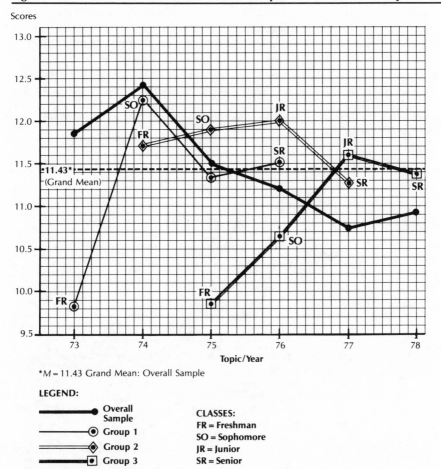

*M = 11.43 Grand Mean: Overall Sample

LEGEND:

	Overall Sample
	Group 1
	Group 2
	Group 3

CLASSES:
FR = Freshman
SO = Sophomore
JR = Junior
SR = Senior

years. The figures thus suggest that in some cases, an unexpected drop in score may be explained by topic effects.

However, topic effects are clearly not the sole contributor to such changes in scores. For example, mean scores for group 3 increase during the years 1975–78 at the same time that the mean scores for the overall sample decrease. But the mean scores for any given topic year also include the scores of randomly selected groups of students in addition to the scores of the sub-samples, and thus the scores for these groups may have been affected by sampling error. Individual differences, quality of instruction, and various factors such as distractions in the test taking environment and lack of motivation may also have contributed to changes in scores.

Obviously, various factors may influence changes in quality ratings and mean scores, but the effect of the topic is clearly an important source of variation. As Figure 11.2 indicates, the overall means for the combined grade levels in the sample show a small but steady improvement from the freshmen mean of 10.37 to the senior mean of 12.10. However, this expected pattern of improvement is not consistent within all topic years. For example, the figure shows that seniors were not consistently better than juniors. Jun-

Figure 11.2. New Score Means for each Grade Level Compared to Overall Sample Means for each Topic/Year

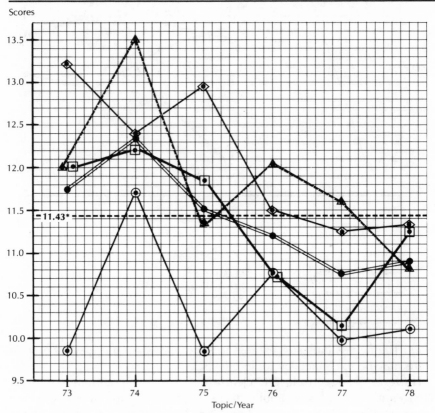

*M = 11.43 Grand Mean: Overall Sample

LEGEND:

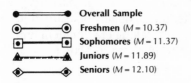

●━━━━━● Overall Sample
⊙━━━━⊙ Freshmen (M = 10.37)
▣━━━━▣ Sophomores (M = 11.37)
▲━━━━▲ Juniors (M = 11.89)
◈━━━━◈ Seniors (M = 12.10)

iors received higher mean scores than other groups in 1974, 1976, and 1977, and sophomores performed better than juniors in 1978. Thus, although the overall mean scores indicate growth with age, the data also suggest that students at different grade levels may respond differently to the same topics and that different topics may produce different manifestations of growth or lack of it.

An additional factor which may contribute to change in quality ratings from one test occasion to the next, and which is impossible to deduce from patterns of scores alone or from differences among topics per se, is task interpretation. It is possible for students to create a variety of task interpretations from the text of any given topic. If the tasks differ in complexity, or if the student has mastered one kind of task but not the other, scores may give misleading indications either of improvement or the lack of it. If students are attempting to employ new and untried rhetorical skills, or if they are attempting more difficult tasks, their scores may even seem to indicate regression with respect to the development of their writing abilities.

Examination of developmental changes in task interpretation over time was difficult in this study because the topics differed from year to year. However, some evidence from the study does suggest that students may define writing tasks differently at different stages in the development of their writing abilities, and that the nature of the change may be from more concrete to more abstract constructions of rhetorical problems. Application of the typology to the sub-sample provided data which suggest a shift in the pattern of preference by grade for particular combinations of function and strategy, a progression which tends to move from narrative strategies and functions based on experience, (primary type 1), to more abstract forms, e.g. the strategy of evaluation (commentary) used to "express an idea" (primary type 3).

The researchers report that freshmen in 1975 showed a low preference for primary type 1 (the use of narration to "tell a story") while sophomores showed a low preference for primary type 2 (the use of description to "reveal an entity"). Moreover, although the use of primary type 3 (the use of commentary to "express an idea") remained relatively constant among freshmen and sophomores (18 and 16% respectively), juniors tended to select this more abstract type more frequently (30% compared to 10% who chose primary type 2). Among seniors, the shift to the more abstract task is even more apparent for this particular topic, with 46% of the students selecting primary type 3. The figures would thus suggest a pattern of developmental progression from more concrete to more abstract formulations of rhetorical tasks.

However, the reader is cautioned to remember that these percentages are based on very small numbers of coded papers for each topic/year and grade level (10–12). Moreover, the papers were not randomly selected from the original population; they were selected only from students whose scores did not show consistent improvement from year to year. Thus it is not possible to draw conclusions from the data about developmental changes in task construction.

It should also be noted that the developmental progression suggested by the figures above did not appear for all of the topics. In fact, the progression appeared to reverse in the responses to the 1973 topic: Fewer freshmen preferred primary type 1, "tell a story" (20%), while half of them preferred primary type 3, "express an idea" (50%). Sophomores were almost equally divided between the two types (30% for primary type 1 and 40% for primary type 3). Juniors shifted even more toward a preference for primary type 1 (50% compared to 30% who chose primary type 3). Finally, seniors showed a strong preference for primary type 1 (70%) with only one student choosing primary type 3 (10%).

The response of the seniors suggests that the nature of the topic should also be considered in developmental research. Some topics appear to more strongly encourage the use of certain text types than others, and these effects may outweigh any general tendency on the part of older writers to exhibit a preference for more abstract types of text. One might also argue that seniors, as older and presumably more advanced writers, would be better able to select the mode that was most strongly cued by the topic. Thus, although one might expect that narrative would be more accessible to younger writers and thus be their preferred task construction, the results for this topic clearly demonstrate that narrative may not always be the preferred response for younger writers, even when the topic strongly cues a narrative framework.

Patterns of Task Interpretation

A number of different patterns of task intepretations appeared for each of the topics. For more complete discussions of each pattern, the reader is referred to Warantz & Keech (1982) and to Keech (1984). The description of two of the patterns should suffice here, however, to demonstrate the complexity of the issues that need to be addressed in future research of this sort. Several variables and their possible interactions will have to be examined, including age, task interpretation, topic and score. In addition, the matter of appropriateness of response must be considered. One might speculate, for example, that the seniors in 1973[2] were more successful at choosing an appropriate response to that particular topic than were the younger writers, and that their chosen response allowed them to employ a text type they presumably had mastered as well as one which was particularly appropriate to the topic. If a student chooses a text type that is familiar, mastered *and* appropriate, one would expect high scores. Conversely, if the student chooses a text type that is unfamiliar *and* unsuited to the given assignment, one would expect lower scores. Thus the student's level of mastery within particular text types also

[2]See text of topic given in list of Topics Used in Six Years of Writing Assessment p. 221.

needs to be considered, along with the appropriateness of the response to the given assignment. Evidence from this study, as well as the study reported in Chapter 9 indicates that the way a student interprets a topic can influence his or her selection of a particular text type. However, the student's sense of the appropriateness of a particular text type to the topic at hand, and his or her preference for certain text types will also influence how the task is ultimately defined.

The interplay of these variables should be examined in future research, as well as the relative difficulty of different kinds of tasks. For example, are abstract tasks (e.g. argument) inherently more difficult for writers than more concrete tasks (e.g. narrative). If so, then one would expect that students who attempt these more abstract tasks might be less likely to earn high scores than students who attempt more concrete tasks, assuming, of course, that the level of mastery is equivalent among the students who attempt the different tasks. On the other hand, if abstract tasks are not inherently more difficult, then future research should examine other factors that might contribute to difficulty. The complexity of the ideas that the student is attempting to communicate and the student's background knowledge about the subject of the topic might serve to make some abstract tasks actually less difficult than other more concrete tasks.

Problems and Limitations of Developmental Studies

The study described above is limited in terms of the conclusions that can be drawn about the effects of different variables on holistic scores. One of its limitations stems from the fact that the topics in the study—as natural data—were not designed with specific research questions in mind. The topics and the compositions written in response to them came from a school district which made its composition files available to the project for the study that was conducted. Thus the topics were not what might have been developed if the study could have been designed in advance. Given provision of long term financial support for true longitudinal studies, it should be possible to construct topics with planned characteristics and to employ them in more tightly controlled research designs so that more definitive conclusions can be drawn about the interactive effects of topic, task intepretation and age on the holistic scores students receive. Nevertheless, evidence from the study does suggest that topics do affect scores, and that as a result, mean scores may decline on subsequent annual assessments. Evidence from the study also suggests that in addition to the effects of the topic per se, scores will vary according to the way the student interprets the task (Keech, 1984).

The study is also limited, however, by the fact that it depends solely on post hoc analyses of written products. Thus it cannot provide much information about developmental process except by way of inference. One cannot really tell, for example, whether different students actually interpreted the texts of the topics in different ways. One can only infer that they may have done so since very different kinds of papers were produced in response to the same topics, a phenomenon that might have been partly the result of the very open ended instructions regarding the form of the response. Moreover, without other kinds of evidence, one cannot know whether to attribute the students' use of a particular text type to their interpretation of the constraints of the topic, to their conscious or unconscious choice of a rhetorical strategy (whether relatively untried or mastered) as a test-taking strategy, or to some combination of the two. As the data from the study suggest, some topics may elicit more uniform task interpretation than others. Until more is learned about the processes of topic interpretation and the construction of the rhetorical problem, conclusions about the relative effects of these variables cannot be made.

Clearly, post hoc analyses of products will always be limited in terms of the kind of information they can provide. It is not enough to examine only the products if one wants to gather information about the effects of processes on products. Task complexity, for example, is defined by the nature of the processes required by any particular task. Complex cognitive processes may be required to produce very simple texts, and conversely, very simple cognitive processes may produce very complex texts (Williams, 1979). Future research in this area might well be directed toward an examination of whatever differences in actual processes are required to produce different types of text. The ways these processes might be facilitated, as well as the ways new discourse types might thus be developed and mastered should also be subjects of research. Therefore, it would seem advisable to collect data on processes as well as the products they engender, and to collect such data from several sources so that conclusions drawn are more likely to be definitive.

A variety of research techniques needs to be used in order to collect data that pertain to both products *and* processes. However, one kind of research technique does not necessarily prohibit the use of another. Rather, one technique can be used to inform and/or to qualify another. The coordination of a variety of research techniques within the context of the same or similar studies might help to elucidate the relationship between products and processes, providing of course, that the limitations of each research technique are also recognized. Protocol techniques, for example, provide direct information about a process *as it occurs,* not after the fact. But with protocol analysis researchers risk interfering with and perhaps altering the very process they wish to study. Questionnaire data can also provide valuable information about students' perceptions of their writing tasks, but here too the procedure is limited. Data from memory about what *happened* may be less accurate than data collected *at the time* that it happens. Moreover, students may be influenced by the wording of the questionnaire itself in unpredictable ways. So questionnaires too are vulnerable to problems of interpretation. However, although each individual approach—product analyses, protocol analyses and the analyses of questionnaire data—may be limited, together they could constitute a powerful research tool. Each procedure provides a slightly different kind of information, which may illuminate only part of the problem, but which also provides a cross-check on the results of the other procedures—a way to validate findings.

The notion of triangulating different sources of information was described in Chapter 7 where the work of Cicourel et al. (1974) is cited as a model for this approach. By itself, any one approach will provide incomplete and probably inaccurate impressions of the data, in much the same way that the blind men who each touched a different *part* of the elephant claimed to be able to describe the *whole* elephant. Together, however, the use of multiple approaches for analysis, and the logical coordination of the results may provide us with the best picture of the whole. For the conduct of research intended to investigate the ways students interpret writing tasks as well as the ways their task constructions might change over time, an approach which triangulates sources and methods of data collection offers promise.

TWELVE

Guidelines for Designing Topics for Writing Assessment

Introduction

As direct assessment of writing has gained favor, more and more attention has been given to the quality of the assessment instrument—the topic or task that is used to elicit a sample of writing. Since each composition in a writing assessment issues from an individual response to a general summons to write, some problems in the papers may originate with the summons, not with the writer.

We need to examine carefully how the topic is stated and how it provides a context for writing to begin. However, as we have already observed, writing tasks themselves have rarely been treated as objects of inquiry; thus, we have almost no literature on the *ways writing tasks function as instruments in either assessment or research.* As far as we know, our own Central High School study described in Chapter 9 is the first qualitative inquiry into the processes of topic comprehension.

We are just beginning to reappraise the nature of topics used in assessments, the principles upon which they are based, and the techniques for generating and evaluating them. For example, the quarterly publication, *ETS Developments,* announced in its Autumn 1984 issue a "quality control" project to develop uniform guidelines for all ETS-administered tests. Mary Fowles, team leader of the guidelines group, says:

> ETS will be helping to set the standards for essay testing. These have never been put down on paper. Even the terms related to essay testing have had imprecise and multiple meanings (Ballas, 1984, p. 8).

In the earlier chapters of this volume, we have presented a comprehensive review of current sources of knowledge for designing topics followed in the later chapters with reports of our own exploratory research studies of topic interpretation. The solutions to the problems facing designers of topics are neither simple nor straightforward. However, even though we are just beginning to understand the issues that designers of writing tasks must consider, it is feasible to consolidate current knowledge in the form of a provisional set of guidelines.

We intend these provisional guidelines to aid in generating questions leading to qualitative investigations of long-ignored problems of meaning and interpretation in using writing tasks for assessments and research. We do not intend these guidelines to be taken as hard and fast rules but as aids to focus the discussions of teachers, researchers, and others who design writing tasks for various assessment contexts. We hope that the topic design process that we are recommending will lead to refinements of the process itself and of the quality of the instruments developed. In the following sections, we offer principles and recommendations derived from the practice, theory, and research described in the foregoing chapters.

Some of the material in Section B of this chapter is based on two manuscripts prepared for the BAWP Writing Assessment Project (Gray & Ruth, 1982) in 1980–81 by Catharine Lucas Keech, a reseacher in the Project. In the fall of 1980, the Project sent the first Keech manuscript to two panels of reviewers selected on the basis of their many years of experience as developers of writing tasks in local, state, and national assessments.[1] We asked the reviewers to comment specifically on the "completeness, accuracy, organization, and style" of the presentation. Subsequently, Keech did a comprehensive revision of the original manuscript for the final report on the Project (Ruth, 1982), incorporating many of the suggestions offered by the panels. This chapter re-analyzes, updates, and expands the 1982 report.

Overview of the Process of Topic Design

Process models of topic design may vary in detail and in specific steps, but we recommend a simple model that depicts the process in three interrelated phases consisting of planning, development, and evaluation. In *the planning phase,* the task design team develops consensus on its theory of language and discourse processes, defines the purpose of the writing assess-

---

[1]We acknowledge Catharine Keech's 1982 report as the source of some of the material presented in this chapter. We also gratefully acknowledge those professional colleagues who aided and encouraged the Project through their responses to the first manuscript in 1980. The panel of writing instructors included Ruby Bernstein, Northgate High School, Concord, California; Mary Francis Claggett, English Department Chairman, Alameda High School, Alameda, California; Kim Davis, Subject A, University of California, Berkeley; Edmund Farrell, Professor of English Education, University of Texas, Austin; Jean Jensen, English Department Chairman, Las Lomas High School, Walnut Creek, California; Irving Peckham, English Teacher, Live Oak High School, Morgan Hill, California; Bill Robinson, Director of Composition, English Department, San Francisco State University; Bernard Tanner, English Teacher, Palo Alto High School, Palo Alto, California. The panel of researchers and professional evaluators included: Evans Alloway, Director of Test Development, Educational Testing Service; Gordon Brossell, Associate Professor of Education, The Florida State University, Tallahassee; Rexford Brown, Editor of Publications and Test Developer, National Assessment of Educational Progress; Gertrude Conlan, Test Developer, Educational Testing Service; Charles Cooper; Coordinator of Writing Programs, University of California, San Diego; Paul Diederich, Senior Research Analyst, Emeritus, Educational Testing Service; Sarah Freedman, Associate Professor of Education, University of California, Berkeley; Ann Humes, Communication Skills Project Assistant, Southwest Regional Laboratory; Ina V. S. Mullis, Senior Research Analyst, National Assessment of Educational Progress; Joe Steele, Research Psychologist, College Outcomes Project, American College Testing Program; Edward White, English Test Center, California State University, San Bernardino. We are especially grateful to Deborah Dashow Ruth for her substantial editorial contribution to the 1982 report and to the present chapter.

ment and the uses of the data derived from it, and determines the nature of the group to be examined and the plan for administering the test and scoring the papers. *The developmental phase* begins after the preliminary analyses have been completed. Here the task design team drafts versions of topics appropriate to purpose and audience, following recommended principles. A language analysis and sensitivity review take place toward the end of the developmental phase. During *the evaluation phase,* the design team arranges for field trial and user interviews that feed back information into the design process. The evaluation phase is intended to gauge the range of responses and to determine whether the task achieves its aims. The evaluation phase continues even after the test has been administered. The results are studied to determine if unanticipated topic effects have affected the performance of either the student writers or the teacher readers. When topic effects are discovered, the topic is redesigned prior to general administrations.

Constant vigilance at every stage of the process assures the validity and fairness of the assessment. The procedure is exacting and time-consuming, but we believe that local test makers as well as professional test developers have a responsibility to validate their tests for uses in particular contexts. Figure 12.1 depicts the topic design process.

The Planning Phase

The conception of a writing task implies a general theory of language, a model of discourse forms and functions, and a theory of the nature of the writing process. Since the writing task itself constitutes a text to be read, it also reflects the designers' tacit assumptions about the process of comprehending and responding to written language. The following section proposes guidelines for establishing the theoretical base and the objectives underlying the topic design process.

Understand and Publicly Acknowledge the Limits of Precision of All Types of Test Instruments.

The restricted samplings of writing performance taken under test conditions are inadequate indicators of levels of competence or of growth. A valid assessment of performance in writing requires a sampling over time of the ongoing work that students produce for classroom writing assignments, e.g., a portfolio of a year's work. The insensitivity of typical standardized achievement tests in detecting differences in accomplishment is illustrated in a study Edna Shapiro (cited in Patton, 1975) conducted to determine *why* standardized test scores showed *no difference* between (1) children in an enriched Follow Through school program and (2) children in comparison schools not involved in such programs. Shapiro actually went to the class-

Figure 12.1. The Process of Designing a Writing Task

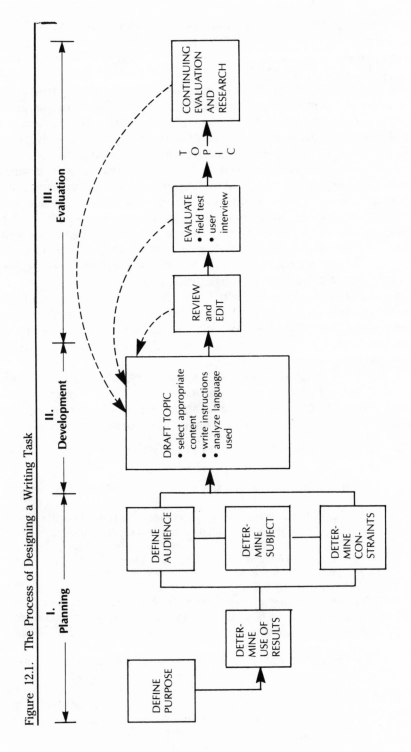

239

rooms of these same children in the two kinds of programs to see what they were doing (Patton, 1975).

Shapiro found that classroom observational data revealed a "marked disparity" in the quality of the performance of the children in the two programs. In other words a genuine "significant" difference had gone undetected by the standardized measures traditionally used to evaluate the effectiveness of different kinds of school experience (Patton, 1975, p. 16).

Neither the multiple-choice test of writing skills nor the writing sample gathered under conditions typical of many large scale assessments can be relied upon to reflect the natural processes of writing in either academic or personal contexts. To write upon demand on a prescribed subject for a fictional audience within a severely restricted time frame denies the writer opportunity for careful planning and revision. No matter how limiting writing under test conditions may be, this kind of test does sample writing capacities that cannot be gauged through existing multiple-choice measures. But as with *all* tests of educational attainment, the direct measure's limits also need to be expressed. Single-sample, impromptu essay test results must be reported and interpreted with extreme caution, for such tests, being only "one probe into a massive competence" (Lloyd-Jones, 1982, p. 3), "by definition understate competence" (p. 9).

Janet Emig is another of the experts in the field of research on writing who has questioned the assumptions behind the practice of relying on a single writing sample—for measuring achievement, for determining placement or for assessing competency. Emig (1982) writes:

Among the assumptions behind the use of a single writing sample are the following:

i)   A single writing sample in a single mode is a reflection of that writer's ability to
   a)   write in that specific mode, not only on the single occasion represented by the testing situation but also on any subsequent occasion;
   b)   write in a related mode: e.g., if the sample involves argument, then exposition;
   c)   write in any mode.

ii)   The piece of writing produced on any one occasion reflects the ability to write another piece of writing on any other occasion: in other words, language is a fixed phenomenon—language 1 is language 2 is language 3.

iii)   A single piece of writing is a sufficiently useful index of ability to "write," "do," or "pass freshman composition," "do college work."

iv)   Decisions by instructors, chairs, deans, departments, admissions offices, and testing agencies can sensibly be made on the basis of this one sample that affect placement in a course, a college career, or, indeed, a full human future. (Emig, 1982, p. 69)

Most teachers recognize that these assumptions are questionable, that performance may not be stable across different kinds of writing tasks, that some tasks may be harder for students than others, and that a host of factors may interfere in a student's ability to perform from one test occasion to the next. Nevertheless, the practice of relying on a single writing sample for assessment and placement purposes has not been abandoned. Indeed, it is extremely wide spread.

Know How Assessment Contexts Can Violate Normal Writing Processes.

As Lloyd-Jones reminds us, "A writing sample is not real writing" (1982, p. 3). Nearly 50 years ago, P.B. Ballard explained precisely why writing done under testing constraints is not real writing:

> When you and I write anything, rarely do we leave it as it first flowed from the pen. We set it aside and read it later; we score out superfluous words, change awkward phrases, rearrange the ideas, and sometimes, indeed, write the whole thing over and over again . . . To revise and remodel, to reflect upon what is written, and to reject even the good in favour of what is better—that is at least part of the secret of clear and vigorous prose. We do this ourselves, but we do not allow our pupils to do it. Often do we expect them to write without preparation; always do we expect them to write without revision. Second thoughts are discouraged. (1939, p. 66)

Various other observers cited in earlier chapters also have declared that much of current practice in writing assessment still is incongruous with the accounts we have of the writing process. Many assessments continue to follow the pattern of eliciting an impromptu essay based on an imposed topic within a time frame that seldom allows the unfolding of a natural process of conception, development, revision, and editing to occur. The evaluators get what is essentially a *rough draft* to rate and rank in relation to the other papers received, or in relation to an arbitrary rating scale or rubric. Such procedures, which do not allow for the prewriting and revision activities which distinguish between skilled and unskilled writers, call into question the validity of this kind of assessment (Polin, 1980, p. 2).

The assessment of writing should call into play the thinking and planning operations involved in the development, expansion, and integration of ideas as well as the articulation of feelings. We need to find ways of collecting samples of actual writing which do not vitiate natural processes.

Preserve as Many Features of the "Real" Writing Process as Feasible Under Assessment Conditions.

Both Canadian and English assessment authorities are showing that it is possible under large scale assessment conditions to preserve more steps of the "real" writing process than normally occurs in many large scale assessments. In England's version of a national assessment of writing, the teachers administering the task are "encouraged to introduce the writing task before the group of pupils begin writing." In an assessment, three samples of writing, each involving different types of tasks, are collected. A portfolio of written work selected by the teacher from writing produced in the normal course of classwork also is collected (Gorman, et al., *Secondary Survey*, 1982, p. 66).

Several of Canada's provinces honor some elements of writing process in their assessments (Evans, 1985a): Ontario calls for "several different examples of the student's work and writing over a period of time . . ." (p. 2). British Columbia's statement of philosophy says that "The test situation should approximate as closely as possible the instructional activities of the writing process—prewriting, writing, and editing" (p. 7). British Columbia's 1980 Achievement Test in Writing (Grade 12) takes two days to administer: On the first day, students are asked only to generate and record ideas "with a little advisory assistance." On the second day, students write the essay, referring back to the ideas and examples list created the day before (p. 6).

We are also seeing greater attention to process in some of our own state and college assessments. The Writing Test for New York State Elementary Schools requires two samples, each done on a separate day. Teachers are allowed to read the directions and the tasks to the students. One hour and 15 minutes are allowed to complete each task and drafting and revising are suggested to the students (Chew, 1983). At the 11th grade, three samples are taken. The three writing tasks—a business letter of complaint, a report, and a persuasive topic—are placed in a rhetorical context with the purpose and audience identified. Stoney Brook, New York has adopted a writing portfolio model of assessment which incorporates some assignments written under relatively controlled conditions (Belanoff, cited in Murphy, 1985). The Minneapolis Benchmark Writing Tests include more than one sample of writing; and "when retention is considered, the decision is based on a portfolio of writing from throughout the year, one impromptu essay, and teacher ratings" (Ballas, 1984, p. 8).

Establish the Purpose of the Writing Assessment.

We determine the purpose of particular assessments of writing when we answer the question: what needs for collecting evidence of progress and for passing judgment on attainments must be satisfied? In establishing assessment purposes, it is well to remember that efficient means of ranking students for administrative purposes seldom produce useful feedback for students. A crucial need for instructional purposes is to develop writing tests that say something—beyond numerical rankings—that is meaningful to students, parents, and especially to teachers. Test scores that assert standings and rankings may serve the politics of school accountability, but they never

explain anything. An examination system has value to the extent that it con-
tributes sound information to improve classroom teaching and educational
guidance for students.

We must remember that no writing examination can substitute for the
judgment of the adequately prepared professional. Yet, Stibbs (1979), writing on behalf of the National Association for the Teaching of English reminds us that

> There are pressures on teachers—often from the least informed about lan-
> guage and education—to teach a narrow set of language skills and uses, and
> to accept teacher-free assessments which seem to measure, more accurately
> than teachers can, the performance of children and schools.

Thus, we need to be wary of using examination data in ways that erode
confidence in teacher judgment and undermine the curriculum. We must be
careful to protect the integrity of our writing curriculum by monitoring the
validity of the content of any writing examinations used in our school system. Tests have a way of feeding back into the educational process in
unintended ways. We must watch with great care what we put into our tests
because what the writing examination sanctifies, we must teach.

The most common purposes of assessing writing are listed below:

Purposes for Assessing Writing

Administrative: To assert standings and assign rankings.

1. General accountability. We need to evaluate the efficiency of educa-
    tional systems and their contribution to the development of society.
2. Program evaluation. If writing programs are to be improved, we need to
    judge the quality of their effectiveness. We need to appraise the success
    of a particular program and its instructors at imparting certain under-
    standings.
3. Certification. We need to be assured that certain levels of professional
    competence in writing have been attained.
4. Selection. We need evidence of entry level competence in writing to
    make admissions and hiring decisions. We need to predict the likeli-
    hood of success at school tasks and life tasks requiring writing.
5. Placement. We need to be assured that certain patterns of writing expe-
    rience have been developed in order to make decisions about exemp-
    tions or assignments to special courses.

Instructional: To guide individual progress.

1. Diagnosis. We need to appraise the student's strengths and weaknesses
    and provide feedback.
2. Progress. We need to estimate how well the student is progressing to-
    ward the goal of mastering effective communication through writing.

3. Self-evaluation. We need to involve students in monitoring their own development as writers, helping them to learn to write with interest and pride in what they have to say.

Research: To attain knowledge of effective instructional procedures and writing processes.

Establish a Definition of Writing Competence in Relation to the Purpose of the Assessment.

The definition of competence will vary according to the purpose of the assessment. For example, a college level proficiency test would require a measure of the kind of academic writing required in most college courses. Academic writing at this level requires the general ability to explain or defend a point of view, report facts and draw conclusions, analyze and summarize a passage, and other more specialized abilities depending on the discipline. Clearly, personal writing tasks that elicit narratives, create mood or expressions of feeling would be inappropriate for showing how students might cope with the expository or persuasive tasks required in much academic writing. General definitions of competence in writing and specifications of the domain of school writing are presented in detail in Chapter 6.

Acknowledge That the Act of Writing in an Assessment Begins with an Act of Reading for Understanding, and Deal with the Implications.

Before starting to write, the test taker must make sense of the topic and understand the task set by the test maker. This initial act or reading by the test taker and subsequent re-readings at any stage of the composing process activate the various elements of comprehension processes: prior experience carried in memory schemata or frameworks, inferential interpretation of the test maker's intentions, identification of the elements in the task statement that are essential to understanding and carrying out the implicit or explicit task demands. Thus, functioning initially as a reader, the writer constructs the meaning of the task and proceeds to act upon his understood meaning. In Chapter 7 we have described a model of topic interpretation which challenges the commonly held psychometric assumption that every test item or essay topic delivers identical messages to different test takers. Consequently, thoughtful and skilled use of topic design guidelines, as well as user interviews after pretesting the topics, are essential to minimize *unexpected* interpretations and *misinterpretations* of the test maker's intentions.

Establish Consensus About Which Writing Tasks Are Significant in Particular Functional Contexts.

In their earliest years children acquire language as part of the experience of growing up. They come to know the forms and functions of spoken language through talking with their family and companions. As their minds develop so does their knowledge of words and their capacity to construct meanings. In the natural course of development children learn to draw on this knowledge to meet the demands of many of the communicative situations that they encounter in the world around them. Children's intuitive understanding of how oral language works in actual use gives them a vital resource to apply to their learning to use written language in school. As they mature into adolescents and young adults, their range of contexts for language use expands in relation to their experience in the world and in school. Thus, in the case of writing, students need to develop their command of language so that they can perform a range of writing tasks in academic settings and beyond. It follows that in writing assessments, students must be offered a range of writing tasks related as closely as possible to ways in which language is actually used. We propose here what is often called a functional perspective on writing and the assessment of competence in its uses.

Identify the Model of Discourse Guiding Assessment Decisions.

The models of discourse described in Chapter 6 have particular implications for structuring writing tasks. Although each model is unique, each shares some features in common. For example, any communicative use of language in spoken or written discourse implies that someone is attempting to say something meaningful to someone else for some purpose. A writer ordinarily addresses someone he wants to influence, inform, or entertain. This special relationship between the writer and his reader is recognized in the concept of "audience." Writing usually takes place in a social context, and competence requires an ability to adjust to different audiences and social relationships. Thus, as topic designers define the scope of the writing task, they need to raise a basic question: "Who is being directed to write what, to whom, and why?". The answers to these questions have profound consequences for the examinees, for they control what can be written and how it can be said. The nature of a person's writing performance varies according to context and audience. It makes a difference whether the writer thinks he is writing something to interest a known audience, or whether he sees his task as an exercise to be evaluated. Even under the contextual constraints of a school assessment, it is important to recognize the need to define meaningful, appealing contexts for writing which correspond as closely as possible to "real world" writing tasks.

Determine Scoring Procedures in Relation to Purpose and Prior to Designing the Topic.

What might be a good topic from one scoring perspective might be a poor one from another scoring perspective. For example, when a writing sample is scored holistically and read quickly for the total impression it makes upon the reader, it is viewed as a total work. However, when a writing sample is scored using the primary trait system, the rater examines the piece focusing on the particular discourse features it is supposed to exhibit according to the precise specifications of the primary trait scoring guide. The various types of scoring procedures are defined in Chapter 1 and elaborated on in Chapter 2 and Chapter 6.

Determine Who Should Be Tested in Relation to the Assessment Purpose.

To accomplish the purpose of the assessment, it is necessary to answer a number of questions: How many students will be tested over what range of ages, grade levels, and ability levels? Is it necessary to test everyone in a targeted population, or will a sample of that population suffice? How old are the students in the sample? Is the population homogeneous? Does the population include a mix of native and non-native speakers? The answers to these questions will affect choice of subject, structure of the whole topic, length of time allowed for writing, and range of scores used.

Be Responsive to New Methods of Assessing Writing.

Because our understanding of the nature of human cognition and writing is changing, we must be responsive to new methods of evaluating development in writing which respect the complexity of the process and the persons engaged in it. There is an emerging literature on approaches to assessment in writing which designers of writing tasks need to take into account. Faigley, Cherry, Jolliffe & Skinner (1985) call for reexamination of the ways we evaluate development in writing, defined as the means we use to describe changes in the writer's knowledge and processes of composing. They argue the need for a theory of writing assessment that takes into acccount the writer's *knowledge and processes.* The authors provide practical examples of theory-based writing tasks and scoring rubrics for college freshmen courses to use in what they call "performative assessments," a method of assessing ability to produce written texts through performance on controlled writing tasks. This research group sees the assessment of changes in writing processes as one of the most critical issues in writing instruction, so it has set forth direct methods for describing changes in composing processes by focusing the writers' awareness on their composing strategies.

Other alternative models of writing assessment are being developed which assure that writing tasks are undertaken in encouraging contexts— with an appropriate time allowance, advice as needed, reference materials, and opportunities to revise and develop several drafts. These attempts to conduct "naturalistic" assessments honoring the individuality of the writers and the complexity of the writing process are being developed in the United States through various forms of "portfolio" assessments (Camp, 1985; Belanoff, 1985); in England through the collection of "exemplar folders" of students' writing (Dixon & Stratta, 1982); and in Australia through "self-reflective monitoring" of one's own development as a writer (Johnston, 1983).

According to Murphy (1985), a recorder at the 3rd Annual Conference on Writing Assessment, both speakers on the panel on Models of Portfolio Assessment, Camp (1985) and Belanoff (1985), raised the issue of the relationship between the curriculum and testing, when they argued that our dominant methods of assessment conflict with our new emphasis on process in writing. They see the "portfolio" approach, where responses are written to a variety of tasks under "natural" classroom conditions and collected over a semester or a term, as a method of assessment more closely tied to the curriculum and one which honors process in writing and provides more comprehensive information.

Johnston (1983) points out that "it is important that students reflect on the quality of their own work, because their involvement in that process determines how much they will learn and how they will think about themselves as learners" (p. 1). Dixon argues for the development of descriptions of growth in writing with each description unique to the student. In Dixon's view, "any evaluation which does not make for better instruction in the classroom, improving the lives of children, is not worth doing" (cited by Robinson, 1985, p. 111).

The Developmental Phase

Someone has said, "Having to say something is not the same thing as having something to say." Too often writing assessments become occasions that demonstrate the truth of these words, providing students with alien subjects leading to falsification of perception and feeling. No one will do his best writing about a topic for which he has no experience, or about which he has little understanding. This section proposes guidelines for designing topics that are understandable, appropriate, and fair to the examinee. It raises questions such as the following: What issues should writing task designers consider as they create a topic for a certain type of test? How do these issues relate to the language of the topic and the purposes of the test? How do these issues relate to the evaluator who will try to read the papers and rank them?

Not all of the great many pitfalls in designing tasks for writing assessment can be considered here. Thus, we will concentrate on what seem to be some of the larger issues in creating a topic: (1) relating task to purpose of assessment, (2) selecting the subject, (3) defining the scope of the rhetorical demands, (4) wording the task clearly, (5) evaluating the quality of the topic. The guidelines that follow do not solve all the problems of topic design identified in the earlier chapters; however, as a beginning effort, we hope they will help designers avoid some of the more serious problems which can produce faulty topics and—the inevitable consequence—faulty data about the competence of the writers responding to them.

Develop a Set of Criteria or Questions to Guide the Topic Design Process and Define Its Scope.

In school districts that are developing their own writing assessments, we have observed that more and more frequently English departments and elementary grade level assessment committees are forming topic writing teams to develop criteria and questions to guide topic development. Departmental cohesion grows stronger as members rotate in serving on the topic writing team because the process of developing and reviewing criteria for designing topics constitutes a form of in-service education that deepens understanding about the nature of the writing process. It is inevitable that such topic design sessions should promote continuing discussions about the teaching and learning of writing, about the nature of the writing process, about the values of certain modes of discourse, about what constitutes "good" writing, and about the central place of writing in the school curricula.

The following "Questions to Consider in Creating Topics" is an example of a set of locally developed guidelines derived from an audio cassette recording made on an occasion when three English teachers convened as a topic design committee and met in a three-hour session to create possible topics for use as an end-of-year tenth grade assessment to be scored holistically.

Questions to Consider in Creating Topics for a Tenth Grade Assessment
Holistically Scored[2]

1. Why are we doing this? What is the purpose of this writing assessment?
2. What will we do with the results?
3. What is the nature of the student population to be assessed?
    a. What is their grade level?
    b. What is their general level of academic competence?
    c. What prior curricular experience have they had that prepares them for this assessment?
4. What is the most appropriate topic subject for this assessment?
    a. What prior knowledge will discussion of this subject require?
    b. Is this subject accessible to a wide range of students?
    c. What is the relation of the topic subject to the students' world?
        Is it connected to real student concerns?
        Is it remote or alien to their world?
        Is it an interesting or involving topic?

---

[2]Abstracted by L. Ruth from a three-hour audio cassette recording of three English teachers in a topic development session conducted during the Central High School study. (May, 1981)

    d. Are there aspects of the subject that may lead to stereotyped thinking, reliance on cliches?

    e. Is there any element of the subject that may be considered unduly threatening to personal values, religious beliefs, self-esteem, etc.?

    f. Is the subject free from biasing effects for different sub-groups within the student population?

        Is it too limiting for upper level ability students?

        Does it presume experience that may have been denied some students for social, cultural, or economic reasons?

        How difficult might the task be for the lowest 25 percent of the student population?

    g. Will the topic lead to diatribes against persons at the school? Parents? Local citizens?

    h. How is the subject related to the school curriculum, and can equal exposure to similar curriculum experiences be assumed?

    i. How does the choice of subject affect choice of rhetorical mode?

5. How should the topic subject be worded?

    a. What do the verbs used communicate to the student? e.g., Describe? Tell? Explain? Illustrate? Analyze? Discuss?

    b. What do the commonly used formal labels actually communicate? Essay? Story? Argument? Persuasive essay? Letter? Journal entry?

    c. Should a range of formal options be proposed?

    d. To what extent should students be cued? e.g., "Write about *one* thing . . ." "Tell about *three* improvements. . ."

    e. What level of background detail should be provided?

    f. Should the subject include specification of an audience?

6. How should instructions be handled? Embedded in the topic or kept separate? Should the topic contain hints about approaches to the subject or suggestions for task management?

Each design team should create and answer its own set of questions for topic development, taking into account the purpose of the assessment, the nature of the student population, and the uses of the results.

Develop a General Task Framework Responsive to Discourse Theory, Writing Process, and Assessment Purposes.

To insure that succeeding assessments cover the full range of writing tasks valued in school, college, and out-of-school adult writing contexts, design teams should set up a general framework which relates writing purposes and tasks in plausible social contexts. The frameworks[3] described below, ranging across elementary through adult levels of proficiency, provide attention to significant dimensions of writing tasks: range of purposes, sources of subject matter, variations in mode, variations in audience, and control over

---

[3]See also our discussion in Chapters 2 and 6 of the National Assessment of Educational Progress and the theory of discourse underlying its primary trait topic development procedures.

appropriate forms. These frameworks should provide useful leads to local writing task designers interested in developing their own task frameworks sensitive to local needs and particular student populations.

The Assessment of Performance Unit of the Department of Education and Science for England and Wales (APU) (Gorman, White, Orchard, Tate, Sexton, 1981) established a framework for their national assessment of writing that indicates four dimensions of writing tasks. This framework arose initially out of the recommendations of a nationally constituted Language Steering Group for the Assessment of Writing, which identified some important considerations in designing the prompts for writing.

> A number of dimensions were considered within which specific writing activities could be sampled. One dimension related to the contrast between different types of writing: narrative/descriptive on the one hand and reflective/analytical on the other. A second dimension concerned the degree of control granted to writer or assessor. At one end of the scale are tasks in which the assessor seeks to define fully as possible the topic and how it is to be dealt with; at the other the selection of both are left to the writer. Thirdly, the source of subject-matter was considered. Some tasks draw on the writer's first hand experience and others on knowledge derived from elsewhere. Finally, it was acknowledged that the range of purposes for which a child might write also differs. Some tasks require a pupil to create a literary work such as a story, and others a piece of writing which sets out to inform, direct or persuade. (p. 82)

An APU research team invited groups of teachers to review the original task proposals. As a result of these discussions and preliminary trials of tasks, the purposes and categories were further refined. For the sake of economy in this discussion, the two separate task lists for 11 year-olds and 15 year-olds have been abridged and merged into the composite framework depicted in Table 12.1.

The tasks for 11 year-olds are framed so that they can be responded to with writing which is predominantly narrative or descriptive or both. Although some tasks for 15 year-olds ask for narrative, a larger proportion of tasks ask for writing which is analytical and/or reflective. Some narrative tasks at age 11 move toward reflection on the subject, asking for expressions of judgment and feeling, and most narrative tasks at age 15 move into reflection.

The degree of control granted to the writer over selection of subject and type of writing is limited in these tasks, with part of the task defined and part left to the writer's choice. There is more emphasis on the ability to write competently within specifications set by others in the tests for 15 year-olds than in the tests for 11 year-olds.

There is a considerable difference in the relative emphasis on writing from first-hand experience or knowledge from elsewhere, with the older stu-

Table 12.1.
Composite Framework of Writing Tasks for Ages 11 and 15*

General Writing Purposes	APU Language Performance Surveys at Elementary and Secondary Level 1981–1982 Written Products to Be Elicited
1. To describe	1.1 Sustained description of person, place, or object (11) 1.2 Description and expression of feelings toward what is described (11) 1.3 Sequenced description from memory (15) 1.4 Description to accompany given pictures (15)
2. To narrate	2.1 Imaginative narrative based on given characters and setting (11) 2.2 Original end to a story selected by the pupil (11) 2.3 Short story (15)
3. To record/report	3.1 Autobiographical account of event experienced recently (11, 15) 3.2 Verifiable account of an event (11) 3.3 An account of something learned (11,15)
4. To explain/direct	4.1 Explanation and reflection on a convention or regulation (11, 15) 4.2 Explanation of a complex skill (15) 4.3 Instructions to accomplish a simple household task (15)
5. To persuade	5.1 Informal letter to a friend to get reader to change mind (11) 5.2 Argument justifying a point of view (15)
6. To request	6.1 Letter to a person in a public/private agency (11) 6.2 Letter of application (15)
7. To plan	7.1 Account of an activity to be undertaken (11)
8. To edit	8.1 Editing of a written account (11)

*Adapted from Gorman, T. P., et al. *Language Performance in the Schools: Primary Survey Report No. 1* (1981), p. 85, and *Secondary Survey Report No. 1* (1982), pp. 66–67. London: Her Majesty's Stationery Office.

dents expected to write about ideas and processes drawn from a variety of sources. Some of the tasks for 15 year-olds still draw on personal experience but ask the writer to provide more detached accounts. Tasks vary audience and the degree of the writer's control over appropriate forms. The general writing purposes set forth in this model reflect the Language Steering Group's view that

"In order to write what they will need to write during their lives, young people need to develop specialized proficiencies. These variations in task and context indicate which these specialized proficiencies are." This statement can never be proved true or false since it rests upon a value-laden view of what constitutes full participation in living. It is thus permanently open to debate (*Language Performance*, 1978, p. 14).

Three theory-based sequences of classroom assignments presented in detail are available for adaptation to assessment contexts. Dixie Dellinger (1982) has developed a guide for the design of writing assignments for high school courses which draws upon the discourse theories of James Moffett (1968), Frank D'Angelo (1975), and James Kinneavy (1971). Scardamalia, Bereiter, and Fillion (1981) have developed a sourcebook of 60 cognitively-oriented activities focused at elementary levels of the following "subskills:" genre tasks, planning tasks, topic development tasks, language tasks, style tasks, coherence tasks, evaluation tasks, and revision tasks. This work should not be confused with narrow skills approaches, for it attends to communicative needs advocated by holistic approaches. It is particularly valuable as a research-tested source of ideas for assessing and developing writing proficiency at the elementary levels, although much of it is also relevant for secondary levels.

Gene Krupa (1982) has developed a sequence of 24 "writing situations" for use in a beginning college level course.[4] Krupa sets forth his assignment or "writing situation," and then his plan gives the student guidelines which discuss the particular rhetorical trait or characteristics that are necessary for success with that task. Each of these assignments is accompanied by four sample student papers followed by a related assessment guide to be used in individual or small group evaluations. A second section provides an additional 24 assignments in a briefer format: situation, guidelines, asssessment form. An appendix classifies all of the writing situations according to five different principles: (1) purpose, (2) thematic sequences, (3) traditional modes, (4) level of abstraction, (5) audience.

Krupa's writing tasks on a given subject interconnect and expand upon one another. One pattern moves students through "situations" that are *expressive* in purpose, then *explanatory,* and then *persuasive.* On the audience dimension, assignments move from an intimate and friendly reader to a more distant and impersonal reader. The assignments also move toward increasing abstraction, from dealing with people and events to ideas and

[4]See also the series of theory-based "performative assessment instruments" (topics plus rubrics) developed and field tested over a three year period to measure the skills that are the target of instruction in freshman English in college (Faigley, Cherry, Jolliffe, & Skinner, 1985, pp. 103–160). We received a report of this work too late to consider it in any detail in this monograph, but we believe that designers of tasks for writing assessments should give this important work careful consideration.

generalizations. For example, in a first assignment, the writer expresses to a close friend how he feels about a job. In a second assignment, the writer explains to a friend how to deal with a particular problem on the job, and in the third assignment the writer attempts to persuade his former employer to hire the friend. An assignment on the subject of injustice asks the writer to tell about his first experience of injustice, what happened, and how it made him feel. In the last assignment on the subject, the writer is asked to discuss the ethical principle underlying the experience.

Other approaches to the classification of writing tasks include the several research-based specification tables described in detail in Chapter 6 (Purves et al., 1984; Bridgeman & Carlson, 1984). Besides these there is the stimulus matrix developed by Forrest & Steele (1982) for the College Outcomes Measures Project. Forrest and Steele's table describes stimulus modes (including written narrative, audiotape, videotape, and others) for each of fifteen general tasks across three content-related domains (functioning in social institutions, using science and technology, and using art). This American College Testing Program COMP project was designed to measure the knowledge and skills (1) that undergraduate students are expected to acquire as a result of general education programs, and (2) that are important to effective functioning in adult society.

Control for Prior Knowledge Demands in Selecting Subjects for Writing Tasks.

No topic can absolutely guarantee equal access to knowledge of the subject matter for all participants in a test. But some topics provide more opportunities than others. Test developers need to be sensitive to the knowledge demands of the writing tasks they create. For testing general writing competency, test makers should select subjects that will give all students "something" to write about. Personal experience subjects meet this criterion. Test makers should recognize, however, that personal experience topics tend to elicit some modes of writing more than others, and that the expressive writing elicited will be more valued in English than in other disciplines which tend to value exposition and argument. Of course, if the object of the test is to assess knowledge of specific content, then the subject will be determined by the content that is to be assessed.

The question of prior knowledge about a subject is particularly pertinent in designing exposition and argument topics for tests of general writing proficiency. The student who is already knowledgeable about the subject presented is likely to produce a more well developed essay. Even the best writers will fail to produce good writing if they do not possess adequate information about the subject presented. What authors of writing tasks assume to be general knowledge may turn out to entail a quite special realm of knowledge. For example, the following topic was eliminated from an assessment testing for general competency after teachers pre-tested it by attempting to write on it themselves (Myers, 1980, p. 13):

Unsuccessful Topic

Explain your agreement or disagreement with the following statement: The history of women in our country is the history of oppression.

Two of the teachers who attempted to write a response to this topic found that they did not know enough about the history of women to write an adequate essay on the subject. For testing general writing competency, the topic was inappropriate. If all students being tested had just completed a course on the history of women, the topic, of course, would be more appropriate. In that case, the topic would test mastery of course content in addition to ability to control the argument mode of discourse.

Subjects for tests of general writing proficiency must be selected very carefully so as not to become tests of special knowledge. For example, the subject of injustice could be structured into a topic that draws on either personal experience or on special knowledge. A writer could be asked for an account of a personal experience in which he was treated unjustly. On the other hand the subject of injustice in South Africa would call for specialized knowledge that all writers might not possess. Topics that allow students to argue directly from their direct experience or reading need not be discriminatory. They become tests of *special knowledge* only when the content is narrowly specified.

Understand How Social Context Influences Interpretation of Subjects Selected for Writing Tasks.

The determination of what constitutes common knowledge for the population to be tested can be more complex than one might expect. The use of school experience as a subject for writing always seems to be a safe topic because students are immersed in the life of schools. The following example was used successfully in several assessments (Keech, 1982, p. 183):

Provisionally Successful Topic

There is probably at least one thing about your school that you would like to see changed. Write a letter to your principal and tell him about the problem. Be sure to describe the situation as it is now and tell why it bothers you, as well as how you would like to change it.

Yet this topic proved to be unsatisfactory in two other schools and had to be abandoned after the field tryout. In one of the schools, teachers monitoring the trial administration reported that students responded to the topic with derisive laughter, complaints, and even refusals to write. These students saw their principal as an uncaring adversary, unwilling to listen to their appeals. At another school where the principal was especially effective in developing a unified, contented student body, the students complained that they couldn't think of a problem worth writing about. The trivial nature of their letters validated their complaints about the topic. Subjects selected for use in assessments can never safely be assumed to be trouble-free. Consider the National Assessment of Educational Progress' experience with certain subjects as reported by Lloyd-Jones (1977):

> Certain images create trouble. *Bananas,* for example, seems to provoke pornographic or scatological responses. *Bill collectors* seem to be exceedingly threatening to some people. When we tried an explantory-persuasive exercise to evoke a serious letter to correct an error in computer billing, we got a number of amusing responses, but when we tried to revise the exercise to encourage humorous literary-expressive responses by making the situation more absurd, we found that the increase in the number who could joke about computers and overdue bills was small and, strangely, the number which dealt with the problem in serious, highly conventional terms became larger. In both versions, a substantial number of respondents were merely hostile (p. 44).

Lloyd-Jones (1977) concluded, ". . . finding likely topics within the range of all the respondents and challenging enough to produce the desirous efforts despite the lack of any 'payoff' remains a problem" (p. 44).

Assessors need to be sensitive to the impact that local environments may have on the meanings and interpretations of particular subjects. For this reason, all topics must be checked out in limited field trial prior to full-scale use.

Understand How Cultural Diversity Affects Response to the Subjects Selected for Writing Tasks.

It is generally assumed that topics which allow students to draw upon personal experience provide better means for assessing general writing competency. However, topic designers need to be aware that teachers of speakers of English as a second language report special problems with personal experience topics. R.V. White (1980) finds that students in ESL classrooms have difficulty with writing assignments in which they are asked to reveal themselves and their personalities, such as in personal letters to friends. Also, White suggests that personal or "creative writing in the native language may be little more than a stringing together of items (often noun phrases) with much emphasis on feeling and little on logic" (p. 15). R.V. White does not recommend outlawing all personal writing for ESL students, but he does say:

> What I am pointing out is that personal writing is very much more difficult to teach and to learn because the conventions which govern interpersonal relationships (as opposed to institutional relationships) are so much more complex and varied than those which govern institutional roles . . . there may well

be a case for giving [ESL] students a basis in institutional language use first, for in learning to write institutional, referential, objective prose, appropriate to a professional or occupational role, they will be acquiring a foundation in the forms and functions of language which will be enormously helpful when they embark on the less clearly mapped seas of interpersonal language use. (pp. 15–16)

Besides the Bridgeman and Carlson (1984) report mentioned above two other works present both practical and technical information valuable to the test designer seeking to assess the writing of limited English speakers: Jacobs, Zingraf, Wormuth, Hartfiel, & Hughey, (1981) *Testing ESL Composition: A Practical Approach* and Dieterich & Freeman (1979), *A Linguistic Guide to English Proficiency Testing in Schools.*

Select Personal Experience Subjects to Test General Fluency of Native Speakers of English.

In general, topics which allow native speaking students to draw on their personal experiences do provide reliable means of assessing general writing fluency. A similar version of the following topic used in grades 7-10 in Canadian schools typically produced straightforward narrative of a single incident within the suggested time limit of 1 - 1¼ hours:

Successful Topic[5]

Narrative: First person (real or imaginary)

Most of us at one time or another are put into a position where we feel we are the victim of circumstances.

Maybe you were all set for a party when you were cornered into babysitting instead, or perhaps an unexpected "pop quiz" caught you without your homework done, or perhaps something more unusual occurred to make you ask, "Why does it always have to be me?"

You are to write a story, of about a page or a page and a half, about a particular time when you felt this way. The story doesn't have to be completely true, but *you* are one of the main characters. *You* are telling the story.

You may want to begin by giving a little background to the incident, but keep it brief. Move quickly to the incident. Make sure your story includes the outcome of the incident.

Narrative tasks should provide a clearly-defined initial incident which has potential for being a problem that the student will be able to resolve. Bernard Tanner, a high school teacher, finds that few students, even students in creative writing, can develop a plot without suggestions. Students

[5]*English I (writing supplement): Intermediate division: Ontario assessment instrument pool* (adapted, p. W-114, 1982). Toronto, Ontario: The Minister of Education.

can develop a chain of happenings, but these do not necessarily add up to a plot. Students tend, even without prompting, to want to write in the first person; they like to use themselves as the central character. But the problem with writing in the first person in their own voice is that they may revert to oral language forms, becoming caught up in their own patterns of speech and thinking, thereby ignoring important shaping conventions of written language. Tanner avoids this problem by prompting his students to role-play and write "in character" from the point of view of someone different from themselves but still easily imagined. But if they are given a specific role too far outside of themselves, they flounder or write only briefly.

Understand How Narratives Based on Imagined Experience Make More Demands on the Writer Than Narratives Based on Personal Experience.

Dixon and Stratta (1980ab) in studying the development of the writing of 14-16 year-olds established that writing an imaginary story makes more demands on the writer than writing a story from personal experience: (1) in assembling imaginative resources; (2) in creating the story; (3) in making rhetorical choices and exploring new forms of language. A much abbreviated account of Dixon and Stratta's discussion of the differences between narratives based on personal and imagined experience follows.

The simplest way to elicit an imagined story is to draw entirely on personal experience but fictionalize it. Another source would be second order experience: books, films, photographs, television, anecdotes heard. Eventually, research into documentary or historical materials might be called for. In personal narratives, the characters, the plot, the setting, and the problems or focus of the story already exist in the writer's memory. But for imaginative stories these elements have to be created or invented (Dixon & Stratta, 1980b). The narrator in the personal experience is the writer, the "I." But the imagined story presents a variety of rhetorical choices: The writer can withdraw from the narrative, as in stream of consciousness; the writer can assign a desired personality to the narrator; or the writer can make the narrator impersonal, an omniscient observer. These more complex choices make great demands on the writer. There are also more complex story forms and their associated language with a range of styles and conventions which may enter into the imagined narrative.

Dixon and Stratta (1981a) also characterize these adolescent writers that they studied as progressing from "staging point 1," writing that is close to speech, to "staging point 4," writing that reaches toward a mature literary model. In the middle are "stage 2," transition from the speech model, and "stage 3," the early stage of the literary model. Dixon and Stratta provide too many details characterizing each of these "staging points" to summarize here, but basically the markers of the changes give evidence of increasing control of the narrative voice and the degree of explicitness in structuring the plot of the text. The complete report of Dixon and Stratta's conception of narrative provides important data to consider when structuring a narrative writing task.

Understand the Potential and the Limits of Images— Photographs, Drawings, Cartoons—for Providing a Common Subject for Initiating Writing.

The use of pictorial stimuli is now commonplace in writing assessments because they provide broadly accessible information content, something for the mind to work on as a starting point for writing. A particular virtue of the photograph, unlike a literary passage or a poem, is that it is a wordless stimulus that enables writers at all levels of literacy to enter varied worlds of information and ideas, providing material for emotional and cognitive response. Photographed subjects are set in a frame, and their organization is uniquely visible. Student writers can take what is available to their "mind's eye" and use it with their own associations and inferences in making meanings for writing.

As Jon Wagner (1979) so aptly puts it, "Looking at photographs can be just as creative an activity as taking them. As a result, there is potential not only for insight and conceptualization, but also for bias and error" (p. 151–152). Films, photographs, drawings, paintings, and other imagistic forms do not ordinarily tell their meanings. What people see in them depends as much on who they are as what the stimulus is. Hence, just as written prompts require interpretive, transactional processes to create meanings, so do various forms of non-verbal prompts. "Seeing" with understanding is a literate process, as well as a physiological one. Consequently, the image reader's lack of knowledge, restricted experience, and limited cognitive processing ability will affect both his visual literacy and his writing proficiency.

Wagner (1979) observes that "the ambiguity of the medium, as both a matter-of-fact record and a complex symbolic language, becomes apparent to anyone who attempts to use it in communicating with students" (p. 171). Yet this inherent ambiguity of the medium seems to go unrecognized by many test-makers. Users of photographs or other pictorial material as prompts in writing assessments need to understand that these materials cannot be expected to function as uniform stimuli with every respondent "reading" the image and receiving identical messages. Deborah Dashow Ruth's (1977) observations about variation of response to films emphasizes and explains this point: "Although a given group may *watch* the same film, they actually *see* different films, since each student's own individual background, preferences, values, and other 'contextual' considerations determine what each student *sees* and how he/she makes meaning out of what is seen" (p. 106).

This cautionary statement is not intended to discourage using visual stimuli as prompts for writing; rather it aims to encourage assessors using pictorial material to learn more about how it convey meanings, how to avoid the "one right answer syndrome" (D. Ruth, 1976), and how to prepare to accept a range of plausible responses. The issues we have presented are illustrated in the following accounts of the use of photographs to stimulate writing under both national assessment and local classroom conditions.

In the early years of National Assessment, a picture of a forest fire was used with the following instructions for 9 year-old students:

> Here is a picture of something sad that is going on in the forest. Look at the picture for a while. Do you see the forest fire? Write a story about what is happening in the picture. This is an important story because you want people to know about this sad event. [The picture depicts a forest fire with animals swimming across the river rapids to safety.] (Mellon, 1975, p. 21)

Mellon reports that "the words 'sad' and 'important' . . . led some writers to downplay what was happening in an attempt to describe their feelings. Others tried to explain why forest fires constitute important events, and a few ventured into the Smokey Bear idiom and wrote essays on fire prevention" (p. 35). Another commentator (Olson, 1976), complained about the lack of reality of the task, noting that the language of the instructions does not "place the writer in a situation which approaches similitude," and that the instructions are also confusing. One doesn't know whether to describe a sad "event" in the *real picture* or whether to pretend the picture is "a fictive picture [about] which he is to frame a *story*" (p. 17).

Harpin's (1976) account of the use of pictures as stimuli in classroom assignments also is instructive. He describes how two teachers working independently in different schools associated with his project used the identical starting point for writing—a picture of fire-fighting in Jacobean times. Each teacher held brief discussions prior to having the student write. One teacher asked his class to "write a story" about the picture and received a set of historical fiction papers, all except one written in the third person. The other teacher discussed with his class a variety of ways the picture might be responded to and received the following range of responses: (1) the historical fiction form, but also an "eye-witness" or "participant" report involving a change from third to first person narrative; (2) an itemizing of the content of the picture; (3) a broadly aesthetic treatment ("all the faces look alike and the colors are very dull"); and, (4) consideration of the historical significance (p. 94). Harpin concluded that

> apparently equivalent images worked fitfully or not at all. From the experiences of these experiments and the evidence of the project, one significant feature is the extent to which interpretation is 'closed' or 'open'. There appears to be a necessary level of ambiguity for a photograph to succeed in arousing

uniquely individual associations. Too much ambiguity and nothing happens: too little and the responses show little or no variation. (p. 106)

It is evident that we need to know a good deal more about how photographs and other sources of images communicate "visual statements," and how to select and introduce them as contexts for writing. Because research in testing has not yet provided us with sufficient information to guide selection of images for assessment purposes, we must turn to works from other disciplines for help, for example, Wagner's collection of sociological studies in *Images of Information* (1979) and Maley, Duff, and Grellet's (1980) language learning activities in *The Mind's Eye*. Wagner's book, intended for social scientists using photographs as "background, data, and information" in teaching and research, does not deal extensively with photographs and writing, but it is nonetheless a source of valuable insights for assessors who desire to understand better the processes by which photographs can be interpreted and meanings assigned to them. Maley, et al., (1980) intend *The Mind's Eye* a book on using pictures, to be employed creatively for second language learning. Anchored in practical experience, the book has broad relevance as a source for assessors who are looking for help in selecting pictures to accomplish specific purposes in stimulating writing.

Avoid Subjects That Encourage Cliches.

Test-makers sometimes unintentionally create topics that encourage cliches. For example, the following topic was pilot-tested at a state university (M. Kirrie, cited in Keech, 1982a, p. 162):

Unsuccessful Topic

Consider the words *trees* and *plastic*. Write a paragraph in which you discuss some aspect(s) of what the words suggest to you.

Many students who responded to this topic simply resorted to cliches about man's abuse of the environment, using "trees" and "plastic" to represent the natural versus the man-made. Those who attempted to reach beyond cliches and generate an original thesis found it difficult to do so, and their essays were disorganized and lacked coherence. Gertrude Conlan (personal communication, August 22, 1980), speaking from the experience of her long service as Senior Examiner at Educational Testing Service, points out that it becomes difficult for readers to make distinctions in the range of quality of essays written to topics that have elicited papers that are "all alike," "mediocre," "cliche-ridden," or composed of "canned responses."

Avoid Subjects with Hidden Biases.

Unintentional bias may occur if the test maker assumes that students perceive themselves exactly as the test maker perceives them. When the following prompt was piloted for a college proficiency test in 1980, the test committee assumed that the subject of personal rebellion would have universal appeal for students because they believed that most young people perceive themselves as rebels at some time (Keech, 1982a, p. 163):

Unsuccessful Topic

Even those of us who may conform outwardly have our private, personal forms of rebellion. Some rebel against society's conventions, some against family values, and others against the attitudes of peers. We might dress in unconventional ways, reject our family's traditions, or disagree with friends' political beliefs. Some of us may simply rebel against popular fads. Many of us are not interested in jogging five miles a day, eating natural foods, or wearing designer jeans.

Instructions:

Describe one way you choose not to conform. Explain why you act as you do and analyze the effect your choice has on your life.

Apparently the group of students who responded to this subject were less familiar with rebelling than with conforming. Their papers revealed that few had actually experienced significant "personal forms of rebellion" in a way they could write about convincingly. Thus, on the whole, they had little to say. Fortunately, pilot testing revealed the inadequacies of the topic, and the test committee chose an alternative prompt.

Avoid Introducing Subjects Dealing with Controversial Issues into Tasks Calling for Argument or Persuasion.

Controversial issues may seem to provide attractive subjects for tasks calling for persuasion or argument. One might expect students to have much to say about a current subject of controversy. However, papers written in response to such topics without recourse to references and adequate time for reflection are likely to contain snap answers or simple parroting of opinions heard in the media or from friends or parents. Profound consideration of serious issues is unlikely to occur with a previously unseen topic during a 50 minute examination. Additionally, topics based on controversial issues often lead to the expression of views which may be offensive to particular evaluators. The controversial subject may arouse strong biases in the readers, distracting them from making valid and careful evaluations of the students' writing ability. Gertrude Conlan's (1980) trenchant observation on this issue needs to be considered very seriously:

Politics, racial issues, and other inflammatory topics are to be avoided. Also to be avoided are topics that are dishearteningly dull. For example, even a seemingly innocuous topic such as *Who has had the greatest influence on your life?*

cannot be scored easily. If the candidate writes on the wrong political figure (from the reader's point of view) the score is either too high—because the reader is making up for his or her own bias—or too low because the reader has succumbed to that bias. On the other hand, the fifth essay on the greatness of the basketball coach is not scored on the same standard as the first. Readers are human; they do become bored. (G. Conlan, personal communication, August 22, 1980)

Even if special training of evaluators could counteract reader bias on controversial subjects, for most test purposes, it would be wise to avoid statements of extreme general propositions such as the following (Keech, 1982a, p. 157):

Unsuccessful Topics

Men are superior to women.

   or

Women are superior to men.

Instructions:

Agree or disagree with the statement, giving reasons for your opinion.

The British researchers, John Dixon and Leslie Stratta (1981) suggest that this general proposition type of topic, which derives from the debating tradition, aims to provoke a response rather than invite real exploration of an issue. They argue that this type of forced-choice categorical response to complex issues without opportunity for preparation pushes writers to levels of abstraction that are self-defeating. Because such topics given under examination conditions do not provide opportunity for real exploration of issues, Dixon and Stratta do not consider them adequate tests of a student's competence in serious argument.

Select Subjects for Argument Topics That Invite Possible and Reasonable Generalization.

Other serious problems in the conception of argument topics are revealed in the report by Dixon and Stratta (1981). Their paper, important for its profound analysis of problems and its recommendations for change, appears to be little known in this country, so it is summarized at some length in this guideline. Dixon and Stratta's discussion assumes application in a classroom context, but it has profound implications for use of any sort of argument topic in an assessment at any level. Dixon and Stratta (1981) cite the following topic as an example of the traditional approach to designing argument topics, and then they proceed to analyze it for the largely unintended problems it poses for the writer:

Unsuccessful Topic

Young people today have no individuality. They conform to the tastes and interests of their friends and seldom think for themselves. Do you agree? (p. 1)

Dixon and Stratta list 7 constraints and interpretive requirements that make the topic unacceptable in their view. These can be summarized as follows:

1. Given proposition to discuss.
2. Proposition deals with highly general category: [all?] "young people."
3. States a categorical truth about all members of the category.
4. Assumes sophisticated sociological knowledge about "young people today."
5. Implies a contrast with a "yesterday" or "bygone years" and thus assumes equally sophisticated sociological knowledge about the past.
6. Closed question form invites "yes" or "no" answer and constrains approach to issue.
7. Question appears in timed exam to be answered in 50 minutes without preparation and without reference to any sources. (adapted, 1981, p. 1)

Dixon and Stratta provide several examples of subjects for argument tasks that draw on personal experience and that do invite, in their view, "possible and sensible" generalization:

1. You want to convince your parents that you should (not) take up a particular week-end job. What arguments would you put forward?
2. You've seen a particular job you would like. How would you go about convincing an employer that you're very suitable?
3. There are some week-end jobs in your area that seem to you particularly interesting. How would you put the case for them to a younger person?
4. Take a range of weekend jobs in your area: which would you not recommend, and why?
5. What sort of young people would benefit most from doing a weekend job, in your experience? (1981, p. 5)

Dixon and Stratta (1981) define good argument tasks as having qualities such as the following: (1) "They demand response to personal experience, mulling it over, and viewing it in the light of further evidence from classmates or 'authorities' outside the school;" (2) They may "arise from a personal, involved position" or they may "encourage a broader, more general perspective;" (3) They are not so general as "to ask huge overarching questions;" (4) They invite consideration of "a specific issue" and judgment of "how far it is possible and sensible to generalize about it;" (5) They "take personal experience as their springboard and often require students to take a personal position;" (6) They need to "start with small-scale generalizations rather than impossibly huge questions, "many of them beyond the competence, we suspect, of the examiners who set them—if they were constrained to answer unseen in fifty minutes or so" (1981, p. 5).

Dixon and Stratta define and summarize the forms of argument and its functions as follows:

Forms and Functions of Argument
(Adapted from Dixon & Stratta, 1981)

1. Ruminative or reflective essay.

Attempts to explore and sift personal experience (and of others) to discover patterns of significance and ways of viewing them. Does not have to take a final position. (e.g., "Some of the problems facing Asian youngsters in Great Britain.")

2. Advocacy.

Desires to recommend a decision or present a point of view. May marshal a number of points together with supporting evidence. Shows a persuasive edge and sometimes emotional appeals are included (e.g., "Why I am well-suited for this job.").

3. Arguing through an issue or justifying a decision.

Takes account of opposing viewpoints, counters or concedes them in a rational manner (e.g., "Why do some parents think it is important to restrict or guide teenagers in their choice of clothes, and which reasons do you think are justifiable?).

When action is implied, the justification of a decision calls for analysis and evaluation of a body of evidence, including a rational review of alternative proposals (e.g., "Set down the reasons why you propose to choose certain courses, and to reject others, from the range of options offered in the 4th or 5th year.").

4. Attempting an Overview.

Tries to organize and represent the range of arguments available on all sides of an issue or decision for the sake of an audience. Readers are left to make own decision on basis of these data (e.g., "Given the current high rate of unemployment, what arguments would you need to take account of before deciding whether to stay on full-time in education or to leave school."). (p. 11)

Assessors will find these recommendations useful for devising good argument topics, but these summaries are merely an introduction to the fresh perspective of Dixon & Stratta on the nature of argument, and they necessarily omit much information of value in the original reports. We recommend that teachers and evaluators consult the complete version in ERIC.

Relate the Rhetorical Specification to the Assessment Purpose.

Decisions about what kind and how much information to include in topics must depend largely upon the *purpose* of the test. For example, if we wish to

see how the student controls language in relation to audience, we can specify a reader, ranging from an intimate, friendly person to a distant, impersonal, or even unfriendly reader. Thus, to some degree, decisions about
what elements of rhetorical specification to include should be based on
what it is we want to learn from the test—either about what students have
learned or what they have the ability to do.

Variability in the ways topics are interpreted creates some difficult problems for those who must design topics to be used for either assessment or
for research. For example, a very briefly stated topic may elicit a broad range
of task interpretations, especially if the topic allows students to select their
own audience, define their own purpose, etc. On the other hand, introducing constraints into the topic may create its own set of problems.
Lengthy topics that contain many instructions for the expected writing performance or that provide detailed fictional rhetorical contexts may create
problems of reading comprehension and unwittingly introduce crippling
constraints for the writer. Ironically, the addition of what is intended to be
"helpful" contextual information to an examination topic may increase the
possibility of variable interpretations while simultaneously narrowing the
rhetorical demands of the writing task to such a degree that it no longer tests
the student's own ability to determine purpose, audience, and organization.
With each added rhetorical specification, we introduce a constraint, increasing the likelihood of eliciting more convergent responses with a corresponding loss of divergent responses. In effect we restrict the scope of the student's response, gaining uniformity and comparability of samples, but there
is also a loss of information about the range of variability. If purpose, audience, and organization are preformulated, the writing task cannot measure
how the student would have determined these unaided.

Assessors and teachers also need to be sure that the rhetorical contexts
they specify are reasonable. The teacher who created the following classroom test on a Chekhov story, "The Lament," was doubtless sincere in his
intention to reduce uncertainty in his students by giving very clear, detailed
rhetorical specification for his writing assignment. "The Lament" depicts a
pathetic situation where Iona, an old cabdriver who has lost his son, can
find no one in the world to whom he can confide his grief. So, in the end, he
goes out to the stable to tell his "little horse" the whole unbearable story.
Our teacher examiner was thus inspired to propose the following assignment:

Unsuccessful Topic

Level: Average 11th grade
Time Limit: 55 minutes

Assume you are Iona's horse. You are describing the same events to a fellow
horse. Keep your paper short—not over 1 typewritten page. You may be com-
ical, ironic, pathetic or unconcerned in your approach.

Your purpose in writing this paper is to show how a different point of view can change a story.

Be consistent. Try to think like a horse and write like you would imagine a horse might, if he could write.

If you are successful, no matter what approach you make to this assignment, you should illustrate irony, and should almost certainly end up by adding a dimension to the same theme Chekhov had in his version.

Remember, it is essential that you include a description of *the events,* or at least those events that seemed important to you. Those events *you* considered important could be different from those Iona considered important.

Providing writers with not only a subject, but also a purpose for writing and an imaginary audience other than the examiner may be an admirable practice in some testing situations, but it may cause problems in others. One does not have to go to the bizarre extreme of rhetorical specification of the teacher examiner above to get into trouble. Sarah Freedman has provided us with a case in point from a freshman English class where a topic seems to offer clear and exact specification of subject, purpose, audience, and form until one thinks more carefully about the effect of these specifications as constraints on the writer:

Unsuccessful Topic

Length: 3 typed pages, double spaced

You are the president of XXX advertising firm. Members of your firm have just completed a poster for Blue Nun wines advertising their wine. Blue Nun contracted 5 firms to do ads for them, and they will only buy one ad. Write a letter to Blue Nun in which you convince them that they should buy your ad. You have not seen any of the other ads so you cannot compare your ad to the others; your sales pitch will consist of an elaboration of the merits of your own ad.

When we examine carefully the task demands of the topic above, we can see that it presupposes the following knowledge: 1) understanding of the role of the chief executive of an advertising firm; 2) knowledge about Blue Nun wines and their virtues; 3) knowledge about the form of an advertisement; 4) knowledge about the form of a persuasive sales letter. Interestingly, the audience for this *dual-form communication* (an ad embedded in a letter) is only vaguely suggested. Who at Blue Nun will be addressed—an advertising account executive? the board of directors? the Blue Nun president? Having little knowledge about ways of life among executives in the business world, we are wondering just how the president of XXX happens to be writing this letter in the first place. This whole exercise is simply not grounded in anyone's reality, and thus it invites falsification of response even though it is presented under the guise of setting up a real, life-like context for writing.

Rosen (1982) criticizes this type of scenario, where a "fiction" is created, as a practice that produces "bogus" writing that is not "genuine communication" (p. 35). In some assessment situations, however, specification of the rhetorical context may actually seem "real" enough to have positive effects. When audience and purpose are specified, by terms of reference to actual local places and agencies, a topic can present students with an interesting, "realistic" writing problem, as in the following topic successfully used at elementary, middle school, and high school levels in the Bay Area (adapted from Myers, 1980, p. 8):

Successful Topic

The following article appeared in the local newspaper:

KDOL BEGINS SURVEY

Why do we remember certain people from our past but forget others? Television station KDOL is preparing a special TV show on personalities people remember from their younger school years—a classmate, a member of the school staff, a family member, or a neighborhood friend. Send your description to:

> Program Producer
> KDOL
> Oakland, CA 94606

Write about someone who made an unusually strong impression on you. Explain why you remember him or her.

Of all the principles recommended for designing writing tasks, specifications of a full rhetorical context is the one most solidly established in the wisdom of practitioners (see Chapters 2 and 5). Yet there is little research to guide decisions in this area of topic design, and what research is available is inconclusive. So we are left at the moment with common sense as our guide. When making decisions about specification of the rhetorical context, test makers will have to weigh potential benefits against the problems such specification may create, taking into account the purpose of the test, the subject, and the mode of writing.

Specifying the rhetorical context may be advisable when the writing task requires communication for business, social or political purposes. In the real world, such tasks relate to known audiences whose special needs influence the writer's choice of what to say and how to say it in relation to clear purposes. On the other hand, specifying audience for expressive or literary tasks seems to make little difference. Harpin (1976) provides insight into this phenomenon:

> Children often see a single demand behind the variety of surface inducements to write. The writing stimulus, whatever its nature, becomes a springboard, lost sight of after initial purpose is served. The most frequent outcome is in

functional terms, a loose kind of expressive writing, occasionally with narrative form, having 'I' as the center. (p. 93)

Possibly, instead of proposing exotic roles or audiences or even prosaic ones such as members of the family, it is only necessary to train the writer to realize that he is writing for a reader. Thus, instead of directing the writer to pretend to be a disk jockey or a business tycoon, ask him to focus on a reader who needs to be pleased, entertained, informed, instructed, persuaded, or won over in an argument. Simple directives such as the following would then suffice:

1. Write X for a reader and try to convince him or her that you are telling the truth.
2. Write a description of X for a reader whose point of view is different from yours.
3. Write instructions about X that are clear enough for a reader to follow.

Supplementary questions may be added as needed: What does the reader need to know? What questions or objections will the reader have to your argument? What will be the effect on your reader of inadequate information? What is your intention or purpose, and what language will you need to use to get it across?

Bernard Tanner (1981) believes that bringing audience into the rhetorical specification can cause "a whale of a problem." He recommends thinking about the aim or purpose of the prompt in this way:

Into what role does the prompt put the writer—self talking about own experience, self talking about imagined experience, self adopting a role comfortable to self in an imagined transaction, self adopting a role quite unlike self in an imagined transaction, etc.? (B.R. Tanner, letter, February 8, 1981)

Edmund Farrell's discussion of the importance of considering *role* and *voice* in creating writing assignments is a valuable resource on this issue (See Chapter 2).

Avoid Special Forms and Audiences That May Trap Writers into Unwittingly Violating the Testing Frame of Reference and the Tacit Demand to Display Formal Competence in Writing.

Something of this sort did happen in the experimental study reported in Chapter 8 where high school students wrote to a topic that was intended to assess their general proficiency. A number of students selected the form option that invited them to write personal letters or diary entries, two very informal genres that frequently tend to lure students into casual writing that violates the testing frame of reference and its implicit demand to display formal levels of competence. In that study the following topic was employed (Leu, et al., 1982):

Provisionally Successful Topic

Think of an occasion when you experienced something for the FIRST TIME. It may have been something you later came to do more easily or something you now take for granted; but, for some reason, your *first time* was memorable. Write about this "first time" experience so that your reader can understand your feelings and why this memory has stayed with you.

You may write an essay, a short story, a letter, or a journal entry as a way of retelling your experience.

During training for holistic scoring sessions, mismatches between teacher and student expectations and evaluative criteria occurred when students were evaluating compositions written in the form of letters to friends or parents or as entries in personal diaries. The students in the study tended to reward verisimilitude in compositions written in these forms, valuing pieces which sounded more like "real letters" than like "real English themes." They saw the use of "school writing" in the other compositions employing these same forms as unnatural pseudo-letters or as "showing-off." Teachers, on the other hand, paid less attention to the distinction between simulated life-like communicative writing and school writing. Moreover, in some cases teachers penalized students for features of their writing which could be justified by the choice of genre (e.g. lack of detail in a letter to parents who could be presumed to share knowledge of the unstated details).

These research findings should lead us to question whether a writing task functions the same way in an assessment as it would if set in the real world. That is, if we want a sample of competent general writing, we may not get it by asking for a "personal letter to a friend." The student who literally follows this directive may get caught up in two conflicting frames of reference, not realizing that the testing frame of reference calling for correctness and logical order must override his natural impulse toward the casual, fragmented, associational expression of real personal letter writing. Thus, students who take the instructions literally, ignoring the special unstated charge of a test to display competence, may risk being penalized unfairly. Only the most able and test-wise students can balance off the conflicting demands introduced unwittingly into some of these more elaborately staged writing tasks.

Determine That Writers and Evaluators Share a Common Understanding of the Requirements of the Task.

It is, of course, appropriate to test students for their knowledge of the special conventions that are employed with different forms of writing: letters (of complaint, thanks, invitation, recommendation, inquiry, application), reviews, instructions, stories, and other types. But, the test maker must do so deliberately, deciding in advance which form suits the assessment purpose and how much value to place upon adherence to the special conventions of the form. In addition, students must be informed of the conventions which are being tested in the writing assessment. For example, if test makers call for students to write business letters but fail to decide in advance how to weight such formal considerations as salutations, closings, return addresses, etc., it would be difficult to evaluate the responses. A problem of this sort arose with the following prompt when it was tested (Myers, 1980, pp. 8–9):

Provisionally Successful Topic

The following advertisement appeared in the local paper:

SUMMER EMPLOYMENT

Earn & Learn

On-the-job training for future positions as:

Medical Services Aide at Highland Hospital

Ticket taker at local theatre

Grocery clerk at local supermarket

Plumbing assistant for plumbing company

Assistant to the manager of a circus

Earn $3.50 or more per hour while you learn a valuable skill.

Send letter of application to:

Ms. Laura Jones, Opportunity Training Center
2212 Fruitvale Ave., Oakland, California 94231

Pretend that you are applying for one of the jobs listed. Write a letter explaining why you should be hired. You should give information about yourself. The information may be actual facts, made-up information, or a combination of fact and fiction.

Students who responded to this topic used a variety of different conventions in setting up their letters, and the readers differed in their understanding of the preferred conventions. Some believed that "correct form" called for no paragraph indentation; others stressed the importance of adequate spacing between the date and the body of the letter.

In reviewing an earlier version of this guideline on assigning letter writing tasks in assessment, Bernard Tanner (1981) placed the issue of the status of conventions in perspective when he wrote:

We all know that English usage and English style change gradually. [But] The form of business letters . . . has changed rapidly over the last hundred years as offices have shifted from manuscript letters to typewritten letters to word processing. Readers who are evaluating the writing skills of students must make allowances for such changes and differences, ignoring petty matters so that important matters of good sense and clarity take priority. Similarly those who write testing prompts must take care not to make mere conventions into important objectives at the same time that the central purpose of the test is to evaluate common sense and the student's ability to communicate. Perhaps matters of convention like the addresses in letters, the salutations, and the closures, and matters of sentence style like the use of a series of fragments to comprise a perfectly clear list are best tested, after all, by multiple-choice objective tests. (B.R. Tanner, letter, February 8, 1981)

If students have been taught the same set of conventions for business letters, and if the evaluators could reach consensus on the preferred form, it would be possible to devise some system for scoring the finer points of layout and presentation. However, it is clear that general impression scoring would not be an efficient or accurate way of measuring mastery of these conventions. Tanner is correct: The multiple-choice format is ideal for discrete point testing of the sort involved in checking on knowledge of letter writing formats.

When designing topics calling for responses in the form of a letter, testers should be aware that in the absence of specific directions to attend to particular conventions, students will differ in their assumptions about what the tester wants. Some students may, under these circumstances, offer only a mere suggestion of letter form (e.g. "Dear Sir," and "Sincerely,") and proceed to write an essay for the teacher. This is the test-wise student who understands the unstated *real* purpose of the examination exercise. Other students will dutifully observe letter form, assuming that this is what is being tested, rather than the content.

Avoid Developing Topics Around Hypothetical Situations Which Can Only Be Written About in Conditional and Subjunctive Modes.

The way a topic is worded can have a profound effect on the writing produced by students and on their success or failure at accomplishing the task. A language trap, unrecognized by many test makers, can be set when topics are worded so that they encourage young writers to project themselves into hypothetical situations. The following topic exemplifies the problem (Keech, 1982a, p. 151).

Unsuccessful Topic

Write about an event you wish you had witnessed or could witness. The event can be real or imagined; the time of the event can be past, present, or future. Make it clear why the event is significant to you.

Irmscher (1979), Kirrie (1979), and Robinson (1981) all counsel against the use of hypothetical situations for testing writing because such situations call for students to use conditional or subjunctive verb phrases. As Robinson says, speaking from his experience with freshmen at San Francisco State University, "When students are put into situations where they have to use the conditional, they invariably demonstrate that they cannot" (W. Robinson, letter, February 16, 1981). Only the very best high school writers who wrote compositions in response to the topic above were able to maintain a consistent point of view throughout their essays.

Ultimately, however, the test's purpose must determine whether or not to use hypothetical situations. If teachers want to test students' abilities to employ the conditional, then the use of topics which call for its use is appropriate. To avoid the "conditional problem," the instructions should place the student writers *inside* the situation, rather than asking them to comment on what *would, should,* or *might happen* if such a situation occurred. The following topic presents an imaginary situation which proved interesting to student writers (adapted from Camp, 1982, p. 342):

Successful Topic

While visiting in your grandmother's house you find a huge trunk. Propped on a chair beside the trunk is an envelope with your name on it. Inside, in your grandmother's handwriting, is a note that reads: "To my grandchild: Inside this trunk you will find some thing that you have always wanted." Describe what you find in the trunk and tell what you will do with it.

Plant Cues in Topics to Guide Writers in Generating Content and in Adopting Appropriate Forms, but Avoid Overprompting.

The judicious use of cues can assist writers in generating ideas, in clarifying the test maker's expectations about content and form, and in directing attention to options. The test designer should be cautious, however, of overprompting. That point has been reached when the writer responds to suggestions as if they were mandates to include particular content. For example, the following topic, recommended by a state agency for use in elementary schools, includes highly directive cuing, intended to ensure that students write at some length and in comparable ways, but the underlined portions also simultaneously restrict what students can choose to write about (Keech, 1982a, p. 146):

Unsuccessful Topic

You have met a man from outer space who has landed on earth near your school playground. He can understand English, but he does not know anything about schools here on earth. Describe your school for him. *Tell him about your school building. Tell how the school building looks on the outside and the inside. Tell him about your teacher and your classmates.*

The topic has several unfortunate characteristics: Designating a space man as the imaginary audience serves no purpose that would not be better served by a "real" human audience. However, more serious problems occur in the cuing for content which distracts students from observing and selecting what they consider to be significant features of the school. The cuing emphasizes what may be the least interesting aspect of the school—the building—and the tone of the cuing allows no freedom for students to choose some other feature of the school which they might prefer to write about. It is extremely difficult to reword this topic in a way that will get an interesting description of a school from elementary school students. Description, one of the most sophisticated modes of writing, requires a purpose and a physical point of view. These are very hard to cue in the early grades. Therefore, we will keep the same subject—school—but we will reword the instructions to cue a more familiar form, the reporting of a past event, a factual narrative in suggesting an alternative.

Revised Topic

Tell about the best or the worst thing that ever happened to you at school.

Because this revised topic has not been field tested, we cannot be certain that it will be successful. However, this version does illustrate several principles of topic design. It proposes a potentially interesting, familiar subject that is more "open" than the "closed" version it replaces. It also presents a more natural rhetorical problem for the writer, cuing a familiar rhetorical form, e.g. telling, in a factual narrative, what actually happened. Although this topic does not state a purpose, fifth graders are able to understand the "real" purpose and the "real" audience of any writing assigned in a testing context. In this version of the topic, the writer-audience relation is simplified: The writer no longer has to address a dual-audience, the *pretended* "man from outer space" as well as the *real* teacher evaluator who will judge the paper on its merits.

There are instances where a topic designer needs to be directive to be sure that the particular purposes of the examination are being served. For example, if the examiner desired to determine how well high school or beginning college students might write a description requiring a higher level of abstraction, the school topic might be recast as follows.

Successful Topic

Schools are places which have strong effects and influences on people. Describe the atmosphere of your present school or one you attended earlier. You are talking about what it feels like to be in this school. Build your description around a particular feeling or tone. What must your reader see and know to gain the same dominant impression of the basic qualities of the school's atmosphere that you have?

This version of the topic is still open, but it cues a pattern of description ordered around a controlling psychological point of view. It makes a higher order cognitive demand on the writer because it requires him to abstract the physical, tangible elements of the place in order to capture the intangible feeling or tone of the school as an environment.

The next topic illustrates another troublesome issue in formulating cues for content, cues which provoke a disjointed collection of answers (Keech, 1982a, pp. 147–148):

Unsuccessful Topic

Write about your favorite place. Name the place and tell where it is. Tell how often you go there. Why is this place special to you? How do you feel when you are there? What are some sights, sounds, colors and or smells in your favorite place?

Writing Sample

Disneyland. Hollywood. Once a year. Because it is fun. I feel good. Happy. Tired. Sights: Mickey Mouse, rides, African house. Sounds: loud roars, lots of people. Colors: red, yellow, blue, all colors. Smells: cotton candy, caramel apples, animal smells, people smells.

Some students responded to this topic as if it were a short-answer quiz. They wrote words and phrases rather than sentences in response to the questions. In the revision below, we have attempted to make the topic seem less like a set of questions to be answered, and more like an invitation to communicate. Of course, our success could only be determined in a pre-examination tryout with a sample of writers from the target population.

Revised Topic

Everyone usually has a favorite place. Write about yours. Tell why you like to go there and what you do when you're there. Write about this place so that your reader will know why it's special to you.

There are also other indications that using questions as part of the task instructions may introduce unanticipated problems. For example, the following topic was employed in England's 1981 Assessment of Performance Unit Primary Survey of 11 year-olds (Gorman, *et al*, 1981, p. 99):

Sample APU Topic

Imagine this scene:

A tall ragged man is trudging up a steep muddy lane. A little girl and an old woman are hurrying after him. It is pouring rain. The man looks grim and determined. The little girl and the old women look frightened.

Write a story about this scene. If you like, your story could answer some of these questions.

> Who are these people?
> Where are they going?
> Where have they come from?
> Is something going to happen, or has it already happened?

Finding content was not a problem for the 11 year-olds writing to this topic, and misinterpretation was rare. However, although the students did not treat the questions as literal demands for answers, they did tend to link their stories to the questions and to the opening description in ways that tied their stories too closely to the suggested pattern. The evaluators comment (Gorman, *et al*, 1981):

> The instructions contained an additional hazard for some writers, that of the management of tense sequence: where stories opened with reference to the questions, they tended to adopt the present tense, then, as the story developed, changed to the more familiar past tense without regard to the coherence of the tale. (p. 100)

To summarize, when testers want to assist students in accessing and selecting personally meaningful content, they would be wise to avoid offering suggestions which seem like questions to be answered. Wagner (1979) noted a dilemma in using questions either as probes or prompts to elicit information in social science research when he wondered: "How can we ask questions without having the questions themselves organize the perceptions of those we interview?" (p. 85). The test maker faces the same danger of overstructuring the response in using sequences of questions to cue writers. To avoid literal-minded quiz-like responses the designer of the writing task must word questions judiciously, making clear their heuristic function. Questions or other types of cues should be logically arranged to suggest natural patterns of development, ordered progressions of ideas, not random lists of elements of content. Cues for content should suggest options, not impose constraints. Elaborate cuing may help students to think of things they can write about, but it can also lead to poor writing.

Avoid Undercueing with Abstract Directives Such as "Describe."

In general, it can be said that any writing instruction consisting only of the simple direction, "describe," is a case of *undercueing* (Keech, 1982a, p. 167). Additional cues should suggest the physical orientation and the purpose of the description. Without the addition of a limiting instruction, the students, in effect, must set their own limits and construct their own rhetorical purposes. For example, in responding to sparely worded topics such as "Describe your school" or "Describe your home" students will define the task differently—some very literally, others very imaginatively.

Topics such as, "Describe your favorite person," "Describe your favorite object," or "Describe your favorite food," can be altered to prompt more interesting writing: "Describe your favorite _____ (person, food, object) so that *your reader will understand why it is your favorite.*" This simple addition clarifies the rhetorical purpose and cues writers to recognize that the test maker is interested in more than just the ability to write accurate physical descriptions. But for topics intended to elicit physical description, it doesn't help much to simply add the instruction: "Describe your school *so that your reader can understand what it looks like.*" Physical description must have a *point of view:* a fixed point, a moving point, or an "omniscient" point. For example, if this task were rewritten as follows, it would work better: "Describe your school the way it looks as you walk through it, taking any path you wish."

The "describe" instruction has been problematic in various ways in other assessments. One school system found that the task, *"Describe* a person who is important to you," elicited only physical descriptions from many writers (Keech, 1982a, p. 167). A revised instruction, *"Tell about* a person who is important to you," led students to be more elaborate in their descriptions. Tanner (1981) illustrates how the substitution of "tell" for "describe" clarifies the meaning of the prompt: "Describe something from which you learned a lesson." Tanner points out that this prompt could be interpreted to mean "describe an object which taught you a lesson." He says:

> A student might scratch his brains for some time to invent a "lesson" taught him by some particular object—a hard sidewalk or something—and end up with a rather silly piece of trumped-up writing. Try "Tell about an experience from which you learned a lesson." (B.R. Tanner, letter, February 8, 1981)

A research study floundered when an entire group of students refused to write on the topic "Describe your home" because they thought it was too childish (Stahl, 1977). What the students did not realize is that in some ways it was also too difficult: Only the most mature and confident writers can take such an underdeveloped topic and define a rhetorical purpose of their own.

Walker Gibson (1959) illustrates the complexity of rendering good descriptions through one of his fifteen composing exercises in *Seeing and Writing*:

> Find a church in your neighborhood that seems to you an interesting building. Describe what you see on its facade in detail and in such a style that your reader sees it as interesting too. (p. 95)

Gibson explains just how complex this apparently simple task is, and why a church is a good subject for this kind of practice. Churches are often loaded with personal meanings and the task of describing one entails working out answers to several questions: "Who are you, who should you be, as you speak to a reader about the appearance of a church?" (p. 86). Description requires both a purpose and a physical point of view in order to re-create the actual experience of looking. Description is a sophisticated exercise even for advanced writers; it is not, as might be expected, the simplest mode of writing, and therefore it should be used judiciously when testing for general fluency.

Keep Instructions as Brief as Clarity Allows.

Test makers need to consider the extent to which they wish to *test* the student's ability to cue himself in choosing organizational schemes and in exploring his own thoughts on the subject, and the extent to which they wish to cue the student to insure fluency. The advice of Knoblauch and Brannon (1984) on this issue deserves consideration:

> When students are asked to memorize and reproduce the five-paragraph theme structure, for example, their performance is certainly measurable—either they reproduce that structure correctly or they don't. But what is measured here is mainly their ability to follow directions, to do things the teacher's way, not necessarily their ability to compose mature discourse. Training students to follow simple orders offers the alluring possibility of "instant improvement," since only obedience is directly at stake, not intellectual development. Multiplying the number of artificial constraints to include the making of an outline, the recollection of some set of prewriting heuristics, the declaring of a thesis statement, the making of topic sentences, the writing of a "conclusion paragraph," and so forth, testing these all in turn, will enhance the illusion that improvement is occurring, thereby making this style of curriculum irresistible to teachers and administrators under public pressure to deliver "results." (p. 154)

Whether particular types of cues function as constraints or as inspiration is of course debatable. The issue can only be resolved in the context of use with particular student populations. The amount and kind of cuing should be considered in relation to the range of student abilities in the target population under assessment. Students of average or underaverage ability may need more cuing if they are expected to write at any length. Cues for such students should be put in an order that leads to coherence, for they tend to follow cues as given. Randomly listed cues or questions will lead these students into incoherence. More able students, on the other hand, need fewer cues in order to write at length. Often a carefully planned sequence of cues that helps the writer of average ability may confound and inhibit the imagination of the more able.

Avoid Specifying Number of Words, Sentences, Paragraphs.[6]

Most writing assessments impose a time limit which, of course, affects the length of what can be written. Therefore, in any timed examination there is always an implied limit, but the number of words produced will vary with the fluency of the individual students. Some assessors, however, directly specify a *minimum* number of words, sentences, or paragraphs in the instructions. It is not uncommon to see:

> Write at least three sentences . . . (elementary)
> Write one paragraph describing . . . (elementary)
> Write two paragraphs in which you . . . (junior high)
> Write an essay of about 300 words . . . (high school, college)

In general such admonitions are unhelpful, both to the students and to the tester. The tester's purposes can be better served in other ways that do not interfere with the primary aim of the testing, which is to see not only how much but how well the student can write in response to the topic. For example, an important thing to measure in elementary school writing is the degree of fluency—the number of sentences or ideas the child can generate when given a stimulating topic to write on. Thus, the instruction to write three sentences probably is intended to encourage students to write more than they might otherwise attempt. But for children who might be able to think of only one sentence to write, the command to write three sentences is simply an assurance of failure before they begin. A more effective way to insure that low fluency students will generate more than one sentence is to give them an interesting rhetorical problem. In fact, the instruction to write a specific number of sentences on a topic may simply encourage redundancy. In one field test in which the topic asked for three sentences, one student even construed the instruction to mean that she should copy her one sentence over three times. Such an instruction may also increase writing anxiety, turning students' attention to arbitrary formulas for composing rather than helping them generate ideas. In the same field test, several third grade students whose sentence combining skills outstripped their peers were penalized because they each wrote one long, layered sentence which included more information than appeared in the three-sentence papers. Most of the third graders in the field test simply ignored the three-sentence instruction and wrote one to six sentences of varying quality.

The problem in specifying "Write one paragraph" is somewhat different. If the focus of teaching has been on the construction of paragraphs, and if students have been practicing this unit of discourse, the instruction will be familiar. The tester might then be able to justify testing for paragraph construction. But the value of this approach, both to teaching and to testing, is

[6]Based on Keech, 1982a, pp. 179–182.

debatable. Teaching the paragraph as a complete unit of discourse rather than as a method of building an edifice for ongoing discourse may be misleading, even at early stages of writing instruction. If our concern in teaching is to enable students to write fluent, coherent discourse that communicates their intentions, then the manner in which we test should reflect what and how we teach. The instruction "Write a paragraph. . .", introduces a concern for the paragraph as a unit of *testing* rather than as a unit for providing structure in an act of communication. Our concern in such tests might be better directed towards determining the extent to which students have learned to use the paragraph to structure their texts. If testers wish to measure the student's ability to recognize the internal coherence of a good paragraph, they can develop reasonably good multiple choice tests. But using a writing sample test to check primarily on this sort of "paragraph skill" is the wrong testing format.

Finally, the admonition to write a specified minimum number of words, whether included in test instructions or on classroom assignments, encourages pointless word counting and attention paid to "padding" rather than to the development of ideas. Most test-makers who include a word-count specification are merely suggesting the general scope of the topic, thereby indicating how much students should attempt to do in the time available. But the specification presupposes that students have a sense of what a "300-word paper" consists of—as if they were newspaper columnists who write regularly to the same given format. In addition, specifying a certain length may actually impose a limit on fluent students. Sufficient limits are already imposed by the amount of time allowed for writing.

These observations remain to be tested in careful research. However, it is fair to say that the amount of time allowed for a writing episode is an important variable that will have to be considered by testers who are developing topics for writing assessment. Evidence cited in Chapter 8 suggests that the amount of time allowed for writing has different effects on writers of different abilities. It is also likely that a time limit would interact with the effects of specific instructions. How much students *need to say* in order to communicate their intentions effectively is the real consideration, not the number of words used. In a testing context, students should be using their energies and time on more important concerns than counting words.

Avoid Setting the "Choose a Form" or "Pick Your Own Subject" Trap.

Sometimes the instructions in a topic will allow students maximum freedom to match form or mode to intention, such as in the topic instruction which follows (Keech, 1982a, p. 174):

Write in whatever form you want—journal, letter, essay, story.

This kind of instruction in classroom assignments allows imaginative students a full range of choices for creative experimentation which can often result in outstanding writing. But in a testing situation this makes scoring difficult. For example, in our discussion of rhetorical specification, we noted that students may select forms that conflict with the purposes of the assessment. Students who choose to write letters or journal entries may write less formally or correctly than they would if they had chosen essay or story forms. Teacher readers scoring such papers find it difficult to avoid penalizing these students for using techniques that are, in fact, appropriate to the form they've selected.

Allowing a choice of forms or modes can have still another unfortunate effect. Even when teacher readers try to be conscientious about giving full credit to forms other than traditional essays, they are likely to find it difficult to make valid comparisons among papers using different forms. For example, it is easier to judge the relative merits of two short stories, than to judge the relative merits of a short story compared with an argument. Allowing a choice of forms or modes is thus likely to decrease inter-rater agreement.

Chapter 4 describes the finding of several studies which indicates that when students are given a choice in the selection of subjects, they do not always choose wisely. There are also indications that the readers may respond differently to different subjects. Thus, allowing a choice of subjects will lead to differentials of performance which will confound the scoring and interpretation of the sample. Hence, to assure greater reliability in holistic scorings, test makers should give only one topic at a time. As Peter Evans (1979) puts it, "Topic restriction is *more* rather than *less* fair" (p. 17).

Strive for Clarity and for Freedom from Bias in the Language of the Topic.

If a topic is to succeed in engaging students to write with integrity and spirit, it must be carefully conceived and crafted. Experienced writers of topics for assessments have suggested several ways to make the language of instruction definite, unambiguous. Gertrude Conlan (personal communication, August 22, 1980), a senior examiner for the Educational Testing Service, recommends using directives such as the following: "Discuss, citing specific examples from one novel;" "Pay attention to the correct form of the business letter;" "Be sure to use complete sentences." She also recommends including an organizing principle in the directions: "Compare and contrast . . .;" "Briefly describe . . . and then analyze;" "Discuss your answer to this question, giving the reasons for your answer and citing specific examples to support those reasons." We should note, however, that the use of these directives does presuppose knowledge of their significance, and that they take on different meanings as their contexts of use vary. For example, *analysis* will connote different forms of discourse in history, chemistry, or English literature.

Bernard Tanner—speaking as a high school English teacher, author of language texts, and long-time table leader in College Board readings—tells how he words topics to avoid confusion:

> I have . . . made it a rule of thumb for myself in attempting to write prompts that I would use an *entirely* limited vocabulary. I use "tell" when I mean either narration or description. "Tell what happened . . ." means narration; "Tell what the place looks like . . ." means description. I use "explain" when I mean either persuasion or exposition. "Explain how it works . . ." means exposition; "Explain what you believe and why . . ." looks toward persuasion. (Naturally I do not mean that I use those quotations; I mean merely that by using "tell" and "explain" and whatever appropriate phrases are needed after these commands, I establish the central mode or intention of the piece of called-for writing.) (B.R. Tanner, letter, February 8, 1981)

The instrument for assessing writing at the earlier levels in elementary school may consist mainly of oral instructions. The wording of oral instructions needs to be carefully determined prior to the administration. One effective elementary school test consists of a piece of lined paper with the words, "I wish I had . . ." at the top of the page where the student would ordinarily begin to write. The teacher then gives the following instructions orally:

Acceptable Topic

> There are lots of things we wish for. Most of us think of something every day that makes us say, "I wish I had . . ." I want you to think of some of these things, and then choose *one* thing you wish for the *very most*. Tell me what it is by finishing the sentence, "I wish I had . . .". What do you wish you had? After you write down its name, then go on writing and tell me all about it. What is it like? Write down everything you think and feel about your wish.

Tannner (1981) analyzes such tasks this way: 1) The beginning sentence establishes a topic sentence suitable for simple exposition; 2) The "write down its name" assures the completion of the topic sentence; 3) The urging to tell "what it is like" suggests description or discussion of its purpose and value; 4) The "think and feel" opens the door for explanatory comments.

The length of oral instructions needs to be controlled so that the writing assessment doesn't require a feat of memory that gives an advantage to the students with better retention. This should be determined in the pretesting.

Conclusion

The formal literature of educational testing says little about the actual wording of topics: We have mainly anecdotal information from veteran essay examiners like Conlan and Tanner, but even very little of this practical wisdom is available in the more accessible professional publications. It still remains to be gleaned, collated, synthesized from myriad sources. Until this serious gap is closed, we must turn to other disciplines that have studied the nature of the language we use in our instruments of inquiry.

The field of survey research is the richest source of both anecdotal and research-based knowledge about how words are used in data collection instruments, interview questions, and printed questionnaires. An invaluable source is Payne's classic work, *The Art of Asking Questions* (1951). Never out of print since its publication, Payne's eloquent little book guides its reader through a range of considerations for question wording. Payne gives explicit examples of problems and their solutions. One of its special features is "A Rogue's Gallery of Problem Words with Case Histories." Other valuable sources to consult on wording questions include Gordon's *Interviewing: Strategy, Techniques and Tactics* (1980), and Oppenheim's *Questionnaire Design and Attitude Measurement* (1966). Many of the ideas in these books are directly applicable to the design of topics for writing assessment.

Probably the most important cross-disciplinary source of knowledge about language problems in institutional documents is the Document Design Center administered through the American Institutes for Research and Carnegie-Mellon University. Two key publications developed through the Document Design Project are *Document Design: A Review of the Relevant Research* (Felker, 1980) and *The Guidelines for Document Design* (Felker, Pickering, Charrow, Holland, & Redish, 1981). The *Review* synthesizes research relevant to document design (and to design of topics by extrapolation) in the following areas: psycholinguistics, cognitive psychology, instructional research, readability, "human factors," and typography. The *Guidelines* develop research-based principles for re-writing public documents into "plain English." The *Guidelines* are especially useful for identifying particular syntactic patterns that make sentences hard to understand. For example, they deal with the problems created by (1) noun strings— sentences in which the first nouns modify later ones (school assessment policies); (2) nominalizations (implementation, utilization); (3) "whiz-deletions—deletions of terms of subordination (The administrator wants the scores determined by holistic scoring procedures. versus The administrator wants the scores that were determined by holistic scoring procedures.).

Professional testing agencies have become so sensitive to the issues of bias and discrimination in tests that they now have specific policies and elaborate procedures for detecting bias in test items and for eliminating ill-chosen content and potentially inflammatory language. (See Chapter 3 for descriptions of these policies.) Both in the design phase and after the pre-test phase, essay topics are checked during a process called a "sensitivity review" for words and phrases that might be construed as inappropriate references to minorities and women. The procedure described in the Educational Testing Service's *ETS Test Sensitivity Review Process* (Hunter &

Slaughter, 1980) is one that could very well be adapted for use at local levels of assessment. The kind of thoughtful and humanistic concern that is reflected in the process of eliminating material that might be unfair or offensive to any group is a "minimum essential" for the scrupulous conduct of topic design procedures at either national or local levels of writing assessment.

The Evaluation Phase

Once the topics have been written, the design team arranges for their administration to sample groups similar to the population for whom the test is intended. New knowledge about the process of interpreting topics makes the refinement of these field tryout procedures desirable. The construction of the writing test, the reading of the prompt followed by the writing of a response by the student, and the evaluation of the student's composition by the test rater—all involve interactions between texts and participants in the assessment episode. Key points of interaction where "misfires" may occur are in the interpretation of the writing task by the student and in the interpretation of the student's writing specimen by the rater. Our investigation of these points of interaction has led us to propose several recommendations.

The Field Trial Should Include Study of the Causes of Variation in Student Response to Writing Prompts: Calculations of Score Distributions Do Not Suffice.

In their attempt to honor the intention of the test maker, different writers will respond to the same text of a topic for writing and come away from it with different notions about the significance of particular features of the topic. As we have seen, different writers begin to write in testing situations according to different views of what the task actually demands. For example, in our study of the writing assessment episode reported in Chapter 9, the topic for writing which focused on widely discussed local school improvement projects was very carefully structured by a team of teacher designers who expected that this very familiar subject would tap knowledge accessible to all tenth grade students at the high school where the assessment was conducted. These teachers assumed that the instruction to "describe one problem" was clearly self-evident, but when we interviewed students about their interpretations of the topic, it was clear that not all students shared the assumed background information and that they had interpreted the test makers' intentions in a variety of ways which resulted in very different types of compositions.

Such variations in interpretation have important implications for the ways we evaluate topics during field trials. As mentioned earlier psychometric procedures which yield only the distributions of scores fail to give adequate information. These numbers do not tell us, for example, whether the differences in scores reflect true differences in students' writing abilities or differences in the ways they have interpreted the test maker's intention. Clearly, the standard pilot testing approaches are inadequate and must be supplemented by individual user interviews such as those described in Chapter 9, and by careful examination of the compositions produced in response to the topic.

The Field Trial Should Include Study of Any Differences Between the Ways Student Writers and Teacher Raters Perceive the Task.

Depending on the knowledge and experience participants bring to an assessment episode, differences will occur between the key groups of participants in a writing assessment episode. Students have their own experience as test takers to rely on, but teachers bring to the interpreting task a wealth of professional experience in the evaluation of writing. Given such differences, it is not surprising that, as groups, their responses to a writing topic might differ. In the study discussed in Chapter 9, for example, teachers' perceptions of the meaning and significance of portions of the writing prompt frequently differed from those of the students. The teachers saw the need for a focus in the student essays, and they recognized the significance of the phrase, *"Describe one problem,"* as an intentional cue to indicate the desirability of focusing on only one problem. Many of the students, however, either failed to notice the cue or to recognize its significance. Students and teachers also held divergent opinions about the significance of the opening sentence of the prompt, *"Many different suggestions for improvement of Central High School have recently been made."* The teachers considered this first sentence of the prompt to be merely an introduction to the real substance of the writing assignment. Some students, however, considered it to be an operative part of the assignment.

The Appraisal of *Growth* of Competence in Writing Requires Development of New Sampling Approaches; the Single Sample Does Not Suffice as a Valid Measure.

Given the same topic student writers may contruct different writing tasks for themselves at different stages in the development of their intellectual and writing abilities. Holistic scores are insufficient to identify this phenomenon. As students mature, as they learn about different forms of discourse, they may, from any given topic, set a more complicated rhetorical task for themselves than they have previously attempted—before they have full control of the new form. Thus, although test makers may be able to control the set of constraints and options expressed or implied in the text of a writing assignment, they are less able to predict the ways the students may interpret the task.

The study of the interpretation of writing tasks is just beginning, but the preliminary investigations conducted by the BAWP Writing Assessment Project have important implications for writing assessment—especially if the purpose of an assessment is to measure growth—because a comparison of holistic scores may ignore the fact that students are attempting more difficult tasks so that apparent regression (a decrease in score) might actually represent progression (an increasee in the student's repertoire of rhetorical abilities). Thus, a student might appear more expert when writing a form he has mastered, but less expert when he attempts a more complex form.

What is needed is the development of methods and procedures for measuring growth in writing ability that can account for variations in the complexity of the task that the student attempts. A promising approach is the use of the writing folder, in which samples of a student's writing—writing of various kinds in response to topics calling for a variety of rhetorical tasks—are collected at intervals, allowing for an analysis of any improvement (or lack of it) that the student has made over time. Analytical procedures can be used to gauge the development of those features of writing that are amenable to statistical analysis (e.g. cohesion, syntax, frequency of error, etc.), taking into account the rhetorical task attempted. Research has shown that some of these features vary according to the rhetorical demands of the writing. General impression holistic scoring can be used to judge the student's earlier and later performance on similar tasks, and, if necessary, against the performance of other students on the same task.

The Field Tryout Must Provide for Qualitative as Well as Quantitative Analyses of the Properties of Topics.

Even the most carefully structured topics may elicit unexpected results in terms of the quality of the writing produced. Topics should always be pretested to determine the range of scores they generate and the demands they place on the writer. It would be unfortunate if some students "failed" a minimal competency test simply because the topic they received was more difficult than the test designers anticipated. Pre-testing topics will usually reveal whether the test maker's assumptions about what the student can understand and do prove to be accurate or not. In addition, topics of different types may differ in terms of the demands they place on the writer. As examples, two topics from England's Assessment of Performance Unit Secondary Survey are presented below:

APU Sample Topics

Opinion Topic

Think of a subject about which you have a particular opinion, perhaps a strong opinion. Write an essay which would persuade somebody who does not share your opinion to change their mind, and see things your way.

Process Topic

Think of something that you are good at doing, perhaps to the extent of being an expert. Describe how it is done for the benefit of someone much less familiar with the process than yourself.

You may include sketches and diagrams if you wish. (Gorman, et al., 1982, p. 74)

Although both topics invite a student to choose what he wants to write about and to write from a position of conviction or authority, more students received higher marks on the process topic than on the opinion topic. The majority of the compositions for the opinion topic were judged to be inadequate in varying degrees. Students with little detailed knowledge of even well-known, controversial subjects found it difficult to rise above cliched or emotional response. Another group of low scorers used the topic as an opportunity to "let off steam" or "air a grievance." In comparing the demands of the two tasks, the evaluators make several astute observations:

The effect of the writer's presuppositions as to the level of the reader's belief or knowledge as a crucial feature. After all, the difference between being asked to defend an opinion and to explain how to carry out a skilled task lies not so much in the complexity of what is to be articulated. Is a belief that racial discrimination is harmful more complex to set down in writing than a precise account of how to play an organ? A more fundamental difference appears to lie in the expectations which the writer has about the reaction of his audience. Thus, when writing to persuade somebody to share an opinion, the state of that person's attitude can only be intuited (is it hostile? sympathetic? stubborn? half-hearted?); when writing from a position of authority to instruct a novice, assumptions about the reader's knowledge are on more stable ground from the start. Additionally, the writer explaining a skill has a potentially easier method of structuring his writing, in that logical and temporal sequences coincide in the breakdown of "how to do X." Sequencing and emphasizing ideas can be a more problematic area for the writer concerned to justify an opinion. (Gorman, et al., 1982, p. 77)

Traditionally, the primary goal of field testing topics has been to determine whether or not a given topic will produce a range of scores so that test administrators will be able to discriminate between writers of various abilities. But comparisons are not always made between scores awarded to *different* topics, and it is impossible to compare such test results unless topics are pretested carefully enough to establish their equivalence in terms of the scores they produce. This is an especially important issue because topics usually change from year to year or from one test administration to the next.

For example, one pilot study (Kinzer & Murphy, 1982), for the Writing Assessment Project employed data that had already been collected by local school agencies. Following traditional field-testing procedures, data on the range of scores generated by each of eight topics had been tabulated. However, the field testing procedures had examined only the range of scores generated by each topic; comparisons had not been made among the scores generated by all eight topics.

The Writing Assessment Project team made comparisons among the mean scores of the topics. Two were found to be significantly different in the mid-range sample:

Topic A

Think of a friend, real or imaginary, that you had when you were younger. Describe something you and this friend did together, try to show your reader the kind of person this friend was and why you chose this person as a friend.

Topic B

The school newspaper has asked students to submit suggestions about how to improve the school. Think of ONE and only one problem which you would like to see solved to make life at school better for you and others. In a letter to the school newspaper, describe the problem and tell how you would like to see it solved.

Both of these topics called for a composition on personal experience, although one was to be presented in the form of a letter. Topics such as these are commonly classified as "personal essays" in the writing assessment literature (Bridgeman & Carlson, 1983). Presumably, for this reason, and because score comparisons between topics were not made, they were considered to be equivalent. The papers from the field test of these two topics provided the data for the pilot study. In that study, an analysis of the compositions produced in response to the two topics indicated that students were more successful at meeting the task demands of topic B than topic A. The findings from this pilot study thus suggested that topic A was more difficult than topic B, even though both of the topics drew upon personal experience and had been classified as "personal essays."[7]

A research group in Scotland (Pollitt, Hutchinson, Entwistle, & De Luca, 1985) also has conducted a study of "what makes exam questions difficult." This research unit carried out a content analysis of Scottish Certificate of Education Ordinary Grade questions identified as difficult, and the pupil's

---

[7]Just as we went to press, we learned about Schwalm's (1985) approach to *degrees of difficulty* in writing tasks. Designers of writing tasks will find Schwalm's insights into the issues of writing task construction for basic writing courses in college to be very helpful.

answers to them. They found that it was possible to identify particular sources of difficulty and that the same question content could lead to ease or difficulty for the writers, depending on the form and wording of the question. The researchers analyzed questions in relation to the range in quality of answers emerging in terms of "outcome space," a concept which refers to the range of the levels of different responses given to the same question about a prose passage or problem. The researchers in this study are able to identify examples of variations in outcome space which reflect the effects of the question form. The implications of this research are that test makers could control the difficulty of examination questions more systematically. In lengthy appendices, the researchers illustrate how questions might be adjusted to control the range of difficulty to suit different purposes in assessing attainment in English and other subjects (pp. 96–185). If their procedures are adopted, the researchers anticipate that:

> The same candidate should show qualitatively different levels of response to questions presented with varying levels of support and specificity, and contrasting forms of questions should create differing outcome space boundaries by either narrowing or broadening the range of possible responses. (Pollitt, et al., 1985, p. 87.)

The Individual User Interview Is an Essential Procedure of the Post-Design Evaluation Phase.

A standard type of pilot testing or group tryout procedure is designed to evaluate the merit of the topic itself and to enable the design team to determine whether the topic actually works in the way expected. Pilot testing does reveal whether most students can respond to the topic, how difficult the task seems to be, and whether the topic "discriminates" between good and poor students. The standard group tryout can reveal such problems as (1) the topic that elicits unexpected response modes, e.g., narration instead of exposition; (2) the topic that elicits trite responses or highly emotional writing—both factors that make it difficult for readers to score the essays reliably; (3) the topic that is ambiguous, misleading, or confusing.

The field tryout of topics typically produces these useful data, but beyond employing conventional statistical procedures to investigate and/or control for topic effects in testing and research, we need more intensive research into the *causes* of topic effects. It is not enough to know that some topics do, in fact, induce better scores than others; we need to know why. If we are to develop systematic procedures for designing topics that will accurately assess writing abilities, then we need to learn why some topics produce better scores than others. However, the standard approach of using a group to pilot test topics is quite unsuited to the detection of individual misunderstandings and to the analyses of the causes. Therefore, we recommend that this tryout procedure be taken one step further to include also a sample of individual user interviews. This further step is essential so that reliable knowledge for improving the design of tasks used for subsequent assessments of writing can be accumulated. Until funding can be found to support long-term research into writing assessment tasks, small-scale field testing that directly samples writers' interpretations of the language of topics is essential. We recommend adopting a modified form of the procedures used in our Central High School study of topic effects. Following these procedures, field-testing would be undertaken as usual, but a sample of writers would be randomly selected and interviewed about their interpretations of the topics. Thus, the topic is pre-tested to determine how well similar potential users will understand the task when they encounter it in a writing assessment.

The task-based interview adopted in the Central High School study provides a rich source of data about a number of crucial issues in designing topics for writing assessments. It provides a means of

1) discovering writers' paths of interpretation in response to the content of particular topics;
2) discovering the relative importance of various properties of the topic *as experienced by the writer*;
3) discovering the frame of reference used by the writer in interpreting the instructions and constraints of the task;
4) discovering the nature of the task as *reconstructed* and acted upon by the writer.

With the information that the interviews provide, a topic designer can uncover the causes of misunderstandings and redesign the tasks accordingly.[8]

The Evaluation Phase Needs to Be Continuous and Focused on Gathering the Kind of Knowledge Required to Improve Practice in Designing Writing Tasks.

With each new field interview that goes beyond numerical scores to reveal what actually causes variations in response, a topic designer adds to a cumulative body of knowledge available for future topic designers to use as they face the questions at the beginning of any topic design cycle:

1. What is a good topic for the purpose of this assessment?
2. How can we tell if the topic will be understood as we intend by the writers receiving it?
3. What can we do to make the topic comprehensible?

The task ahead in the improvement of practice in the design of topics for

---

[8]A greatly detailed account of user interviews in establishing the nature and range of understanding survey questions is provided in the research of Belson (1981). As one of a handful of qualitative studies of response to questions, Belson's work is important for designers of tests to consider.

writing assessments is to take steps to gather, analyze, and preserve knowledge that practical experience provides.

Conclusion

The model of the assessment episode that we have described in Chapter 7 and the guidelines for designing topics that we have proposed in this chapter challenge commonly held psychometric assumptions that each statement of the writing task is interpreted in the same way by the different participants in a writing assessment episode—the test designers, the test takers, and the test raters. Our model of the writing assessment episode, which focuses on interactions of participants with the written texts that engage them, is designed to guide study of the nuances of *individual* interpretations. The usual accumulation of massed data descriptive of the performance of sample *groups* does not yield the kind of information that we need for the refinement and evolution of practice in designing topics.

We need to move toward developing a model of writing assessment that respects the complexity of individual responses to writing topics. That model must accommodate a range of reasonable interpretations of the task, for the potential meaning will vary from writer to writer. Contemporary reading theory provides insight into ways that personal meanings are created in the minds of the writers not only as they read the text of the prompt, but also as they write, read, and re-read the text that they are creating.

The poet and scientist, Jacob Bronowski ([1956] 1975), writing in *Science and Human Values,* shared his insight into the process of creative readings of both poetry and scientific theorems:

> We re-make nature by the act of discovery, in the poem or in the theorem. And the great poem and the deep theorem are new to every reader, and yet are his own experiences, because he himself recreates them . . . The poem or the discovery exists in two moments of vision: the moment of appreciation as much as that of creation. (pp. 20, 19)

Although Bronowski is discussing great "moments of vision," his observation holds true for all other kinds of texts—even the prosaic texts of writing assessment tasks. Thus, we could say that the text of a writing task lives in *three* "moments of vision:" The first "moment" occurs when it is created by the test maker; the second, when it is read by the student writer; and the third, when it is read by the teacher rater or judge. The more congruent we can make all three visions, the more we will improve the stability of the measure that we use in assessment, and the closer we will come to providing students with writing tasks that will stimulate their powers of expression to the maximum, enabling them to write with interest, effort, and pride in what they have to say.

References

Abelson, R.P. (1981). Constraint, construal and cognitive science: In *Proceedings of the Third Annual Conference of the Cognitive Science Society.* Berkeley: University of California.

Anastasi, A. (1976). *Psychological testing.* New York: Macmillan.

Angoff, W.H. (1982). Use of difficulty and discrimination indices for detecting item bias. In R.A. Berk (Ed.), *Handbook of methods for detecting test bias* (pp. 96–116). Baltimore: John Hopkins University Press.

Applebee, A.N. (1980). *A study of writing in the secondary school.* (Final Rep. NIE-G-79-0174). Urbana, IL: National Council of Teachers of English.

Applebee, A. N. (1984). *Contexts for learning to write: Studies of secondary school instruction.* Norwood, NJ: Ablex.

Atkins, L., & Jarrett, D. (1979). The significance of 'significance tests'. In J. Irvine, I. Miles, & J. Evans (Eds.), *Demystifying social statistics.* London: Pluto Press.

Atwater, J.D. (1980). *Better testing, better writing: Papers on research about learning.* New York: Ford Foundation.

Austin, J.L., & (Eds.), Urmson, J.O., & Sbisà M. (1975). *How to do things with words* (2nd ed.). Cambridge, MA: Harvard University Press.

Ballard, P.B. (1939). *Teaching and testing English.* London: University of London Press.

Ballas, M.S. (1984, Autumn). Writing: New approaches to teaching and assessment raise new questions for researchers. *ETS Developments, 30*(2), 5–8.

Bartlett, E.J. (1981). *Learning to write: Some cognitive and linguistic components.* Washington, DC: Center for Applied Linguistics.

Belanoff, P. (1985, November). In S. Murphy (Recorder), Models of portfolio assessment. In K.L. Greenberg and V.B. Slaughter (Eds.) *Notes from the National Testing Network in Writing.* (pp. 2 & 7) New York: City University of New York, Instructional Resource Center.

Belson, W.A. (1981). *The design and understanding of survey questions.* London: Gower Publishing.

Bereiter, C., & Scardamalia, M. (1983). Does learning to write have to be so difficult? In A. Freedman, I. Pringle, & J. Yalden (Eds.), *Learning to write: First language, second language* (pp. 20–33). London: Longman.

Bereiter, C., Scardamalia, M., & Bracewell, P.J. (1978, March). *Writing and decentered thought: The development of audience awareness.* Paper presented at American Educational Research Association, Toronto, Ontario, Canada.

Berk, R.A. (Ed.). (1982). *Handbook of methods for detecting test bias.* Baltimore, MD: John Hopkins University Press.

Bernstein, B. (1971). *Class, codes and control: Theoretical studies towards a sociology of language* (Vol. 1). London: Routledge & Kegan Paul.

Bizzell, P. (1984). William Perry and liberal education. *College English, 46,* 447–454.

Bloom, B.S. (Ed.). (1956). *Taxonomy of educational objectives: Classification of educational goals. Handbook I: Cognitive domain.* New York: McKay.

Booth, W.C. (1961). *The rhetoric of fiction.* Chicago: The University of Chicago Press.

Braddock, R., Lloyd-Jones, R., & Schoer, L. (1963). *Research in written composition.* Urbana, IL: National Council of Teachers of English.

Breland, H., Camp, R., Jones, R., Morris, M., & Rock, D. (1987). *Assesssing writing skills.* New York: College Entrance Examination Board.

Bridgeman, B., & Carlson, S. (1983, September). *Survey of academic writing tasks required of graduate and undergraduate foreign students* (Research Rep. 15). Princeton, NJ: Educational Testing Service.

Bridgeman, B., & Carlson, S. (1984). Survey of academic writing tasks. *Written Communication, 1,* 247-280.

Britton, J., Burgess, T., Martin, N., McLeod, A., & Rosen, H. (1975). *The development of writing abilities (11–18).* London: Macmillan Education.

Bronowski, J. ([1956] 1975). *Science and human values.* New York: Harper & Row Torchbook.

Brossell, G. (1983, February). Rhetorical specification in essay examination topics. *College English, 45,* 165–173.

Brossell, G. (1986). Current research and unanswered questions in writing assessment. In K. Greenberg, H. Wiener, & R. Donovan (Eds.), *Writing assessment: Issues and strategies.* New York: Longman.

Brown, R. (1978). Choosing and creating an appropriate writing test. In L. Kasdan & D. Hoeber (Eds.), *Basic writing.* Urbana, IL: National Council of Teachers of English.

Bruce, B., Collins, A., Rubin, A.D., & Gentner, D. (1978, June). *A cognitive science approach to writing* (Tech. Rep. No. 89). Urbana, IL: University of Illinois, Center for the Study of Reading.

Cameron, W.B. (1963). *Informal sociology.* New York: Random House.

Camp, G. (1982, November). A field test of eight prompts: Santa Clara County writing assessment. In J. Gray, & L. Ruth, *Properties of writing tasks: A study of alternative procedures for holistic writing assessment.* (pp. 341–385) Berkeley: University of California, Graduate School of Education, Bay Area Writing Project. (ERIC No. ED 230 576)

Camp, R. (1985, November), In S. Murphy (Recorder), Models of portfolio assessment. In K.L. Greenberg & V.B. Slaughter (Eds.). *Notes from the National Testing Network in Writing* (pp. 2 & 7). New York: City University of New York, Instructional Resource Center.

Campbell, D.T., & Stanley, J.C. (1966). *Experimental and quasi-experimental designs for research.* Chicago: Rand McNally.

Cannell, C.F., & Robinson, S. (1971). Analysis of individual questions. In J.B. Lansing, S.B. Withey, & A.C. Wolfe (Eds.), *Working papers in survey research in poverty areas.* Ann Arbor, MI: University of Michigan, Institute for Social Research.

Carleton, S.T., & Marco, G.L. (1982). Methods used by test publishers to "debias" standardized tests: Educational Testing Service. In R.A. Berk (Ed.), *Handbook of methods for detecting test bias* (pp. 278–313), Baltimore, MD: Johns Hopkins University Press.

Carr, A.J. (1965). A student writing assignment based on 'Fire Walking in Ceylon'. In *Commission on English kinescripts (Set 1)*. New York: College Entrance Examination Board.

CCCC resolution on testing. (1979, December). *College Composition and Communication, 30,* 391.

Chafe, W.L. (1979). The flow of thought and the flow of language. In T. Givon (Ed.), *Syntax and semantics: Discourse and syntax* (Vol. 12). New York: Academic Press.

Chafe, W.L. (1980). The deployment of consciousness. In R.O. Freedle (Ed.), *The pear stories: Advances in discourse processes* (Vol. 3). Norwood, NJ: Ablex.

Chew, C.R. (1983, January). A competency test in writing: An impetus for change. In D.A. McQuade & V.B. Slaughter (Eds.). *Notes from the National Testing Network in Writing* (pp. 3 & 14). New York: City University of New York, Instructional Resource Center.

Choppin, B.H., & Purves, A.C. (1969). A comparison of open-ended and multiple-choice items dealing with literary understanding. *Research in the Teaching of English, 3,* 15–24.

Cicourel, A., Jennings, K., Jennings, S., Leiter, K., MacKay, R., Mahan, H., & Roth, D. (1974). *Language use and school performance.* New York: Academic Press.

Clark, C.M., & Florio, S. (1982). *Understanding writing in school: A descriptive study of writing and its instruction in two classrooms* (Research Series No. 104. NIE 400-81-0014). East Lansing: Michigan State University, Institute for Research on Teaching.

Clark, M. (1980). There is no such thing as good writing (so what are we looking for?). In A. Freedman & I. Pringle (Eds.), *Reinventing the rhetorical tradition.* Conway, AR: University of Central Arkansas, L&S Books.

Clark, M. (1983). Evaluating writing in an academic setting. In P. Stock (Ed.), *FForum: Essays on theory and practice in the teaching of writing.* Upper Montclair, NJ: Boynton/Cook.

Clark, R., et al., (Eds.). (1968). *A quest for questions: English series* (rev. ed.). New York: AEVAC, Inc.

Coffman, W.E. (1971a). Essay examinations. In R. Thorndike (Ed.), *Educational measurement* (2nd ed.). Washington, DC: American Council on Education.

Coffman, W.E. (1971b). On the reliability of ratings of essay examinations in English. *Research in the Teaching of English, 5,* 24–37.

Cohen, L., & Manion, L. (1980). *Research methods in education.* London: Croom Helm.

Cole, M., & Means, B. (1981). *Comparative studies of how people think: An introduction.* Cambridge, MA: Harvard University Press.

Collins, J.L., & Williamson, M.M. (1984). Assigned rhetorical context and semantic abbreviation in writing. In R. Beach & L.S. Bridwell (Eds.), *New directions in composition research* (pp. 285–296). New York: The Guilford Press.

Commission on English. (1965). *Freedom and discipline in English.* New York: College Entrance Examination Board.

Commission on English. (1967). *End-of-year examinations in English for college bound students grades 9–12.* Princeton, NJ: College Entrance Examination Board.

Conlan, G. (1982, October). Panning for gold: Finding the best essay topics. In H.S. Weiner, K.L.

Greenberg, & R.A. Donovan (Eds.), *Notes from the National Testing Network in Writing* (p. 11). New York: City University of New York, Instructional Resource Center.

Conlan G. (1983, December). In A. Danzig (Recorder), Research findings: A panel discussion. In K.L. Greenberg, & V.B. Slaughter, (Eds.). *Notes from the National Testing Network in Writing* (p. 10). New York: City University of New York, Instructional Resource Center.

Connors, R.J. (1983, January). Composition studies and science. *College English, 45,* 1–20.

Cooper, C.R., & Odell, L. (Eds.). (1977). *Evaluating writing: Describing, measuring, judging.* Urbana. IL: National Council of Teachers of English.

Cooper, C.R., & Watson, C. (1980). *The sentences of nine-year-old writers: Influences of ability and discourse type.* Unpublished manuscript, La Jolla, CA: University of California, San Diego, Department of Literature.

Cooper, M., & Holzman, M. (1983, October). Talking about protocols. *College Composition and Communication, 34,* 284–293.

Cronbach, L.J. (1980). Validity on parole: How can we go straight? In W.B. Schrader (Ed.), *New directions for testing and measurement: No. 5. Measuring achievement: Progress over a decade* (pp. 98–108). San Francisco: Jossey-Bass.

Crowhurst, M.C. (1978). *Syntactic complexity in two modes of discourse at grades 6, 10, and 12.* Brandon, Manitoba, Canada: Brandon University. (ERIC No. ED 168 037)

Crowhurst, M., & Piche, G.L. (1979). Audience and mode of discourse effects on syntactic complexity in writing on two grade levels. *Research in the Teaching of English, 13,* 101–109.

D'Angelo, F.J. (1975). *A conceptual theory of rhetoric.* Cambridge, MA: Winthrop.

D'Angelo, F.J. (1976). Modes of discourse. In G. Tate (Ed.), *Teaching composition: 10 bibliographical essays.* Fort Worth, TX: Christian University Press.

D'Angelo, F.J. (1980). *Process and thought in composition* (2nd ed.). Cambridge, MA: Winthrop.

Dellinger, D.G. (1982). *Out of the heart: How to design writing assignments for high school courses.* Berkeley: University of California, Graduate School of Education, The National Writing Project.

Diederich, P.B. (1965). Grading and measuring. In A. Jewett & C. Bish (Eds.), *Improving English composition.* Washington, DC: National Education Association.

Diederich, P.B. (1974). *Measuring growth in English.* Urbana, IL: National Council of Teachers of English.

Dietrich, T.G., & Freeman, C. (1979). *A linguistic guide to English proficiency testing in schools* (Language in Education: Theory and Practice 23). Arlington, VA: Center for Applied Linguistics.

Dixon, J., & Stratta, L. (1980a). *Achievements in writing at 15 + : Paper 1. Staging points reached in narratives based on personal experience.* London: Schools Council. (ERIC No. ED 209 389)

Dixon, J., & Stratta, L. (1980b). *Achievements in writing at 16 + : Paper 2. Narratives based on imagined experience: Possible staging points.* London: Schools Council. (ERIC No. ED 216 366)

Dixon, J., & Stratta, L. (1981). *Achievements in writing at 16+:* 'Argument': *What does it mean to teachers of English?* London: Schools Council. (ERIC No. ED 216 357)

Dixon, J., & Stratta, L. (1982). Changing the model for "examining" achievements in writing. In D. Eagleson (Ed.), *English in the eighties.* (Adelaide, Australia: Australian Association for the Teaching of English). Upper Montclair, NJ: Boynton/Cook. (U.S. distributor).

Donaldson, M. (1978). *Children's minds.* London: Fontana/Collins.

Ede, L. (1984, May). Audience: An introduction to research. *College Composition and Communication, 35,* 140–154.

Ede. L., & Lunsford, A. (1984, May). Audience addressed/audience invoked: The role of audience in composition theory and pedagogy. *College Composition and Communication, 35,* 155–171.

Emig, J. (1971). *The composing processes of twelfth graders* (NCTE Research Rep. No. 13). Urbana, IL: National Council of Teachers of English.

Emig, J. (1982). Inquiry paradigms and writing. *College Composition and Communication, 33,* 64–75.

English I: Intermediate division: Ontario assessment instrument pool. (1979). Toronto, Ontario, Canada: The Minister of Education.

English I (writing supplement): Intermediate division: Ontario assessment instrument pool. (1982). Toronto, Ontario, Canada: The Minister of Education.

Evans, P. (1979). Evaluation of writing in Ontario: Grades 8, 12, and 13. *Review and Evaluation Bulletins, 1* (2). Toronto, Ontario, Canada: The Minister of Education.

Evans, P. (1985a, March). *Large scale assessment in Canada.* Paper presented at National Testing Network in Writing Third Annual Conference, San Francisco, CA.

Evans, P. (Ed.). (1985b). *Directions and misdirections in English evaluation.* (Canadian Council of Teachers of English Monographs and Special Publications). Upper Montclair, NJ: Boynton/Cook. (U.S. distributor).

Evertts, E. (1980, Fall). A thousand topics for composition: Plus practical ideas and strategies for teaching (2nd ed., Elementary level). *Illinois English Bulletin, 68,* 3–48.

Expressive writing: Selected results from the second national assessment of writing. (Writing Report No. 05-W-02) (1976, November). Denver, CO: National Assessment of Educational Progress.

Faigley, L. (1980). Names in search of a concept: Maturity, fluency, complexity, and growth in written syntax. *College Composition and Communication, 31,* 291–300.

Faigley, L., & Skinner, A. (1982, August). *Writers' processes and writers' knowledge: A review of research* (Tech. Rep. No. 6. FIPSE Grant No. G008005896). Austin, TX: University of Texas, Writing Program Assessment Project.

Faigley, L., Cherry, R.D., Jolliffe, D.A., & Skinner, A.M. (1985). *Assessing writers' knowledge and processes of composing.* Norwood, NJ: Ablex.

Farr, M. (1981). Moving between practice and research in writing. In A Humes (Ed.), *Proceedings of the NIE-FIPSE Grantee Workshop* (pp. 11–14). Los Alamitos, CA: SWRL Educational Research and Development.

Farrell, E.J. (1969). The beginning begets: Making composition assignments. *English Journal, 58,* 428–431.

Felker, D.B. (Ed.). (1980, April). *Document design: A review of the relevant research* (Contract No. NIE-400-78-0043). Washington, DC: American Institutes for Research, (Carnegie-Mellon University & Siegel & Gale), Document Design Project.

Felker, D., Pickering, F., Charrow, V., Holland, V., & Redish, J. (1981). *Guidelines for document designers* (Contract No. NIE 400-78-0043). Washington, DC: American Institutes for Research, (Carnegie-Mellon University & Siegel & Gale), Document Design Project.

Fillmore, C.J., & Kay, P. (1980, November). *Progress report: Text semantic analysis of reading comprehension.* Unpublished manuscript. Berkeley: University of California.

Finley, C.J., & Berdie, F.S. (1970). *The national assessment approach to exercise development.* Ann Arbor, MI: National Assessment of Educational Progress.

Fish, S. (1980). *Is there a text in this class?* Cambridge, MA: Harvard University Press.

Flower, L.S. (1981). *Problem solving strategies for writing.* New York: Harcourt, Brace and Jovanovich.

Flower, L.S., & Hayes, J.R. (1979). *A process model of composition* (Document Design Project Tech. Rep. No. 1. NIE-G-79-0174). Pittsburgh, PA: Carnegie-Mellon University, American Institutes for Research, Document Design Project.

Flower, L.S., & Hayes, J.R. (1980, February). The cognition of discovery: Defining a rhetorical problem. *College Composition and Communication, 31,* pp. 21–32.

Foley, J.J. (1971). Evaluation of learning in writing. In B. S. Bloom (Ed.), *Handbook on formative and summative evaluation of student learning* (pp. 767–814). New York: McGraw-Hill.

Forrest, A., & Steele, J.M. (1982). *Defining and measuring general education knowledge and skills* (Tech. Rep. 1976-1981). Iowa City: American College Testing Program, College Outcome Measures Program.

Freedle, R., & Duran, R.P. (Eds.). (in press). *Cognitive and linguistic analyses of test performance: Advances in Discourse Processes.* Norwood, NJ: Ablex.

Freedman, A., & Pringle, I. (1980a, June). *The writing abilities of a representative sample of grade 5, 8, and 12 students: The Carleton writing project* (Part 2. Final report). Carleton, Ontario, Canada: Carleton Board of Education. (ERIC No. ED 217 413)

Freedman, A., & Pringle, I. (1980b). Writing in the college years: Some indices of growth. *College Composition and Communication, 31,* 311–324.

Freedman, A., & Pringle, I. (1981). *Why students can't write arguments.* Unpublished manuscript. Ottawa, Ontario, Canada: Carleton University, Linguistics Department.

Freedman, A., Pringle, I., & Yalden, J. (Eds.). (1983). *Learning to write: First language/second language.* London: Longman.

Freedman, S.W., (1983, December). Student characteristics and essay test writing performance. *Research in the Teaching of English, 17,* 313–325.

Freedman, S.W., & Robinson, W.S. (1982, December). Testing proficiency in writing at San Francisco State University. *College Composition and Communication, 33,* 393–398.

French, J.W. (1966). Schools of thought in judging excellence in English themes. In A. Anastasi, (Ed.), *Testing problems in perspective: Twenty-fifth anniversary volume of topical readings from the Invitational Conference on Testing Problems* (pp. 587–596). Washington DC: American Council on Education.

Gage, N.L. (1972). *Teacher effectiveness and teacher education: The search for a scientific basis.* Palo Alto, CA: Pacific Books.

Gere, A.R. (1980, September). Written composition: Toward a theory of evaluation. *College English, 42,* 44–58.

Gibson, W. (1959). *Seeing and writing.* New York: Longmans, Green and Co.

Giddens, A. (1976). *New rules of sociological method: A positive critique of interpretive sociologies.* New York: Basic Books.

Giddens, A. (1979). *Central problems in social theory: Action, structure and contradiction in social analysis.* Berkeley: University of California Press.

Godshalk, F.I., Swineford, F., & Coffman, W.E. (1966). *The measurement of writing ability.* New York: College Entrance Examination Board.

Gordon, R.L. (1980). *Interviewing: Strategy, techniques and tactics.* Homewood, IL: The Dorsey Press.

Gorman, T.P., White, J., Orchard, L., Tate, A., & Sexton, B. (1981). *Language performance in schools* (Primary Survey Rep. No. 1). London: Her Majesty's Stationery Office, Department of Education and Science.

Gorman, T.P., White, J., Orchard, L., Tate, A., & Sexton, B. (1982). *Language performance in schools* (Primary Survey Rep. No. 2). London: Her Majesty's Stationery Office, Department of Education and Science.

Gorman, T.P., White, J., Orchard, L., Tate, A., & Sexton, B. (1982). *Language performance in schools* (Secondary Survey Rep. No. 1). London: Her Majesty's Stationery Office, Department of Education and Science.

Gorman, T.P., White, J., Orchard, L., Tate, A., & Sexton, B. (1983). *Language performance in schools* (Secondary Survey Rep. No. 2). London: Her Majesty's Stationery Office, Department of Education and Science.

Graves, D.H. (1978). *Balancing the basics: Let them write.* (Papers on research about learning series). New York: Ford Foundation.

Graves, D.H. (1979, January). Research doesn't have to be boring. *Language Arts, 56,* 76–80.

Graves, D.H. (1983). *Writing: Teachers & children at work.* Exeter, NH: Heinemann.

Gray, J.R., and Ruth, L.P. (1982, November). *Properties of writing tasks: A study of alternative procedures for holistic writing assessment.* (Final Rep. NIE-G-80-0034). Berkeley: University of California, Graduate School of Education, Bay Area Writing Project. (ERIC No. ED 230 576)

Green, D.R. (1982). Methods used by test publishers to "debias" standardized tests: CTB/McGraw-Hill. In R.A. Berk (Ed.), *Handbook of methods for detecting test bias* (pp. 229–240). Baltimore, MD: Johns Hopkins University.

Greenberg, K.L. (1981a). *The effects of variations in essay questions on the writing perfor-

mance of CUNY freshmen. New York: City University of New York, Instructional Resource Center.

Greenberg, K.L. (1981b). *Some relationships between writing tasks and students' writing performance* (with WAT Question Pilot Series attachment). Paper presented at the 71st Annual Convention of the National Council of Teachers of English, Boston, MA.

Greenberg, K., Wiener, H., & Donovan, R. (Eds.). (1986). *Writing assessment: Issues and strategies.* New York: Longman.

Halliday, M.A.K., & Hasan, R. (1976). *Cohesion in English.* London: Longman.

Hamp-Lyon, L. (1987). The product before: Task-related influences on the writer. In P. Robinson (Ed.) *Academic writing: Process and product.* London: Pergamon

Harpin, W. (1976). *The second "r": Writing developments in the junior school.* London: George Allen and Unwin.

Hays, J.N. (1983). The development of discursive maturity in college writers. In J.N. Hays, P.A. Roth, J.R. Ramsey, & R.D. Foulke, *The writer's mind: Writing as a mode of thinking.* Urbana, IL: National Council of Teachers of English.

Hendrick, F.A., & Loyd, B.H. (1982). Methods used by test publishers to "debias" standardized tests: The American College Testing Program. In R.A. Berk (Ed.), *Handbook of methods for detecting test bias* (pp. 272–278). Baltimore, MD: Johns Hopkins University.

Henkel, R.E. (1976). *Tests of significance* (Sage University Papers Series: Quantitative Applications in the Social Sciences, Series No. 07-001). Beverly Hills, CA: Sage.

Hoetker, J. (1982, December). Essay examination topics and student's writing. *College Composition and Communication, 33,* 377–392.

Hoetker, J., Brossell, G., & Ash, B. (1981). *Creating essay examination topics.* Unpublished manuscript, Florida State University, Tallahassee.

Hopkins, K.D., & Stanley, J.C. (1981). *Educational and psychological measurement and evaluation.* Englewood Cliffs, NJ: Prentice-Hall.

Hunt, K.W. (1965). *Grammatical structures written at three grade levels* (NCTE Research Report No. 3). Urbana, IL: National Council of Teachers of English.

Hunter, R.V., & Slaughter, C.D. (1980, July). *ETS test sensitivity review process.* Princeton, NJ: Educational Testing Service.

Interviewer's manual. (1969). Ann Arbor, MI.: Institute for Social Research, Survey Research Center.

Irmscher, W.F. (1979). *Teaching expository writing.* New York: Holt, Rinehart and Winston.

Jacobs, H.L., Zingraf, S.A., Wormuth, D.R., Hartfiel, V.F., & Hughey, J.B. (1981). *Testing ESL composition: A practical approach.* Rowley, MA: Newbury House.

Johnston, B. (1983). *Assessing English: Helping students reflect on their work.* (Sydney, Australia: St. Clair Press). Urbana, IL: National Council of Teachers of English. (U.S. distributor).

Johnson, P.H. (1983). *Reading comprehension assessment: A cognitive basis.* Newark, DE: International Reading Association.

Johnson-Laird, P.N., & Wason, P.C. (Eds.). (1977). *Thinking: Readings in cognitive science.* Cambridge, MA: University Press.

Kandel, I.L. (1936). *Examinations and their substitutes in the United States.* New York: The Carnegie Foundation for the Advancement of Teaching.

Kaplan, A. (1964). *The conduct of inquiry: Methodology for behavioral science.* San Francisco: Chandler.

Katzer, J., Cook, K.H., & Crouch, W.W. (1978). *Evaluating information: A guide for users of social science research.* Reading, MA: Addison-Wesley.

Keech, C.L. (1982a, November). Practices in designing writing test prompts: Analysis and recommendations. In J.R. Gray, & L.P. Ruth, *Properties of writing tasks: A study of alternative procedures for holistic writing assessment* (pp. 132–214). Berkeley, University of California, Graduate School of Education, Bay Area Writing Project. (ERIC No. ED 230 576)

Keech, C.L. (1982b, November). Unexpected directions of change in student writing performance. In J.R. Gray, & L.P. Ruth, *Properties of writing tasks: A study of alternative procedures for holistic writing assessment* (pp. 472–508). Berkeley: University of California, Graduate School of Education, Bay Area Writing Project. (ERIC No. ED 230 576)

Keech, C.L. (1984). *Apparent regression in student writing performance as a function of unrecognized changes in task complexity.* Unpublished doctoral dissertation, University of California, Berkeley.

Keech, C.L., and McNelly, M.E. (1982, November). Comparison and analysis of rater responses to the anchor papers in the writing prompt variation study. In J.R. Gray, & L.P. Ruth, *Properties of writing tasks: A study of alternative procedures for holistic writing assessment* (pp. 260–315). Berkeley: University of California, Graduate School of Education, Bay Area Writing Project.

Kerlinger, F.N. (1964). *Foundations in behavioral research.* New York: Holt, Rinehart, & Winston.

Kincaid, G.L. (1953). *Some factors affecting variations in the quality of students' writing.* Unpublished doctoral dissertation, Michigan State University.

Kinneavy, J.L. (1971). *A theory of discourse.* Englewood Cliffs, NJ: Prentice-Hall.

Kinneavy, J.L. (1980). A pluralistic synthesis of four contemporary models for teaching composition. In A. Freedman, & I. Pringle (Eds.), *Reinventing the rhetorical tradition.* Conway, AR: University of Central Arkansas, L&S Books.

Kinzer, C., & Murphy, S. (1982, November). The effects of assessment prompt and response variables on holistic score: A pilot study and validation of an analysis technique. In J.R. Gray, & L.P. Ruth, *Properties of writing tasks: A study of alternative procedures for holistic writing assessment* (pp. 316–340). Berkeley: University of California, Graduate School of Education, Bay Area Writing Project. (ERIC No. ED 230 576)

Kirrie, M. (1979, May). Prompt writing is not impromptu. *National Writing Project Newsletter, 1,* 6–7.

Knoblauch, C.H., & Brannon, L. (1984). *Rhetorical traditions and the teaching of writing.* Upper Montclair, NJ: Boynton/Cook.

Krupa, G. (1982). *Situational writing.* Belmont, CA: Wadsworth.

Labov, W. (1971). The study of language in its social context. In J.A. Fishman (Ed.), *Advances in sociology of language* (Vol. 1) pp. 152–216. The Hague, Holland: Mouton.

Labov, W. (1972). *Language in the inner city: Studies in the Black English vernacular.* Philadelphia: University of Pennsylvania Press.

Labov, W., & Waletzky, J. (1966). Narrative analysis: Oral versions of personal experience. In J. Helm (Ed.), *Essays on the verbal and visual arts: Proceedings of the 1966 Annual Spring Meeting of the American Ethnological Society.* Seattle: University of Washington Press.

Langer, J.A. (1984). Where problems start: The effects of available information on responses to school writing tasks. In A.N. Applebee, *Contexts for learning to write: Studies of secondary school instruction* (pp. 135–148). Norwood, NJ: Ablex.

Language performance. (1978, May). London: Department of Education and Science, Assessment of Performance Unit.

Lanham, R.A. (1979). *Revising prose.* New York: Charles Scribner's Sons.

Lenke, J.M. (1982). Methods used by test publishers to "debias" standardized tests: The Psychological Corporation. In R.A. Berk (Ed.), *Handbook of methods for detecting bias* (pp. 255–260). Baltimore, MD: Johns Hopkins University Press.

Leu, D.J., Jr., Keech, K.L., Murphy, S., & Kinzer, C. (1982, November). Effects of two versions of a writing prompt upon holistic score and writing processes. In J.R. Gray, & L.P. Ruth, *Properties of writing tasks: A study of alternative procedures for holistic writing assessment* (pp. 215–259). Berkeley: University of California, Graduate School of Education, Bay Area Writing Project.

Lloyd-Jones, R. (1977). Primary trait scoring. In C. Cooper, & L. Odell (Eds.), *Evaluating writing: Describing, measuring, judging* (pp. 33–36). Urbana, IL: National Council of Teachers of English.

Lloyd-Jones, R. (1982, October). Skepticism about test scores. In D.A. McQuade, & V.B. Slaughter (Eds.), *Notes from the National Testing Network in Writing* (pp. 3, 9). New York: City University of New York, Instructional Resource Center.

Loban, W. (1963). *The language of elementary school children* (NCTE Research Report No. 1). Urbana, IL: National Council of Teachers of English.

Long, R.C. (1980, May). Writer-audience relationships: Analysis or invention? *College Composition and Communication, 31,* 221–226.

Maley, A., Duff, A., & Grellet, F. (1980). *The mind's eye: Using pictures creatively in language learning.* Cambridge, England: Cambridge University Press.

Matsuhashi, A. (1981). *Producing written discourse: A theory-based description of the temporal characteristics of three discourse tasks from four competent grade 12 writers.* Unpublished manuscript, University of Illinois, Chicago Circle.

Matsuhashi, A. (1982). Explorations in the real-time production of written discourse. In M. Nystrand (Ed.), *What writers know: The language, process and structure of written discourse.* New York: Academic Press.

Mehrens, W., & Lehman, I. (1973). *Measurement and evaluation in education and psychology.* New York: Holt, Rinehart, and Winston.

Meier, D. (1973, February). *Reading failure and the tests.* New York: The Workshop Center for Open Education.

Mellon, J.C. (1975). *National assessment and the teaching of English.* Urbana, IL: National Council of Teachers of English.

Mellon, J.C. (1977, June). *A taxonomy of compositional competencies.* Paper presented at the Minnesota Perspectives on Literacy Conference, Minneapolis. (ERIC No. ED 157 058)

Miles, J. (1979). *Working out ideas: Predication and other uses of language* ((Bay Area Writing Project Curriculum Publication No. 5)). Berkeley: University of California, Graduate School of Education, Bay Area Writing Project.

Miller, C., & Swift, K. (1980). *The handbook of nonsexist writing for writers, editors, and speakers.* New York: Lippincott & Crowell.

Mitroff, I.I., & Kilmann, R.H. (1978). *Methodological approaches to social science.* San Francisco: Jossey-Bass.

Moffett, J.W. ([1968] 1983). *Teaching the universe of discourse.* Upper Montclair, NJ: Boynton/Cook.

Moffett, J.W. (1981). *Active voice.* Montclair, NJ: Boynton/Cook.

Morrison, D.E., & Henkel, R.E. (1969, May). Significance tests reconsidered. *The American Sociologist, 131–139.*

Mullis, I.V.S. (1976, April). *The primary trait system for scoring writing tests.* Paper presented at the Annual Meeting of the American Educational Research Association, San Francisco. (ERIC No. ED 124 942)

Mullis, I.V.S. (1981, April). *Highlights and trends in writing achievement, 1969-79: Results from the National Assessment of Educational Progress.* Paper presented at the Annual Meeting of the American Educational Research Association, Los Angeles.

Mullis, I.V.S. (1984, Spring). Scoring direct writing assessments: What are the alternatives? *Educational Measurement: Issues and practice, 16–20.*

Murphy, S. (1985, November). (Recorder), Models of portfolio assessment. In K.L. Greenberg, & V.B. Slaughter (Eds.). *Notes from the National Testing Network in Writing* (p. 2 & 7). New York: City University of New York, Instructional Resource Center.

Murphy, S., Carroll, K., Kinzer, C., & Robyns, A. (1982, November). A study of the construction of the meanings of a writing prompt by its authors, the student writers, and the raters. In J.R. Gray, & L.P. Ruth, *Properties of Writing Tasks: A study of alternative procedures for holistic writing assessment.* (pp. 336–471). University of California, Graduate School of Education, Bay Area Writing Project. (ERIC No. ED 230576)

Myers, M.A. (1980). *A procedure for writing assessment and holistic scoring.* Urbana, IL: ERIC Clearinghouse on Reading and Communication Skills and the National Council of Teachers of English.

Neilson, B. (1979). *Writing as a second language: Psycholinguistic processes in composition.* Unpublished doctoral dissertation, University of California, San Diego.

Newkirk, T. (1983, Third Quarter). Why bother with William Perry? *The English Record.* 9–11.

Nold, E., & Freedman, S. (1977). An analysis of readers' responses to essays. *Research in the Teaching of English, 11,* 165–174.

Ochs, E. (1979). Planned and unplanned discourse. In T. Givon (Ed.), *Syntax and semantics: Discourse and syntax* (Vol. 12). (pp. 51–80). New York: Academic Press.

Odell, L. (1977). Measuring changes in intellectual processes as one dimension of growth in writing. In C.R. Cooper, & L. Odell (Eds.), *Evaluating writing: Describing, measuring, judging* (pp. 107–132). Urbana, IL: National Council of Teachers of English.

Odell, L. (1979, February). Teachers of composition and needed research in discourse theory. *College Composition and Communication, 30,* 39–43.

Odell, L. (1981). Defining and assessing competence in writing. In C. Cooper (Ed.), *The nature and measurement of competency in English* (pp. 95–103). Urbana, IL: National Council of Teachers of English.

Odell, L. (1983). How English teachers can help their colleagues teach writing. In P. Stock (Ed.), *FFORUM: Essays on theory and practice in the teaching of writing.* Upper Montclair, NJ: Boynton/Cook.

Odell, L., & Cooper, C.R. (1980, September). Procedures for evaluating writing: Assumptions and needed research. *College English, 42,* 35–43.

Odell, L., & Cooper, C.R., & Courts, C. (1978). Discourse theory: Implications for research in composing. In C.R. Cooper & L. Odell (Eds.), *Research on composing: Points of departure.* Urbana, IL: National Council of Teachers of English.

Olson, P. (1976, December). *A view of power: Four essays on the National Assessment of Educational Progress.* Grand Forks: University of North Dakota Press, Center for Teaching & Learning, North Dakota Study Group on Evaluation.

Ong, W.J. (1977). *The interface of the word: Studies in the evolution of consciousness.* Ithaca, NY: Cornell University Press.

Ong, W.J. (1979). Literacy and orality in our times. *Profession 79.* New York: Modern Language Association.

Oppenheim, A.N. (1966). *Questionnaire design and attitude measurement.* New York: Basic Books.

Park, D.B. (1982). The meanings of "audience". *College English, 44,* 247–257.

Patton, M.Q. (1975). *Alternative evaluation research paradigm.* Grand Forks, ND: University of North Dakota, Center for Teaching & Learning, North Dakota Study Group on Evaluation.

Payne, D.A., & McMorris, R.F. (1967). *Educational and psychological measurement.* Waltham, MA: Blaisdell.

Payne, S.L. (1951). *The art of asking questions.* Princeton, NJ: Princeton University Press.

Pearce, J. (1974). Examinations in English language. In I.J. Forsyth, & J. Pearce (Eds.), *Language: Classroom and examinations* (Schools Council Programme in Linguistics and English Teaching, Papers Series II, Vol. 4) (pp. 37–82). London: Longman.

Perron, J.D. (1977, April). Written syntactic complexity and the modes of discourse. Paper presented at the meeting of the American Educational Research Association, New York.

Perry, W.G. (1968). *Forms of intellectual and ethical development in the college years.* New York: Holt, Rinehart and Winston.

Peterson, B.T. (1982, September). Writing about responses: A unified model of reading, interpretation, and composition. *College English, 44,* 459–468.

Pianko, S. (1979). A description of the composing processes of college freshmen writers. *Research in the Teaching of English, 13,* 5–24.

Polin, L. (1980) *Specifying the writing domain for assessment: recommendations to the practioner* (CSE Report No. 135). Los Angeles, CA: University of California, Graduate School of Education, Center for the Study of Evaluation.

Pollitt, A., Hutchinson, C., Entwistle, N., & De Luca, C. (1985). *What makes exam questions difficult? An analysis of "0" grade answers and questions.* Edinburgh: Scottish Academic Press.

Powell, D. (1981). *What can I write about? 7,000 topics for high school students.* Urbana, IL: National Council of Teachers of English.

Purves, A.C., & Takala, S. (Eds.). (1982). An international perspective on the evaluation of written composition [Special Issue]. *Evaluation in Education: An International Review Series, 5,* (3).

Purves, A.C., Söter, A., Takala, S., & Vähäpassi, A. (1984), Towards a domain-referenced system for classifying composition assignments. *Research in the Teaching of English, 18,* 385–416.

Quellmalz, E.S. (1984, Spring). Toward successful large-scale writing assessment: Where are we now? Where do we go from here? *Educational Measurement: Issues and practice, 3,* 29–32.

Quellmalz, E.S., Capell, F.J., & Chou, C.P. (1982). Effects of discourse and response mode on the measurement of writing competence. *Journal of Educational Measurement, 19,* 241–258.

Raju, N.S. (1982). Methods used by test publishers to "debias" standardized tests: Science Research Associates. In R.A. Berk (Ed.), *Handbook of methods for detecting test bias* (pp. 251–272). Baltimore, MD: Johns Hopkins University Press.

Reid, W.A. (1978). *Thinking about curriculum: The nature and treatment of curriculum problems.* London: Routledge & Kegan Paul.

Reynolds, J., & Skilbeck, M. (1976). *Culture and the classroom.* London: Open Books.

Robinson, S. (1985). Afterward, a reflective reaction. In P. Evans (Ed.), *Directions and misdirections in English evaluation* (pp. 111–115). (Canadian Council of Teachers of English, Carleton College, Department of Linguistics) Upper Montclair, NJ: Boynton/Cook. (U.S. distributor).

Rockas, L. (1964). *Modes of rhetoric.* New York: St. Martin's Press.

Rosen, H. (1969). *An investigation of the effects of differentiated writing assignments on the performance in English composition of a selected group of 15/16 year old pupils.* Unpublished doctoral dissertation, University of London, London, England.

Rosen, H. (1982). *The language monitors: A critique of the APU's Primary Survey Report, Language Performance in Schools* (Bedford Way Papers, No. 11). London: University of London, Institute of Education.

Rosenblatt, L.M. ([1938], 1976). *Literature as exploration* (3rd ed.). New York: Noble and Noble.

Rosenblatt, L.M. (1978). *The reader, the text, the poem: The transactional theory of the literary work.* Carbondale, IL: Southern Illinois University Press.

Rosenblatt, L.M. (1985, February). Viewpoints: Transaction versus interaction—A terminological rescue operation. *Research in the Teaching of English, 19,* 96–107.

Rowntree, D. (1977). *Assessing students: How shall we know them?* London: Harper and Row.

Rowntree, D. (1981). *Statistics without tears.* New York: Charles Scribner's Sons.

Rumelhart, D.E. (1977). Toward an interactive model of reading. In S. Dornic (Ed.), *Attention and performance* (Vol. 6). Hillsdale, NJ: Erlbaum.

Rumelhart, D.E. (1978). Understanding and summarizing brief stories. In D. Laberge, & S. Samuels (Eds.), *Basic processes in reading: Perception and comprehension.* Hillsdale, NJ: Erlbaum.

Rushton, J., & Young, G. (1974). Elements of elaboration in working class writing. *Educational Research, 16,* 181–188.

Ruth, D.D. (1976, April). *Views of nonprint media: A case for expanded literacy.* Paper presented at the Annual Meeting of the Secondary Section English Conference (National Council of Teachers of English), Boston, MA.

Ruth, D.D. (1977). The next language art: Views of nonprint media. In J.R. Squire (Ed.), *The teaching of English: The Seventy-Sixth Yearbook of the National Society for the Study of Education: Part 1* (pp. 96–125). Chicago: University of Chicago Press.

Ruth, L.P. (1980). *Questions and answers: A model of relations, forms and functions.* Unpublished doctoral dissertation, University of California, Berkeley.

Ruth, L.P. (1982, November). Sources of knowledge for designing writing test prompts. In J.R Gray, & L.P. Ruth, *Properties of writing tasks: a study of alternative procedures for holistic writing assessment.* (pp. 31–131). Berkeley: University of California, Graduate School of Education, Bay Area Writing Project. (ERIC No. ED 230 576)

Ruth, L.P., & Murphy, S. (1984, December). Designing topics for writing assessment: Problems of meaning. *College Composition and Communication, 35,* 410–422.

Sachse, P.P. (1984, Spring). Writing assessment in Texas: Practices and problems. *Educational Measurement: Issues and Practice, 3,* 21–26.

Sanders, N.M. (1966). *Classroom questions: What kinds?* New York: Harper & Row.

Sanders, S., & Littlefield, J. (1975). Perhaps test essays can reflect significant improvement in freshmen composition, *Research in the Teaching of English, 9,* 145–153.

San Jose, C.P.M. (1972). *Grammatical structures in four modes of writing at fourth-grade level.* Unpublished doctoral dissertation, Syracuse University, NY.

Sax, G. (1974). *Principles of educational measurement and evaluation.* Belmont, CA: Wadsworth.

Scardamalia, M., Bereiter, C., & Fillion, B. (1981). *Writing for results: A sourcebook of consequential composing activities.* Toronto, Ontario, Canada: The Ontario Institute for Studies in Education.

Scheuneman, J.D. (1982). A posteriori analyses of biased items. In R.A. Berk (Ed.), *Handbook of methods for detecting test bias* (pp. 180–198). Baltimore, MD: Johns Hopkins University Press.

Schon, D.A. (1983). *The reflective practioner: How professionals think in action.* New York: Basic Books.

Schwalm, D.E. (1985, October). Degree of difficulty in basic writing courses: Insight from the Oral Proficiency Interview Testing Program. *College English, 47,* 629–640.

Scott, F.N. (1903). The teacher and his training. In G.R. Carpenter, F.T. Baker, & F.N. Scott (Eds.), *The teaching of English in elementary and secondary school.* New York: Longmans, Green and Co.

Scriven, M. (1972). Objectivity and subjectivity in educational research. In L.G. Thomas (Ed.), *Philosophical redirection of educational research.* Chicago: University of Chicago Press.

Shepard, L.A. (1982). Definition of bias. In R.A. Berk (Ed.), *Handbook of methods for detecting test bias* (pp. 9–30). Baltimore, MD: Johns Hopkins University Press.

Shuy, R. (1981). Closing remarks. In A. Humes (Ed.), *Moving between practice and research in writing: Proceedings of the NIE-FIPSE grantee workshop* (pp. 161–174). Los Alamitos, CA: SWRL Educational Research and Development.

Smith, L.S. (1980). *Measures of high school students' expository writing: Direct and indirect strategies* (CSE Report No. 133). Los Angeles: University of California, Graduate School of Education, Center for the Study of Evaluation.

Snow, R.E. (1973). Theory construction for research in teaching. In Travers, R.M.V. (Ed.), *Second handbook of research on teaching* (pp. 77–113). Chicago: Rand McNally.

Spandel, V., & Stiggins, R.J. (1980). *Direct measures of writing skill: Issues and applications.* Portland, OR: Northwest Regional Educational Laboratory.

Stahl, A. (1977). The structure of children's compositions: Developmental and ethnic differences. *Research in the Teaching of English, 11,* 156–164.

Starch, D., & Elliott, E.C. (1912). Reliability of the grading of high school work in English. *School Review, 20,* 442–457.

Starch, D., & Elliott, E. ([1912,1913] 1967). The reliability of grading work in English, mathematics, and history. In D. Payne, & R. McMorris (Eds.), *Educational and psychological measurement.* Waltham, MA: Blaisdell.

Staton, J. (1981). Introduction. In E. Bartlett (Ed.), *Learning to write: Some cognitive and linguistic components* (Linguistics and Literacy Series 2). Washington, DC: Center for Applied Linguistics.

Steinberg, E.R. (1980). A garden of opportunities and a thicket of dangers. In L.W. Gregg & E.R. Steinberg (Eds.), *Cognitive processes in writing* (pp. 156–168). Hillsdale, NJ: Erlbaum.

Steinman, M. (1967). A conceptual review [Review of *The measurement of writing ability*]. *Research in the Teaching of English, 1,* 79–94.

Stenhouse, L. (1981). What counts as research? *British Journal of Educational Studies, 20,* 103–114.

Stibbs, A. (1979). *Assessing children's language: Guidelines for teachers.* London: Ward Lock Educational.

Sudman, S., & Bradburn, N.M. (1982). *Asking questions: A practical guide to questionnaire design.* San Francisco: Jossey-Bass.

Sutherland, J.W. (1973). *A general systems philosophy for the social and behavioral sciences.* New York: George Braziller.

Tannen, D. (1984). *Coherence in spoken and written discourse: Advances in discourse processes.* (Vol. 12). Norwood, NJ: Ablex.

Thomas, L.G. (Ed.). (1972). *Philosophical redirection of educational research: The Seventy-First*

Yearbook of the National Society for the Study of Education. Chicago: University of Chicago Press.

Thorndike, R.L., & Hagen, E. (1969). *Measurement and evaluation in psychology and education.* New York: John Wiley.

Thousand topics for composition (4th ed., secondary level). ([1947] 1980, Spring). *Illinois English Bulletin, 67*(3), 1–32.

Travers, R.N.W. (Ed.). (1973). *Second handbook of research on teaching.* Chicago: Rand McNally.

Vähäpassi, A. (1982). On the specification of the domain of school writing. *Evaluation in Education: An International Review Series. 5,* (3), 265–290.

Voss, R.F. (1983, October). Janet Emig's "The composing processes of twelfth graders": A reassessment. *College Composition and Communication, 34,* 278–283.

Vygotsky, L.S. (1978). *Mind in society: The development of higher psychological processes.* Cambridge, MA: Harvard University Press.

Wagner, J. (Ed.). (1979). *Images of information: Still photography in the social sciences.* Beverly Hills, CA: Sage.

Warantz, E., & Keech, C.L. (1982, November). Beyond holistic scoring: Rhetorical flaws that signal advance in developing writers. In J.R. Gray, & L.P. Ruth, *Properties of writing tasks: A study of alternative procedures for holistic writing assessment* (pp. 509–542). Berkeley: University of California, Graduate School of Education, Bay Area Writing Project. (ERIC No. ED 230 576)

Wesman, A.G. (1971). Writing the test item. In R. Thorndike (Ed.), *Educational measurement* (2nd ed.) (pp. 81–128). Washington, DC: American Council on Education.

Whale, K.B., & Robinson, S. (1978). Modes of students' writing: A descriptive study. *Research in the Teaching of English, 21,* 349–355.

White, E. (1973). *Comparison and contrast.* Los Angeles: California State Universities and Colleges, Office of the Chancellor.

White, E. (1984, May). Post-structural literary criticism and the response to student writing. *College Composition and Communication, 35,* 186–195.

White, E. (1985). *Teaching and assessing writing.* San Francisco: Jossey-Bass.

White, R.V. (1980). *Teaching written English.* London: George Allen & Unwin.

Wilkinson, A. (1983). Assessing language development: The Crediton project. In A. Freedman, I. Pringle, & J. Yalden (Eds.), *Learning to write: First language, second language.* London: Longman.

Wilkinson, A., Barnsley, G., Hanna, P., & Swan, M. (1980). *Assessing language development.* Oxford: Oxford University Press.

Williams, J. (1979). Defining complexity. *College English, 40,* 595–609.

Winters, L. (1980). *The effects of differing response criteria on the assessment of writing competence* (CSE Report No. 131). Los Angeles: University of California, Graduate School of Education, Center for the Study of Evaluation.

Witte, S.P., & Faigley, L. (1983). *Evaluating college writing programs.* Carbondale, IL: Southern Illinois University Press.

Woodworth, P., & Keech, C. (1980). *The write occasion.* Berkeley: University of California, Graduate School of Education, Bay Area Writing Project.

Author Index

A

Abelson, R., 17, *291*
Anastasi, A., 39, *291*
Angoff, W.H., 61, *291*
Applebee, A.N., 52, 77, 108, 109, *291*
Ash, B., 56, 57, *298*
Atkins, L., 47, *291*
Atwater, J.D., *291*
Austin, J.L., 118, *291*

B

Ballard, P.B., 69, 241, *291*
Ballas, M.S., 236, 242, *291*
Barnsley, G., 213, 214, 216, *306*
Bartlett, E.J., 109, *291*
Belanoff, P., 246, 247, *291*
Belson, W.A., 289, *291*
Berdie, F.S., 62, 63, 132, *296*
Bereiter, C., 3, 98, 211, 212, 213, 252, *291*, *304*
Berk, R.A., 60, 61, *291*
Bernstein, B., 54, *291*
Bizzell, P., 213, 216, 217, 218, *291*
Bloom, B.S., 66, *292*
Booth, W., 134, *292*
Bracewell, P.J., 3, *291*
Bradburn, N.M., *305*
Braddock, R., 12, 42, 43, 79, *292*
Brannon, L., 277, *299*
Breland, H., 43, *292*
Bridgeman, B., 110, 111, 112, 113, 253, 256, 287, *292*
Britton, J., 22, 76, 94, 95, 110, 207, *292*
Bronowski, J., 290, *292*
Brossell, G., 12, 56, 57, 71, 72, 124, 140, *292*, *298*
Brown, R., 33, *292*
Bruce, B., 98, 99, 119, 220, *292*
Burgess, T., 22, 76, 94, 95, 110, 207, *292*

C

Cameron, W.B., 17, *292*
Camp, G., 271, 272, *292*
Camp, R., 43, 246, 247, *292*
Campbell, D.T., 125, *292*
Cannell, C.F., 119, *292*
Capell, F.J., 82, *303*

Carleton, S.T., 60, *292*
Carlson, S., 111, 112, 113, 253, 256, 287, *292*
Carr, A.J., 25, *293*
Carroll, K., 133, 134, 155, *301*
Chafe, W.L., 159, 166, 171, *293*
Charrow, V., 282, *296*
Cherry, R.D., 246, 252, *295*
Chew, C.R., 242, *293*
Choppin, B.H., 45, 46, *293*
Chou, C.P., 82, *303*
Cicourel, A., 117, 123, 126, 235, *293*
Clark, C.M., 85, 86, 87, *293*
Clark, M., 83, 84, *293*
Clark, R., 25, 26, *293*
Coffman, W.E., 22, 40, 41, 42, 43, 44, 56, 58, 60, *293*, *297*
Cohen, L., 68, *293*
Cole, M., 63, *293*
Collins, A., 98, 99, 119, 220, *292*
Collins, J.L., 77, 78, *293*
Conlan, G., 30, 31, 32, 41, 260, 261, 280, *293*, *294*
Cook, K.H., 47, 48, *299*
Connors, R.J., 17, 20, *294*
Cooper, C., 13, 79, 80, 206, *294*, *302*
Cooper, M., 125, *294*
Courts, C., 13, *302*
Cronbach, L.J., 61, *294*
Crouch, W.W., 47, 48, *299*
Crowhurst, M., 3, 70, 79, 205, *294*

D

D'Angelo, F., 88, 89, 90, 91, 110, 252, *294*
Dellinger, D., 252, *294*
De Luca, C., 287, 288, *303*
Diederich, P.B., 7, 139, *294*
Dietrich, T.G., 256, *294*
Dixon, J., 82, 247, 257, 262, 263, 264, *294*, *295*
Donaldson, M., 117, 132, *295*
Donovan, R., *298*
Duff, A., 260, *300*
Duran, R.P., 12, *296*

E

Ede, L., 75, *295*
Elliott, E., 44, *305*

Emig, J., 95, 96, 125, 240, *295*
Entwistle, N., 287, 288, *303*
Evans, P., 58, 59, 114, 115, 116, 242, 280, *295*
Evertts, E., *295*

F

Faigley, L., 46, 205, 206, 246, 252, *295, 307*
Farr, M., 16, 18, *295*
Farrell, E.J., 26, 27, 268, *296*
Felker, D., 282, *296*
Fillion, B., 98, 252, *304*
Fillmore, C.J., 117, 122, *296*
Finley, C.J., 62, 63, 132, *296*
Fish, S., 121, *296*
Florio, S., 85, 86, 87, *293*
Flower, L.S., 69, 70, 75, 95, 97, 119, 125, 220, *296*
Foley, J.J., 55, *296*
Forrest, A., 253, *296*
Freedle, R., 12, *296*
Freedman, A., 12, 80, 81, 82, 98, 207, 208, 209, 225, *296*
Freedman, S., 58, *296, 301*
Freeman, C., 256, *294*
French, J.W., 41, 55, *297*

G

Gage, N.L., 125, *297*
Gentner, D., 98, 99, 119, 220, *292*
Gere, A.R., *297*
Giddens, A., 18, 19, *297*
Godschalk, F.I., 41, 43, 44, 55, 56, 58, *297*
Gordon, R.L., 282, *297*
Gorman, T.P., 113, 114, 242, 250, 251, 274, 275, 286, *297*
Graves, D.H., 83, 213, *297*
Gray, J.R., 4, 117, 131, 237, *297*
Green, D.R., 60, *297*
Greenberg, K.L., 12, 13, 57, 62, 64, 65, 66, 67, 68, 124, *297, 298*
Grellet, F., 260, *300*

H

Hagen, E., 1, 16, 39, 41, *306*
Halliday, M.A.K., 78, *298*
Hamp-Lyons, L., 13, *298*
Hanna, P., 213, 214, 216, *306*
Harpin, W., 51, 62, 220, 221, 259, 267, *298*
Hartfiel, V.F., 256, *298*

Hasan, R., 78, *298*
Hayes, J.R., 69, 70, 95, 97, 119, 125, 220, 225, *296*
Hays, J.N., 213, 216, 217, 218, 219, *298*
Hendrick, F.A., *298*
Henkel, R.E., 47, 48, 49, *298, 301*
Hoetker, J., 12, 13, 42, 43, 56, 57, 67, 70, 71, 72, 117, 124, 139, 141, 150, 190, *298*
Holland, V., 282, *296*
Holzman, M., 125, *294*
Hopkins, K.D., 48, 59, *298*
Hughey, J.B., 256, *298*
Hunt, K.W., 205, *298*
Hunter, R.V., 283, *298*
Hutchinson, C., 287, 288, *303*

I

Irmscher, W.F., 27, 271, *298*

J

Jacobs, H.L., 256, *298*
Jarrett, D., 47, *291*
Jennings, K., 117, 123, 126, 235, *293*
Jennings, S., 117, 123, 126, 235, *293*
Johnston, B., 247, *298*
Johnson, P.H., 122, *298*
Johnson-Laird, P.N., 125, *299*
Jolliffe, D.A., 246, 252, *295*
Jones, R., 43, *292*

K

Kandel, I.L., 39, 42, *299*
Kaplan, A., 127, *299*
Katzer, J., 47, 48, *299*
Kay, P., 117, 122, *296*
Keech, C.L., 11, 31, 82, 124, 131, 132, 134, 135, 137, 138, 139, 142, 150, 151, 192, 193, 194, 195, 196, 197, 198, 199, 221, 224, 225, 227, 228, 232, 233, 237, 254, 268, 271, 272, 274, 275, 276, 278, 279, *299, 300, 306, 307*
Kerlinger, F.N., 125, *299*
Kilmann, R.H., 125, *301*
Kincaid, G., 43, *299*
Kinneavy, J.L., 80, 88, 91, 92, 109, 205, 252, *299*
Kinzer, C., 124, 132, 133, 134, 138, 142, 155, 268, 287, *300, 301*
Kirrie, M., 32, 271, *299*

Knoblauch, C.H., 277, *299*
Krupa, G., 252, *299*

L
Labov, W., 83, 171, 174, *300*
Langer, J.A., 53, 54, *300*
Lanham, R.A., 67, *300*
Lehman, I., 59, 60, *300*
Leiter, K., 117, 123, 126, 235, *293*
Lenke, J.M., 60, *300*
Leu, D.J., Jr., 124, 132, 138, 142, 268, *300*
Littlefield, J., 13, *304*
Lloyd-Jones, R., 1, 12, 32, 33, 34, 35, 41, 42,
        43, 79, 110, 240, 241, 255, *292, 300*
Loban, W., 205, *300*
Long, R.C., 73, *300*
Loyd, B.H., *298*
Lunsford, A., 75, *295*

M
MacKay, R., 117, 123, 126, 235, *293*
Mahan, H., 117, 123, 126, 235, *293*
Maley, A., 260, *300*
Manion, L., 68, *293*
Marco, G.L., 60, *292*
Martin, N., 22, 76, 94, 95, 110, 207, *292*
Matsuhashi, A., 82, *300*
McLeod, A., 22, 76, 94, 95, 110, 207, *292*
McMorris, R.F., 41, 44, *302*
McNelly, M.E., 134, 191, 193, 194, 195, 196,
        197, 198, 199, 200, 225, *299*
Means, B., 63, *293*
Mehrens, W., 59, 60, *300*
Meier, D., 117, *300*
Mellon, J., 35, 36, 41, 100, 101, 259, *301*
Miles, J., 10, 22, 23, 27, *301*
Miller, C., *302*
Mitroff, I.I., 125, *301*
Moffett, J., 22, 92, 93, 94, 95, 110, 206, 207,
        208, 252, *301*
Morris, M., 43, *292*
Morrison, D.E., 47, *301*
Mullis, I.V.S., 1, 32, 33, *301*
Murphy, S., 37, 124, 128, 132, 133, 134, 138,
        142, 155, 242, 247, 268, 287, *299, 300,
        301, 304*
Myers, M.A., 3, 254, 267, 270, *301*

N
Neilson, B., 77, 78, *301*

Newkirk, T., 213, 216, 217, 218, *301*
Nold, E., *301*

O
Ochs, E., 166, *301*
Odell, L., 13, 100, 102, 103, 104, 105, 210,
        211, *294, 302*
Olson, P., 259, *302*
Ong, W., 73, 78, *302*
Oppenheim, A.N., 282, *302*
Orchard, L., 113, 114, 242, 250, 251, 274,
        275, 286, *297*

P
Park, D.B., 73, 74, 75, *302*
Patton, M.Q., 238, 240, *302*
Payne, D.A., 41, 44, *302*
Payne, S.L., 282, *302*
Pearce, J., 81, 82, *302*
Perron, J.D., 79, 205, *302*
Perry, W.G., 213, 216, 217, 218, 219, *291*
Peterson, B.T., 121, *302*
Pianko, S., 85, *302*
Piche, G.L., 79, 205, *294*
Pickering, F., 282, *296*
Polin, L., 3, 99, 241, *303*
Pollitt, A., 287, 288, *303*
Powell, D., 10, *303*
Pringle, I., 80, 81, 82, 98, 207, 208, 209, 225,
        296
Purves, A.C., 12, 45, 46, 47, 100, 105, 106,
        108, 113, 220, 253, *293, 303*

Q
Quellmalz, E.S., 82, *303*

R
Raju, N.S., *303*
Redish, J., 282, *296*
Reid, W., 20, *303*
Reynolds, J., 118, *303*
Robinson, S., 79, 119, 247, *292, 303*
Robinson, W.S., *296*
Robyns, A., 133, 134, 155, *301*
Rock, D., 43, *292*
Rockas, L., 89, *303*
Rosen, H., 22, 55, 76, 79, 81, 82, 94, 95,
        110, 207, 266, *292, 303*
Rosenblatt, L.M., 119, 120, 121, *303*
Rowntree, D., 47, 72, 73, *304*

Rubin, A.D., 98, 99, 119, 220, *292*
Rumelhart, D.E., 120, *304*
Rushton, J., 54, 55, *304*
Ruth, D., 258, 259, *304*
Ruth, L.P., 4, 37, 51, 117, 118, 119, 121, 126, 128, 131, 237, 248, *297*, *304*

S

Sachse, P.P., 80, *304*
Sanders, N.M., *304*
Sanders, S., 13, *304*
San Jose, C.P.M., 79, 205, *304*
Sax, G., 40, 44, *304*
Sbisà, M., *291*
Scardamalia, M., 3, 98, 211, 212, 213, 220, 252, *291*, *304*
Scheuneman, J.D., 61, *304*
Schoer, L., 12, 42, 43, 79, *292*
Schön, D.A., 37, *304*
Schwalm, D.E., 287, *304*
Scott, F.N., 21, 22, 27, 37, *305*
Scriven, M., 126, 127, *305*
Sexton, B., 113, 114, 242, 250, 257, 274, 275, 286, *297*
Shepard, L.A., *305*
Shuy, R., 83, *305*
Skilbeck, M., 118, *303*
Skinner, A., 46, 246, 252, *295*
Slaughter, C.D., 283, *298*
Smith, L.S., 41, *305*
Snow, R.E., 127, *305*
Söter, A., 12, 47, 100, 105, 106, 108, 220, 253, *303*
Spandel, V., 1, *305*
Stahl, A., 276, *305*
Stanley, J.C., 48, 59, 125, *292*, *298*
Starch, D., 44, *305*
Staton, J., 83, *305*
Steele, J.M., 253, *296*
Steinberg, E.R., 70, *305*
Steinman, M., 55, *305*
Stenhouse, L., 19, 36, *305*
Stibbs, A., 243, *305*
Stiggins, R.J., 1, *305*
Stratta, L., 82, 247, 257, 262, 263, 264, *294*, *295*
Sudman, S., *305*
Sutherland, J.W., 126, *305*
Swan, M., 213, 214, 216, *306*
Swift, K., *301*
Swineford, F., 41, 43, 44, 55, 56, 58, *297*

T

Takala, S., 12, 47, 100, 105, 106, 108, 113, 220, 253, *303*
Tannen, D., 166, *305*
Tate, A., 113, 114, 242, 250, 251, 274, 275, 286, *297*
Thomas, L.G., 126, *305*
Thorndike, R.L., 1, 2, 16, 39, 41, *306*
Travers, R.N.W., 125, *306*

U

Urmson, J.O., *291*

V

Vähäpassi, A., 13, 47, 100, 105, 106, 108, 220, 253, *303*, *306*
Voss, R.F., 125, 132, *306*
Vygotsky, L.S., 78, 203, 225, *306*

W

Wagner, J., 258, 260, 275, *306*
Waletzky, J., *300*
Warantz, E., 135, 221, 223, 224, 225, 227, 228, 232, *306*
Wason, P.C., 125, *299*
Watson, C., 79, 80, 206, *294*
Wesman, A.G., 2, 16, 40, 41, *306*
Whale, K.B., 79, *306*
White, E.M., 121, 122, *306*
White, J., 113, 114, 242, 250, 251, 274, 275, 286, *297*
White, R.V., 255, *306*
Wiener, H., *298*
Wilkinson, A., 213, 214, 215, 216, *306*
Williams, J., 234, *306*
Williamson, M.M., 77, 78, *293*
Winters, L., 41, *306*
Witte, S.P., *307*
Woodworth, P., 137, 139, 150, 151, *307*
Wormuth, D.R., 256, *298*

Y

Yalden, J., 98, *296*
Young, G., 54, 55, *304*

Z

Zingraf, S.A., 256, *298*

Subject Index

A

Abstraction, degrees of
  in speaker-audience relations, 93
  in speaker-subject relations, 93
Analytic scoring, 7
Argument (persuasion)
  as rhetorical mode (aim), 79, 80–81
  Dixon and Stratta's forms and functions
    of, 264
  narrative and evaluative elements,
    171–175
  tasks, 64–68, 262–263, 264, 286
Assessment, conditions, 83–85, 100,
    149–154, 238–242
Assessment, large scale
  Assessment of Performance Unit
    (England), 113–114, 242, 250–252,
    286
  International Association of Educational
    Achievement, 105–108
  National Assessment of Educational
    Progress (U.S.), 32–36, 110–111
  Ontario Ministry of Education (Canada),
    114–115, 242
Assessment, planning for, see also,
    Evaluation of school writing,
    approaches to
  adopting a theory of discourse, 245
  defining competence, 244
  determining uses of results, 243
  exploring new sampling approaches,
    284–285
  planning user review and pretesting,
    283–284
  using professional judgment, 243
Assessment, purposes of
  administrative, 243
  instructional, 243–244, 244–245
Assessment of Performance Unit, see
    Assessment, large scale
Assessment tasks, see Writing tasks
Assignment, classroom writing, 8–9
  as occasion for writing, 24–25
  as subject without predication, 23, 81
  as subject with predication, 22–23, 24
  basic patterns of, 25

  criteria for, 25–32
  philosophy of, 21–22
Audience, concepts of,
  actual (real), 74–75, 149–150
  as a created fiction, 70, 73, 74, 149–150
  implied, 74, 266
  invoked (imagined), 75, 265–267
Audiences for school writing, 76–78, 245
  actual (real), 74–75
    general readers, 75
    peers as readers, 74, 144
    self, 76
    teacher as evaluator, 77
    teacher as trusted adult, 77
    unknown, 77
    inappropriate, 79, 266, 268–269,
      272–273

B

Bias,
  concepts of,
    psychometric, 60–61
    social, 61
  control for,
    in reader responses, 32, 260–261
    in test instruments, 32, see also,
      Sensitivity review

C

Classification of writing tasks, 124, see also
    Discourse, systems of classification
  domain of school writing, 106–107
  survey of classification systems, 220–221
  taxonomy of student text types, 223
College Entrance Examination Board, 24
Commission on English, 24, 25
Commission on Writing, 25–26
Community of readers, see Readers
Comparability of writing tasks, 64–68,
    70–73, 141
Competencies in writing, 99–101, 244
  Mellon's taxonomy of, 101–102
  Odell's sugestions for measuring,
    102–104

313

Comprehension of writing tasks, 118–119, 129–130, 244
  and cognitive theory, 110
  and literary theory, 119–122, 134
  and reading theory, 122–123
Contexts for writing, 8–9, 244–245
  classroom, 85–87
  natural, 69, 85
  task environment, 69–70
  testing, 67, 83–85, 123, 149–154

D

Definitions of terms
  assessment and evaluation, 6
  assessment and scoring, 7
  competence in writing, 102
  given task and constructed task, 7, 130, see also Meanings of writing tasks, understood
  rhetorical problem or situation, 70
  significance, 47–48
  writing assignments and writing tests, 8–9
  writing sample, 6
  writing test and essay test, 6
Demands of writing tasks, see also Difficulty of tasks
  cognitive, 10, 12n, 64–68
  prior experience, 3, 67
  rhetorical situation (problem), 70–73
Description
  as mode, 275–276
  tasks, 273
Development of proficiency, see Progress in writing
Difficulty of tasks
  argument, 78–82, 219
  description, 275–276
  narration based on imagined experience, 257–258
  reporting versus generalizing, 82
Difficulty, psychometric measures of, see Item analysis
Directions for writing, see Instructions
Discourse, systems of classification,
  categorical, 88–92
    Bain, 88
    De Angelo, 90
    Kinneavy, 91
    Rockas, 89
  relational, 92–95

Britton, 94
Moffett, 93

E

Educational Testing Service, 110, 236
Effects on performance, 46–47
  of audience specification, 3, 70, 77–78
  of freedom to select
    subject, 55–59
    mode, 43, 46, 79
  of wording variation, 53
Elements in (dimensions of) writing tasks, see Subjects, Instructions, Rhetorical specification
English as a Second Language (ESL) writing, see Personal experience tasks, problems for ESL students
Equating tasks, problems of, 144
Essay topics, see Writing tasks
Evaluation of school writing, approaches to, 103–104, 242, see also, Assessment, large scale models
  plan for a school system, 115
  portfolio approaches, 246–247
  primary trait model, 110–111
  self-assessment, 247
  skills models and discrete point measures, 108–110
  validation of topic types, 111–113
Evaluation of task adequacy, see, Bias, Field test, Sensitivity review, Reliability, Validity
Evaluators, see Readers
Exposition, 27–28, 81
Explanatory discourse, 111
Expressive discourse, 90, 94, 96, 111
Extensive discourse, 96

F

Features of topics, see Definitions of Terms, Subjects, Instructions, Rhetorical specification
Field test
  inadequacy of statistical procedures, 40–44, 283–284
  interviews with users, 288–289, 289n

G

General impression scoring, 8
Genre, see Argument, Description, Exposition, Narrative

Growth in writing, *see* Progress in writing
Guidelines for designing writing tasks, 21,
24, 26, 27, 31–38, 248–249, 251,
249–290, *see also* Subjects,
Instructions, Rhetorical specification,
Wording

H
Holistic scoring, 7

I
Informative discourse, 90
Instructions, 7, 10–12, 31, 37, 267–268,
272–274, 277–278
International Association for the Evaluation
of Educational Achievement, *see*
Assessment, large scale
Interpretation of topics, differences in, 3, 15,
35–36, 82, 118–119, 156–158,
182–188, 269–271
Interpretation of topics, sources of variation
context of test situation, 176
learned strategies, 176–177
misreading, 178
prior knowledge, 179
selective reading, 178
wording, 71–73, 178–179, *see also*,
Wording
Interview protocols, 132–133
idea unit as unit of analysis, 159
Item analysis
misconceptions about, 2, 40–42
Item writing, *see* Guidelines for designing
writing tasks

L
Language effects, *see* Wording
Letters, 78–80, 144

M
Meanings of writing tasks
intended, 130
understood (constructed), 130, 134–135,
156–170, 220–225, 231–233 *see also*,
Comprehension of writing tasks
Measurement issues in writing assessment,
see Psychometric measures of
writing, Reliability, Validity
Mode, effects of, 79–82 *see also* Argument,
Exposition, Description, Narrative

Models
nature of, 126–127
writing processes of
Bereiter and Scardamalia, 98
Bruce, et al., 98–100
Emig, 95, 96
Flower and Hayes, 69–70, 95–97
and assessment, 100
Motivation, effect on test results, 58, 67, 85

N
Narrative
based on imaginative experience,
257–258, 271–272
based on personal experience, 257–258
National Assessment of Educational
Progress (NAEP), *see* Assessment,
large scale

O
Ontario Ministry of Education, *see*
Assessment, large scale

P
Personal experience tasks,
problems for ESL students, 255
criticized, 23, 27, 255
recommended, 255, 256, 257
Persuasive discourse, 111
Pictures as writing tasks, 33–34, 258–260
Poetic discourse, 94
Portfolio assessment, *see* Evaluation of
school writing, approaches to
Pre-testing writing tasks, *see* Field test
Primary trait scoring, 7, 32–36, 110–111
Problems in topics,
audience specification, 3, 29, 140, 266,
272
clarity of language, 280–281
hypothetical elements, 29, 219, 265–266,
271–272
overprompting, 272–275
prior knowledge requirements, 3, 35, 36,
47, 53, 54
specification of length, 278–279
undercueing, 275–277
unintended effects, 86
Progress in writing and
affective and moral development,
214–220
cognitive development, 206–214

Progress in writing (*cont.*)
  false impressions of regression, 203–204, 225
  linguistic development, 205–206
Proficiency, development of, *see* Competencies in writing, Progress in writing
Psychometric measures of writing
  history of, 39–42
  limits of indirect measures, 36–37
Purposes (aims, functions) for writing
  described, 90
  effects of, 79–80

Q
Questions, *see* Writing tasks
Questionnaire data, limitations of, 133, 154

R
Readers (evaluators), 134, 181, 185–191, 202
  expert teachers as raters, 196, 199, 200, 201
  novice teachers as raters, 196, 199
  students as peer raters, 199–200
  students as topic readers, 185–191
  teachers as raters, 184
  teachers as topic authors, 182–184
Reading process and writing tasks,
  patterns of task interpretation, 159–176
  studies of, 132–133, 155–156
Reflexive discourse, 96
Reliability, 42, 44
Research methods, explanatory power of
  case study, 36
  experiment, 68, 124–125
  field test, 40–44, 283–284, 288–289
  interview protocol analysis, 132–133
  linguistic analysis, 122, 159
  model (theory) building, 127–128
  naturalistic, 85–87, 126
  survey, 119
  think-aloud, 117
  triangulation, 68, 126
Research on writing tasks,
  failure to provide topic texts, 43–44
  need for contextual research, 18, 123
  limits of experimental models, 17, 68
  questions needing answers, 4, 13–15, 131
  problems with
    control of variables, 140–141
    constraints of psychometric methods, 41–42, 124–125

developmental studies, 233–235
  measuring writing development over time, 225–233
  topic effects, 42–47, 55–58, 62–66, 141–149, 227–229
  the unstudied assignment variable, 12, 41, 43, 47, 117
Resolution on testing, 1
Response modes
  essay, 6
  free answer, 39
  multiple-choice, 43–44, 45
  short answer, 52
  structured answer, 39
Response error in survey research, 118–119, 123
Rhetorical specification, 7, 26–27, 266–268, *see also,* Audience, Genre, Mode, Role, Voice
  effects on
    performance 137–140
    choice of form, 142–145
    composing strategies, 145–149
Role, 26–27

S
Scores, change over time, 228–231
Scoring procedures, 245–246, *see also,* Analytic, General impression, Holistic, Primary trait
Sensitivity review, 282
Significance,
  practical, 48
  statistical, 47–49
Single-sample testing
  limitations of, 82, 284
  overgeneralization from, 240
Stimuli for writing, 10, *see also,* Personal experience tasks, Pictures as writing tasks, Text-based writing tasks
Subjects
  effects, 51–55, 253–256
  nature of, 8–10, 71
  popularity indexes, 57
  selection of, 14, 22, 37, 260–261, 260–264

T
Tenor of discourse, 96
Text-based writing tasks, 10, 24, 45
Time limit effects, 151–153, *see also* Writing process, violation of

Topics, *see* Writing tasks, Subjects
Transactional writing, 94

U
Unsuitable topics, 30, 52, 254, 260, 261, 262, 263, 265–266, 271, 272, 274, *see also,* Problems in topics

V
Validation of tasks, 110–113
Validity, 40–42, 61, 118, 240–242, 290
Voice, 26–27

W
Wording
    problem words
        demonstrate, 10
        describe, 275–276
        discuss, 60
        list, who, what, whether, 60
    words to cue mode, 281
Writing assessment episode, 127–130
Writing process, violation of, 100, 240–241

Writing task design process
    as an art, 2–3, 25
    planning phase, 238–247
    development phase, 247–283
    evaluation phase (field trial), 283–290
Writing task design, sources of information
    common sense, 18–19
    composition research, 16, 95–100
    document design research, 282
    educational research, 17, 99–113
    literary theory, 73–75, 119–122, 134
    professional knowledge, 18–38, 131
    psychometric research, 111–113
    rhetorical theory, 88–95
Writing tasks, examples
    for college students, 11, 71, 84–85, 264, 273, 276
    for elementary students, 11, 33, 35, 98, 259, 267, 273, 274, 281
    for secondary students, 11, 53, 55–56, 137, 138, 155, 221–222, 254, 256, 264, 267, 270, 273, 276, 276, 287